Civil Procedure in Greece

Civil Procedure in Greece

Third Edition

Pelayia Yessiou-Faltsi
Apostolos Anthimos

This book was originally published as a monograph in the International Encyclopaedia of Laws/Civil Procedure.

Founding Editor: Roger Blanpain
General Editor: Frank Hendrickx
Volume Editor Wannes Vandenbussche

Wolters Kluwer

Published by:
Kluwer Law International B.V.
PO Box 316
2400 AH Alphen aan den Rijn
The Netherlands
E-mail: lrs-sales@wolterskluwer.com
Website: www.wolterskluwer.com/en/solutions/kluwerlawinternational

Sold and distributed by:
Wolters Kluwer Legal & Regulatory U.S.
920 Links Avenue
Landisville, PA 17538
United States of America
E-mail: customer.service@wolterskluwer.com

DISCLAIMER: The material in this volume is in the nature of general comment only. It is not offered as advice on any particular matter and should not be taken as such. The editor and the contributing authors expressly disclaim all liability to any person with regard to anything done or omitted to be done, and with respect to the consequences of anything done or omitted to be done wholly or partly in reliance upon the whole or any part of the contents of this volume. No reader should act or refrain from acting on the basis of any matter contained in this volume without first obtaining professional advice regarding the particular facts and circumstances at issue. Any and all opinions expressed herein are those of the particular author and are not necessarily those of the editor or publisher of this volume.

ISBN 978-94-035-4417-5

e-Book: ISBN 978-94-035-4427-4
web-PDF: ISBN 978-94-035-4437-3

This title is available on www.kluwerlawonline.com

© 2024 Kluwer Law International BV, The Netherlands

All rights reserved. No part of this publication may be reproduced, stored in a retrieval system, or transmitted in any form or by any means, electronic, mechanical, photocopying, recording, or otherwise, without the prior written permission of the publisher.

Permission to use this content must be obtained from the copyright owner. More information can be found at: www.wolterskluwer.com/en/solutions/legal-regulatory/permissions-reprints-and-licensing

The Authors

Pelayia Yessiou-Faltsi studied at the Law School of the Aristotle University of Thessaloniki, Greece and as an Alexander von Humboldt Stiftung scholar at the University of Cologne and Munich, Germany. She received a doctorate degree in law from Thessaloniki (1960–1964) and presented her habilitation in 1970. She has been a member of the Thessaloniki bar since 1960, a professor in Thessaloniki (*Ordinarius*) since 1979, and was also the Director of the Department of Civil Law, Civil Procedure and Labour Law from 1988 to 1990. From 1994 to 1997, Yessiou-Faltsi was the Dean of the Faculty of Law and a Member of the Senate of the University of Thessaloniki. She is a Member of the Teaching Staff of the National School for the Judiciary, a Member of the Council of the International Association of Procedural Law, and a Member of the International Academy of Comparative Law. She was a member of the Special Highest Court of Greece (1987–1989), President of the Committee for International Relations of the Aristotle University (1989–1997) and Director of the European Community Programme (Erasmus) 'Elpis' at the Law Faculty of Thessaloniki. She has lectured and has given seminars in the United States of America (USA), the United Kingdom (UK), Germany, Austria, Poland, Bulgaria, India and Japan and has been a visiting Professor at Tulane Law School, USA.

In May 2006, she was awarded a PhD h.c. from the Faculty of Law of the University of Athens. On 27 March 2008, Yessiou-Faltsi was elected a cor. Member of the Academy of Athens. The official ceremony took place on 25 November 2008.

The Authors

Apostolos Anthimos: Attorney at law, Thessaloniki Bar, Greece; working languages: English, German, Spanish; Greek. PhD in International Civil Litigation (Aristotle University Thessaloniki, 2002); two Masters of Laws from the University of Hanover, Germany (1994) and Thessaloniki (1997). Four monographs on Civil Procedure and Conflict of Laws; co-editor and main author of the volume 'The EU Service Regulation, a Commentary' (Edward Elgar, 2023); various publications on topics related to European & International PIL, Arbitration and Dispute resolution, EU law and Civil Procedure. Focal point, European Judicial Network in civil matters; Member of the UIHJ Expert Panel. European Judicial Training Network and Hellenic School of Magistrates Instructor; Trainer of Judges, lawyers, and MoJ staff in East & Southeastern Europe, Africa, the Middle East, and Central & Southeastern Asia. Panelist at the Czech Arbitration Court [.eu ADR]. Editor for PIL, European & International Civil Procedure in the following law reviews: European Legal Forum; Thessaloniki Bar Review 'Armenopoulos'; Civil Procedure Law Review (GR); Commercial Law Survey (GR). Editor in chief in Lex & Forum – a law review on conflict of laws (GR). Co-editor, www.conflictoflaws.net / www.eapil.org/blog; Founding, Board and Steering Committee Member of the European Association of Private International Law. Member of International Association of Procedural Law. Member of the European Union (EU) expert groups (DG JUSTICE AND CONSUMERS) on: Modernization of Judicial Cooperation in Civil and Commercial Matters (2018); Expert Group against SLAPP [Strategic Lawsuits Against Public Participation] (2021). CoE expert: Legal aid and legal representation (2020–2021). Accounts: Academia.edu [https://independent.academia.edu/ApostolosAnthimos]; SSRN [http://papers.ssrn.com/sol3/1735857]; International Civil Litigation in Greece: blog featuring reports on Greek case law [https://icl-in-greece.blogspot.gr].

Table of Contents

Table of Contents

List of Abbreviations

In the interest of greater clarity and for the convenience of foreign readers, the citation forms of the Greek Codes or other legislative materials (Legislative Decrees, Presidential Decrees, etc.) of the different types of Greek courts and legal periodicals include their entire title, rather than an abbreviation, as in most instances a uniform system of citation forms in English is still absent.

The names of the Greek statutes, courts and legal periodicals are exclusively cited in an English translation, with the exception of the Greek Supreme Court for civil and criminal matters, which is referred to by its original Greek name (*Areios Pagos*).

Abbreviations listed below are of frequent recurrence:

B.C.	Before Christ
CC	Civil Code
cf.	*confer* (compare with)
Const.	Constitution
CPC	Civil Procedure Code
Czech Yb Int'l	Czech Yearbook of International Law
ed.(s)	edited, editor(s)
e.g.	*exempli gratia* (for example)
etc.	et cetera (and so forth)
EU	European Union
ff.	following
gen. ed.(s)	general editor(s)
GPR	European Union Private Law Review
i.e.	*id est* (that is)
IDME (IΔΜΕ)	Institute for Procedural Studies
IPRax	Praxis des Internationalen Privat- und Verfahrensrechts
MDR	Monatsschrift für Deutsches Recht
Min. Dec.	Ministerial Decision
n.	Note
No.(s)	number(s)
p., pp.	Page, pages

RHDI	Revue hellénique de droit international
RIW/AWD	Recht der Internationalen Wirtschaft
Vol.(s)	volume(s)
YPIL	Yearbook of Private International Law
ZfRV	zeitschrift für Europarecht Intern. Privatrecht und Rechtsvergleichung
ZZP	Zeitschrift für Zivilprozess
ZZZ	Schweizerische Zeitschrift für Zivilprozess- und Zwangsvollstreckungsrecht

Prefaces

In Greece, some of the most eminent legal scholars are known for their works on procedure. Thus, a great part of the discussions of European legal doctrine in the nineteenth and early twentieth centuries, introduced in Greece by the founder of modern Greek Civil Procedural Law, V. Oikonomidis, and further developed by leading scholars such as G. Rammos, Ch. Fragistas and G. Mitsopoulos have been implemented in the present Civil Procedure Code (CPC) of 1967/1971. This Code, a modernized and refined version of the Code of 1835, which was modelled on a mixture of both German and French prototypes, is still continually supported by an active and influential legal scholarship, which, as a rule, has a considerable impact on the interpretation and practice followed in the courts. Traditionally, Greek procedural doctrine strongly relies on the comparative method, and the institutions of domestic procedure are most often examined in light of the German, Austrian, French, Belgian, Italian and Swiss Codes.

A monograph of this length on the Greek Civil Procedure appears for the first time in English or in any language other than Greek. It could not be our intention, however, to present a detailed study. Rather, we have chosen to describe the basic elements of Greek Procedural Law, with emphasis on those institutions that are of particular interest to a foreign lawyer. The reader will thus find more comprehensive presentations in the area of International Procedural Law. Territorial competence, since this currently functions as a basis for the determination of the international jurisdiction of Greek courts, and recognition and enforcement of foreign judgments are two examples. In the context of international litigation, enforcement proceedings also had to be treated rather extensively, as foreign instruments continue to be executed through the operation of domestic institutions.

Since the exclusive objective of this monograph is to present the national system of Civil Procedure rather than to deal with comparative law aspects, the exposition mainly encompasses the system of the Greek Code of 1967/1971. On some occasions, however, it seemed necessary to also highlight the historical and comparative perspectives. Moreover, the chapters on the Fundamental Guarantees and on the Organization of the Courts had to primarily cover their constitutional backbones.

References to works written in Greek state the English translation of their original title. Works written in languages other than Greek are always referred to with their original titles. Special care has been taken to indicate the books, essays or articles written by Greek scholars in foreign languages.

During the preparation of this monograph, the Greek CPC underwent rapid changes. An effort was undertaken to take due account of these modifications even as regards chapters that had been already completed. The book is now based on the CPC as most recently revised by Laws 2145/1993, 2172/1993, 2207/1994, 2298/1995 and 2331/1995. These Laws have been respectively enacted on 28 May and 16 December 1993, on 25 April 1994, on 4 April 1995 and on 4 September 1995.

The author is sincerely grateful to Mr Geoffrey H. Mead, Lecturer in Law at the Faculty of Law of the University of Southampton, UK, and Barrister at Law, for his precious assistance in improving the English text. The author is also indebted to Miss Lena Pipinika for her skill and efforts during the technical preparation of the English manuscript.

Pelayia Yessiou-Faltsi
Professor of Law, Aristotle University of Thessaloniki
October 1995

Preface to the 2003 Edition

The 2003 edition of this monograph presents all the successive modifications of the Greek CPC through several recent Laws (2207/1994, 2298/1995, 2447/1996, 2462/1997, 2479/1997, 2521/1997, 2721/1999, 2741/1999, 2819/2000, 2915/2000 and 3043/2002). In addition, it takes due account of the amendments of the Greek Const. in 2001 and the pieces of legislation which have been issued to implement the newly introduced constitutional provisions

Among the Laws mentioned above, Law 2915/2001 in particular, in force since 1 January 2002, as revised by Law 3043/2002, has brought about a momentous change to the structure of the CPC. To achieve acceleration and immediacy, this Law has now established a unified model of normal proceedings in all Greek civil courts based on the attempt to concentrate all relevant material in one single oral hearing.

Pelayia Yessiou-Faltsi
Professor of Law
October 2003

Preface to the 2011 Edition

The main purpose of this 2011 edition is to update the 2003 monograph. In the process, the opportunity has been taken to improve its contents and add some important references to recent legislation and court decisions, as well as to recent legal scholarship.

Pelayia Yessiou-Faltsi
Professor of Law
January 2011

Preface to the 2019 Edition

The 2019 edition of the monograph 'Civil Procedure in Greece' presents the major changes of the Greek CPC 1968/1971, imposed in the midst of the country's economic crisis, as a measure to treat its side-effects by achieving simplification and, thus, acceleration of civil trials.

Although the basic institutions and concepts of the Code have remained intact, there has been a radical revision regarding the mode of conducting the first-instance proceeding as well as the means of evidence to be produced. Ordinary first instance, as well as, in principle, second instance proceedings, are now purely written, while testimony may be allowed only in exceptional cases. In addition, the enforcement proceeding for money claims has been almost totally revised. Most of the enforcement acts must now be conducted through electronic means since February 2018, including the auction. Beyond the simplification of the revised proceedings, the possibilities of debtors opposing execution have been considerably eliminated.

Pelayia Yessiou-Faltsi
Professor of Law
January 2019

Preface to the 2023 Edition

The 2023 edition features the amendments made in the Code of Civil Procedure between 2019–2023. Out of 1054 provisions of the Code, eighty-four articles were amended. In particular, the changes may be classified as follows: nineteen concerning first-instance proceedings; five concerning evidence; two concerning small claims proceedings; thirteen concerning appeals; four concerning particular (special) proceedings; ten concerning provisional measures; one concerning non-contentious proceedings; three concerning arbitration; four concerning the general, and twenty-three concerning the special part of the monograph on execution. The amendments are elaborated on the respective chapters of this monograph.

The 2023 edition is based on the following principles: first, reference to Greek literature was made redundant, given that the volume is addressed to the international legal community; second, efforts have been made to collect and include any publications authored by Greek scholars in foreign languages, such as English, German, French, and Spanish; third, beyond the 'traditional' legal scholarship published in established law journals and collective volumes, valuable material available in pertinent international legal blogs has been included, so as to enrich the volume with notes and comments on recent Greek case law presented in English.

Last but surely not least, the author wishes to express his deepest gratitude to Professor Pelayia Yessiou-Faltsi, who was the initiator of the first fully-fledged presentation of Civil Procedure in Greece in English. The 2023 edition is founded upon the laborious efforts of Professor Yessiou-Faltsi, reflected in four consecutive editions since 1995. It is a great honour and an enormous challenge to be assigned to the continuation of this unique work. Naturally, any mistakes or omissions in this volume are of course my own.

Apostolos Anthimos
August 2023

General Introduction

§1. General Background

1. According to the Const. of 1975,[1] as amended in 1986, 2001 and 2008, Greece (*Hellas*) is 'a parliamentary republic' (Article 1, §1). The referendum of 8 December 1974 abolished the monarchy (with 69.2% of the valid votes in favour of a republican regime), whereas Article 110, §1, of the Const. of 1975 forbids its restoration. In contrast to the crowned democracy of the previous Const. of 1952 (Article 21, §1), the present Const. has introduced a 'presidential democracy'.

2. Greece became a member of the European Community on 1 January 1981. The Treaty of Accession, signed on 28 May 1979, was ratified by the Greek Parliament on 29 June 1979 (with 193 votes out of 300). Transition periods have expired since 31 December 1985 and 31 December 1987. The 'Single European Act' was signed by Greece on 28 February 1986 and was ratified by Law 1681/1987. The Maastricht Treaty 'On European Union' of 7 February 1992 was ratified by Law 2077/1992 (7/7 August 1992), the Amsterdam Treaty of 2 October 1997 by Law 2691/1999, the Treaty of Nice Amending the Treaty on European Union (EU) of 26 February 2001 by Law 3001/2002 (8 April 2002), and the Lisbon Treaty of 13 December 2007 by Law 3671/2008.

Greece's accession to the European Community had been prepared through certain constitutional provisions, which permitted restrictions of national sovereignty by law (Article 28, §3) and the exercise of powers provided by the Const. by institutions of international organizations, in both cases when this serves an 'important national interest' (Article 28 §§2, 3). According to an interpretative statement, which was added under Article 28 during the revision of 2001, this article constitutes the foundation for the country's participation in the process of European integration.

I. Historical Evolution

3. The contemporary significance of the Ancient Greek Law for the modern Greek legal system, as it did not enjoy a continuous historical development throughout the centuries but was still capable of indirectly influencing some basic

1. *Constitution of Greece*, voted by the fifth Revisionary Parliament of the Hellenes on 9 Jun. 1975 and entered into force on 11 Jun. 1975 (English translation of the House of Parliament, Athens 1975).

orientations of contemporary Greek and overall continental law, can be best examined on the level of principles rather than on the basis of concrete and specific institutions.

4. The origins of modern Greek law are marked by the National Revolution for Independence of 1821. Despite the strong impact of French doctrine and legislation, starting even before this revolution (especially in the field of Individual Rights and Commercial law), the first major Greek codes were based on both French and German models. They were drafted by Ludwig von. Maurer, the Bavarian law professor and scholar,[2] in his capacity as a member of the regency council of King Otto.[3] This admirable work of codification comprised four codes: (a) the Civil Procedure Code (CPC) of 2/14 April 1834; (b) the Code for the Organization of Courts and of Notaries of 21 January/2 February 1834; (c) the Criminal Code of 18/30 December 1833; and (d) the Code of Criminal Procedure of 10/22 March 1834. These were published in the German language and decisively influenced the development of the modern Greek legal system. Whereas the latter two codes remained in force until 1951, the CPC was replaced only in 1968 and the Code for the Organization of Courts and of Notaries in 1988.

However, due to the legal aspects of *Ludwig von Maurer*, who was a supporter of the historical school of law, no Civil Code was drafted. Thus, Byzantine Law became the main source of Civil law for more than a century and totally oriented the Greeks towards the German doctrine.[4] Yet, the gradual adoption of new legislation, inspired by the Austrian, German and French Civil Code (CC), created a mosaic of modern features which, supported through court rulings and the Greek scholars, was reproduced by the Greek CC (in force since 23 February 1946).[5] The CC of 1946 also extended its force to the areas previously dominated by local CCs (*Ionian Islands*: Ionian CC of 1841 (of French origin); *Crete*: CC of Crete, 1904 (of German origin); *Samos*: CC of Samos, 1899 (of French and Italian origin)) and thus unified Civil Law throughout the Greek State.

II. Classification

5. In light of its long historical evolution, the classification of modern Greek law within one of the main modern branches of European legal systems (Roman,

2. K. Dickopf, *George Ludwig von Maurer 1790–1872 – Eine Biographie* (Kallmünz 1960).
3. Ludwig von Maurer's conceptions about his mission in the new-founded State of Greece are discussed in detail in his work: *Das griechische Volk in öffentlicher, kirchlicher und privat-rechtlicher Beziehung vor und nach dem Freiheitskampfe bis zum 31 Juli 1834*, Vols 1–3 (Heidelberg 1835).
4. K. Zweigert, & H. Kötz, *Einführung in die Rechtsvergleichung*, Vol. 1 (Mohr, Tübingen 1971), pp. 186–187; same authors, *Introduction to Comparative Law*, translated in English by T. Weir, Vol. 1 (Clarendon Press, Oxford 1987), pp. 160–161.
5. P. Zepos, 'The Historical and Comparative Background of the Greek Civil Code', (*Inter-American Law Review* 1961), pp. 285–299.

Germanic, Nordic)[6] would not give the exact picture despite its undeniable Roman-Byzantine backbone. Due to the diversified impact of several legal systems, depending on the specific field, Greek law has been accordingly defined[7] as belonging to a 'selective' or 'mixed' branch. By picking up the appropriate sources from both the German and the French systems and also elaborating on some other mixed elements, it results in its own original form.

III. Legal Sources

6. Greek legal norms are, to a great extent, codified. The cornerstone of the Greek legal system is the Const. of 1975. Among the more significant codifications, one should include: (a) The CC of 1946; (b) the CPC of 1967; (c) the Commercial Code of 1835, as extensively amended; (d) the Code of Private Maritime Law of 1958 (radically amended by Law 5030/2023); (e) the Criminal Code of 1950; (f) the Code of Criminal Procedure of 1950; (g) the Code of Administrative Procedure of 1999. There are also some more specific codifications, such as the Code of Civil Servants, the Code of Greek Nationality, the Lawyers' Code, the Notaries Code, the law on judicial officers, the law on court clerks, the Forest Code, the Agricultural Code, the Military Penal Code, and others.

The sources of law are defined by Article 1 of the CC, a provision that contains a general principle of the Greek legal system whose significance reaches beyond the scope of Civil law. Though in practice of only minor importance, apart from statute law, customary law is also accepted as a source of law (*praeter*, but not *contra legem*: Article 2 §2 Legislative Decree 7/10 May 1946).[8]

With some very specific exceptions (*see*, e.g., Articles 321–333 CPC, referring to the binding force of res judicata), the Greek legal system does not include any rules regarding the binding effect of judicial precedents. Thus, case law is not considered to be a source of law.

IV. Distinctions and Basic Elements

7. Following the civil law tradition, the Greek legal system is based on the distinction between *Private* and *Public law*. Contrary to Private law, provisions of Public law govern relations among persons, at least one of which is vested with public authority. Two main branches of Private law are Civil and Commercial law.

---

6. Zweigert & Kötz, *supra,* (No. 5, n. 5), pp. 65–80; same authors, *supra,* (No. 5, n. 5, Engl. transl.), pp. 63–75; R. David & J. Brierly, *Major Legal Systems in the World Today*, (Stevens 3rd ed., London 1985), pp. 20–34.
7. G. Michaelides-Nouaros, 'Les systèmes juridiques des peuples Européens', *RHDI* 1957, pp. 40 ff. (67, 106, 110 ff.). *Cf.* Ch. Fragistas, 'L'usage qui est fait par la jurisprudence du droit comparé', *RHDI* 1950, pp. 30 ff. Also, ZweigertKötz, *supra,* (No. 4, n. 5), p. 79; same authors, *supra,* (No. 5, n. 5, English translation), p. 74, speak of a 'hybrid system'.
8. Zepos, 'The Greek Legal System', *RHDI* 1961, pp. 1 ff. (8–10).

Commercial operations are thus treated by a separate branch of legislation, which is distinct from Civil law.

Public law is mainly divided into constitutional law and Administrative law. Criminal law, Criminal Procedural law, Ecclesiastical law and Civil Procedural law also belong to Public law.

§2. Delimitation of the Subject Matter

I. Definition of the Term 'Civil Procedure'

8. Civil Procedure refers to the totality of rules regulating the organization and the dispensing of justice in the field of private law.

9. Unlike differentiation developed within other legal systems, in Greek law, both terms 'Civil Procedure' and 'Civil Procedural Law' are equally used. Whereas a significant number of the standard procedural manuals or commentaries have been edited under the title of 'Civil Procedure' (the present Code of 1967 has also been enacted under this title), most recent works seem to prefer the title of 'Civil Procedural Law', despite its narrowness compared to the fields treated. All those books certainly comprise methods and forms of remedies regarding not only *civil* but also all *private* cases, i.e., labour, commercial, and maritime law cases. Yet, the prevalence of this term, covering the older and most significant branch of private law, must be attributed to historical reasons.

10. Contrary to some formerly expressed opinions, according to which Civil Procedure should be considered a mixed discipline, combining both public and private law provisions, the currently prevailing conception unanimously accepts that Civil Procedure belongs entirely to public law.

Classification of Civil Procedure to public law is nowadays justified in particular through the consideration that in the same manner as the rest of public law, Procedural law in general, and consequently Civil Procedure, by dealing with the dispensing of justice as a State activity, regulates relations dominated by the element of public authority. This overall qualification helps to consistently decide over a series of controversial matters, such as the applicability of private law on procedural acts (i.e., those affecting the validity of procedural contracts), the legal nature of relations developed between organs and parties during the enforcement proceedings, the nature of public auction, etc. However, despite this predominant consideration of Civil Procedure as entirely belonging to public law, neither the fact that some procedural rules are subject to private autonomy (*jus dispositivum*)[9] nor its close connection to private law was ever denied.

9. The division of procedural rules according to whether or not they are subject to modifications through contrary agreements of the parties is generally accepted.

II. Distinction from Other Types of Procedure Separate

11. Similar to most civil law systems and unlike the conception of common law, Greek codifications and legal scholarship have both been developed under the basic idea of a clear distinction between substantive and procedural law.[10] Under this conception, the need for introducing several types of procedural law becomes apparent.

Greek procedural law is accordingly divided into several branches, each corresponding to the equivalent field of substantive law: one speaks of a series of subdivisions, which, besides Civil Procedure, comprise Administrative Procedure (or Administrative Procedural Law, or Procedure of the Administrative Conflicts), Criminal Procedure (or Criminal Procedural Law), Disciplinary Procedure (or Disciplinary Procedural Law), Social Insurance Procedure (or Procedural Law of Social Insurance), Tax Disputes Procedure (or Tax Procedural Law), etc. These branches are dominated by common principles, the most important of which are: publicity of the hearing (Article 93 §2 Const.), protection of the right of defence (Article 20 §2 Const.), thorough reasoning of court decisions and publication of the dissenting opinion (Article 93 §3 Const.).[11] Common procedural features are moreover distinct (e.g., recognition of the right to appeal, the structure of the cassation proceedings, some principles of evidence, etc.), while most procedural institutions and concepts have essentially developed the same content. In this sense, one may speak of a common backbone and also of a certain degree of uniformity. Yet, given that the differentiation between the objectives and principles of each substantive law branch requires an elaboration of the appropriate type of procedures, it is also true that each of the above branches of procedural law has its own structure and principles.

III. Are There Separate Court Systems and Rules of Procedure?

12. The most significant branches of procedural law within the Greek legal system are: (1) Civil Procedure or Civil Procedural Law; (2) Administrative Procedure or Administrative Procedural Law; (3) Criminal Procedure or Criminal Procedural Law. The above *three separate* systems of procedural rules correspond to only *two separate* court systems. While ordinary justice includes: (1) the civil (Articles 93 §1; 94 §§2, 3 Const.); (2) the criminal (Articles 93 §1; 96 §1 Const.); and (3) the administrative (Articles 93 §1; 94 §1; 95 Const.) courts, the judiciary is the same for both civil and criminal courts. A special body of judges has been recently formed specifically for the ordinary administrative tribunals. This inconsistency between systems of procedural rules and court system has resulted from the overall historical evolution of the Greek judicial system.

---

10. Substantive and procedural law are treated in separate codes (e.g., CC and CPC; Criminal Code and Code of Criminal Procedure). Moreover, most of the procedural treatises offer an extensive analysis on the differentiation of these notions.
11. *See* particularly *infra*, Nos 47 ff.

13. The field of Civil Procedure has a long tradition and has always enjoyed the special attention of both scholars and practitioners. The old CPC of 1835 was, for over a century, the main statute regulating both civil and administrative litigation; until 1983, the new CPC continued to provide the main procedural structure for administrative disputes, while the incidental review of administrative acts is still operating.

§3. Sources of Civil Procedural Law

I. A Brief Historical Perspective

A. General Remarks

14. For the purposes of this chapter, Civil Procedural Law will be understood in its wide sense, comprising both the organization of the courts and the methods for dispensing civil justice. Apart from the Const., which is regarded as a fundamental source of Procedural Law, the specific statutory source directly devoted to Civil Procedure in Greece is currently the CPC of 1967, as subsequently modified. However, judicial organization is determined by Law 4938/2022, which recently replaced Law 1756/1988 ('Code for the Organization of Courts and the Status of Judicial Functionaries').[12]

B. Ancient Greek Law

15. The evidence for judicial proceedings in Greece goes back to the seventh century B.C. Despite the lack of any direct impact of Ancient Greek law on the sources of modern Greek Procedural Law, it is necessary to stress that it was in the justice-making process of the sixth, fifth and fourth centuries B.C. that the system of trial by jury and some fundamental procedural guarantees of contemporary significance originally developed.[13] Within the Ancient Greek machinery of justice, the roots of some of our contemporary fundamental procedural institutions or principles, e.g., the judicial review of unconstitutional state acts, the rights of access to justice and defence, the principle of publicity and the free disposition of the parties, and, in particular, arbitration, can be revealed.[14]

12. *See infra*, Nos 64 ff.
13. P. Yessiou-Faltsi, 'The Public Trial in Ancient Athens: Basic Principles of Contemporary Significance', *Volume in Honour of A. Manessis*, III (Sakkoulas, Athens 1999), pp. 315–342. This report has been initially published in a Japanese translation by the Institute of Comparative Law in Japan, Chuo University, special volume, 1993. It has also appeared in English in the volume Kojima et al., (eds), Europe's Judicial Systems, Past and Future (Chuo University Press, Tokyo 1998).
14. K. Beys, 'Die Ausstrahlung des deutschen zivilprozessualen Denkens auf das griechische Recht der Privatrechtsstreitigkeiten, Ein Beitrag zur Geschichte der griechischen Prozessrechtswissenschaft',

C. Period of the Turkish Domination

16. During the period of Turkish domination, and before Greece was recognized as an independent State (London Protocol of 1830), the dispensing of civil justice was undertaken, either by the Greek Orthodox church through 'episcopal' courts[15] or by certain notable persons, adjudicating through elaborate procedures of arbitration. It is assumed that episcopal courts applied Roman-Byzantine procedural law. Additionally, a whole system of alternative extrajudicial methods for dissolving civil disputes had been developed.

D. Period of the War of Independence

17. Until the establishment of the first Greek King in 1833, the following statutory Regulations concerning civil proceedings had been promulgated, although never essentially applied: (1) 'Resolutions for the Procedure and the Organization of the Courts' of 30 April and 2 May 1822, strongly oriented towards oral procedures and modelled on the French CPC of 1806; (2) The Resolution of the Governor I. Kapodistrias for the 'Organization and the Competence of the Courts' of 15 December 1828; (3) The Resolutions of the Governor I. Kapodistrias (a) for the 'Organization of the Courts' and (b) for the 'Civil and Criminal Procedure' of 15 August 1830, instituting written procedures known as the first Greek CPC (including 562 articles).

E. Period of the Codes of 1835[16]

18. Among four Codes elaborated by *Ludwig von Maurer*,[17] two concerned civil matters: (1) The Code on Civil Procedure, issued on 2 April 1834, published on 16 June 1834 and in force from 25 January 1835 until 15 September 1968; (2) the Code on the Organization of the Courts and Notaries, issued on 21 January 1834, published on 10 April 1834 and in force from 25 January 1835 until 1988. These Codes were published in both Greek and German.[18] However, the German text was considered authentic and thus prevailed in cases of a wording divergency.

---

in *Grundlagenberichte für die Tagung der Wissenschaftlichen Vereinigung für Inter-nationales Verfahrensrecht, Verfahrensrechtsvergleichung und Schiedsgerichtswesen e.V.* (Passau 1989), zum Thema 'Das deutsche Zivilprozessrecht und seine Ausstrahlung auf andere Rechtsordnungen', p. 173.

15. P. Zepos, 'Mixed Jurisdiction in Greece', (*The American Journal of Comparative Law* 1974), pp. 221–229.
16. D. Tsikrikas, 'Die Entstehung und Entwicklung des griechischen Zivilprozessrechts im rechtshistorischen und rechtsvergleichenden Zusammenhang', *ZZPInt* 2011, pp. 111–133.
17. *See supra*, No. 4.
18. *Gesetzbuch ueber das Zivil-Verfahren, Beilage zu Nr. 22 des Regierungsblattes, Nauplia 1834; Gerichts – und Notariats – Ordnung, Beilage zu Nr. 13 des Regierungsblattes*, Nauplia 1834.

19. Until 1968, Greece operated under two Codes of Civil Procedure. Whereas the Code of 1835 successively extended its force to all new areas of the Greek State (the Ionian Islands, Thessaly, Epirus, Macedonia, Thrace, Islands of the Aegean, Islands of the Dodecanese), Crete was allowed to maintain[19] its own local procedural codes, i.e, the Cretan CPC of 1903,[20] partly modelled after the Austrian CPC of 1900, and the Organization of the Courts in Crete, also of 1903.

II. Contemporary Sources of Civil Procedural Law

A. The Constitution of 1975

20. The Const. of 1975, as subsequently amended, is a direct source of Civil Procedural Law.[21] The present Constitution comprises numerous provisions regarding procedural issues and has supported, even more distinctly than its predecessors, a predominant consideration of procedure as being a kind of 'applied constitutional Law'.

In section V, Part Three of the 1975 Const., fifteen articles of the Const. are devoted to the 'Judicial Power', including all fundamental rules with regard to the administration of justice (Articles 87–100A). They are divided into two chapters: the first one (Articles 87–92) covers the 'Judicial Functionaries and Staff', and the second (Articles 93–100A) the 'Organization and Jurisdiction of the Courts'. Section V naturally refers to all three branches of ordinary justice (*cf.* Article 93 §1), thus also comprising civil justice as one of the state functions. However, the 1975 Const. provides for a series of general fundamental principles, directly or indirectly, regarding the administration of justice. Several of those principles are repeated in the CPC under the same or a more concrete formulation. They introduce a complex of constitutional guarantees. Among them, Article 20 §1 safeguards the right of access to courts particularly.[22]

B. The CPC of 1967/1971: Subsequent Modifications

21. The New CPC was enacted in 1967[23] and entered into force on 16 September 1968. The Code of 1967 is to a great extent based on German, Austrian and some other continental, mainly French models. Given that this work of codification derived from the experience gained through the application of the previous Code, it has been considered an original synthesis of purely Greek character.[24]

19. Law 291/1914.
20. Law 571/1903.
21. In particular P. Yessiou-Faltsi, 'Les bases constitutionnelles de l'organisation judiciaire en Gréce', *RHDI* 1979, pp. 62 ff.
22. *See* more precisely *infra*, No. 47 and Nos 52–55.
23. By-Law 44/1967.
24. R. Stürner, 'Das deutsche (österreichische) Zivilprozess und seine Ausstrahlung auf andere Rechtsordnungen', in W. Habscheid (ed.), *Das deutsche Zivilprozessrecht und seine Ausstrahlung auf andere Rechtsordnungen* (Gieseking, Bielefeld 1991), pp. 27–28.

22. The principal objectives of the Code were: an overall simplification through the unification of particular proceedings when possible; acceleration through the categorization of procedures and the elaboration of appropriate mechanisms to serve specific groups of disputes; a stronger orientation towards substantial truth through the institution of a more activist judge; emphasis on oral procedures and direct communication between the judge and the interested parties; larger operation of the principle of free evaluation of evidence; and, finally, 'humanization' of proceedings.

23. However, due to the fact that judicial practice could not be easily adjusted to the new Code, a special committee of experts was assigned to proceed to modifications in 1971. The objective of the 1971 amendment was to make the necessary corrections to the Code and treat its practical shortcomings satisfactorily. Royal Decree 657/1971 recodified both the initial text of the Code (Law 44/1967) and the 1971 amendments (Legislative Decree 958/1971), introducing a new enumeration. This unified text resulted in the current CPC of 1967/1971.

Some additional modifications of a lesser extent followed. Beyond a series of amendments caused by the revision of the CC in 1983, the more significant reforms include: introduction of particular proceedings for car accident disputes (Article 681A), maintenance and custody (Article 681B), simplification of divorce proceedings through abrogation of the pretrial stage before the bishop (Articles 593–597).

The second and even more important revision was attempted in 1984, basically due to the long duration of litigation. The new statutory provisions were the result of experience gained through the application of particular proceedings for labour cases. These operated successfully, as they provided for a more flexible procedural structure and a much wider admissibility of evidence. The main points of this amendment were: (a) the substitution of the non-final decision, which was rendered after the first hearing, in order to determine the questions of evidence (and was indeed time-consuming for the court), by a simple 'act' of the court, relieved from the demands and guarantees of a genuine judicial decision; (b) the extension of the subject matter competence of one-member district courts; (c) the attempt to eliminate the number of hearings before one-member district courts, by introducing an oral first hearing of the case, during which the parties were obliged to appear, the means of proof (mainly witnesses and documents) were subject to an early presentation and evidence approached the model of free proof taking.[25]

Some partial modifications of the Code have also been enacted by Laws 1545/1985, 1649/1986, 1653/1986, 1682/1987, 1738/1987, and 1868/1989, again oriented towards the need for acceleration.

The next amendments to the Code were affected by Laws 2145/1993, 2172/1993, 2207/1994, 2298/1995, 2331/1995, 2721/1999, 2741/1999 and 2819/2000. Among a series of changes,[26] the most important include: (a) Restoration of the non-final decision to deal with questions of evidence. Beyond the determination of matters

25. *See infra*, No. 417.
26. Especially for Laws 2145/1993, 2172/1993, 2207/1994, *see* N. Klamaris, 'Die prozessuale Aktualität in Griechenland, in: *Festschrift für Wolfram Henckel zum 70. Geburtstag'* (Walter de Gruyter, Berlin, New York 1995), pp. 437–454.

related to the taking of evidence, and in contrast to the aforementioned act, this decision ought to contain full reasons regarding the admissibility and the legal foundation of the parties' requests. (b) Abandonment of the 'unjustified' opposition against default.[27] (c) Introduction of a mandatory pretrial stage (Article 214A CPC) for actions belonging to the subject matter competence of three-member district courts for attempting a conciliation.[28]

One of the most important amendments dates from 2001.[29] Law 2195/2001, as modified by Law 3043/2002, has indeed introduced a momentous change to the structure of the CPC. According to this new system, all kinds of proceedings in both one- and three-member district courts ought to follow the same pattern. This unified model of normal proceedings had been based on the attempt to concentrate all relevant material for the adjudication of civil cases in a single oral hearing. Factual allegations of the parties, as well as means of evidence, ought to be thus introduced during this sole hearing on penalty of inadmissibility. The judge was relieved of the rules dominating rigid evidence in all civil courts, with the exception of those rules imposing limitations on the use of testimony.[30]

24. A legislative intervention related to the peculiarity of the Greek linguistic evolution was attempted in 1985 to secure greater accessibility to judicial mechanisms, along with the rest of the Greek Codes, as most of them had been initially formulated in the archaic form of the Greek language, called 'purified' (*katharevousa*), the CPC was changed to the contemporary linguistic form (*dimotiki*) and was as such enacted by Presidential Decree 503/1985. The archaic text, nevertheless, prevails when a divergency between the authentic initial and the new formulation appears.

25. A series of partial amendments to the CPC were carried out between 2002 and 2008. They introduced modifications regarding the disqualification of judges; the allocation of court costs and legal aid; some family matters in both adversary and voluntary proceedings, mostly due to innovations in the area of substantive family law; certain special issues of labour proceedings, e.g., the granting of standing to sue to trade unions, chambers or other associations in all court instances.

Three important modifications concerned provisional remedies. First, upon rendering a provisional order, a time limit of thirty days was provided for the hearing of the application for granting injunctions; in case a provisional order was connected to labour disputes, the summoning of the adversary party to the hearing ought to take place twenty-four hours in advance (Article 691, §4 CPC). Second, after a decision granting provisional relief was rendered, a time limit of thirty days was provided for bringing the principal action on penalty of expiry of the provisional measure *ipso iure* (Article 693 CPC). Third, where the State or other public

27. *Infra*, No. 285.
28. *Infra*, No. 204.
29. N. Klamaris, 'Die aktuellen bzw. bevorstehenden Reformen im Bereich des griechischen Zivilprozeßrechts. Reformtendenzen und verabschiedete ZPO-Modifizierungen', in Rolf A. Schütze, *Einheit und Vielfalt des Rechts, Festschrift für Reinhold Geimer zum 65, Geburtstag* (Verlag C.H. Beck, München 2002), pp. 437–447.
30. For more details *infra*, Nos 412–417.

law entities are parties, the Public Prosecutor of *Areios Pagos* was exceptionally authorized to attack all decisions issuing or revoking an injunction by filing a cassation, in case the injunction pertains to matters of general interest, and despite the general rule under which, provisional remedies may not be attacked by any methods of review (Article 699 CPC). Another group of amendments may be evaluated as tending to accelerate the proceedings, directly or indirectly (*see* Article 226 §5, CPC; Article 307; Article 748 §1). Finally, some important changes were designed to modernize or promote the efficiency of enforcement proceedings (*see* Article 982, §2e, CPC; Articles 954 and 1003; Articles 959, 965, 982, 995 and 998). However, the most recent reforms, affected by Laws 4335/2015, 4772/2017, 4475/2017, 4512/2018, 4842/2021, 4855/2021, 4912/2022 and 5023/2023, have brought about the most radical change ever attempted to its entire structure. The modifications introduced by the new rules will be discussed later on in this monograph.

26. In its present form, the CPC consists of eight Books, each one divided into several chapters. The first Book (twenty-three chapters) comprises the 'General Provisions' (Articles 1–207), while part of its second Book (Articles 208–334) deals with the 'Procedure before the Courts of First Instance' (eleven chapters). Articles 335–465 of the second Book are devoted to 'Evidence' (Chapter 12). The rest of the provisions of this Book (Articles 466–494) contain particular rules for small claims and actions seeking an accounting or partition (three chapters). Appeals and other methods of review are treated in the third Book (Articles 495–590, in six chapters), while the fourth Book provides for the 'Particular Proceedings' (Articles 591–636, in four chapters) and the fifth Book for 'Provisional Remedies' (Articles 682–738, in eight chapters). The sixth Book covers 'Voluntary Jurisdiction' (Articles 739–866, in two chapters), the seventh Book 'Arbitration' (Articles 867–903, in one chapter) and the eighth Book 'Enforcement Proceedings' (Articles 904–1054, in nine chapters). The Introductory Law of the Code, in its present form (after 1971), comprises seventy-six articles.

C. The Code on the Organization of the Courts of 1988

27. The Code on the Organization of the Courts and Notaries of 1835[31] was not replaced with the CPC. Due to the decision of the Revision Committee of the CPC in 1964 to postpone the elaboration of a new Code on the Organization of the Courts, the Code of 1835 survived until 1988. The 'Code on the Organization of the Courts and the Status of Judicial Functionaries' (Law 1756/1988) contained an extensive regulation about the structure, composition and functioning of the courts (Articles 1–130), thus concretizing the basic provisions of the Const. (Articles 87–92). The law was recently replaced by Law 4938/2022.

---

31. N. Klamaris, 'Das neue griechische Gerichtsverfassungsrecht oder 'Die Rache der Wittelsbacher', *Festschrift für W. Habscheid* (Gieseking, Bielefeld 1989), pp. 161–166.

D. Special Laws

28. Numerous statutory regulations supplement the three basic sources of Civil Procedural Law aforementioned.

A very important group of special procedural laws has been provided by the Const. of 1975 itself. They are designed to deal more extensively with some constitutional institutions: (a) Law 345/1976 on the 'Code of the Special Highest Court Provided by Article 100 of the Constitution.' regulates both organization and proceedings before this Special Supreme Judicial Organ;[32] (b) Law 184/1975 on 'The Formation of the Supreme Judicial Council and the Supreme Disciplinary Councils provided by Articles 90 and 91 of the Const. etc.';[33] (c) Law 693/1977 on 'The Adjudication of Actions for ' mistrial' (civil actions against judges); (d) Law 3038/2002 on 'The Resolution of Disputes Related to Article 88 §2 Const. and Other Provisions' (remunerations and pensions of judges); (e) Law 3068/2002 on 'The Compliance of the Administration to Judicial Decisions and the Promotion of Judges of the Ordinary Administrative Courts to the Post of Councillor of State' (implementation of new Articles 94 and 95 Const.).

E. International Conventions

29. Greece is a party to several international conventions, both multilateral and bilateral, dealing with civil procedural matters, of which only the most important can be mentioned. According to Article 28 §1 Const., By the time they are sanctioned by law and have become operative according to the conditions therein, these conventions constitute thereafter an integral part of domestic law and prevail over any provisions contrary to this law.

The European Convention on Human Rights (Article 6 §1) was ratified in 1974 (Legislative Decree 53/1974).

Greek membership in the European Community (1 January 1981) resulted in the adherence to the Brussels Convention on Jurisdiction and the Enforcement of Judgments in Civil and Commercial Matters of 1968 (Ratification: Law 1814/1988). The Brussels Convention, which has been replaced by Council Regulation 44/2001 on 1 March 2002 and currently by (recast) Regulation 1215/2012, in force since 10 January 2015, governed the relations of Greece with all Community Member States since 1 April 1989. Greece ratified (Law 2004/1992) the San Sebastian Convention of 1989, which entered into force on 1 July 1992, as well as the Convention of 1996 for the accession of Austria, Sweden and Finland (Law 2727/1999).

The Lugano Convention of 16 September 1988 was ratified by Law 2460/1997 and entered into force on 26 February 1997. A revision of the Lugano Convention, signed on 30 October 2007, was ratified by the EU on 18 May 2009 and started to apply in all Member States on 1 January 2010.[34]

32. *Infra*, No. 73.
33. *Infra*, Nos 50 and 83.
34. *See Official Journal of the European Union*, No. L 339/1 of 21 Dec. 2007.

Furthermore, Greece was party to the two Geneva Conventions on Arbitration: (1) of 24 September 1923, Protocol on the Arbitral Clauses (Ratification: Legislative Decree of 4/27 March 1926); and (2) of 26 September 1927 on the Execution of Foreign Arbitral Awards (Ratification: Law 5013/1931), and to the New York Convention of 10 June 1958 on the Recognition and Execution of Foreign Arbitral Awards (Ratification: Legislative Decree 4220/1961).

Greece has ratified the following conventions of the Hague Conference of Private International Law:

(1) Convention of 5 October 1961 on Abolishing the Requirement of Legalization for Foreign Public Documents (Ratification: Law 1497 of 21/27 November 1984). The Convention has been in force in Greece since 18 May 1985.
(2) Convention of 15 November 1965 on the Service Abroad of Judicial and Extrajudicial Documents in Civil or Commercial Matters (Ratification: Law 1334/1983). The Convention has been in force in Greece since 18 September 1983.
(3) Convention of 18 March 1970 on the Taking of Evidence Abroad in Civil or Commercial Matters (Ratification: Law 3287/2004). The Convention has been in force in Greece since 19 March 2005).
(4) Convention of 2 October 1973 on the Recognition and Enforcement of Decisions Relating to Maintenance Obligations (Ratification: Law 3171/2003). The Convention has been in force in Greece since 1 February 2004).
(5) Convention of 29 May 1993 on Protection of Children and Co-operation in Respect of Intercountry Adoption (Ratification: Law 3765/2009). The Convention has been in force in Greece since 1 January 2010).
(6) Convention of 19 October 1996 on Jurisdiction, Applicable Law, Recognition, Enforcement and Co-operation in Respect of Parental Responsibility and Measures for the Protection of Children (Ratification: Law 4020/2011). The Convention has been in force in Greece since 1 June 2012).
(7) Convention of 13 January 2000 on the International Protection of Adults (Ratification: Law 4898/2022). The Convention has been in force in Greece since 1 November 2022).
(8) Convention of 30 June 2005 on Choice of Court Agreements (Ratification: Greece is bound by the Convention as a result of the approval by the EU). In force since 1 October 2015).
(9) Convention of 23 November 2007 on the International Recovery of Child Support and Other Forms of Family Maintenance (Ratification: Greece is bound by the Convention as a result of the approval by the EU). In force since 1 August 2014).
(10) Convention of 2 July 2019 on the Recognition and Enforcement of Foreign Judgments in Civil or Commercial Matters (Ratification: Greece is bound by the Convention as a result of the approval by the EU). In force since 1 September 2023).

Finally, Greece has become a party to the following multilateral conventions dealing with procedural matters:

(1) The European Convention of 7 June 1968 on Information of Foreign Law and its Additional Protocol of 15 March 1978 (Ratification: Law 593 of 6/7 June 1977). The Convention has been in force in Greece since 6 January 1978.
(2) The European Convention of 27 January 1977 on the Service Abroad of Documents Relating to Judicial Assistance (Ratification: Law 1456 of 16/6 June 1984).
(3) The ICSID Convention of 16 March 1966 on the Settlement of Investment Disputes Between States and Nationals of Other States (Ratification: Law 608 of 11/11 November 1968). The Convention has been in force in Greece since 21 May 1969.
(4) The Convention of 10 May 1952 on the Unification of Certain Rules Relating to the Arrest of Sea-going Ships (Ratification: Legislative Decree 4570 of 22/26 October 1966). The Convention has been in force in Greece since 28 August 1967.
(5) The Convention of 10 May 1952 on the Unification of Certain Rules Concerning Civil Jurisdiction in Matters of Collision of Ships (Ratification: Law 4407 of 4/11 November 1964). The Convention has been in force in Greece since 16 September 1965.
(6) The United Nations Convention of 20 June 1956 on the Recovery Abroad of Claims for Maintenance (Ratification: Legislative Decree 4421 of 7/11 November 1964). The Convention has been in force in Greece since 1 December 1965.
(7) The Vienna Convention of 18 April 1961 on Diplomatic Relations (Ratification: Legislative Decree 530 of 14 April/15 May 1970). The Convention has been in force in Greece since 15 August 1970.
(8) The Vienna Convention of 24 April 1963 on Consular Relations (Ratification: Law 90 of 23/23 July 1975). The Convention has been in force in Greece since 13 November 1975.
(9) The Hague Convention of 25 October 1980 on International Child Abduction (Ratification: Law 2102/1992). The Convention has been in force in Greece since 1 June 1993.

Among the various bilateral conventions of which Greece is a party, directly regulating procedural matters, one can distinguish the following groups:

(1) Conventions dealing with recognition and enforcement of judgments. Contracting States: *Albania* (Convention of 17 May 1993, in force since 15 September 1995; ratified in Greece by Law 2311/1995, Articles 23–30); *Armenia* (Convention of 21 November 2000, in force since 21 July 2002; ratified in Greece by Law 3007/2002, Articles 17–23); *Bulgaria* (Convention of 10 April 1976, in force since 26 April 1980; ratified in Greece by Law 841 of 21/21 December 1978, Articles 27–33); *China* (Convention of 17 October 1994, in force since 1 July 1996; ratified in Greece by Law 2358/1995, Articles 20–27); *Cyprus* (Convention of 5 March 1984, in force since 25 August 1985; ratified in Greece by Law 1548 of 17/23 May 1985, Articles 21–26); (former) *Czechoslovakia* (Convention of 22 October 1980, in force since 16 July 1983; ratified

in Greece by Law 1323 of 12 January 1983, Articles 22–28); *Georgia* (Convention of 10 May 1999, in force since 5 June 2000; ratified in Greece by Law 2813/2000, Articles 21–29); *Germany* (Convention of 4 November 1961, in force since 18 September 1963; ratified in Greece by Law 4305 of 22/30 May 1963); *Hungary* (Convention of 8 October 1979, in force since 14 August 1981; ratified in Greece by Law 1149 of 22 April/5 May 1981, Articles 24–25); *Lebanon* (Convention of 5 April 1975, in force since 4 August 1986; ratified in Greece by Law 1099 of 12/17 December 1980, Articles 3–9); *Poland* (Convention of 24 October 1979, in force since 23 December 1981; ratified in Greece by Law 1184 of 23/29 July 1981, Articles 21–31); *Romania* (Convention of 19 October 1972, in force since 29 April 1977; ratified in Greece by Legislative Decree 429 of 20 May/27 June 1974, Articles 21–28); (former) *Soviet Union* (Convention of 21 May 1981, in force since 1 September 1982; ratified in Greece by Law 1242 of 23 March/6 April 1982, Articles 23–34); *Syria* (Convention of 2 June 1981, in force since 5 April 1985; ratified in Greece by Law 1450 of 16/16 June 1984, Articles 21–29); *Tunisia* (Convention of 12 April 1993, in force since 21 January 1995; ratified in Greece by Law 2228/1994, Articles 28–36); *Ukraine* (Convention of 2 July 2002, in force since 27 January 2007; ratified in Greece by Law 3281/2004, Articles 20–25); (former) *Yugoslavia* (Convention of 18 June 1959, in force since 1 April 1960; ratified in Greece by Legislative Decree 4007 of 27 October/3 November 1959).

(2) Conventions dealing with matters of legal aid and service abroad. Contracting states: *Albania* (Convention of 17 May 1993, *see supra*, Articles 1–22); *Armenia* (Convention of 21 November 2000, *see supra*, Articles 1–16); *Austria* (Convention of 6 December 1965, in force since 13 January 1971; ratified in Greece by Legislative Decree 137 of 1/11 March 1969); *Bulgaria* (Convention of 10 April 1976, in force since 26 April 1980; ratified in Greece by Law 841 of 21/21 December 1978); *China* (Convention of 17 October 1994, *see supra*, Articles 1 ff.); *Cyprus* (Convention of 5 March 1984, *see supra*, Articles 2–15); (former) *Czechoslovakia* (Convention of 22 October 1980, *see supra*, Articles 2–16); *Georgia* (Convention of 10 May 1999, *see supra*, Articles 1–20); *Germany* (Convention of 11 May 1938, in force since 31 May 1939, suspended since 6 April 1941, again in force since 1 February 1952; ratified by Law 1432 of 19/25 October 1938); pursuant to an Official Announcement of the Greek Ministry of Foreign Affairs (1 May/10 September 1992), the convention with East Germany concerning legal aid (Law 1618/1986) has ceased to operate; *Great Britain* (Convention of 27 February 1936, in force since 16 December 1937; ratified in Greece by Law 730 of 8/15 June 1937); *Hungary* (Convention of 8 October 1979, *see supra*, Articles 2–14); *Lebanon* (Convention of 5 April 1975, *see supra*, Articles 36–45); *Poland* (Convention of 24 October 1979, *see supra*, Articles 6–12); *Romania* (Convention of 19 October 1972, *see supra*, Articles 7–19); (former) *Soviet Union* (Convention of 21 May 1981, *see supra*; Articles 2–13). *Switzerland* (Convention of 30 March 1934, in force since 27 January 1938; ratified in Greece by Law 729 of 8/15 June 1937); *Syria* (Convention of 2 June 1981, *see supra*, Articles 6–20); *Tunisia* (Convention of 12 April 1993, *see supra*); *Ukraine* (Convention of 2 July

2002, *see supra*);(former) *Yugoslavia* (Convention of 19 June 1959, in force since 1 April 1960; ratified in Greece by Legislative Decree 4009 of 27 October/5 November 1959).

(3) Conventions Securing Legal Protection. Contracting States: *Switzerland* (Convention of 1 December 1927, in force since 30 November 1928; ratified in Greece by Law 3610 of 9 July/22 September 1928); *United States of America* (Convention of 3 August 1951, ratified in Greece by Law 2893 of 23 June/10 July 1954, Article 6).

F. Customary Law

30. Procedural customs are also covered by the general rule of Article 1 of the CC[35] and are commonly accepted as a source of Greek Civil Procedural Law under the same general conditions despite their minor practical significance. Some procedural institutions have been indeed considered, under the previous Code of 1935, as being created by procedural custom. The limited space given to the creation of a customary rule of procedural law is primarily attributed to the ever-expanding enacted law and, consequently, to the de facto primacy of procedural legislation. However, procedural law, as a branch of law mainly regulating actions by state organs, is not regarded as a suitable field for the development of customary law.

G. Judicial Precedents

31. Notwithstanding the creative role of judicial decisions, this role in Greece being particularly distinct in relation to procedural issues, judges are not admitted as creators of the law. Nevertheless, although judicial decisions are not formal sources of Civil Procedural Law, the practical significance of the technically non-binding judicial precedents has been fully revealed, not only when the orientations of the New Code of 1967 were elaborated but also after this Code started to operate.

H. Legal Doctrine

32. Legal doctrine of Civil Procedure, as well as the overall legal scholarly production, is not a source of Greek law. Nevertheless, Civil Procedure has been and is still regarded in Greece as a major discipline directly dealing with the process of law. The development of Greek Civil Procedural Law, based on a relatively long tradition under leading representatives, is currently oriented mostly to the German, Austrian, Swiss, Belgian, Italian and French doctrine. Beyond its direct impact on the orientations of judicial decisions, procedural legal doctrine has strongly influenced the overall evolution of Greek Civil Procedural Law.

35. *Supra*, No. 6.

§4. General Features of the Administration of Justice in Civil Matters

I. Characteristics of the Procedure

A. General Remarks

33. Articles 106–116 CPC (Chapter II) are devoted to the 'fundamental procedural principles'. Under this general title, the above provisions either contain some basic rules which regulate relationships between the court and the parties throughout the procedure (Articles 106, 107, 108) and also its main characteristics (Article 115) or institute several fundamental guarantees for the parties (Articles 109, 110, 111, 112, 113, 114, 116).[36]

The following parts of this section will present the rules of the first category, while the fundamental guarantees will be treated in section II.

B. The Principle of Free Disposition of the Parties (Article 106 CPC)

34. According to the main principle of the CPC, the parties control civil litigation in several aspects. This dominant position of the parties with regard to civil action goes hand in hand with the principle of private autonomy prevailing in the CC. It is, thus, provided (Article 106) that the power to determine whether or not to commence a civil action or to specify the extent of the contested claims belongs entirely to the parties (principle of free disposition). With the exception of some very limited cases referring to the voluntary jurisdiction (i.e., Articles 826 §1, 831, §1, 838 §1),[37] since civil rights are concerned, a civil court may not originate a civil process ex officio. Furthermore, adjudication over non-requested claims or beyond the claims of the parties, being the practically relevant cases of violating the above principle, is sanctioned even through a ground for cassation (Article 559 No. 9 CPC).[38] Accordingly, the effect of res judicata extends only insofar as a relevant claim has been raised (Article 322 CPC).[39] In a similar fashion, enforcement proceedings commence only upon the creditor's motion (Article 927).[40]

35. It is moreover conversely understood that beyond the normal mode of terminating civil proceedings through the rendition of a judicial decision, pending civil litigation may also terminate on the plaintiff's initiative (i.e., abandonment), in principle, without any further inquiry by the court.[41] From the principle of private autonomy, it is finally assumed that not only the plaintiff but also the defendant must

36. N. Klamaris, 'Verfahrensgrundsätze nach dem griechischen Zivilprozessrecht', *MDR* 2016, pp. 947–951.
37. *See infra*, Nos 96 and 276.
38. *See infra*, No. 299. *See*, e.g., *Areios Pagos* 892/1980, *Legal Tribune* 1981, p. 284; *Areios Pagos* 451/1980, *Dike* 1980, p. 930.
39. *See infra*, No. 245.
40. *Infra*, No. 479.
41. *See infra*, Nos 318–326.

be primarily entitled to abandon civil rights and terminate a civil dispute (i.e., admission) at any time before a judgment is pronounced.[42] The validity of procedural contracts, however, which are basically connected to the right of free disposition of civil rights (i.e., conciliation), is through explicit provisions (i.e., Article 293: conciliation) dependent on the relevant conditions of substantive law.[43]

Although the principle of free disposition as such has not yet been explicitly considered enjoying a constitutional pre-eminence in relation to civil rights, any restrictions in this respect would certainly be regarded as a prohibited intervention in private personal freedom and free development and contrary to the conception of civil proceedings designed to be consistent with the policies embodied in substantive law.

C. The Principle of Party Presentation (Article 106 CPC)

36. The adversary element in Greek Civil Procedural Law has been developed under the CPC of 1835 in the form of rules known as the 'conversational system' or 'conversational principle'. It refers to a procedural structure based on party presentation.

Whereas the principle of free disposition is regarded by most Greek authors as technically referring to the parties' claims, the principle of party presentation exclusively deals with the overall facts based on those claims. This last notion is defined as referring to allegations containing relevant facts, in the sense of the overall elements of a legal norm, which are instituted as the necessary conditions for its legal consequences. More specifically, Article 106 provides that the court may take into consideration only facts alleged and proven by the parties. Privately acquired cognizance by the court is thus not allowed. Reliance by the judge on facts not submitted by the parties[44] or not proven through the relevant means of proof[45] constitutes grounds for review even in cassation proceedings (Article 559 No. 8 and No. 10). Finally, the principle of party presentation is safeguarded by one more ground (Article 559 No. 11), which sanctions consideration of evidence not presented or not produced by the parties.[46]

The existing two exceptions are evidently of limited practical significance: Facts which are notorious, either to everyone, beyond any reasonable doubt (Article 336 §1), or only to the court in its official capacity through another judicial activity (Article 336 §2), may be taken into consideration by the court ex officio, and do not need to be previously proven. There is also a third category of elements, called 'teachings of common experience', which may be the object of the court's judicial notice (Article 336 §4). These are, however, not regarded as an exception to the rule of party presentation. 'Teachings of common experience' comprise all human

42. *See infra*, No. 326.
43. *See infra*, Nos 327–330.
44. *Areios Pagos* 1111/1984, *Hellenic Justice* 1985, p. 220; *Areios Pagos* 1398/1982, *Dike* 1984, p. 131; *Areios Pagos* 750/1980, *Legal Tribune* 1981, p. 38; *Areios Pagos* 204/1976, *Legal Tribune* 1976, p. 723.
45. *Areios Pagos* 571/1980, *Legal Tribune* 1981, p. 29; *Areios Pagos* 198/1976, *Legal Tribune* 1976, p. 722; *Areios Pagos* 1285/1974, *Archives of Judicial Decisions* 1975, p. 418.
46. *Areios Pagos* 816/1982, *Journal of Greek Jurists* 1983, p. 407.

knowledge, accessible through the average education or the everyday social experience in various fields (grammar, history, psychology, mathematics, etc.), and are used by the court while (a) interpreting rules of law, (b) subordinating facts to the rules of law, (c) evaluating means of proof, and (d) drawing off conclusions through syllogisms based on indirect evidence (Article 336 §3).[47] Accordingly, they are subtly distinguished from notorious facts.

37. Following the common conception in civil law countries, the application of legal norms does not principally depend on the parties. Regardless of whether it is public or private, substantive or procedural, domestic, international, private international or foreign, written or unwritten (custom) law, it belongs to the domain of the court, which is entitled to determine the applicable rules ex officio. This power of the court, which is regarded as originating from the nature of the judicial function as such, is not subject to any exceptions under the current Code. Unlike the previously prevailing conception within a long series of judicial decisions, foreign and customary law nowadays enjoy a similar procedural treatment with the rules of domestic or enacted law. This certainly means that they are principally applied by the court on its own motion (Article 337).[48] Moreover, violation of such rules under the present Code also constitutes a ground for cassation (Article 559 No. 1).[49] If, however, the court does not possess the proper sources for cognizance over the content of these two particular categories of legal norms, it enjoys the discretionary power to order the taking of evidence, or to use any appropriate means without any restrictions (free evidence).

D. The Principle of Parties' Motion (Article 108 CPC)

38. Greek Civil Procedural Law follows the system of party prosecution, called 'principle of parties' initiative'. Actually, introducing a type of procedure almost entirely departing from the contrary system of the court's motion, Article 108 indeed declares that all procedural acts have to be carried out on the parties' motion unless otherwise provided. As a result, the advancement of procedure in civil litigation depends entirely on any party's diligence. This rule applies throughout all stages of first instance or appellate proceedings, comprising all relevant procedural steps. The first hearing of the case must be fixed, and service of the action must be carried out on the initiative of the plaintiff; all subsequent hearings of the case, even after appeal (Article 498), and service of various documents, including decisions (Article 123), again depend on the motion of any diligent party. Even enforcement proceedings are subject to the initiative of the petitioning creditor. According to Article 927 CPC, not only commencement but also advancement of execution proceedings depends on this party.[50]

---

47. *See infra*, No. 350.
48. K. Makridou, *The Procedural Treatment of Foreign Law in Greek Civil Trials: Questions of Fact or Questions of Law?*, *ZZP International* 2016, pp. 143 ff.
49. K. Kerameus, *Revisibilität ausländischen Rechts*, *ZZP* 1986, pp. 166 ff.
50. *Infra*, No. 479.

E. The Principle of Concentration (Article 269 CPC)

39. For reasons directly related to the need for acceleration, Article 269 §1 CPC[51] explicitly required that, in principle, all factual allegations by the parties must be submitted to the court in a 'concentrated' manner, i.e., through pleadings of the hearing, which were expected to be deposited twenty days earlier (Article 237 §1, as amended by Law 2915/2001 and 3043/2002), otherwise sanctioning their inadmissibility on the court's own motion.

The principle of concentration applied to appellate proceedings (Article 527) as well, under equal conditions to the first instance.

Article 269 CPC was abolished by Law 4335/2015 in the context of the modification of the CPC, which has been operative since 1 January 2016.[52] Under this system, the parties re obliged to file their pleadings and provide all evidence in support of their claims or factual allegations within one hundred days from the filing of their legal action (new Article 237 §1). Reply submissions could be filed within the next fifteen days from the date of expiry of the one-hundred-day time limit (new Article 237 §2). Pursuant to an explicit new rule (Article 237 2c), submissions filed after the above time limits are absolutely inadmissible and cannot be taken into account by the court. The so-called principle of concentration has thus become even stricter, as, since 1 January 2016, it is no longer subject to the exceptions previously recognized by former Article 269. These exceptions, however, can still apply to appellate proceedings (Article 527) under similar conditions to those provided by former Article 269.[53]

Article 237 CPC was again amended in 2022 and has been in force since 1 January 2022. According to this provision, the parties are obliged to file their pleadings and provide all evidence in support of their claims or factual allegations within ninety days following the lapse of the term for service of the claim. Reply submissions could be filed within the next fifteen days from the date of expiry of the time limit aforementioned (new Article 237 §2).

F. Oral and Written Procedure

40. After successive amendments,[54] the CPC (Articles 115, 237, 238), in its present form (since the amendments of Law 4335/2015, in force after 1 January 2016, and Law 4842/2021, in force after 1 January 2022), has introduced a mixed system, combining both oral and written procedures, basically depending on the nature of the dispute.

Proceedings before the justice of the peace, both ordinary and particular (Articles 115 §3; 649–650; 666, 671; 679, 681; 681A; 681B; 681D),[55] were mainly oral,

51. P. Mainas, *Die Eventualmaxime nach griechischem Recht* (Diss. Köln, 1970); G. Baumgärtel, 'Welche Anregungen vermag das neue griechische ZPGB für die in Deutschland geplante Prozess-beschleunigung zu geben?', *ZZP* 1968, pp. 6 ff.

52. *See supra*, No. 25.

53. *See infra*, No. 292.

54. Legislative Decrees 958/1971 and 490/1974; particularly Law 1478/1984, in force since 1 Mar. 1985; and Law 2915/2001, in force since 1 Jan. 2002.

55. *See infra*, Nos 419 ff.

whereas both one-member and three-member district courts also adjudicated on the basis of oral procedures. However, proceedings before the justice of the peace and three-member and one-member district courts varied: in the latter case, written pleadings remained mandatory (Article 115 §3), again with the exception of some particular proceedings (Articles 649 §1; 666 §1; 679 §1; 681A; 681B; 681D). Depending on subject matter competence or the type of proceedings (ordinary or particular), the CPC, in its endeavour to secure immediacy, strongly supported oral proceedings.

Contrary to the previously dominant role of oral proceedings, Law 4335/2015 has brought about a radical change with regard to ordinary proceedings before all first-instance courts, as the newly introduced Article 237 CPC has provided for an overall written procedure. As a rule, all first-instance courts are expected to issue a final judgment based on the written contents of the file. However, particular proceedings remained oral (new Article 591 §2). However, as far as ordinary proceedings are concerned, a number of explicit stipulations have still allowed the judge to develop a more active role in the process of their administration, a possibility not very often utilized in court practice.

Cassation proceedings[56] have always been oral (Article 574 CPC). This remains the most renowned example of oral civil proceedings within the Greek procedural system.

41. In conclusion, the various combinations of oral and written elements in Greek civil proceedings are currently as follows: (a) Ordinary proceedings before all first-instance courts are since 1 January 2016 mandatorily written (Articles 115 and 237); (b) Particular proceedings before the one-member district courts and the justice of the peace are mandatorily oral, while written pleadings are also required (new Article 591); (c) Appellate proceedings are, since 2002, only in some occasions mandatorily oral (Articles 524 §2 and 528, as amended by Law 2915/2001, Law 4335/2015, and currently Law 4842/2021); (d) Cassation proceedings are mandatorily oral, while written pleadings are principally only optional (Articles 570 and 574).

G. Role of the Judge

42. In the context of the principle of party presentation, before the 2001 amendments, the Greek civil judge emerged as a more or less passive figure, with authorities mainly related to the application of legal norms and the examination of lack of procedural prerequisites (Article 73). The generalized operation of oral proceedings introduced on the basis of the 2001 amendments was, however, distinctly oriented towards the contemporary model of a more active judge. Some particular rules allowing the judge to play a more active role, which already existed before the 2015 amendments, have also survived in the context of the written procedure introduced.

---

56. *Infra*, Nos 293 ff.

43. Notwithstanding restrictions deriving from the principle of party presentation (Article 106), the court has the duty to intervene and help the parties to expose their factual statements properly (Article 236).[57] In addition, the court may order the personal appearance of the parties during the hearing of the case on its own motion[58] for the clarification of their factual allegations (Article 245 §1).[59] Finally, according to an amendment of 1984, even after the hearing of the case, the court must communicate with the parties or their lawyer through a written invitation or a telephone call for the correction of eventual formal omissions in their pleadings (Article 227).

44. The principle of party presentation (Article 106) does not completely apply in relation to means of proof. The court may act on its own motion, being free to use any legal means of proof proper for the case, even if not proposed by the parties (Article 107). Article 232, §1b and c goes further and permits the judge to demand any document possessed by public authorities, even before the first hearing of the case, or to order the parties to present such documents during oral hearings. Nevertheless, the court may use such means of proof only for the production of evidence of factual statements already presented by the parties. However, the production of evidence is always carried out by the parties, even if the judge has required the use of certain means of proof ex officio (party motion).

45. Moreover, the CPC provides for some flexibility of the judge in order to control the unfolding of the case and the duration of litigation:[60] The court may also order the procedural connection of several pending cases or the procedural separation of those already connected (Articles 218 §2; 246; 247 CPC) if this facilitates or accelerates the procedure or reduces the expense of the trial.[61]

The most important exception to the party's dominant role in civil proceedings is recognized in connection with provisional remedies, which in recent years have become quite popular.[62] Article 691(1) declares that the judge may act on his own motion and select all the necessary material for his decision. According to one opinion, Article 691(1) may apply to both means of proof and facts. The prevailing conception does not accept that during these proceedings, the inquisitorial system may be adopted.

46. In conclusion, a traditional conviction that civil litigation procedures must preserve principles suitable to private law rights did not allow the prevailing

57. N. Katephores, *Darf die richterliche Prozessleitung den Kläger zur Stellung der erforderlichen Anträge veranlassen (grZPO Arts 224–236)*, *ZZPInt* 2007, pp. 119–125.
58. K. Polyzogopoulos, *Parteianhörung und Parteivernehmungen in ihrem gegenseitigen Verhältnis* (Diss. Tübingen, 1976).
59. *See also* Art. 232, §1a; its application, however, depends on a request by the parties.
60. *See infra*, Nos 208 ff.
61. *See* moreover Art. 248 (possibility of successive hearings in case of more self-standing defences on the discretion of the court); Art. 267 (separation of procedural matters on the court's motion); Arts 249 and 250 (stay of the proceedings on the motion of the court in case of pending preliminary matters).
62. *Infra*, Nos 250 ff.

conception of the parties being *domini litis* to be disputed. In so far as private law rights are involved, the CPC has not gone beyond the basic consideration that the interested parties must remain free to initiate litigation, determine its subject matter, or declare its termination. Apart from this general view, a more or less effective power of the court in managing civil proceedings has not been considered necessarily involving an intervention in private personal freedom and free development. The idea of this procedure as also possessing a social welfare function has not been rejected. Yet, judges are usually reluctant to undertake the role of an 'activist' judge in connection with civil proceedings. This situation may be attributed to two reasons: First, to the still strongly held conviction that a civil trial must be administered exclusively by the parties; second, to the heavy caseload a Greek civil court is expected to manage.

II. Fundamental Guarantees

A. *General Remarks: The Convention of Rome for the Protection of Human Rights*

47. The Const. of 1975, as amended in 1986, 2001, and 2008, contains a series of guarantees referring to the dispensing of justice.[63] As already explained, the basic guidelines for the administration of justice in Greece emanate from this hierarchically superior source of law. Accordingly, ordinary legislation is most often destined only to concretize such provisions.

This section will discuss briefly each one of those guarantees.

48. Greece is a member of the Convention of Rome for the Protection of Human Rights and Fundamental Freedoms of 4 November 1950, with its Protocols (1, 2, 3, 5, 6, 7, 8, 11, 13 and 14).[64] Fundamental guarantees of this Convention, and more specifically Article 6 §1, have become 'an integral part of domestic law' and 'prevail over any contrary provision of the law' (Article 28 §1 Const.).[65] The Convention and its 'Additional' (First) Protocol of 1952 were initially ratified in 1953, renounced on 12 December 1969 by the military junta (1967–1974), and re-ratified in 1974. The jurisdiction of the European Court of Human Rights has been recognized since 30 January 1979. The right to individual petition ('application') under Article 34 of the European Convention has been recognized since 20 November 1985. Greece has ratified Protocol No. 11, which has amended the European Convention and is in force since 1 November 1998 (Law 2400/1996). Finally, Greece ratified the Protocol No. 16 in 2019 (Law 4596/2019).

---

63. G. Mitsopoulos, *Der Einfluss der Verfassung auf das Zivilprozessrecht*, *RHDI* 1982–1983, pp. 219–226.
64. Ratified respectively by Legislative Decree 215/1974, Law 1705/1987, Law 1841/1989, Law 2400/1996, Law 2610/1998, Law 3289/2004, and Law 3344/2005.
65. K. Beys, *Grundgedanken des griechischen Zivilprozeßrechts in ihrer Fortentwicklung durch die EMRK*, *ZZP* 109 (1996), pp. 29–60.

By Law 2462/1997, Greece has finally ratified the International Covenant on Civil and Political Rights of 16 December 1966.[66] Articles 2 §3, 11 and 14 §1 have been, accordingly, integrated within the domestic legal order.[67]

B. Establishment of Courts by Law (Article 8 Const.)

49. According to Article 8 §1 of the Const. of 1975, 'No person shall against his will be deprived of the judge assigned to him by law'. Article 8 §2 of the Const. additionally declares that 'Judicial committees or extraordinary courts, under any name whatsoever, shall not be constituted' unless allowed exclusively by the Const. itself (*see* Article 48 §1). This backbone of the principle of 'natural judge' certainly prohibits its violation by ordinary legislation. It has been, therefore, repeatedly argued that regulations about the method of designating particular judges as members of court panels are likely to entail infringements of this guarantee if such method is not based on objective criteria. For this reason, it has been provided[68] that, in some of the biggest courts (Court of Appeal in Athens, Thessaloniki and Piraeus, Courts of First Instance in Athens, Thessaloniki and Piraeus; justices of the peace in Athens and Thessaloniki), the exact composition of each court is formed through decisions of a three-member council before the beginning of each judicial year.

A direct reservation in favour of the volition of the parties (Article 8 §1: 'No person shall *against his will*') confirms the constitutionality of both (non-compulsory) arbitration and prorogation.

C. Independence and Impartiality of the Judiciary (Article Const.)

50. The Const. of 1975 not only explicitly declares the independence of the judiciary but also contains guarantees of its realization. According to Article 87 §§1, 2, 'judges … enjoy functional and personal independence.[69] Judges shall in the discharge of their duties be subject only to the Constitution and the laws … '.

Functional independence of the judge refers, on the one hand, to the freedom from interference by the Legislature or Executive and, on the other hand, to the lack of any hierarchical control of the inferior by superior courts.

The principle of independence of the judicial function against the Legislature has resulted in an important rule: Since the close of the last century, Greek courts have reviewed laws, denying application of those opposed to the Const. In addition, Greek courts, based on their independence against the Executive, proceed to review the legality of administrative acts, though to an extent which is still under discussion

66. UN General Assembly Resolution 2200 A (XXI) of 16 Dec. 1966. Entry into force of the Covenant: 23 Mar. 1976, in accordance with Art. 49.
67. For the impact of Art. 11 in particular *see infra*, No. 449.
68. Article 17 Law 4938/2022 on the Code for the Organization of Courts and the Status of Judicial Functionaries.
69. D. Papaphilippou, *Guarantees for judicial independence*, *RHDI* 1980, pp. 203–240.

(as to whether correctness of the factual statements of the administrative organs is also included). Civil courts may not abolish the acts of the Executive but only deny applying them (Article 2 CPC). The power to declare illegal administrative acts as null and void belongs to the administrative courts and is subject to a review by the Council of State.

The hierarchical independence of the judge seems to have only theoretical value: the inferior courts, although not obliged, usually follow the legal opinion of superior courts in order to avoid review of their decision.

The personal independence of the judge aims to guarantee the freeing of judicial action from any influence due to political interventions. Since 1892, Greece has provided for a career in the judiciary upon condition of successful participation in a special examination. Judges are promoted from the inferior to the superior courts until the age limit designated for their retirement (Article 88 §5 Const.).[70]

However, judges are not permitted to exercise another salaried service or profession (Article 89 §1 Const.).[71] Judges are also not permitted to be members of the Government (Article 89 §4 Const.).

Since the Const. of 1911, justice in Greece has its own administration: the promotions and transfers of judges are realized upon decision of a Supreme Judicial Council.[72] This council is composed of the President and judges of the Supreme Courts of each branch (Article 90 §1 Const.).[73]

A fundamental guarantee of judicial independence is the judges' appointment for life (Article 88 §1 Const.). They remain even though their post is abolished and must vacate their office on the day on which they reach the age of 67 if they belong to a superior court, or of 65 if they belong to an inferior one (Article 88 §5 Const.). Judges are dismissed only on the basis of a judicial decision in case of a criminal sentence against them, a grave disciplinary fault, sickness, invalidity or service inefficiency (Article 88 §4 Const.).

D. Review of Unconstitutional Ordinary Legislation (Article 93, §4 Const.)

51. Article 93 §4 Const. explicitly provides that 'The courts shall be bound not to apply laws, the contents of which are contrary to the Constitution.' Thus, the

70. K. Kerameus, 'National Report for Greece', in Sh. Shetreet & J. Deschênes (eds), *Judicial Independence the Contemporary Debate* (Martinus Nijhoff Publishers, Dordrecht/Boston/Lancaster 1985), pp. 123–140 (123).
71. With the exception of the post of a Professor at the University, membership of the Academy of Athens or in special courts or councils (Art. 89, §2 Const.) *See also infra*, No. 79.
72. With the disputed exception of the appointment to the posts of the President and Vice President of *Areios Pagos*, the Council of State and Exchequer's Tribunal, and the Public Prosecutor of *Areios Pagos*, which are carried out by the Government; *see* more specifically Art. 90 §5 Const. The 2001 amendment of the Constitution has provided that this appointment can be effected for a term of only four years. In addition, Art. 59 §3 of the new Code (Law 4938/2022) provides that such decisions of the Government must be based on a previous proposal by the Parliament (the so-called deliberation of its Presidents), which, however, is not binding.
73. For the Supreme Judicial Council for Civil and Criminal Justice, *see* Art. 91 of Law 4938/2022.

official form has been given to a practice already known in Greece since the end of the nineteenth century.[74]

E. Access to Justice (Article 20 §1 Const.)[75]

52. According to Article 20 §1 Const., 'Every person shall be entitled to receive legal protection by the courts as specified by law.' Similar to the Italian Const. (Article 24 §1), and through a wider wording than that of the German Const. (Article 19 §4), this provision is regarded as belonging to the highest level of guarantees, containing a procedural individual right. It is defined as guaranteeing the rendition of a judicial decision on the merits, in the sense of the right to a due process of law and a completely accessible, accelerated and effective system of justice. However, it is considered to cover all three forms of legal protection (contentious/voluntary proceedings, provisional remedies, and enforcement proceedings).[76] It is moreover unanimously accepted that the guarantee of legal protection also comprises the right to proof. Ordinary legislation may provide for appropriate legal remedies or specific procedural hindrances unless the right of legal protection is deprived by any means whatsoever, directly or indirectly.

On the contrary, it is almost unanimously accepted that the right to appeal (Article 12 CPC) does not fall within the scope of the guarantee of legal protection. According to the prevailing opinion, ordinary legislation may, but is not bound to provide access to a Court of Appeal.

53. Under Article 20 §1 Const. of 1975, legal scholarship and courts of law have quite often encountered problems related to the constitutionality of statutes, whether pre-existing or not. Examples: restrictions to the right of execution for money claims against the State (Article 8 Law 2097/1952);[77] restriction to the right of garnishment on bank accounts (money deposits) due to secrecy imposed on the banks (Article 1 Legislative Decree 1059/1971);[78] restriction of legal aid to foreigners upon the condition of reciprocity (Article 195 CPC).

---

74. *See* Ph. Vegleris, 'La Constitution, le loi et les tribunaux en Grèce', *Annales de la Faculté de Droit de Liege,* 1967, pp. 439 ff. (446/447); E. Spiliotopoulos, 'Judicial Review of Legislation Acts in Greece', *Temple Law Quarterly*, Vol. 56 (1983), pp. 463–502; P. Yessiou-Faltsi, 'Judicial Review of Unconstitutional Legislation in Greece', *Festschrift Für Hideo Nakamura Zum 70. Geburtstag am 2. März 1996* (de Gruyter; Tokyo 1996, Reprint 2013), pp. 697 ff.

75. N. Klamaris & P.M. Estratiou, *Access to Justice as a Fundamental Right, RHDI* 1998, pp. 291–310.

76. N. Klamaris, *Die Grundstruktur des griechischen Zwangsvollstreckungsrechts als des effektiven Teils des prozessualen Grundrechts auf Justizgewährung*, in *Festschrift Für Hideo Nakamura Zum 70. Geburtstag am 2. März 1996* (de Gruyter; Tokyo 1996, Reprint 2013), pp. 253–280.

77. *See also* Legislative Decree 31/1968 (extension of this privilege to municipalities and village communities). This specific problem has been now treated by an explicit positive provision (Art. 94 §4c), inserted in the Constitution of 1975 by the 2001 amendment.

78. Law 2915/2001 (Art. 24) has now settled this question, by providing that such garnishments are permissible. In detail, *see* A. Bolos, *Die Pfändung von Bankkonten im griechischen Recht*, zugl. Diss. Berlin, Berlin, 2004; D. Tekidou, *Der Vollstreckungszugriff auf Bankkonten. Eine rechtsvergleichende Betrachtung des griechischen und deutschen Rechts*, Europäische Hochschulschriften, Reihe 2, Bd. 4142, zugl. Diss. Hannover 2004, Frankfurt/ M. u.a., 2005; A. Kaissis, *Wandlungen des*

F. Right of Defence (Article 20 §1 Const.)

54. The second part of Article 20 §1 Const. explicitly guarantees the right of defence before courts: 'Every person … may plead before them his views concerning his rights or interests as specified by law'. However, the CPC, beyond a generally formulated requirement for the summoning of the parties in all hearings of the case as provided by law (Article 110 §2), which naturally refers to the need only for a proper service and not for a compulsory appearance, also contains a series of specific provisions based on the underlying idea of defence.

Article 343 CPC demanded the summoning of the parties throughout all steps of the evidence procedure. This provision was removed by Law 2915/2001 as not being in conformity with the newly introduced system of a single oral hearing. The court is obliged to declare on its own motion all hearings inadmissible if a party has not been duly summoned by his opponent (Article 108) and thus fails to appear (Articles 271 §§1, 2).[79] The party's right to be heard is additionally protected by an application to stay the default proceedings (Article 501)[80] and further by virtue of a special ground for cassation (Article 559 n. 6).[81]

55. Ex parte proceedings are allowed only in exceptional cases. Beyond voluntary jurisdiction,[82] the most striking examples are related to the proceedings for provisional remedies and for the issue of payment orders.[83] Relief may thus be granted, without summoning the adversary party, through a provisional remedy at the discretion of the court, under particularly urgent circumstances (Article 687 §1CPC), or through the rendition of a provisional order immediately after the filing of an application for a provisional remedy, also on the motion of the court (Article 691A §1 CPC). However, an order of payment is always rendered without the debtor's summoning (Article 627 CPC). Doubts about the constitutionality of these proceedings, particularly in view of the prompt enforcement given to such orders (Article 631CPC), are not supported by most authors. The right of the debtor for defence may be indeed materialized by filing an opposition (Articles 632–633 CPC), which also stays execution if ordered by the court (Article 632 §3 CPC).

According to Articles 134–136 CPC, service of documents abroad or to persons of unknown residence is effected through delivery to the public prosecutor (Articles 134, 136: system of the '*remise au parquet*') and some publications in the latter case (Articles 135, 136), regardless of whether (or when) these documents are actually served on their addressees. Nevertheless, the essential operation of this system, often resulting in violations of this right, has been altered: beyond the impact of Articles 15 and 16 of the 1965 Hague Service Convention, Greek courts have repeatedly accepted applications for relief and reopened decisions which had been rendered in Greece after service by publication.

Bankgeheimnisses in Griechenland am Beispiel der Pfändbarkeit von Bankeinlagen, in *Festschrift für Erik Jayme* (Sellier European Law Publ. Munich 2004), pp. 1475–1486.

79. *See infra*, No. 270.

80. *See infra*, Nos 285–286.

81. *See infra*, No. 299.

82. *Infra*, Nos 96, 276.

83. *Infra*, Nos 278, 464.

G. Equality of the Parties (Article 4 §1 Const.)

56. Article 4 §1 Const. provides that 'All Greeks are equal before the law'. This fundamental individual right is naturally regarded as also comprising civil procedure in the sense of prohibiting unequal procedural treatment between the parties, both by ordinary legislation or the courts. Article 110 §1 CPC specifically provides that 'The parties have the same rights and obligations and are equal before the court.' This provision is accordingly regarded as establishing two basic principles: on the one hand, equality of the parties before the law, and on the other hand, equality of the parties before the court. The first principle refers to the 'equality of weapons', whereas the latter obliges the judge to treat both parties in a strictly equal procedural manner. The right of each party to be heard is also regarded as a specific expression of the principle of equality.

57. Actual situations of 'unequal weapons' between the parties, due to purely economic factors, have been treated in Greece by Law 3226/2004, which has implemented the European Directive 2003/8 of 27 January 2003 on legal aid. With regard to civil and commercial matters, the provisions of Articles 194–204 CPC, which have proven to be insufficient, do not apply any longer (Article 16 §1 Law 3226/2004).[84]

58. The principle of equality of the parties before the law is subject to some traditional exceptions, most of which are favourable to the defendant (e.g., Article 22 CPC: dependence of the territorial competence principally on the defendant's domicile; Article 169 CPC: eventual obligation of the plaintiff to deposit a guarantee at the discretion of the court, for the expenses of the proceedings).

59. Procedural provisions involving discrimination against foreign parties,[85] as in the previous Code of 1835, do not exist any longer.[86]

H. Publicity (Article 93 §§2, 3 Const.)

60. The Const. guarantees publicity of both the courts' sittings (Article 93 §2) and the pronouncement of the courts' judgement (Article 93, §3α). Publicity of the courts' sittings is subject to rather limited exceptions, namely when it is 'detrimental to moral principles' or when 'special reasons call for the protection of the private or family life of the litigants' (Article 93 §2; *see also* Article 6 §1 European Convention of Human Rights). The CPC, however, includes a detailed regulation

84. *Infra*, Nos 333–335 α.
85. *See* the reports for the Congress of 'Wissenschaftliche Vereinigung für Internationales Verfahrensrecht' 1987, by P. Gottwald, 'Die Stellung des Ausländers im Prozess' and N. Klamaris, 'Der Ausländer im Prozess', in *Grundfragen des Zivilprozessrechts – die internationale Dimension*, edited by W. Habscheid & K. Beys (Gieseking/IΔME, Bielefeld/Athens, 1991), pp. 7 ff. and 103 ff.
86. Ch. Fragistas, 'Nationaux et étrangers en droit de Procedure Civil de la Grèce', *Thesaurus Acroasium*, Vol. IV, Miscellanea in honour of D.S. Constantopoulos (Institute of International and Public Law and International Relations, Thessaloniki), pp. 543 ff.; Klamaris, *supra* (n. 1), pp. 103–153.

regarding the principle of publicity (Articles 112–114), which has been elaborated and entered into force before the present Const. The deliberation of the court for rendering its decision takes place in chambers (Article 113 §1 b).

61. Decisions of any court for a closed sitting are subject to a series of conditions, all aiming to safeguard the principle of publicity (Article 114 CPC). Among the more significant of those guarantees, one must include: the right of the parties to be heard before the decision is rendered (Article 114 § 2a); publicity of the relevant hearing, unless otherwise ordered by the court (Article 114 § 2b), and pronouncement of the decision at a public hearing (Article 93 § 3a Const.; Article 114 §3 CPC (*see also* Article 304 §2); an exceptional right of the parties to attack this non-final decision by a regular appeal or even a cassation (Article 114 §4). These last methods of appeal, however, do not hinder the advancement of the closed proceedings.

Any illegally performed restriction of the publicity of civil proceedings institutes a ground for cassation (Article 559 No. 7).

62. Fundamental guarantees for the publicity of civil proceedings currently have very limited practical relevance in Greece if publicity is understood as direct accessibility to a civil court's session. In this sense, the extent of publicity with regard to civil cases is inevitably dependent on whether proceedings remain oral. On the contrary, indirect publicity, i.e., press reporting of judicial decisions or judicial conduct, has been playing a steadily increasing role. Nevertheless, it is still under discussion as to whether, and if so, on what conditions television should be allowed to enter courtrooms; moreover, if the guarantee of publicity should be interpreted as also comprising access of television to civil trials. Article 8 Law 3090/2002 has forbidden the transmission of civil trials through television, cinema, radio, and tape recording. By way of exception, the court has the authority to allow such activities under the condition that both parties and the public prosecutor consent in order to serve an essential public interest.

I. Reasoning of Judicial Decisions (Article 93 §3 Const.)

63. According to Article 93 §3 Const., 'all court judgments must be specifically and thoroughly reasoned'. Concretization of this guarantee with regard to civil proceedings consists of three different provisions of the CPC, which, directly or indirectly, oblige civil courts to provide reasons for their decisions. They are mainly based on the conception that only the statements of the court on its reasoning, when covering both facts and law, may allow a proper judicial review through methods of appeal.

In the first place, Article 305 CPC explicitly relies on the reasoning of judicial decisions as an integral part of their content.[87] Second, Article 340 requires the

87. G. Rammos, 'Die Entscheidungsbegründung im griechischen Verfahrensrecht', in *Die Entscheidungsbegründung in europäischen Verfahrensrechten und im Verfahren vor internationalen Gerichten* (Springer, Wien/New York 1974), pp. 399–422.

inclusion of the factual statements of the parties and the evaluation of the means of evidence in the court's reasoning. Finally, beyond a regular appeal, Article 559 No. 19, under the definition 'lack of legal base', establishes a specific ground for cassation related to non-existent, contradictory or insufficient reasoning with regard to the subordination of facts to the rules of law. Having a French origin ('*manque de base légale*'), this ground for cassation has been operating since 1937 on a grand practical scale.[88]

Judicial decisions of *Areios Pagos* usually contain rather brief statements on their reasoning. On the contrary, decisions of Courts of Appeal or Courts of First Instance most often contain analytical reasoning with regard to legal matters, including references to scholarly works or court decisions. However, reasoning on the factual part of the case, as a rule, is extremely brief.

According to Article 93 §3b Const., 'Publication of the minority opinion shall be compulsory. A law shall specify matters concerning the entry of any minority opinion into the minutes, as well as the conditions and prerequisites for the publication thereof'. This provision, supplemented by Articles 35–38 Law 184/1975, has modified Article 302 § 1b CPC, which previously allowed the publication of dissenting opinions only in regard to decisions rendered by lower courts, not those of *Areios Pagos*. The underlying idea of this exception was to sustain the prestige of the Supreme Court's decisions. Currently, on the basis of Article 93 § 3b Const. and Article 35 Law 184/1975, all judicial decisions, including decisions of *Areios Pagos*, must also comprise minority opinions, with reference to the number of judges who supported it. Hence, in quite a number of *Areios Pagos*' decisions, and most often in decisions of the court's plenary session, significant minority opinions are appearing. Article 40 Law 2172/1993 provides that the names of the judges holding the dissenting opinion must also be included in the judgment.

88. *See infra*, No. 298.

Part I. Judicial Organization

Chapter 1. The Courts and Their Members

§1. Courts

I. Structure of the Courts' System

64. The most important branch of the courts in Greece is the branch of ordinary justice. It includes the ordinary civil,[89] criminal,[90] and administrative[91] courts. Ordinary courts have a general jurisdiction, except in some limited cases for which the Const. allows the functioning of the so-called special and extraordinary courts.

Special courts have jurisdiction for special cases according to their nature or the identity of the interested parties (for instance, juvenile or military courts).[92] Extraordinary courts may function only under the conditions specifically described by Article 48 §1 Const. concerning the state of siege.

II. Administration of the Courts

A. Separation of the Three Jurisdictions

65. With regard to judicial organization, the Const. introduces the concept of the complete separation of criminal, civil and administrative jurisdictions (Article 93 §1). According to Article 94 §2, all private matters, contentious and non-contentious, belong to the ordinary civil courts, while, under Article 96 §1, the jurisdiction of ordinary criminal courts shall comprise the punishment of crimes and the adoption of all measures provided by criminal laws. Finally, Article 94 §1 provides that the administrative disputes belong totally to the Council of State and the ordinary administrative courts.

66. In conclusion, the general picture of the Greek judicial system is currently the following: three separate systems of jurisdictions and three separate Codes of

89. Article 93, §1; Art. 94 §§2, 3, of the Constitution of 1975.
90. Article 93, §1; Art. 96 §1; Art. 97 of the Constitution of 1975.
91. Article 93, §1; Art. 94 §1, of the Constitution of 1975.
92. Article 96 §§3, 4, of the Constitution of 1975.

Procedure coexist (Civil Procedure of 1967, Criminal Procedure of 1950, and Administrative Procedure of 1999, all extensively modified). However, only two branches of courts exist. The judiciary has remained the same for both criminal and civil cases, whereas administrative disputes belong either to the Council of State, as the Supreme Administrative Court, or to the separate branch of ordinary administrative courts.

B. Ordinary Civil Courts of First Instance

67. Justices of the peace, one-member district courts and three-member district courts are the three types of civil courts, which adjudicate cases at first instance.

Justices of the peace are usually defined as the courts of rural areas. However, they also function within urban zones for adjudicating urgent matters or disputes of lower value.[93] Justices of the peace constituted, until 1985, a separate body of judges within the overall judiciary of ordinary civil justice. Law 1578/1985 (Article 120) abolished this separate rank and incorporated justices of the peace within a unified career structure of judicial functionaries. This experiment, however, did not seem successful. Therefore, Law 1968/1991 (Article 9) restored the separate branch of the justices of the peace. Yet again though, the new Code (Article 130 Law 4938/2022) has abolished the aforementioned rule.

One-member district courts were first instituted by the CPC of 1967. They are formed either by the president of the district court or by one of its members (Article 4 § 1b Law 4938/2022) and a secretary (Article 8 §1 Law 4938/2022). This single-judge court sits in the same jurisdictional districts as the three-member district courts. Beyond adjudicating over disputes of medium value,[94] one-member district courts have been gradually enjoying a steadily increasing role as the competent courts in special kinds of litigation (i.e., labour and car accident disputes, and family matters),[95] especially with regard to provisional remedies[96] and particular proceedings. One-member district courts are entrusted with a double function: since 2011, they also adjudicate over appeals against decisions of the justices of peace (Article 17A CPC).[97]

Three-member district courts, the traditional type of first-instance courts in Greece ever since the previous Code, are formed by three judges, including the president of the court and a secretary (Articles 4 §1c; 7 §1, Law 4938/2022). They have a general jurisdiction regarding all civil matters which do not belong to the types of first-instance civil courts above-mentioned (Article 18 No. 1 CPC). Their districts are most often delimited through the same boundaries as the country's prefectures.

93. *See* more particularly *infra*, Nos 103–105.
94. *Infra*, No. 106.
95. *Infra*, Nos 107–108.
96. *Infra*, No. 253 ff.
97. *See also infra*, No. 109.

Article 51 of Law 2172/1993 has provided for the operation of special panels within the Court of First Instance and Courts of Appeal of Piraeus to handle maritime disputes. Judges of these panels are expected to have specialized knowledge of Maritime Law (Article 51 §7). Also, on the basis of Article 91 of Council Regulation 40/1994 of 20 December 1993, Articles 6–10 of Law 2943/2001 have created special panels within the Courts of First Instance and Courts of Appeal in Athens and Thessaloniki for the adjudication of certain special disputes of commercial law. Finally, according to Law 2447/1996 (Article 48), all Family Law matters must be entertained by special panels in all courts.

C. The Special Court of 'Mufti'

68. Pursuant to the Convention of Athens of 1/14 November 1913 (Article 11 §§9, 11, and Article 5 §2 Law 1920/1991), disputes of Greek Muslims related to family and succession matters have remained under the jurisdiction of the Muslim priests, the 'Muftis', who thus, beyond their religious functions, are also entrusted with special judicial tasks.[98] The 'Muftis' adjudicate by applying the religious (Muslim) laws. Their judgments may be officially declared enforceable and obtain a res judicata effect through the special proceedings of voluntary jurisdiction, without any review on the merits, on the conditions, that they have been decided within the limits of the 'Muftis' jurisdiction and have not applied rules which are contrary to the Greek Const. (Article 5 §3 Law 1920/1991).

69. Following the judgment of the ECHR in the *Molla Sali v. Greece* case,[99] the previous law was amended by Law 4511/2018, providing that, in principle, Greek nationals of the Muslim minority are also subject to the jurisdiction of Greek courts.[100] The Mufti may exceptionally adjudicate over such disputes whenever *both* parties opt to bring their case before him. Finally, according to Article 1 §3 Law 4511/2018, the judgments of the Mufti may not apply rules contrary to the ECHR.

D. The Courts of Appeal

70. The CPC provides (Article 12 §1) that all civil disputes are principally subject to an ordinary appeal (also Article 512 *e contrario*) and that no civil dispute may be directly brought before a Court of Appeal unless otherwise stipulated (Article 12 §2).

---

98. Ch. Fragistas, 'Le Droit Musulman en Grèce', *Annales de la Faculté de Droit d'Istanbul* 1955, pp. 129 ff., A. Grammaticaki-Alexiou, *Mixed Jurisdictions, RHDI* 1985–1986, pp. 315–321.

99. *Case of Molla Sali v. Greece* (Application No. 20452/14), Grand Chamber, 18 Jun. 2020.

100. *See A. Anthimos, Sharia Law in Greece: Blending European Values with Islamic Tradition,* https://conflictoflaws.net/2018/sharia-law-in-greece-blending-european-values-with-islamic-tradition/.

The Courts of Appeal sit in panels of only three judges, including the president (Article 4 §1d Law 4938/2022).[101] Participation of a secretary is also necessary (Article 8 §1 Law 4938/2022). They adjudicate over appeals against decisions of three-member district courts (Article 19 CPC) by dealing with questions of both fact and law. Since 2011, appeals against decisions of the one-member district courts are treated by the newly created one-member Court of Appeal.

E. The Court of *Areios Pagos*

71. *Areios Pagos* is the civil and criminal Supreme Court of Greece.[102] It sits in Athens and is constituted of seventy-four supreme Justices,[103] including the President of the Court and its ten Vice Presidents. The public prosecutor's office includes the Public Prosecutor of *Areios Pagos* and nineteen Deputy Prosecutors.[104] The court functions either through its plenary session, comprising all supreme Justices, the number of at least half being sufficient.[105] The panels of *Areios Pagos* are formed by five supreme Justices, including the President or the presiding Vice President.[106] Additionally, in the court of *Areios Pagos*, when functioning in plenary session, the Public Prosecutor or one of his Deputy Prosecutors must necessarily join;[107] the presence of a court clerk is also imperative.[108] According to Article 27 §2 Law 4938/2022), decisions of the plenary session can be taken by only twenty-nine members in case of death, retirement or other grave hindrance of the rest of the supreme justices who have participated in the hearing of the case.

72. The legendary name of *Areios Pagos* comes from the ancient Greek Judicial Council, so called because it met on the hill Ares west of the Akropolis. The contemporary Supreme Court of Greece was initially constituted following the example of the French *Cour de Cassation*. The review exercised by *Areios Pagos* was strictly limited to points of law. This court is, therefore, not regarded as a court of third instance. From 1957 until 1993,[109] however, *Areios Pagos* was allowed to extend adjudication to questions of facts in case of cassation of the attacked judgment.

Starting from its foundation, *Areios Pagos* has gradually developed a highly significant role in both securing the uniformity of law and in adjusting legal norms to current situations.

---

101. Previously they consisted of five judges. Five judges sat in the exceptional case of Legislative Decree 1266/72, Art. 17 (disputes related to 'Public Constructions'). This proceeding is now governed by Art. 3 of Law 2229/1994 and Art. 3 §3 of Law 2940/2001.
102. Ach. Bakopoulos, '*The Role of the Supreme Courts at the National and International Level*, Greek Law', in the volume Yessiou-Faltsi (ed.), *The Role of the Supreme Courts at the National and International Level,* Reports for the Thessaloniki International Colloquium (1996), pp. 149 ff.
103. Article 43 B No. a, Law 3659/2008, as revised.
104. Article 43 B No. b, Law 3659/2008.
105. However, Art. 27 §2 Law 4938/2022 has now provided that in ordinary cases the plenary session functions with only seventeen supreme justices (so-called ordinary plenary session).
106. Article 27 §1, Law 4938/2022.
107. Article 27, §§5, 6, Law 4938/2022. *See also infra*, No. 76.
108. Article 8 §1, Law 4938/2022.
109. For details *infra*, No. 294.

F. The Special Highest Court

73. The Special Highest Court[110] has been founded by Article 100 Const., which has also directly stipulated its jurisdiction.[111]

Beyond matters related to parliamentary elections (Articles 100 §1a and 58), referendums (Articles 100 §1b and 44 §2), and the office of members of Parliament (Articles 100 §1c; 55 §2; 57), the Special Highest Court's jurisdiction comprises: (a) Settlement of conflicts between courts and administrative authorities (Article 100 §1d first part). (b) Settlement of conflicts between the Council of State and ordinary administrative courts, on the one hand, and civil and criminal courts, on the other hand, or between the Exchequer's Tribunal and any other courts (Article 100 §1d second part). On the basis of this jurisdiction, the Special Highest Court has developed a decisive role during the recent years of transition in delimiting authorities between civil and administrative courts. (c) Settlement of controversies on whether a law enacted by Parliament is fundamentally unconstitutional when conflicting judgments have been pronounced by the Council of State, by *Areios Pagos,* or by the Exchequer's Tribunal (Article 100 §1e). (d) Settlement of controversies on the interpretation of a provision of enacted law when conflicting judgments have been rendered as in (c). During recent years, the Special Highest Court has indeed pronounced a number of judgments reviewing the interpretation of various statutes, thus establishing uniformity of their application by all branches of Greek courts. The Special Highest Court's decision is binding and develops an effect erga omnes.[112] (e) Settlement of controversies related to the designation of rules of international law as generally acknowledged (Articles 100 §1f and 28 §1).[113]

The mixed character of its jurisdiction reveals that the need for establishing the Special Highest Court in Greece has primarily derived from the parallel functioning of more than one court branch, hence, of Supreme Courts, within the same judicial organization. Therefore, its creation covers principally the demand of avoiding conflicts with regard to the interpretation of laws by those courts, and the determination of limits related to their jurisdiction. Under this aspect, the Special Highest Court is not regarded as a constitutional Court in a genuine sense.

The Special Highest Court does not function on the basis of a permanent judiciary. It is rather formed on the basis of a two-year term by members either participating ex officio or being selected by lot (Article 100 §2 Const.). The Court is thus constituted of: The President of the Council of State, the President of *Areios Pagos*, and the President of the Exchequer's Tribunal; four Councillors of State and four members of *Areios Pagos,* chosen by lot for a two-year term. Depending on seniority, the Court is presided over either by the President of the Council of State or by the President of *Areios Pagos*. In case of conflicts related to the jurisdiction of each

110. Translation of its title in English follows the one included in the '*Constitution of Greece*' as translated by the Greek House of Parliament, Athens 1975 (Art. 100).
111. Law 345/1976 'For the Code on the Special Highest Court', as modified by Law 2479/1997 (Art. 1), has more extensively provided about the organization and functioning of the court, as also about the appointment, replacement and assistance of its members, as well as the procedure to be followed, according to Art. 100, §3, of the Constitution.
112. Article 51 §§1, 2 of Law 345/1976.
113. *See* in particular Decision No. 83/1991.

branch of courts or to the review of statute laws with respect to their C constitutionality or their real meaning, as discussed above, the composition of the Special Highest Court is expanded and additionally includes two ordinary professors of the country's Law Faculties, also chosen by lot.

G. The Limited Role of Lay Participants

74. Justice in Greece is administered by courts composed of ordinary judges who enjoy functional and personal independence. The Const. regards ordinary courts as the exclusively competent organs for the dispensation of justice. Thus, the Greek judiciary is primarily identified with professional judges.

The Const. (Article 87 §1) has not allowed the establishment of justice-making bodies other than courts to dispense civil justice. Any attempt to organize special civil courts with lay members has been defined as unconstitutional. Even the historical background of the Greek judicial organization cannot favour such alternative methods. The lay element never participated greatly in the adjudication of civil controversies. The establishment of special courts competent for private cases was always considered to be the exception. Moreover, it proved to be unsuccessful.

Lay participation is today allowed only in the criminal courts according to Article 97 §1, Const. of 1975. Felonies and political crimes are, thus, to be adjudicated by the felony courts consisting of ordinary judges and jurors.

III. Bench and 'Ministère Public'/Public Prosecutor

75. Public prosecutors in Greece must be understood as an independent body of judicial functionaries, which is attached to the courts throughout the country and is hierarchically organized, with the Public Prosecutor of *Areios Pagos* being at the top.[114] Their role is to secure, by acting uniformly and indivisibly, 'legality, protection of the citizen and guardianship of the rules of public policy'. Public prosecutors' tasks are, thus, much more significant within criminal rather than civil proceedings. Public prosecutors are known in Greece as 'the standing judiciary'. They are gradually promoted from the Courts of First Instance to those of the Courts of Second Instance and then to *Areios Pagos*, passing in each court also from the stage of deputy prosecutor.

Public prosecutor's role with regard to civil proceedings may be either the role of an independent organ within the court panel but with no right to vote, or the role of a principal party. Participation of the public prosecutor, practically minimal in civil proceedings before lower courts,[115] is compulsory in *Areios Pagos*[116] and indeed a

114. Article 27, §§5, 6 Law 4938/2022. According to Art. 28 Law 4938/2022, although public prosecutors must carry out the orders of their superiors, they are henceforth free in expressing their opinions, being subject only to the law and to their own conviction.

115. Participation of public prosecutors is explicitly provided in some cases of voluntary jurisdiction. *See* Arts 748, §2, 750 and 760 CPC. The public prosecutor is also allowed to attack decisions through appeals. *See* Art. 761.

very significant part of the oral proceedings of cassation. The official speech of the Public Prosecutor of *Areios Pagos* or the Deputy Prosecutor, comprising his legal opinion on the pending case (Article 574b), has been one of the highlights of this procedure. The Public Prosecutor of *Areios Pagos*, like in French law, is moreover entrusted with the authority to attack decisions of any civil court, even those which are not or no longer subject to methods of appeal by the aggrieved parties, in the interest of the law (Article 557).[117] Decisions of *Areios Pagos* rendered after a cassation brought by the Public Prosecutor of *Areios Pagos* do not affect the interested parties.

The role of the public prosecutor as a principal party in civil proceedings is limited to some rather rare cases, specifically provided by statute law.[118]

76. Public prosecutors also perform quasi-administrative tasks regarding service of documents to persons abroad (Articles 134, 136 §1 CPC) or to persons of unknown residence (Articles 135, 136 §1 CPC). Greek procedural law, like French law, operates in such cases through service of documents to the public prosecutors, a practice known as the system of the '*remise au parquet*'.[119] However, public prosecutors are the supervisors of some auxiliary judicial organs, such as notaries, bailiffs, etc. They are also obliged to officially deliver their legal opinions when demanded. Finally, the Public Prosecutor of *Areios Pagos* delivers legal opinions on matters of general interest.

IV. Appointment of Judges and of Public Prosecutors

77. Pursuant to Article 88 §1 Const.,[120] Law 4938/2022 'On the Code for the Organization of the Courts and the Status of Judicial Functionaries' has extensively provided for the appointment of judges and public prosecutors, who are thus subject to the same regulation.[121]

Although the Const. does not directly provide for a concrete method to be applied in order to appoint judges, their selection has been effected through an established system of a special introductory examination since 1892. Law 2236/1994, as amended (last amendment made by Law 4871/2021), founded the 'National School of the Judiciary', which sits in Thessaloniki and is designed to train those who are successful with the introductory examination for a period of sixteen months.

---

116. However, since the amendment by Law 2298/1995 (Art. 2), this, currently, concerns only the plenary session of *Areios Pagos*. Participation of the Public Prosecutor of *Areios Pagos* at its civil panels has, since 1995, become only optional *see* now Art. 27 §5 Law 4938/2022.
117. For more details, *infra,* No. 304.
118. *See*, e.g., Arts 1378 No. 1 (action for annulling a marriage), 1667 (appointment of a guardian) CC.
119. *See infra*, No. 210.
120. Article 88 §1, of the Constitution reads as follows: 'Judicial functionaries shall be appointed by presidential decree in compliance with a law specifying the qualifications and the procedure for their election; the appointment shall be for life'.
121. Articles 40–46, 82–84 Law 4938/2022.

Greek citizens[122] between the age of 28 and 40[123] who have obtained a degree from one of the Law Faculties of the country or formally recognized foreign law schools[124] are generally qualified for participation. Nevertheless, a detailed list of hindrances[125] mostly related to a criminal condemnation or mental and physical incapacities prohibits appointment to the office.

The introductory examination is held by a committee consisting of a vice president of *Areios Pagos*, a law professor and a lawyer.[126] The examination, both written and oral, covers the most important branches of law and one or more foreign languages (English, French, German, Italian).[127]

Judges and prosecutors are initially appointed for a probationary period of six months, during which they are allowed to perform most of their usual duties. Prolongation of this probationary period for one more year is not prohibited.[128]

§2. Members of the Judiciary[129]

I. Incompatibilities

78. In order to safeguard their personal independence,[130] some principal incompatibilities related to judicial functionaries have been dealt with in the Const.

First, judicial functionaries may neither perform any other salaried service nor practice any other profession (Article 89 §1 Const.).[131] Exceptionally, they may be elected members of the Academy of Athens or professors of Greek Law Faculties at all levels. Furthermore, under certain conditions, they may sit on special councils or committees (Article 89 §2 Const.).[132] Judicial functionaries are moreover allowed to be assigned duties for drafting new statute laws, training judicial functionaries, or representing the country in international organizations (Article 89 §3 of the Const.).

Second, participation of judicial functionaries in the Government is prohibited (Article 89 §4 Const.).[133] Furthermore, they may neither stand for election nor be elected to Parliament unless they resign prior to their nomination (Article 56 §1 Const.), and they may not become members of municipal councils.[134] Additionally,

122. Article 43 §1–3 Law 4938/2022.
123. Article 17 §1b Law 4871/2021.
124. Article 43 §7 Law 4938/2022; Art. 17 §1a Law 4871/2021.
125. Articles 44 and 45 Law 4938/2022.
126. Article 18, §3 Law 4871/2021.
127. Article 17 §2 Law 4871/2021.
128. Article 88 §3, of the Constitution provides for a training and trial period of up to three years. *See* currently Art. 31 §1 Law 4871/2021. Justices of the peace probationary period is currently six months. *See* Art. 77B of Law 1868/1989, as added by Art. 10 of Law 1968/1991.
129. P. Yessiou-Faltsi & A. Tamamidis, *Recent Tendencies in the Position of the Judge*, *RHDI* 1999, pp. 459–484.
130. *See supra*, No. 50.
131. *See also* Art. 48 §1 Law 4938/2022.
132. Article 48 §2 Law 4938/2022.
133. *See also* Art. 47 §5 Law 4938/2022.
134. Article 29 §1a Law 3643/2006 'On the Municipal Code'.

activities of any nature whatsoever in favour of political parties by judicial functionaries are absolutely prohibited.[135] However, the establishment of associations by judicial functionaries for the improvement of their overall professional interests has been permitted (Article 89 §5 Const.). Nevertheless, strikes by judicial functionaries of any nature[136] and participation in associations whose purposes or activities are secret or which impose secrecy on their members are absolutely prohibited.[137]

Incompatibilities with regard to the specific districts judicial functionaries sit play a rather limited role in recent years, as the big cities (Athens, Piraeus, Thessaloniki, Patras, Larissa, Volos, Heraklion, Rhodes, Chania) have been excluded.[138] There, nevertheless, still exist certain stipulations[139] which prohibit judges and prosecutors from exercising their judicial functions within smaller cities or districts where they, or their wives, have been born or, under certain conditions, had or still have their residence or had been appointed as lawyers.

II. End of Functions

79. End of functions of the judiciary may result through resignation, dismissal and retirement.

Judicial functionaries have the right to resign from their office, this being effected through a written declaration. Resignation is deemed to have been accepted if the relevant presidential decree has not been rendered within ninety days.[140]

80. There are three reasons for the dismissal of judicial functionaries: criminal punishment, grave breach of discipline and physical or professional inefficiencies. Article 88 §4 Const. reads as follows: 'Judicial functionaries may be dismissed only in consequence of a court judgment brought about by criminal conviction or a grave breach of discipline,[141] illness, or disability, or professional incompetence confirmed as specified by law,[142] and in compliance with the provisions of Article 93 §§2 and 3'. The latter refers to the guarantees of publicity of judicial proceedings and to the specific and thorough reasoning of judgments.

81. Pursuant to Article 88 §5 Const.,[143] retirement from the service of the judiciary is compulsory upon attainment of the age of 65 years for all functionaries up to and including the rank of the judges or the Deputy Prosecutors of the Courts of Appeal. For judicial functionaries holding a higher rank, retirement is compulsory at the age of 67 years.

---

135. *See* Art. 47 §6 Law 4938/2022.
136. Article 47 §5 Law 4938/2022.
137. Article 47 §7 Law 4938/2022.
138. Article 49 §§4, 5 Law 4938/2022.
139. Article 49, §§1–3, 5–6 Law 4938/2022.
140. Article 70 Law 4938/2022.
141. *See infra*, No. 83.
142. *See* the detailed regulation by Art. 72 Law 4938/2022.
143. *See also* Art. 71 Law 4938/2022.

III. Discipline[144]

82. Article 91 Const. limits considerably the powers of the executive in relation to the disciplinary control of judges. The Minister of Justice is no longer competent to judge disciplinary actions against judges; neither can he review the disciplinary decisions rendered by other disciplinary jurisdictions.

According to the Const. there are three levels of disciplinary control of judicial functionaries:

(1) The jurisdiction for disciplinary actions against the superior judges, namely the members of the Council of State of *Areios Pagos* (including the Prosecutor and the Deputy Prosecutor of *Areios Pagos*), and of the Exchequer's Tribunal belongs to a Supreme Disciplinary Council, which may impose all kinds of disciplinary penalties, except permanent removal from office.[145] It is formed every year by lot, and it is composed of the President of the Council of State, as its President, two judges of the Council of State, two judges of *Areios Pagos*, two members of the Exchequer's Tribunal and two full professors of Law.[146] Judges who belong to the same branch of justice as that of the accused judge are excluded, four so that the Council always has seven members. The disciplinary action against superior judges is raised by the Minister of Justice.[147]

(2) According to Article 91 §3 Const., the disciplinary actions against the rest of the judges are brought before disciplinary councils, which are formed each year by lot, by seven members within the court of *Areios Pagos*, and by five members in each of the Courts of Appeal.[148] The disciplinary councils of the Courts of Appeal have jurisdiction over the inferior judges of the civil and criminal courts. The decisions of the five-man disciplinary councils of the Courts of Appeal are attacked before the seven-man disciplinary councils of *Areios Pagos*. The decisions of the disciplinary councils of seven members of *Areios Pagos* may again be attacked before disciplinary councils consisting of nine members in the same court.[149] Article 91 §3β Const. declares that a disciplinary action is also raised by the Minister of Justice. In accordance with this regulation, Law 4938/2022 (Article – 117 §1a) provides that the Minister of Justice has a general jurisdiction to exercise disciplinary actions against all judges. Furthermore, disciplinary actions against the judges are exercised by superior judges or prosecutors.[150] Disciplinary councils may impose any disciplinary penalty, again with the exception of the penalty of permanent removal from office.[151]

144. P. Yessiou-Faltsi, *Judicial Responsibility in Greece*, *RHDI* 1982–1983, pp. 281–312.
145. Article 91 §§1, 2 Const.; *see also* Art.113 §4 Law 4938/2022.
146. Article 91 §2 Const.; Art. 114 Law 4938/2022.
147. Article 91, §1b, Const.; Art. 117 §1 Law 4938/2022.
148. *See* currently Art. 117 Law 4938/2022.
149. Article 123 Law 4938/2022.
150. Article 117 Law 4938/2022 contains a detailed regulation.
151. Article 113 §2 Law 4938/022.

(3) According to Article 88 §4 Const., judges may not be dismissed for disciplinary violations except on the basis of a judicial decision.[152] In accordance with this rule, Article 113 Law 4938/2022 declares that if the competent disciplinary council judges that the proper penalty for the accused judge is the permanent removal from office, it must transfer the case to the competent courts which are thus also considered having disciplinary jurisdiction. Such permanent removal from office is imposed by the plenary session of the Supreme Courts (Council of State with regard to members of *Areios Pagos* or its Prosecutors and Deputy Prosecutors; *Areios Pagos* with regard to the rest of civil judges),[153] even if the accused judge is subject to the jurisdiction of the Supreme Disciplinary Council.

152. *See supra*, No. 81.
153. Article 113 §2 Law 4938/022.

Chapter 2. The Bar

§1. Exercise of the Legal Profession

I. Conditions for Admission

83. Greek law does not distinguish between solicitors and barristers or similar separate categories. There is one unique kind of advocate, known by the general term of 'lawyers', regulated by the Lawyers' Code (Law 4194/2013, as subsequently modified). Lawyers in Greece are regarded as unsalaried public functionaries who must be 'respected and honoured by all courts and public authorities'.[154]

Greek citizens who have obtained a law degree in a Greek or an equivalent foreign Law Faculty are accepted to the bar after completing a period of eighteen months' practice in a lawyer's office and after passing the introductory examinations organized nationwide twice a year in each Court of Appeal.[155] Within a reasonable time after having obtained their law degree, they are obliged to apply for registration to the special Registry of Apprentice Lawyers of one of the country's bar associations.[156] A detailed regulation stipulates the bar members or other institutions who are entitled to accept apprentice lawyers,[157] their status, duties and rights.[158] The examination is written and oriented to practical problems of law, covering Civil, Civil Procedural, Commercial, Criminal and Criminal Procedural, Public, and Administrative Procedural Law, and Lawyers Code.[159] It is held by a central committee, seated at the Ministry of Justice, and several decentralized committees.[160]

Upon successful completion of this examination, lawyers are appointed to the particular district court they applied for through an act of the Minister of Justice.[161] There are no limitations involving the number of vacancies to be filled. Unlike judicial functionaries, lawyers are not obliged to retire upon attainment of a certain age. Lawyers may start to exercise their profession as soon as they are registered to the official list of the Bar Association, where they have been appointed.[162] Under certain conditions, judges who have abandoned their office may also be accepted as members of the bar.[163]

154. Articles 1 and 34 §1 Lawyers' Code.
155. According to Art. 3 §§2, 3, of the former Lawyers' Code of 1954, as substituted by Art. 1 of Law 723/1977, only candidates below the age of 35 were qualified for participation. According to the Council of State 727/1985, *Hellenic Justice* 1985, p. 350, this limit did not violate the constitutionally guaranteed professional liberty.
156. Article 10 Lawyers' Code.
157. Article 13 Lawyers' Code.
158. Articles 11, 12 Lawyers' Code.
159. Article 19 Lawyers' Code.
160. Detailed regulation in Arts 20–22 Lawyers' Code.
161. Detailed regulation in Arts 23, 24 Lawyers' Code.
162. Articles 28, 29 Lawyers' Code.
163. *See* Art. 27, §1 Lawyers' Code.

II. Rights and Duties

84. Despite their overall definition of public functionaries,[164] lawyers' relationship with their clients is governed by private law rules. This is most often regarded as a salaried mandate (Articles 713 ff. CC).

Lawyers are exclusively entitled to represent and defend their mandators before all courts, public authorities and disciplinary councils by freely carrying out all necessary steps, provide legal advice, and conduct tax, duty and other administrative cases.[165] While representation by a lawyer before administrative authorities is generally optional, conducting litigation in person is, on the contrary, considered to be the exception.[166] Only before lower criminal courts, justices of the peace (in small claims cases), and ecclesiastical courts, or for the avoidance of imminent danger, or for carrying out procedural acts abroad, may the interested parties act in person without being represented by a lawyer.[167]

With certain exceptions, including members of the Parliament, ministers of the government, staff of Law Faculties and journalists, the lawyers' function is incompatible with any other public or private salaried activity.[168] Lawyers are, thus, not allowed to be involved in any kind of commercial activity.[169] Professors of Law Faculties are entitled to practice law only before Courts of Appeal or *Areios Pagos*.[170]

Legal activities by lawyers remunerated on a permanent scale are not prohibited.[171] Due to the steadily increasing number of lawyers, it has been provided[172] that they may not be occupied on a permanent remuneration by more than one mandator if in the public sector.

Since 1986, lawyers have been allowed to establish law firms (partnerships) whose detailed regulation is 'aiming at commonly providing legal services'.[173] A detailed regulation is provided in the Lawyers Code (Articles 49–56).

Lawyers appointed as members of a bar association are obliged to submit an official declaration each year, confirming that they have been actually practising law and the absence of the respective incompatibilities.[174] The submission of such a declaration is not compulsory if no changes have occurred. According to the former Code of 1954, lawyers were primarily allowed to exercise their legal profession only within the territorial limits of the bar association where they belong, except in criminal cases.[175] The present Code has abandoned such restrictions.[176] Transfer of

164. Article 1 §1 Lawyers' Code.
165. Article 36 Lawyers' Code.
166. Article 36 §1 Lawyers' Code.
167. Article 36 Lawyers' Code. *See also* Art. 94 CPC.
168. Article 32 Lawyers' Code; Art. 8 Code of Lawyers' Duties.
169. Article 8 Code of Lawyers' Duties.
170. Article 32 §1 Lawyers' Code.
171. Articles 42 ff. Lawyers' Code.
172. Article 43, §2e, Lawyers' Code. This restriction extends to only the public sector. Lawyers seeking to be occupied in the public sector on a permanent remuneration are now selected through a special procedure (Art. 43 §2, Lawyers Code).
173. Article 47 §2 former Lawyers' Code. *See* the detailed regulation of Presidential Decree 81/2005 'On the Law Firms'.
174. Details are stipulated in Art. 30 Lawyers' Code.
175. *See* Arts 54–55, 56, 57 former Lawyers' Code.

lawyers to another bar association is, under certain conditions, permissible.[177] Lawyers are initially appointed to perform their legal activities before the Courts of First Instance. Under certain conditions, lawyers may be promoted to superior courts.[178]

Fees of lawyers, basically arranged by a free agreement,[179] are subject to specific statutory regulations in the absence of such an agreement.[180] Under certain conditions and up to a certain limit, fees must be deposited to the bar associations before the trial,[181] which may decide to distribute a certain percentage to their members.[182] Settlement of lawyer's fees depending on the outcome of litigation is not excluded, although it may not exceed 20% of the contested objects' value.[183]

Lawyers are obliged to maintain confidentiality with regard to facts confided by their mandators.[184] This also applies to information attained through the exercise of their legal profession.[185] If summoned as witnesses, advocates are either excluded upon an exception of their mandator or entitled to deny their testimony.[186]

III. Discipline

85. Members of the bar are subject to the competent disciplinary councils[187] of their bar associations[188] or the courts with respect to violations committed during their public sessions.[189] Disciplinary proceedings against lawyers may be initiated by the President of the Bar Association ex officio.[190] These councils are formed by the drawing of lots between lawyers who have served for at least fifteen years.[191] Specific disciplinary penalties which are statutorily provided[192] include disbarment. Decisions of the disciplinary councils of the bar associations may be reviewed by a Supreme Disciplinary Council.[193] This sits in Athens and is formed every year, principally by the President of *Areios Pagos*, as its President, one Supreme Court judge and three lawyers.[194]

176. Article 28 Lawyers' Code provides for a detailed regulation.
177. Article 25 §§1–3 Lawyers' Code.
178. Article 28 Lawyers' Code.
179. Article 58 §1 Lawyers' Code.
180. Articles 58, §3 Lawyers' Code and Supplement No. 1. *See also* Arts 63–86 Lawyers' Code.
181. Article 61 Lawyers' Code.
182. Article 62 Lawyers' Code.
183. Article 60 Lawyers' Code.
184. Article 38 Lawyers' Code.
185. Article 38 of the Lawyers' Code.
186. Articles 400 No. 1, 401 No. 1, 402 No. 2, and 403 CPC. For details *see* J. Tompaidis & K. Voulgarakis, in *Professional Secrecy of Lawyers in Europe*, Compiled by the Bar of Brussels, (Cambridge University Press 2013), pp. 200–221.
187. Articles 139–159 Lawyers' Code.
188. Articles 146,147 Lawyers' Code. *See also* Arts 149–151.
189. Article 155 Lawyers' Code.
190. Details in Arts 152, 153 Lawyers' Code.
191. Details in Art. 147 Lawyers' Code.
192. Article 142 Lawyers' Code.
193. Article 157 Lawyers' Code.
194. Article 148 Lawyers' Code.

§2. Organizations of Lawyers[195]

86. All lawyers appointed to the jurisdictional area of a district court constitute a bar association and are compulsory members. Hence, bar associations have the same seat and bear the same title throughout the country as the respective district courts.[196]

Bar associations are public law entities.[197] They are administered by councils, elected for a four years term.[198] Bar associations are entrusted with the task of proposing legislative improvements or the conditions regarding the dispensation of justice and the exercise of the legal profession.[199] Administration councils of bar associations are vested with disciplinary powers[200] and decide on the promotion of lawyers, disputes of lawyers related to the exercise of their functions, and the administration of the bar association's property.[201]

87. Since 1989, presidents of bar associations throughout the country have constituted a special coordinating organ known as 'the Plenary Session of the Presidents of the Bar Associations' of Greece'.[202] This has its seat in Athens and is administered through a directorate consisting of the Presidents of the Athens, Thessaloniki and Piraeus bars and presided by the Athens President.[203] Beyond coordinating the activities of all bar associations nationwide, the 'Plenary Session of the Presidents' is also entrusted with the task of representing the Greek bar in international organizations and in EU bodies and of organizing Panhellenic congresses in order to decide on general matters related to the dispensation of justice, legislation and the exercise of the legal profession.[204]

195. Nerlich J.& Papaioannou B., *Rechtsanwälte in Griechenland*, in Martin Henssler & Jörg Nerlich (Hrsg.), *Anwaltliche Tätigkeit in Europa; Schriftenreihe des Instituts für Anwaltsrechts* (NOMOS; Bonn 1994), pp. 195 et seq.
196. Articles 87, 88 Lawyers' Code.
197. Article 89, §1 Lawyers' Code.
198. Article 97, §4, of the Lawyers' Code.
199. Article 90 Lawyers' Code.
200. *See supra*, No. 86.
201. Article 95 Lawyers' Code.
202. Details in Art. 133 Lawyers' Code.
203. Details in Art. 133 §§5, 6 Lawyers' Code.
204. Article 134 Lawyers' Code.

Chapter 3. The Bailiffs

§1. Exercise of the Profession

88. Under Greek law,[205] bailiffs (i.e., judicial officers, which is the term used by the International and European Association of the profession) are generally regarded as auxiliary organs of civil justice and, contrary to some older opinions, as unsalaried public servants.[206] Their tasks include:[207] (a) service of judicial or extrajudicial documents involving civil litigation; and (b) performance of acts of execution in their capacity as carriers of enforcement proceedings. Because they are not regarded as representing the interested parties through a legal relationship of private law but as acting rather under rules of public law, bailiffs are on specific conditions personally liable for injuries caused by their acts or omissions, as also other judicial functionaries or organs, while carrying out their duties.[208] Nevertheless, it is at the same time accepted that their relationship to the parties is also governed by the private law rules of 'mandate' (Articles 713–728 CC), if necessary (e.g., involving payment of their fees), whenever these regulations do not contradict its peculiar character. Remuneration of bailiffs, in principle, is calculated on a permanent scale. Nevertheless, additional fees have been allowed whenever acts of execution are affected, depending on the value of the claim which is being enforced.[209]

89. Greek citizens may be appointed as bailiffs if they have obtained a law degree from a Greek or an equivalent foreign Law Faculty or if they have successfully completed a yearly organized introductory examination for the provided number of places.[210] Qualified for participation are only those candidates who are between the age of 22 and 35 and have completed one year of training with a bailiff, already practising for four years.[211] The examining committee consists of Members of the Courts of Appeal or District Courts, the local Bar Association and one bailiff.[212] Examination is written; it covers the fields of Civil Procedure, Criminal Procedure and Criminal Law Civil and Commercial Law to the extent that they involve the bailiffs' activities.[213]

Bailiffs are appointed to each district court and are entitled to perform their tasks only within this district court's jurisdictional area.[214] A special presidential decree

205. Law 2318/1995 'On the Code for Bailiffs', as amended.
206. Article 1 §1 Law 2318/1995.
207. Article 1 §2 Law 2318/1995.
208. Article 73 of the Introductory Law of the CPC.
209. Articles 49–52 Law 2318/1995.
210. Article 2 Law 2318/1995.
211. Articles 3–6 Law 2318/1995.
212. Article 9 §2 Law 2318/1995.
213. For details: Arts 10–14 Law 2318/1995, as supplemented by Art. 22 §9, Law 2521/1997.
214. Article 2, §1 Law 2318/1995.

regulates the establishment of civil law Bailiffs companies.[215] Bailiffs are subject to the supervision of the competent public prosecutor at each respective district court.[216]

90. Disciplinary control of bailiffs is effected by the competent judicial councils before the Courts of First Instance and, eventually, Courts of Appeal.[217]

Disciplinary actions against bailiffs are raised by the public prosecutors of district courts[218] or upon the Minister of Justice's order.[219]

§2. Public Institutions of Bailiffs

91. Bailiffs who are appointed to the jurisdictional areas of the same Court of Appeal constitute the respective Bailiff's Association and are its compulsory members.[220] These associations are public law entities[221] administered by special, elected councils.[222] Their tasks include all kinds of activities involving the administration, supervision and improvement of the bailiffs' profession.[223]

215. Article 2 Presidential Decree 68/2011
216. Articles 19 §2, 20, 45 Law 2318/1995.
217. Articles 53–76 Law 2318/1995.
218. Article 62 §1, Law 2318/1995.
219. Article 62 §2, Law 2318/1995.
220. Article 90 Law 2318/1995.
221. Article 91 Law 2318/1995.
222. Articles 96–116 Law 2318/1995.
223. Detailed regulation by Arts 111–112 Law 2318/1995.

Part II. Jurisdiction

Chapter 1. Domestic Jurisdiction (Article 1 of the CPC)

§1. Factors to Be Taken into Account

92. The notion of jurisdiction in Greek law refers to the overall power of the State to exercise its judicial function.[224] As such, jurisdiction is allocated to different branches of ordinary courts, which, under the Const. include criminal, civil, and administrative courts. Article 1(a) CPC declares that all disputes of private law fall under the jurisdiction of civil courts.

§2. Criteria for Distinguishing Jurisdiction of Civil and Administrative Courts

93. While the distinction between criminal and civil or administrative matters has not caused difficulties, determination of the limits between the jurisdiction of civil and administrative courts has caused significant problems.[225] The separation of jurisdictions described above has placed the determination of 'civil' and 'administrative' disputes at the centre of the judicial system. In principle, the separation of jurisdictions for civil, criminal, and administrative matters must be followed by ordinary legislation when allocating cases to different court branches. Opposite legal norms are unconstitutional, and every court in Greece enjoys the power to determine a norm as such. However, to safeguard the uniform application of the same set of legal rules, the 2001 amendment of the Const. has provided that allocation of certain civil disputes to ordinary administrative courts, and vice versa, is exceptionally permissible (Article 94 §3).

According to an opinion and a rather permanent case law of the Council of State during the past decades, all disputes dealing with the function of a public service must be regarded as administrative. On the contrary, older decisions of *Areios Pagos* and some eminent Greek scholars followed a stricter criterion: only disputes

224. Or, exceptionally, of the legal persons of public law.

225. K. Beys, 'Der Bereich der Privat- und Verwaltungsrechtsstreitigkeiten im hellenischen Recht', in *Festschrift Für Hideo Nakamura Zum 70. Geburtstag am 2. März 1996* (Tokyo, 1996, de Gruyter; Reprint 2013), pp. 51–72.

provoked by acts or omissions of public organs while exercising their public authority may be regarded as administrative. During the last decade, the prevailing opinion has been following a definition, which considers as a main characteristic point of each dispute the legal norms to be applied. Disputes regulated by provisions belonging to substantive Administrative law are regarded as administrative and come under the jurisdiction of administrative courts. On the contrary, if private law applies, we may only speak of civil litigation.

Despite this theoretical support, difficulties in exactly defining disputes as civil or administrative remain; hence, conflicts of jurisdiction between civil and administrative courts are still emerging. Most often, they are caused by the peculiar character of parties, which, while legal persons of private law, are entrusted with tasks entailing public authority. In this case, the Special Highest Court is entrusted to determine the appropriate jurisdiction by precisely defining the nature of the contested dispute as civil or administrative.

Pursuant to an express provision (Article 17 §4a Const.), disputes involving a determination of compensation for expropriated property, despite their administrative character, had exceptionally remained under the jurisdiction of civil courts. The revision of the Const. in 2001 has now provided (Article 17 §4α) that such disputes must be adjudicated by ordinary administrative courts, according to Article 94 Const., as these are purely administrative. If the need to institute a uniform jurisdiction for all matters involving such disputes prevails, it is permissible, in exception to Article 94 Const., to provide that civil courts are competent (Article 17 § 4a Const.). Legislative Act of 21 December 2001 (Article 1), ratified by Law 2990/2002 (Article 'First'), has accordingly opted in favour of the subordination of disputes involving determination of compensation in cases of expropriation of private property again to the jurisdiction of civil courts, on the basis of their connection to disputes concerning determination of the persons being the holders of such rights.

§3. Voluntary Jurisdiction of Civil Courts

94. Following the example of other civil law countries, the Greek CPC (Article 1a and b, Article 94 §2 Const.) distinguishes between the jurisdiction for 'disputes' and a wide competence over non-contentious matters, such as questions of personal status or capacity (Articles 782, 783 ff., 796 ff., 799, 801 ff., 803 ff.), inheritance (Article 810 ff.), publication of wills (Articles 807 ff.), etc. The standard requirement for allocating a matter to the voluntary jurisdiction of civil courts is the existence of a relevant statutory provision (Article 739, Article 121 of the Introductory Law of the CC, while the lack of an adversary element is regarded as this jurisdiction's main characteristic.[226] Procedure in non-contentious matters is therefore flexible and informal. Although tending to the protection of private interests, this judicial activity is regarded as having more or less a strong administrative element.

226. *Infra*, No. 276.

Consequently, the court may normally exercise powers which belong to the inquisitorial system (Article 744) and is not subject to the usual limitations of the admissibility of evidence, which is characteristic of the procedure for contentious matters (Article 759).

95. Similar to voluntary jurisdiction on private law matters, according to Article 1c CPC, the jurisdiction of civil courts may also extend to 'affairs' of public law by a specific statute (i.e., the official proclamation of candidates to be elected as members of Parliament). Article 94 §4 Const. has expressly allowed subordination of matters of an administrative nature either to civil or administrative courts.

§4. Lack of Jurisdiction of Civil Courts

96. Jurisdictional issues are regarded as constituting a basic procedural prerequisite. Thus, they must be examined by civil courts ex officio before they proceed to the merits of each case. When a civil court lacks jurisdiction, the case may not be transferred to another jurisdictional branch of courts; it is dismissed as inadmissible (Article 4 CPC). Decisions of civil courts on matters not belonging to their jurisdiction are null and void (Article 313 §1b CPC). This severe sanction is not provided for lack of the courts' competence.

§5. Subject Matter Jurisdiction

I. Factors to Be Taken into Account

A. Definition of Subject Matter Competence

97. Subject matter competence under Greek law must be understood as the part of jurisdiction granted to specific categories of courts. Subject matter competence refers to the allocation of jurisdictional power among the courts of each branch. Pursuant to the present CPC, subject matter competence of civil Courts of First Instance is determined with regard to each of the coexisting three types of courts, i.e., justices of the peace, one-member and three-member district courts. Unlike in venue (territorial competence), the subject matter competence of civil courts may not be modified through a procedural contract of the parties, expressly or tacitly agreed (prorogation).[227]

Allocation of subject matter competence among civil Courts of First Instance is effected in context with the significance of each matter. Despite their equality in jurisdictional rights, civil Courts of First Instance actually function in a hierarchical rank. The justices of the peace belong at the lowest level, whereas the three-member district courts, which adjudicate over disputes of the highest value and enjoy a presumption of subject matter competence for the overall spectre of civil disputes (Article 18 No. 1 – CPC), stand at the top of this hierarchy.

227. Article 42 §1 CPC.

B. Role of the Value of the Claim

98. A principal criterion for allocating disputes among the aforementioned types of First-Instance civil courts is the value of the contested claim (Articles 7–11, 14 and 16 CPC). Thus, in order to effectuate distribution of civil matters among the hierarchy of First-Instance civil courts in accordance with their significance, quantitative criteria are primarily used. Evidently, this method can only be applied with regard to those civil disputes which may be valued in money terms.

The respective limits have been repeatedly modified following the inflation rates.[228] Since 1 January 2016, they are as follows: Justices of the peace are granted subject matter competence whenever the value of the contested claim does not exceed EUR 20,000[229] (Article 14 §1a CPC), whereas one-member district courts are adjudicating over actions if the amount in controversy extends over EUR 20,000 up to EUR 250,000[230] (Article 14 §2 CPC). Finally, whenever the value of the contested claim exceeds EUR 250,000, the subject matter competence belongs to the three-member district courts (Article 18 CPC).

C. Role of the Nature of the Claim

99. Beyond quantitative criteria, the CPC applies an additional method for determining the subject matter competence. In principle, this is not related to the amount in controversy but rather to the nature of some disputes or the simplicity of legal or factual matters involved. It seeks to allot competence to justices of the peace and one-member district courts as the most appropriate jurisdictional organs with regard to the specific nature of certain disputes. These have been included in particular statutory lists regarding both the justices of the peace (Article 15 CPC) and the one-member district courts (Articles 16 and 17 CPC). Hence, the distinction of the subject matter competence of those courts refers to two categories: ordinary and extraordinary competence. While the first is determined by the amount in controversy, the latter does not principally depend on the value of the contested claim.

II. Main Claims and Ancillary Claims

100. The value of the claim, as a means for allotting disputes to the subject matter competence of civil courts (Article 7 CPC), is determined by the judge (Article 8), in principle, following the amount specified by the plaintiff's complaint (Article 9a). This determination is exclusively based on the main claim. Ancillary claims regarding interest, profits and costs are not taken into account (Article 9b). When

228. *See* Art. 7 §§1, 2 Law 2145/1993; Art. 3 Law 2207/1994; Art. 9 Law 2225/1994; Min. Dec. 40320/14-6-95.
229. For the conversion in Euro *see* Arts 3–5 Law 2943/2001.
230. *See* n. 227.

non-money claims are involved, the estimation of the claim value is affected following the existing circumstances at the time when the action is commenced (Article 10). The judge, nevertheless, is free to order the taking of evidence if needed (Article 8). This kind of evidence is defined as free in the sense that it is not subject to common procedural restrictions. If the plaintiff abandoned part of his claim until the first hearing of the case (Article 295 § 1b), determination of the value of the claim is based on the remaining request.

There are some more detailed rules to assist the judge in estimating the value of the claim: First, in the case of joinder of parties, this estimation depends on whether the disputed substantive right is divisible. In the last case, the subject matter competence is, in principle, determined on the basis of each claim raised by or against the joined parties (Article 9 d), whereas otherwise, the value of the whole is taken into account. If, however, the parties' claims are not equal and, thus, this mode for determining the subject matter competence does not lead to the subordination of all co-plaintiffs or co-defendants to the same court, subject matter competence is granted to the hierarchically superior court (Article 9 d). Second, in case the plaintiff joins more causes of actions against the same defendant in one complaint, subject matter competence is determined on the basis of a co-estimation of the total of claims raised (Article 9 c), with the exception of subsidiary joinder, where, under Article 9 e), the claim with the highest value is taken into account. Third, a number of specific stipulations contain technical rules with regard to the estimation of real rights value (Article 11 Nos 1–4), of the action for partition (Article 11 No. 5), of the contract of lease (Article 11 No. 6), and of legal relationships producing periodic claims (Article 11 No. 7).

III. Overview of the Different Rules

A. *Subject Matter Competence of Justices of the Peace*

101. Subject matter competence of the justice of the peace may be either ordinary (Article 14 §1a CPC) or extraordinary (Article 15 CPC).

Ordinary competence covers small-sized claims. Consequently, it depends exclusively on whether the object of litigation may be valued in money terms and on whether the sum claimed does not exceed EUR 20,000. Estimation of property value follows the rules already discussed, with the exception of certain lease disputes.

All disputes involving the lease of things, whether of commercial or of civil character, must be now entertained by the Justices of the Peace in case the monthly price of the lease does not exceed EUR 600 and irrespective of the value of the claim (Article 14 § 1b CPC). If this monthly amount is higher, competence belongs to the one-member district courts (Article 16 No. 1). In addition, following Article 14 §1c CPC, disputes arising out of ownership involving the horizontal division of a building were transferred to the subject matter competence of the justices of the peace, in case the value of the claim does not exceed EUR 20,000.

102. The extraordinary subject matter competence of the justices of the peace must be understood as extending to a quite wide range of disputes, independently from the value of the contested claim, even if this exceeds the sum of EUR 20,000 (Article 15, Nos 1–13 CPC). The extraordinary character refers not only to its non-dependence on quantitative criteria but also to the nature of disputes involved. However, this covers mostly litigation of an urgent or a simple nature.

103. An attempt to categorize disputes referred to in Article 15 CPC results in the following groups:

(a) Rural disputes. This category includes actions involving: (1) the delivery or the return of a leased farm in case the agreed price is a percentage of the crop (Article 641 CC; Article 15 No. 1 CPC); (2) all kinds of damage to trees, plants, fruits or growing crops (Article 15 No. 2); (3) boundary lines in certain cases of farming (Article 15 No. 4); (4) the use of passages and the respective damages or the use of public water (Article 15 Nos 5 and 6); (5) defects or lack of agreed qualities in case of sale of animals (Article 15 No. 13).
(b) Controversies involving certain limits to the right of ownership provided by the CC (Articles 1003–1009, 1018–1020 and 1023–1031) with regard to immovables in rural or urban areas or damages caused by the violation of such limits (Article 15 No. 3 CPC).
(c) Disputes involving hotel services (Article 15 Nos 7 and 8 CPC) and contracts for the transport of persons (only with regard to the claims of the carrier, Article 15 No. 9 CPC).
(d) Controversies involving remuneration of lawyers for services in trials before the justices of the peace (Article 15 No. 11) and compensation or costs of witnesses (in any court or arbitration), interpreters, custodians and guardians (Article 15 No. 12 CPC). Disputes involving lawyers' claims for services in other courts, if the requested sum exceeds EUR 20,000, belong exclusively to the one-member district courts.
(e) Disputes involving the relationship between associations or cooperative societies and their members (Article 15 No. 10). Practically, the most important case of this last category included the declaration of nullity of the decisions of the general assemblies of associations or cooperative societies (Article 15 No. 14), but this was transferred to the one-member district courts (Article 17 No. 4). A considerable number of decisions of justices of the peace had extended their subject matter competence to declare the nullity of the decisions of their councils of administration.

B. Subject Matter Competence of One-Member District Courts

104. As in the case of the justices of the peace, subject matter competence of one-member district courts must be understood as ordinary when based on the amount in controversy and as extraordinary when independent from the sum claimed.

Ordinary competence of one-member district courts currently extends to cases where the amount in controversy, while bigger than EUR 20,000, does not exceed EUR 250,000 (Article 14 §2 CPC).

105. Extraordinary subject matter competence of one-member district courts has been gradually extended to a quite significant number of disputes (Articles 16 and 17 CPC). This must be distinguished into two kinds: The first and most important list of disputes included in Article 16 are brought before one-member district courts even if the amount in controversy exceeds EUR 250,000. Nevertheless, these disputes are partly dependent on the sum claimed: if the value is lower than EUR 20,000, such disputes remain under the subject matter competence of the justices of the peace. The second and shorter list (as included in Article 17)[231] is entirely independent of quantitative criteria.

106. If the amount in controversy exceeds the sum of EUR 20,000, the following categories of disputes are brought before the one-member district courts, even if the claim is over the threshold of EUR 250,000:

(a) Disputes involving all kinds of lease on condition that they do not belong to the subject matter competence of the justices of the peace (ordinary or extraordinary). Thus, one-member district courts enjoy a general subject matter competence for disputes involving leases (Article 16 No. 1 CPC).
(b) Labour disputes. In Greek civil procedural law, the single-judge court has been the traditional court for adjudicating labour disputes. One-member district courts are currently enjoying a far-reaching subject matter competence for hearing all kinds of suits between employers and employees, or between workers, arising out of individual employment contracts or during the delivery of any kind of work (Article 16 Nos 2, 3 and 5), unless they refer to public law relations. Even collective labour disputes are brought before one-member district courts (Article 16 No. 5). These disputes are handled in particular proceedings.
(c) Disputes involving the remuneration of certain professionals. Disputes involving various types of remuneration of lawyers, unless they concern legal services for trials before the justices of the peace, bailiffs, notaries, medical doctors, dentists, veterinarians, engineers, chemists, etc. (Article 16 No. 7) fall within the extraordinary subject matter competence of the one-member district courts. This also concerns remuneration or compensation of some other persons or organs, such as experts, arbitrators, etc. (Articles 16 Nos 8 and 11). Disputes involving remuneration of professionals are also adjudicated following particular proceedings.

231. *See infra*, No. 108. Since its amendment by Art. 8 §1 Law 2145/1993, Art. 17 now contains also cases referring to the declaration of nullity of the decisions of general assemblies of associations or cooperative societies.

(d) Insurance disputes. In contrast to disputes involving social security, which since 1977 are transferred to the jurisdiction of administrative courts, all controversies arising out of insurance contracts and tending to the determination and payment of the premium belong to the subject matter competence of one-member district courts (Article 16 Nos 6, 9).
(e) Disputes arising out of the use of cars. Since 1977, all disputes -quite numerous in recent years – deriving from the cars' circulation, including claims arising out of car insurance contracts,[232] are brought before one-member district courts (Article 16 No. 11). Additionally, since 1977, such disputes have been handled in particular proceedings (Article 614 CPC).
(f) Disputes involving the possession or detention of movables or immovables (Article 16 No. 12). These were transferred to one-member district courts in 1994.

107. For this next group of actions (Article 17 CPC), one-member district courts are the absolutely appropriate courts, whether the amount in controversy is lower than EUR 20,000 or exceeds EUR 250,000. Such subject matter competence concerns:

(a) All family law actions (which, naturally, cannot be valued in money terms), including the exercise of parental care,[233] the use of the family home, and the partition of movable property in case marital life is disturbed, are exclusively heard by one-member district courts (Articles 17 Nos 1 and 2, 592 Nos 2 and 3). Litigation involving the overall family relations has been thus concentrated in courts consisting of a single judge.
(b) All disputes arising out of ownership involving the horizontal divisions of a building (Article 17 No. 3), with the exception of those provided in Article 14 §1 c.
(c) Actions seeking the declaration of nullity of the decisions of general assemblies of associations and cooperative societies (Article 17 No. 4).

One-member district courts are now simultaneously Courts of First Instance and Courts of Appeal. Notwithstanding cases where no appeal is possible (small claims: Article 512 CPC), one-member district courts are also the appropriate courts to hear the appeals against decisions of the justices of the peace (Article 17A CPC).

C. *Subject Matter Competence of Three-Member District Courts*

108. Three-member district courts enjoy a presumption of subject matter competence. According to Article 18 CPC, they must indeed hear all disputes which do not belong to any other court. This presumption of subject matter competence must be understood under two aspects: first, it covers all civil disputes exceeding the sum

232. Law 489/1976, Art. 10 §1.
233. Articles 1510–1541 of the CC, as modified by Art. 17 Law 1329/1983.

of EUR 250,000, whenever not belonging to the extraordinary subject matter competence of one-member district courts (Articles 16 and 17 No. 2) and of the justices of the peace (Article 15). Second, it extends to various disputes which may not be valued in money terms (i.e., divorce cases). While in most cases, there exists unanimity as to whether a specific dispute may not be valued in money and thus belong to this last category, some difficulties have also emerged in relation to specific cases (e.g., negatory action, defrauding of creditors).

D. *Subject Matter Competence of Courts of Appeal*

109. The principal subject matter competence for adjudicating in second instance has been allocated to the Courts of Appeal. These courts hear appeals against decisions of all Courts of First Instance, with the exception of decisions of the justices of the peace, namely of all three-member and one-member district courts (Article 19 CPC).

In some exceptional cases, Courts of Appeal adjudicate as Courts of First Instance over: (a) disputes involving the definite determination of compensation when private property is expropriated;[234] (b) disputes emerging from contracts for 'Public Constructions' when these are regarded as private law contracts;[235] (c) lastly, all disputes regarding the interpretation, or the overall operation of testaments or other acts, comprising donations of property for a public purpose,[236] have been allocated exclusively to the Court of Appeal of Athens and are adjudicated following the procedure of voluntary jurisdiction (Article 825 CPC).

E. Subject Matter Competence of *Areios Pagos*

110. Areios Pagos, the unique Supreme Civil Court of Greece, has as its principal subject matter competence to adjudicate over cassations against decisions of all Greek civil courts, namely, the Courts of Appeal, the three- and one-member district courts, and the justices of the peace (Articles 20 §1, and 552 CPC). In the course of the efforts to accelerate civil and commercial proceedings, a new Article 20A was introduced in the CPC, stating that, in cases where a new difficult legal issue affecting the public at large is in need of interpretation, the matter may be

---

234. Articles 20–21 Law 2882/2001. *See also supra*, No. 95.
235. Such disputes, initially allocated to the civil Courts of Appeal (Art. 61 §3d, of the Introductory Law – CPC), were subsequently transferred to the administrative courts. The Special Highest Court, however, when called to settle the respective conflicts of jurisdiction arising between civil and administrative courts, has ruled that this transfer covers exclusively disputes of a purely administrative nature. Hence, conflicts emerging from public constructions operated by legal persons of private law, despite the fact that such entities are devoted to a public purpose, have retained their private character and have thus remained under the jurisdiction of civil courts. Exception: Presidential Decree 361/1991, in force since 20 Aug. 1993, for OTE (telecommunications) and ΔΕΗ (electricity production).
236. *See* Emergency Law 2039/1939.

directly addressed to the Full Bench of the Supreme Court upon request of a party or a preliminary question submitted by the court seized with the proceedings. The rule applies after 1 January 2022.

§6. Venue (Territorial Jurisdiction)

I. Factors to Be Taken into Account

A. *Definition and Distinctions of Territorial Competence*

111. There are two rather similar terms to express the territorial links of a particular court to a party or a case, namely *territorial competence* and '*jurisdiction*'. Territorial competence is defined as the quantum of subject matter competence vested in a particular court, among those of the same hierarchical level, in the context of its territorial links to each specific case. The notion of 'jurisdiction' (forum)[237] is exclusively used to determine the subordination of a certain case or party to a territorially competent court.

Territorial competence is determined by statute (Articles 22–40 CPC: legal jurisdiction). Such statutory regulations are based on the strength of the ties between the litigants or the subject matter of the action and a given place. Under certain conditions, territorial competence may be either modified by agreement of the parties (Articles 42–44 CPC: *prorogation*) or (only exceptionally) be fixed by a court's decision (Articles 46, 48–51 CPC: judicial jurisdiction). The mere presence of a person in a certain place and his availability for service is neither sufficient nor necessary to establish territorial competence. The doctrine of *forum non conveniens* has not developed in Greece.

112. Territorial competence is either general or special. The jurisdiction regarding a person is defined as general when it covers all actions addressed against him/her unless a special exclusive jurisdiction exists. Special jurisdiction refers to a certain complex of disputes, which, on the basis of a particular statutory provision, are being brought before particularly defined courts, i.e., other than the courts of the general jurisdiction, depending on the connection of their district to the contested claim.

Special jurisdictions are further distinguished into concurrent and exclusive. A concurrent special forum may coexist with the general jurisdiction of a person or even other concurrent jurisdictions in the sense that it allows an option to the plaintiff among either the court of the general or the courts of special forums. The Greek CPC has introduced seven categories of concurrent jurisdictions (Articles 33, 35–40).

Unlike the concurrent, an exclusive jurisdiction is mandatory, as it excludes both general and special jurisdiction. Seven categories of exclusive jurisdictions are featured in the CPC (Articles 27–31, 34, 933).

---

237. The German term 'Gerichtsstand' was used by the previous Code of 1835 in its original German text (*see* Arts 16–22).

In case of co-existence of more concurrent jurisdictions, it is the plaintiff's privilege to choose the more appropriate (Article 41 CPC) by bringing the action in that forum (Article 221, §1c, CPC). This is the proper time for determining the priority among more actions which have been eventually brought (Article 41).

B. *Relevant Connecting Factors and the Conflicting Interests Served*

113. General jurisdiction is primarily based on the defendant's domicile. The underlying idea is evidently related to the need to protect the defending parties. For the purpose of facilitating or accelerating the process, rules of special territorial competence usually take into account, after weighing the conflicting interests, the substantial links between the competent courts' district and the elements of an action. However, when the interest to bestow territorial competence to courts related to the action, rather than to protect the defendant, seems predominant, exclusive jurisdictions are provided.

II. Overview of the Different Rules

A. *General Territorial Competence*

1. Domicile as the Principal Connecting Factor

114. Pursuant to Article 22 CPC, unless otherwise provided, a general territorial competence is bestowed to the courts of the district where the defendant has his domicile. The time relevant for this determination is when the action has been brought (Articles 45, 215, 221, §1b, CPC).

The concept of *domicile* is defined in the CC[238] as a person's principal and permanent establishment. This notion is accordingly regarded as comprising both a corporal (*corpus*) and a non-material element (*animus*). This latter expresses the intent for permanence. In cases of lack of such an intention, which is usually proven only through indirect evidence, the existing physical links of a person to a given place (*corpus*) constitute the notion of residence. When the domicile of a person cannot be identified, residence is deemed as its equivalent.[239] Although a person may not have simultaneously more than one domicile,[240] the CC introduces the notion of special domicile which particularly denotes the place of a person's professional establishment.[241]

A person is deemed to have retained his domicile until the acquisition of a new one.[242] The cases of persons without a domicile are, hence, rather rare. The notion

238. Article 51, as modified by Art. 2 Law 1329/1983.
239. Article 53 CC.
240. Article 51 al. b CC.
241. Article 51 al. b CC.
242. Article 52 CC.

of domicile in Greek law is, moreover, defined on an international basis. Lack of domicile means the absence of domicile in any state of the world.

Three categories of persons have a 'legal' domicile, i.e., a domicile attributed by statute. All public functionaries who have been appointed for life (i.e., members of the judiciary) are deemed to be domiciled at the place where they render their services.[243] Second, all minors under parental care have the domicile of their parents or of the parent who has their care.[244] Finally, in both cases of guardianship (Articles 1589–1654 CC) and interdiction (Articles 1666–1688, especially Articles 1676, 1678 CC), minors or the persons involved have the domicile of their guardians.[245]

2. Rules Founding General Jurisdiction

115. The complex of rules for the foundation of general territorial competence, as provided by the CPC, is quite extensive. They will be treated in this part briefly since they also serve for the establishment of the international jurisdiction of Greek courts:

(a) In principle, general territorial competence depends on the domicile of the defendant (Article 22).
(b) When such domicile does not exist, neither within the Greek territory nor any other state (Article 23 § 1a), or when such domicile cannot be determined (Article 53 CC), residence within the district of a Greek court may take its place, thus functioning as a subsidiary base of general territorial competence. On the contrary, when the given defendant has a domicile abroad, Greek courts may not exercise their international jurisdiction.
(c) If in the above circumstances, the residence of a defendant is unknown, territorial competence is established following the last domicile of the defendant in Greece or, in case such domicile does not exist, his last residence (Article 23, § 1b).
(d) When the defendant is engaged in a profession or trade, disputes involving these activities may be brought, apart from the courts of his general domicile, also before the courts of his special domicile (Articles 23 §2 CPC and 51c CC). Hence, both courts have concurrent jurisdiction. It is moreover assumed that, under this rule, each person may have even more than one special domicile depending on the places of his business.
(e) When the residence of the defendant has a longer duration than in normal cases due to particular circumstances (as in the case of employees serving away from their domicile, servants, students, etc.), and those defendants have the capacity to conduct proceedings in their own name, and the object of litigation is a monetary claim, domicile *and* residence may both exceptionally function as main

243. Article 54 CC.
244. Article 56 §1 CC.
245. Article 56 §2 CC.

bases of territorial competence. In this sense, they serve as concurrent jurisdictions, available at the plaintiff's option (Article 38 CPC). This option seeks to facilitate suing debtors who have a residence of a longer duration in places other than their domicile. It is based on the idea that a defendant does not have a legal interest to avoid being sued in places where he resides for a rather longer time. Since it involves only monetary claims, this option between domicile and residence is regarded as establishing a concurrent special jurisdiction under the name of forum of longer residence.

(f) The general forum for certain categories of persons is determined through connecting factors other than domicile. Beyond the public functionaries for whom the place where they render their services is deemed to be their domicile pursuant to the CC,[246] the CPC (Article 26) provides that lawyers and notaries belong to the general jurisdiction of the courts where they exercise their duties. The same is true for all public servants and the military (place of service), with the significant difference that the latter may additionally be sued before the courts of their domicile (Article 32 CPC). Lastly, all Greeks who enjoy immunity from suit while serving abroad, and all state employees appointed to serve abroad, and also their wives and children, may be sued before the courts where they were domiciled before this mission, and, if they had not such domicile, before the courts of the district of Athens (Article 24). This last provision seeks to secure a forum in Greece regarding persons who are entitled to immunity or who serve abroad.

3. Actions Against the State

116. A special rule governs territorial competence for actions against the State. Pursuant to Article 25 §1 CPC, the State may be sued before the courts of the district where the authority representing it has its seat. As a rule, the State is represented by the Minister of Finance, who sits in Athens.[247] There are, however, cases determined by various statutes where the State is also represented by other authorities, sitting in various districts nationwide, e.g., by the director of the public office charged with the collection of public revenues according to the Code for Collecting the Public Revenues (Article 77 Law 4978/2022); and the general secretary of the region, in disputes involving expropriation (Article 14 §§2, 3 law 2882/2001 'On the compulsory expropriation of immovable property').

4. Actions Against Legal Entities

117. When the defendant is a legal person, the general territorial competence depends on its seat (Article 25 §2 CPC). According to a prevailing opinion in both

246. *See supra,* No. 116.
247. *See* Decree of 26 Jun./10 Jul. 1994 'On the Code of Laws Regarding the Trials of the State'.

theory and case law,[248] which also considerably influences the determination of international jurisdiction of the Greek courts, the relevant factor is the real seat of the legal entity, the place actually maintained by its headquarters, rather than any other place stated in its charter. In addition, branch offices of legal persons (companies) are deemed to also have special seats (Article 23 §2, applicable by analogy;) and may thus be sued in the place of their establishment with respect to disputes concerning the subject matter of their operations.

Similar rules apply with regard to associations of persons or partnerships not vested with legal personality which, although not legal entities, have the capacity to be parties (Articles 25 §2, 62b CPC).

B. Jurisdictions Concurrent to the General Territorial Competence

1. The Forum Involving Juridical Acts (Article 33 CPC)

118. Disputes involving all kinds of juridical acts *inter vivos*, be they contracts or unilateral acts, civil or commercial, may be brought, at the plaintiff's option, apart from the courts of the general jurisdiction, also before the courts of either the district where the juridical act has been drawn or at the place of the contested obligation's performance (Article 33, *Forum contractus*). The wide scope of this forum results in extremely significant practical applications.[249]

According to a traditional view, both places (formation or performance of the act) must be determined following the substantive law rules of the *lex fori*, i.e., the CC (Articles 167, 192–194, 320–322). Recent case law, however, has accepted the relevancy of the *lex causae.*[250] It must be stressed that, under the Greek CC (Article 321), when the claim involves a pecuniary obligation and the place of its performance has not been fixed, expressly or tacitly, by the contracting parties and may not be deduced from the circumstances, it is deemed to be the domicile of the creditor at the time of payment. Moreover, when the claim arises in the course of the creditor's business, the place of business substitutes the creditor's domicile (Article 321b CC). Consequently, all actions which involve pecuniary claims arising from commercial or civil contracts or other juridical acts may be brought before the courts of the plaintiff's domicile or the plaintiff's business if the place of payment

---

248. Plenary Session of *Areios Pagos* 461/1978, *Legal Tribune* 1979, p. 211; Plenary Session of *Areios Pagos* 2/1999, *Legal Tribune* 1999, pp. 1113 ff.; Plenary session of *Areios Pagos* 2/2003, *Legal Tribune* 2003, pp. 1392 ff.; *Areios Pagos* 178/1991, *Hellenic Justice* 1991, p. 1240; *Areios Pagos* 186/2008; Court of Appeal of Athens 2561/1976, *Harmenopoulos* 1976, p. 607.

249. For example: According to several decisions, in case, e.g., of an automobile accident, the action of the victim against the insurer can be brought before the Greek courts by virtue of a contract formed between the victim and the insurer on the basis of the assumption of debt by the insurer. *See* the Plenary Session of *Areios Pagos* 715/1978, *Review of Commercial Law* 1979, p. 284; Court of Appeal of Athens 5614/1978, *Hellenic Justice* 1979, p. 57. There are, however, doubts involving actions for unjust enrichment.

250. *See* Court of Appeal of Thessaloniki 2541/1983, *Harmenopoulos* 1984, pp. 308 (309).

has not been fixed directly or indirectly in the above sense. This result is of particular significance when it serves as a base for the international jurisdiction of Greek courts.

2. The Forum for Tort Disputes (Article 35 CPC)

119. All actions arising from tort, independently of whether this tort constitutes a criminal act or not, can also be brought beyond the courts of the defendant's domicile, either before the courts of the district where the tortuous act occurred or the courts of the district where its effects have appeared.

3. The Forum Related to the Management of Property Other Than under a Court Order (Article 36 CPC)

120. Disputes involving the management of property, when such management is not based on a court order but: (a) on a contract (e.g., contract for work, Article 685 CC), (b) on a testament (e.g., administration of the executor of the will, Articles 2017–2031 CC), (c) on statutory provisions (e.g., administration of parents, Articles 1510, 1523 CC) are adjudicated either by the courts of the defendant's domicile or by the courts of the place of management (*Forum gestae administrationes ex causis variis*).

4. The Forum Involving the Joinder of Defendants (Article 37 §1 CPC)

121. In case of joinder of two or more co-defendants in one action, the plaintiff may sue all co-defendants in the court of the place where any of them is domiciled or, when domicile lacks, where he has a residence (*Forum continentiae causarum ex identitate personali, litis consortium*). The jurisdiction of the joinder of co-defendants depends on the assertion by the plaintiff that the joinder is proper in the sense that it is based on the respective procedural conditions.

This jurisdiction is concurrent not only because it permits an option between several domiciles of the co-defendants but also because the plaintiff may additionally bring the connected actions in the courts of a special concurrent jurisdiction which covers all co-defendants. If, however, such common special jurisdiction is exclusive, the connected actions against the co-defendants may be brought only in the court of the exclusive forum. Due to the narrowness of the wording of Article 37 §1 (which does not expressly cover cases where a special forum involves only one or some of the co-defendants), a question has emerged as to whether the plaintiff has an additional option to sue all co-defendants also before the court of the special forum of one. The divergence of views is particularly intense when such special jurisdiction, related to only one of the co-defendants, has an exclusive nature. The significance of such questions is evident whenever Greek courts are required to determine their international jurisdiction.

5. The Forum Related to Actions Involving Multiple Immovables (Article 37 §2 CPC)

122. Actions based on similar causes by the same plaintiff(s) against the same defendant(s), involving a real right on two or more immovables, situated in the districts of different courts, may be brought in the courts of the location of any one immovable (*Forum continentiae causarum ex identitate reali*). This forum is regarded as simultaneously exclusive in the sense that, beyond the option between the location of the different immovables, it does not allow territorial competence of any other courts (e.g., of the domicile).

6. The Forum for Matrimonial Disputes (Article 39 CPC)

123. All disputes called 'matrimonial' (namely those involving divorce, the declaration of the existence or inexistence of marriage, the annulment of marriage and the personal relationship between spouses) are also adjudicated by the courts of the spouses' last common residence (Article 39, *Forum matrimonii*). The concept of matrimonial disputes is precisely defined by the CPC (Article 592 §1)[251] for the purpose of providing a particular proceeding for their adjudication (new Articles 592–613). This list is for this reason exclusive. However, despite their pecuniary nature, claims involving maintenance between the spouses and reparation in money for moral harm in divorce are allowed to be connected with purely 'marital' matters and, thus, be brought before the same forum by virtue of special rules (Articles 592 §§3, 4, and 610 CPC). The same is true for the list of various family law disputes (Article 592 §§3, 4), evidently for reasons of concentration.

The notion of the spouses' common residence must be distinguished from domicile. It is, however, stressed that residence in the sense of this concurrent jurisdiction must be real and have a rather longer duration than normal cases. Matrimonial cases may also be heard by the court which has the general territorial competence according to the basic rule (defendant's domicile).

7. The Forum Based on Property (Article 40 CPC)

124. The special jurisdiction called 'forum of property' was first introduced by the 1967 Code, based on the German model (*Gerichtstand des Vermögens*). Accordingly, an action of a pecuniary nature against a defendant who has not a domicile within the Greek territory may be brought before the courts where any property of this defendant is situated (Article 40), even if the action is not related to that forum. Its main objective is to extend the international jurisdiction of national courts

251. As modified by Art. 36 of Law 1329/1983; and subsequently by Art. 1, Article 'Fourth', of Law 4335/2015.

whenever the defendant is not domiciled in Greece. With the exception of domicile, this forum may, however, function despite the existence of other general or special jurisdictions. Relevant jurisdictional bases are all kinds of property (movables, immovables, claims) on the condition that they represent a certain value. Pursuant to an explicit rule (Article 40 §2 CPC), when a claim of the defendant is used as a jurisdictional base for an action against him, this claim is deemed to be located at his debtor's domicile. The forum of property is, by most authors, regarded as exorbitant.

C. *Exclusive Jurisdictions*

1. The Exclusive Forum for Company Disputes (Article 27 CPC)

125. All disputes between a company and its partners or among partners themselves, emerging from internal company affairs, must be adjudicated exclusively by the courts of the company's seat (Article 27 §1 CPC, *Forum societatis*). Even disputes appearing after a company's dissolution and liquidation involving property partition must be brought before this exclusive forum on condition that the respective action is being brought within two years after the termination of partition (Article 27 §2). This rule is regarded as covering all kinds of companies, whether commercial or non-commercial. According to the prevailing opinion, it is also irrelevant whether such companies are vested with legal personality. On the one hand, it must be stressed that this exclusive jurisdiction covers solely the internal matters of a company and does not extend to actions between third persons and the company. On the other hand, one must also take into account that the latter, by virtue of the rule about general jurisdiction (Article 25 §2), are also brought before the same forum. Those combined rules, hence, result in the concentration of all corporate claims in the same courts.

2. The Exclusive Forum Related to the Management of Property When This Is Based on a Judicial Order (Article 28 CPC)

126. While disputes involving the management of property in all other cases belong either to the general or the concurrent jurisdiction of the courts where this management was effected, when such management has been ordered either by a court or by another judicial authority (e.g., the public prosecutor), the CPC establishes an exclusive jurisdiction of this court, which has also appointed the administrator (Article 28, *Forum gestae administrations ex decreto iudicis*). This exclusive jurisdiction, however, covers solely disputes emerging between the owner of the property and the administrator; it does not extend to litigation involving third parties, even if related to the respective management.

3. The Exclusive Forum in Actions Involving Real Rights on Immovable Property (Article 29 CPC)

127. All actions involving real rights on immovables must be brought exclusively at the location of the land (Article 29 CPC, *Forum rei sitae*). However, this traditional forum does not solely cover actions related to purely real rights but also some more categories, including actions involving personal rights. The actions to which this forum extends are the following:

(a) All revendicatory (Article 1094 CC), negatory (Article 1108 CC) and public (Article 1112 CC) actions raised to protect ownership, and also those seeking to protect the real rights of predial and personal servitudes, when involving immovable property (Articles 1132, 1173, 1187, 1191 CC), even of a mere declaratory nature. According to some authors and recent decisions, actions tending to the cancellation of the recordation of a mortgage (Articles 1324, 1327, 1328 CC) must also belong to the scope of the exclusive forum of the situs.
(b) Actions involving possession and detention on land. It must be stressed that pursuant to the CC (Article 974), neither possession nor detention is included in the enumeration of real rights and, hence, are rather regarded as sui generis rights.
(c) Actions seeking the partition of an immovable (Articles 799, 1113 CC; *actiones communi dividundo*) or the settlement of boundaries (Article 1020 CC; *actiones finium regundorum*). These actions are defined as of a 'mixed' nature (*actiones mixtae*)[252] in the sense that they combine both real and personal elements.
(d) Personal actions which, by virtue of substantive law rules (e.g., Articles 599 §2, 819, 913, 1126 CC) can be raised against any owner, possessor or detentor of the thing at the time the action is being brought ('*actiones in rem scriptae*').
(e) Actions involving compensation on the ground of expropriation of immovable property.
(f) Actions concerning all kinds of leases or other rights related to the exploitation of immovables (Articles 574, 619, 638, 641 CC). Nevertheless, disputes involving other personal rights on immovable property, such as those deriving from a contract of sale, are not brought in the courts of the situs.

4. The Exclusive Forum Concerning Succession (Article 30 CPC)

128. All actions involving a deceased's estate assets, namely those seeking recognition of a succession right, partition of a deceased's estate among coheirs (*actiones familiae herciscundae*), satisfaction of a heir's claims against possessors of this estate (e.g., *hereditatis petitio*, Articles 1871–1883 CC), satisfaction of claims involving legacies (Articles 1967–2010 CC), or other gifts *mortis causa*

252. The third kind of these mixed actions, known as '*actiones familiae herciscundae*', belongs to the forum involving succession. *See infra*, No. 130.

(Articles 2032–2035 CC), forced heirship (Articles 1825–1838 of the CC), and claims against executors of a will involving the execution of dispositions therein contained (Articles 2017–2031 CC), are exclusively tried by the courts of the deceased's domicile or, when such domicile is absent, his residence at death (Article 30 §1 CPC; *Forum hereditatis*).

In addition, if the action is being brought within two years after the deceased's death, the same courts have an exclusive territorial competence for claims among heirs, eventually arising before the partition of the estate assets has been effected, for debts of the deceased or of the succession against third persons, and for all actions involving real rights on movables, in case they are not covered by the aforementioned list (of Article 30 §1), e.g., revendicatory actions of third persons against heirs claiming ownership on movables included in the deceased's estate (Article 30 §2 CPC). When actions belonging to this second category are being brought after the time limit of two years, they may be adjudicated by the courts of either the general or any eventually existing special jurisdiction since the connecting factors founding the operation of this exclusive forum are deemed to have been already exhausted.

Finally, all succession matters belonging to the scope of voluntary jurisdiction[253] (e.g., the granting of a certificate of inheritance,[254] the appointment of the administrator of a vacant succession,[255] the appointment of a liquidator[256]) are entertained by the 'court of succession'. Under Article 810 CPC, this is the justice of the peace of the district where the deceased was domiciled at the time of death and, in case such domicile is absent, where he was a resident. If the deceased had neither domicile nor residence in Greece, such matters may be brought before the Athens justice of the peace.

These rules are of noteworthy importance with regard to the international jurisdiction of Greek courts, in particular when this involves a succession of Greek nationals dying domiciled outside Greece. In contrast to matters of voluntary jurisdiction, the rules governing territorial competence with regard to disputes emerging from succession do not provide for bases of international jurisdiction of Greek courts when the deceased were not domiciled within Greek territory, even if Greek nationals or their property is located in Greece. A tendency of Greek courts to extend under various formulations[257] their international jurisdiction, also in those cases, has been supported by leading Greek authors.

5. The Exclusive Forum for Related Actions (Article 31 CPC)

129. The exclusive forum involving related actions (*Forum connexitatis*) covers the substantially connected claims, whether main and ancillary or all independent.

253. Articles 811–824 CPC.
254. Articles 819–824 CPC.
255. Article 813 CPC.
256. Article 814 CPC.
257. *Areios Pagos* 400/2009, *Civil Procedure Law Review* 2010, pp. 47 ff., has recently accepted the exclusive jurisdiction of Greek courts for succession disputes related to immovables located in Greece, even if the deceased was not domiciled in Greece.

The notion of related actions primarily refers to cases being contingent upon another to the extent that they may not be logically decided in a contradictory manner. The existence of such a relation between several actions is determined by the court. This exclusive forum relies on avoiding multiplicity of suits and contradictory decisions rather than satisfying any special connecting factors for territorial competence, as the other exclusive jurisdictions. For this reason, it partly also affects determination of the subject matter competence.

Accordingly, all ancillary proceedings, e.g., incidental actions (claims for interest or fruits; actions involving the production of documents),[258] actions against guarantors,[259] interventions[260] and other accessory claims (e.g., impleaders),[261] are exclusively tried by the court which is territorially competent in the principal case (Article 31 §1 CPC). This exclusive territorial competence is not affected by a lack of subject matter competence when ancillary actions, per se, belong to the subject matter competence of an inferior court (Article 31 §2 CPC). Additionally, when several independent claims are regarded as related in the sense already discussed, determination of the exclusively competent court depends on priority. The subsequently raised action belongs to the exclusive competence of the court first seized. This is, however, true only on condition that the subsequently raised action belongs to the subject matter competence of the first court or, at least, an inferior court (Article 31 §3 CPC).

6. The Exclusive Forum for Cross-Actions (Article 34 CPC)

130. A counterclaim may be brought before the court of the main claim on condition that it belongs to the subject matter competence of this court or, at least, an inferior one (Article 34, *Forum reconventionis*). This forum is regarded as exclusive in the sense that, in case the defendant uses his right to bring a counterclaim, rather than raising an independent action, it must be exclusively brought before the court of the main claim.

7. The Exclusive Forum for Litigation Involving Enforcement Proceedings (Article 933 CPC)

131. There is an exclusive forum involving litigation in enforcement proceedings (Article 933). This is discussed in the respective chapter.[262]

258. *See infra*, No. 416.
259. *See infra*, No. 232.
260. *See infra*, Nos 227 ff.
261. *See infra*, Nos 231 ff.
262. *Infra*, No. 490.

III. Prorogation of Territorial Competence

A. General Remarks

132. Unlike subject matter competence, venue can also be based on agreement of the parties (Articles 42–44 CPC), provided that this refers to the territorial competence of the Courts of First Instance. Such agreements may be either explicit or tacit.

Unless strong reasons of public policy demand their application, parties are allowed to derogate from rules establishing both general and special territorial competence. Accordingly, when they involve disputes of a pecuniary nature, all rules of general and special jurisdictions may be modified (Article 42 §1a, CPC). On the contrary, when litigation is related to personal matters (e.g., matrimonial disputes, Article 592, §1 CPC) or disputes concerning relationship between parents and children (Article 592 §2, CPC), prorogation of territorial competence is not allowed. Exclusive forums may be derogated solely by an express agreement (Article 42, §1b, b CPC). Such agreements must be in writing when involving future disputes. In this case, it is additionally required that agreements for prorogation exactly define the legal relationships to which they refer (Article 43 CPC).

Unless a contrary provision has been included in the respective agreements, territorial competence based on prorogation is exclusive, compared to all other jurisdictions, whether concurrent or also exclusive (Article 44 CPC).

133. The prevailing opinion in Greek law regards agreements on prorogation as of a purely procedural nature, even if made before proceedings are commenced.

B. Explicit Agreements

134. An explicit agreement may give competence to a court which otherwise would not have, either before or after lis pendens. It does not need to determine whether the courts have subject matter competence. It is sufficient that it generally confers jurisdiction to the courts of a certain district.

Such agreements quite frequently consist of clauses of various substantive law contracts, most often inserted in a printed form. They are regarded as purely procedural clauses which are being effectuated as soon as contracting parties have become involved in judicial proceedings. When related to an already existing dispute, an explicit agreement conferring territorial competence may also be oral. In such a case, it needs to be proven. This is allowed by using the relevant means of proof CPC, including witnesses, provided that this agreement does not fall within the restrictive limits of testimony.[263]

263. *See infra*, No. 373.

C. Tacit Agreements

135. Failure to object to the territorial competence of a court during the initial phase of litigation, i.e., the initial hearing of the case, precludes the defendant from doing so at a later stage (Article 263a CPC). In such a case, provided that a pecuniary dispute is involved and that a non-exclusive legal jurisdiction is derogated, the defendant is deemed to have tacitly agreed that the initially incompetent court will be accepted as competent (Article 42 §2 CPC).

Nevertheless, a tacit prorogation of territorial competence requires that the involved defendant be present. In case of default, the court must transfer the case to the competent court on its own motion.

§7. Resolution of Jurisdiction Conflicts

I. 'Affirmative' Conflicts

136. As has been already stated,[264] conflicts of jurisdiction between several court categories are brought before the Special Highest Court.

When the same case is pending before both a civil and an administrative court, without any of these courts denying their jurisdiction, this so-called affirmative conflict is settled on the initiative of the parties.[265] At the first phase of this procedure, an application must be brought by the interested party before the court, which, according to the applicant's assertions, lacks jurisdiction, along with the documents indicating that the same case is also pending before a court of another jurisdictional branch.[266] As soon as this application has been brought, both courts are obliged to stay the proceedings.[267]

The next phase of the procedure before the Special Highest Court is initiated, again on the initiative of an involved party, only in case none of the aforementioned courts has stated that it lacks jurisdiction.[268]

II. 'Negative' Conflicts

137. When a 'negative' conflict of jurisdictions emerges, in the sense that the courts of both jurisdictional branches have ruled by successive decisions, which are no longer subject to regular methods of appeal, that they lack jurisdiction on the same case, this is also settled by the Special Highest Court.[269] The procedure is again commenced through an application brought by the interested party directly

264. *See supra*, Nos 73, 95.
265. Article 44 §1f Law 345/1976.
266. Article 44 §2 Law 345/1976.
267. Article 44 § 3c Law 345/1976.
268. Article 45 Law 345/1976.
269. Article 46 Law 345/1976.

before the Highest Court within a time limit of ninety days after the more recent decision denying jurisdiction has been rendered.

III. Effects of the Ruling

138. The decision of the Special Highest Court settles the jurisdictional question only within the limits of the concrete case by reversing the wrongful decision and transferring the case to the court which has been considered enjoying jurisdiction.[270] Unlike other decisions of the Special Highest Court, a ruling settling jurisdiction is binding only against the involved parties.

IV. Relevant Moment for the Existence of Jurisdiction

139. The relevant moment for the existence of jurisdiction is the moment at which the action is deemed to have been commenced (Article 221 §1b CPC). After a case has been brought, the jurisdiction of civil courts may be no more effected, even if modified by statute and the pending case has been transferred to another branch of courts (e.g., from civil to administrative courts).

V. Review of Subject Matter and of Territorial Competence

A. *Relevant Moment for the Existence of Facts Basing Competence*

140. The relevant moment for the existence of facts that form the basis of competence (i.e., domicile, residence, value of the claim, etc.) is the moment at which the action is commenced (Articles 10, 45, 215 §1 CPC). Neither subject matter nor territorial competence may be affected in the event that those facts change (Articles 45, 221 §1b CPC, *perpetuatio fori*).

B. *Lack of Competence*

141. When a court lacks either subject matter or territorial competence, and in the latter case, this cannot be conferred through a tacit prorogation agreement (Article 42), the issue may be raised by both the defendant (Articles 263a, 527 Nr 3) and the court on its own motion. An incompetent court is moreover obliged to determine which court is competent and transfer the case (Article 46a CPC). Thus, unlike the lack of jurisdiction (Article 4 §2 CPC), a lack of competence may not result in the dismissal of a case. A decision ordering transfer does not affect the procedural and substantive consequences already produced at the time the action was brought (Article 46c).

270. Article 47 §4 Law 345/1976.

The court which was determined as the sole competent by the parties, may transfer the case further to another court (or even back to the same court) unless the decision for transfer – which is defined as final and is subject in principle to the normal methods of attack[271] – is no longer appealable. In this case, the determination of subject matter and territorial competence through a decision for transfer is compulsory, regarding both the incompetence of the first and the competence of the second court (Article 46 b). Conversely, a decision on the merits may be attacked for lack of competence unless the court which rendered it is higher than the court which challenged its subject matter competence (Article 47 CPC) and, therefore, is offering increased guarantees. However, it is not correct to assume that superior Courts of First Instance (i.e., three-member district courts) enjoy discretionary powers to adjudicate disputes belonging to the subject matter competence of inferior courts (i.e., of one-member district courts or of justices of the peace).

271. Articles 513 §1a, and 553, §1a, of the CPC. A cassation is admissible only where subject matter (but not territorial) competence is contested (Arts 553 §1a, and 559 No. 5 CPC).

Chapter 2. International Jurisdiction

§1. Rules Applicable in the Absence of a Treaty

I. The Historical Background

A. Nationality as a Main Connecting Factor under the CPC of 1834

142. Under the CPC of 1834 (Articles 27 and 28), international jurisdiction was mainly based on nationality, following the French pattern.[272]

B. Modification of the Critical Factor of Nationality in 1946

143. Articles 27 and 28 CPC of 1834 were repealed in 1946 and simultaneously substituted by Article 126 of the Introductory Law of the CC. Under this regulation, foreign nationals were assimilated as Greeks insofar as the international jurisdiction of Greek courts was dependent on territorial competence.

II. International Jurisdiction According to the Present CPC

A. Territorial Competence as the Main Connecting Factor

144. Article 3 CPC has more emphatically than the previous regulation stressed the total departure from the nationality criterion. According to a unanimous conception in both theory and case law, the sole criterion to be currently applied for the determination of international jurisdiction of Greek courts depends on territorial competence.[273]

In principle, the nationality of the litigants is no longer relevant.[274] Rules establishing general or special jurisdiction are consequently regarded as designed to play an additional role. While allocating disputes to Greek courts only as far as they are territorially competent or to use a classical doctrinal expression, as if the whole world consisted of one state, they are based on considerations tending to the equal distribution of civil disputes on an international scale. Under this aspect, all defendants having a domicile or (in case of a legal entity) a seat[275] in Greece are primarily subject to the jurisdiction of Greek courts, whether Greeks or aliens. When

272. 'Report by D. Evrigenis and K. Kerameus on the Accession of the Hellenic Republic to the Community Convention of Jurisdiction and the Enforcement of Judgements in Civil and Commercial Matters', *Official Journal of the European Communities*, C 298/6, Nos 9–16.
273. *See* A. Anthimos, *Online Defamation, Centre of Interests, and Place of Harmful Event*, http://icl-in-greece.blogspot.com/2016_10_23_archive.html; A. Anthimos, *Defamation Through Wikipedia Postings*, http://icl-in-greece.blogspot.com/2014_09_07_archive.html.
274. *Areios Pagos* 439/1983, *Legal Tribune* 1983, p. 1605, has moreover ruled that the application of the principal of territoriality with respect to Greek nationals does not violate the constitutional guarantee (Art. 20) of free access to the courts of law.
275. Under a predominant conception, relevant is the 'real' seat of legal persons. *See supra*, No. 249.

domicile or seat is lacking, as well as other substitute links and any other special jurisdiction, even Greek nationals cannot be sued before Greek courts unless otherwise provided.

In order to present the current system of international jurisdiction pursuant to the CPC, it is thus sufficient to refer to the rules of territorial competence, which are discussed in the previous chapter.[276] Insofar as the requirements of at least one of those jurisdictional bases are met, be it general or special, concurrent or exclusive, Greek courts are allowed to exercise their adjudicatory powers.

145. Similar to the case of territorial competence, the availability of a litigant for service of process in Greece may not serve as a jurisdictional base in Greek law.

B. Role of Nationality in Exceptional Cases

146. Despite the total disconnection of the international jurisdiction of Greek courts from the litigants' nationality since 1967, this has exceptionally remained relevant with regard to matrimonial disputes and disputes between parents and children (Article 601 CPC): whenever one of the litigants is a Greek national, the international jurisdiction of Greek courts is established,[277] even in the absence of domicile or residence.[278] Where there are no territorially competent courts to entertain such actions, these are allocated to the courts of Athens (Article 601 §3). It is, however, stressed that the rationale of these rules does not consist in introducing an exclusive jurisdiction of Greek courts, i.e., for adjudicating divorces of Greek nationals, but rather in providing an additional jurisdictional base for them. On the contrary, in case an exclusive jurisdiction of a foreign court has been provided for matrimonial disputes by the law of nationality of one or both alien litigants, Greek courts are not vested with jurisdiction (Article 605 §1 CPC), despite the existence of territorial competence,[279] except if a marriage is valid under Greek law, but non-existent or null and void under the spouse's law of nationality.

C. International Jurisdiction Based on Public Policy

147. Greek legal theory accepts international jurisdiction based on public policy, even where territorial competence is lacking. This covers extreme situations where denial of international jurisdiction contradicts the fundamental principles of the national legal order and has been quite often related to provisional remedies.

---

276. *See supra*, Nos 113–137.
277. The same is also true with regard to those who were Greek nationals at the time of the marriage, but who have lost Greek nationality because of it. *See* Art. 601 §1, CPC.
278. Normally, international jurisdiction may be based on the special jurisdiction for matrimonial disputes, aside from the general jurisdiction. *See supra*, Nos 116 ff., 123.
279. The obvious rationale of this stipulation is to avoid the rendering of judgments which will not be recognized.

D. International Jurisdiction with Regard to Matters of Voluntary Jurisdiction

148. The international jurisdiction of Greek courts in matters of voluntary jurisdiction is primarily based on territorial competence (Article 3 CPC). The exact determination of the territorially competent courts is, however, most often governed by the specific rules of the procedure of voluntary jurisdiction. These rules do not follow the same system of establishing jurisdiction as in adversary proceedings.

III. The Impact of Private Agreements on International Jurisdiction

A. Prorogation of the International Jurisdiction of Greek Courts

1. The Permissibility of Private Agreements

149. Since private agreements may serve as a basis for the allocation of territorial competence to a court, it is by analogy accepted that, under a system which connects international jurisdictions to territorial competence (Article 3 CPC), such agreements also result in establishing international jurisdiction. This general rule is moreover deduced from the express provision of Article 4, which, in principle, allows international jurisdiction to be based on a tacit acceptance by the defendant. Accordingly, Articles 42–44 CPC, which govern prorogation of territorial competence, are regarded as offering the relevant rules for the prorogation of international jurisdiction, irrespective of any substantial links of the dispute to the Greek State. Under an express provision (Article 4a CPC), prorogation of international jurisdiction of Greek courts is, however, not permissible where immovables situated outside Greece are involved.

The validity of private agreements affecting the international jurisdiction of Greek courts is governed by the *lex fori*.[280]

2. Explicit Agreements

150. Explicit agreements bestowing international jurisdiction to Greek courts are basically subject to the same requirements as those prorogating territorial competence. They are accepted only if they concern purely pecuniary matters[281] and if they determine which particular Greek court has territorial competence. Such agreements need not be in writing except when they involve future disputes. Unless otherwise deduced from a certain agreement, agreements prorogating the international jurisdiction of Greek courts must be regarded as establishing exclusive jurisdiction.[282]

280. P. Kargados, *Rules Declining to Exercise Jurisdiction in Civil and Commercial Matters in Greece: Forum Non conveniens and Foreign Choice of Jurisdictional Clauses*, *RHDI* 1994, p. 161 f.
281. By analogy of Art. 42, §1 CPC.
282. By analogy of Art. 44 CPC.

3. Tacit Agreements

151. A tacit prorogation agreement is deemed to have been formed through a defendant's tacit acceptance of the international jurisdiction of Greek courts in case territorial competence is lacking. This is effected when a present defendant fails to challenge the international jurisdiction of a Greek court at the hearing of the case. However, tacit acceptance may not be inferred from a defendant's default (Article 4a CPC).

B. Derogation of Greek Adjudicatory Power

152. Despite the lack of explicit regulations, private agreements comprising a derogation of the international jurisdiction of Greek courts are also accepted under the same conditions as those referring to territorial competence, again by analogy, since stipulations regarding prorogation of territorial competence conversely cause the avoidance of the adjudicatory power of another court. These agreements are frequently of practical application, mostly in the form of special clauses, e.g., within employment contracts, contracts for carriage of goods (mainly by sea), or principal/agent agreements.[283] It is, however, required that such avoidance of Greek courts must additionally include the determination of a certain foreign court vested with jurisdiction. A reference to the rules of procedure of a foreign state for this purpose is regarded as sufficient. To avoid an international denial of justice, derogation of the international jurisdiction of Greek courts is usually considered null and void when the foreign courts do not enjoy international jurisdiction under foreign procedural law. This is also true when the decision of a foreign court cannot be recognized in Greece, pursuant to the relevant rules (Articles 323, 905 CPC),[284] or when Greek courts are deemed to have an exclusive international jurisdiction, e.g., in cases of immovables situated in Greece (Article 4 CPC).

In order to protect Greek nationals, Law 1429/1984 (Articles 1, 4 §§1, 2) has moreover stipulated that private agreements concerning contracts for employment in Africa or Asia between Greek nationals and companies, which have their seat or economic interests in Greece, derogating the jurisdiction of Greek courts are null and void. Agreements providing that those disputes belong to foreign courts are deemed to establish only an additional jurisdiction at the side of the jurisdiction of Greek courts. Actions seeking the annulment of an agreement which derogates the international jurisdiction of Greek courts on the ground of a vice of consent may be brought in Greece.

Finally, of major importance are the agreements concluded under the scope of EU Regulations.[285]

283. *See* A. Anthimos, *Greek Supreme Court No. 423/20198*, *International Journal of Procedural Law* (Intersentia 2021), pp. 157–159.

284. *See infra*, Nos 505 ff.

285. *See* A. Anthimos, *International Journal of Procedural Law* (Intersentia 2021), pp. 157–159, *concerning a choice of court clause between a dutch principal and a greek commercial agent.*

IV. Review of International Jurisdiction

153. Lack of international jurisdiction is examined by the court ex officio, but only in case of the defendant's default (Article 4a CPC). When a defendant is present and remains silent in the first hearing of the case, the question cannot be raised by the court; the defendant is then deemed to have accepted the court's international jurisdiction. By way of exception, despite the defendant's appearance, the court must proceed to this examination when immovables situated abroad are involved or when the requirements of a prorogation agreement are lacking.

Whenever a court is not vested with international jurisdiction, the pending action may not be transferred to a foreign court; it is dismissed as inadmissible (Article 4b CPC). A court's decision may be challenged on the grounds of lack of international jurisdiction through an appeal or even through a cassation (Article 559 No. 4 CPC).

§2. International Treaties

I. Multilateral Conventions

A. The Convention on Jurisdiction and the Enforcement of Judgments in Civil and Commercial Matters and Its Successors (EU-Regulations)

154. As a member of the EU since 1981, Greece has adopted the entire *acquis Communautaire* in the field of civil and commercial matters, which includes a large number of EU Regulations, covering – among other issues – the grounds for international jurisdiction. The first step was the ratification of the Community Convention on Jurisdiction and the Enforcement of Judgments in Civil and Commercial Matters of 1968/1978/1982 by Law 1814/1988, which entered into force on 1 April 1989. Greece also ratified the San Sebastian Convention of 1989, the Convention of 1996 (accession of Austria, Sweden and Finland), and the Convention of Lugano of 16 September 1988. Its revised version of 15 October 2007 has entered into force on 1 January 2010.[286]

The application of the Brussels Convention did not cause major difficulties.[287] However, some specific jurisdiction rules of Greek law, such as Articles 24 and 38 CPC, deviated from the Convention's stipulations. Also, a number of special jurisdictional bases established by the Convention were either new to Greek internal law

286. *See Official Journal of the European Union*, No. L 339/1 of 21 Dec. 2007.

287. For a presentation of the differences between the Convention and internal Greek law *see* D. Evrigenis & K. Kerameus, 'Report on the Accession of the Hellenic Republic to the Community Convention on Jurisdiction and the Enforcement of Jurisdiction and the Enforcement of Judgments in Civil and Commercial Matters', Official Journal of the European Communities, No. C298/11–18; K. Kerameus, 'Aktuelle Probleme der internationalen Zuständigkeit im Bereich des Brüsseler Übereinkommens von 1968 und die Deutsch-Griechischen Rechtsbeziehungen', Europa-Institut der Universität des Saarlandes 1987; the same author, 'Das Brüsseler Gerichts-standsübereinkommen und das griechische Recht der internationalen Zuständigkeit', Festschrift für G. Baumgärtel (K. Heymanns, Köln/Berlin/Bonn/München, 1990), pp. 215–227. A more recent survey was prepared by A. Archontaki & P. Simsive, *Chapter 18. Greece*, in Paul Beaumont et al. (eds), *Cross-Border Litigation in Europe* (Hart Publishing 2017) pp. 315–327.

(this refers, e.g., to Article 5 point 2 involving maintenance claims, Article 5 point 6 involving trusts, Articles 7 to 12 involving insurance contracts and Articles 13 to 15 involving consumer contracts), or were provided by the Convention under a variant form (this refers, e.g., to Article 5 points 1, 3, 4, 7, Article 16 points 1, 2, 3 and 5). Finally, the jurisdictional base related to property of the defendant within the Greek territory (Article 40 CPC) could not provide a connecting factor for the establishment of the jurisdiction of Greek courts anymore when the defendant was domiciled in any of the Contracting States (Article 3 of the Convention). On the contrary, this jurisdiction (Article 40 CPC), regarded as exorbitant, could still operate against defendants not domiciled within the EU territory as, according to the Brussels Convention (Article 4), in such cases, national law was applied. Sporadically, the field of application of the Regulation was challenged.[288]

International jurisdiction of Greek courts for civil and commercial matters was subsequently governed by Regulation 44/2001 on Jurisdiction and Recognition and Enforcement of Judgments in Civil and Commercial Matters,[289] and now by Regulation 1215/2012, in force since 10 January 2015.[290] Regulation 1215/2012 applies where the defendant is a domiciliary of the EU, irrespective of his or her nationality (Article 4). Basically, both European pieces of legislation have introduced the same jurisdictional bases as the Brussels Convention.[291] Beyond the Regulations aforementioned, Greece is bound by the following EU Regulations:

(i) Regulation (EC) No. 1346/2000 of 29 May 2000 on insolvency proceedings, which was replaced by Regulation (EU) 2015/848 of the European Parliament and of the Council of 20 May 2015 on insolvency proceedings.
(ii) Council Regulation 1111/2019, on jurisdiction, the recognition and enforcement of decisions in matrimonial matters and the matters of parental responsibility, and on international child abduction (recast), replacing Regulation (EC) No. 2201/2003 of 27 November 2003 concerning jurisdiction and the recognition and enforcement of judgments in matrimonial matters and the matters of parental responsibility, repealing Regulation (EC) No. 1347/2000 ('Brussels IIa'), which replaced Council Regulation 1347/2000 of 29 May 2000 on Jurisdiction and the Recognition and Enforcement of Judgments in

288. A. Anthimos, *Nichtanwendung der EUGVVO 2001 für einen KV-Bescheid in Griechenland* (zu LG Thessaloniki, 19 Dec. 2017 – 19865/2017), *IPRax* 2019, pp. 343–344.
289. *See* A. Anthimos, *Greek Supreme Court on the Interpretation of Art. 23 & 24 Brussels I Regulation*, http://icl-in-greece.blogspot.com/2014_08_03_archive.html; A. Anthimos, *Greece no Forum for Summary Proceedings Against Facebook*, http://icl-in-greece.blogspot.com/2014_02_23_archive.html.
290. With respect to the case law on international jurisdiction according to the Brussels I bis Regulation in Greece, *see* A. Anthimos, *Regulation BIa: A Standard for Free Circulation of Judgments and Mutual Trust in the European Union.* (JUDGTRUST) – National Report Greece (2019), ww.asser.nl/media/795624/greece_report.pdf.
291. In this context, a recent decision of the Supreme Court has ruled that relatives of persons killed in accidents are to be considered immediate victims, *see* A. Anthimos, *The Greek Supreme Court has Decided: Relatives of Persons Killed in Accidents are Immediate Victims.* https://conflictoflaws.net/2023/the-greek-supreme-court-has-decided-relatives-of-persons-killed-in-accidents-are-immediate-victims/.

Matrimonial Matters and in Matters of Joint Parental Responsibility for Children entered into force on 1 March 2001.[292]

(iii) Council Regulation (EC) No. 4/2009 of 18 December 2008 on jurisdiction, applicable law, recognition and enforcement of decisions and cooperation in matters relating to maintenance obligations.[293]

(iv) Council Regulation (EU) 2016/1103 of 24 June 2016 implementing enhanced cooperation in the area of jurisdiction, applicable law and the recognition and enforcement of decisions in matters of matrimonial property regimes.

(v) Council Regulation (EU) 2016/1104 of 24 June 2016 implementing enhanced cooperation in the area of jurisdiction, applicable law and the recognition and enforcement of decisions in matters of the property consequences of registered partnerships.

(vi) Regulation (EU) No. 650/2012 of the European Parliament and of the Council of 4 July 2012 on jurisdiction, applicable law, recognition and enforcement of decisions and acceptance and enforcement of authentic instruments in matters of succession and on the creation of a European Certificate of Succession.

(vii) Regulation (EC) No. 805/2004 of the European Parliament and of the Council of 21 April 2004, creating a European Enforcement Order for uncontested claims.

(viii) Regulation (EC) No. 1896/2006 of the European Parliament and of the Council of 12 December 2006 creating a European order for payment procedure.

(ix) Regulation (EC) No. 861/2007 of the European Parliament and of the Council of 11 July 2007 establishing a European Small Claims Procedure.

(x) Regulation (EU) No. 655/2014 of the European Parliament and of the Council of 15 May 2014 establishing a European Account Preservation Order procedure to facilitate cross-border debt recovery in civil and commercial matters.

B. Hague Conference Conventions

155. Greece has ratified the following conventions of the Hague Conference of Private International Law, which contain rules on international jurisdiction:

(1) Convention of 29 May 1993 on Protection of Children and Co-operation in Respect of Intercountry Adoption (Ratification: Law 3765/2009). The Convention has been in force in Greece since 1 January 2010.

---

292. E. Vasilakakis & V. Kourtis, *The Impact and Application of the Brussels II Bis Regulation in Greece*, in K. Boele-Woelki (ed.), *Brussels II bis: Its Impact and Application in the Member States* (Oxford, Antwerp 2007) pp.133–143; A. Archontaki & P. Simsive, *Chapter 18. Greece*, in Paul Beaumont et al.(eds), *Cross-Border Litigation in Europe.* (Hart Publishing 2017) pp. 322 ff.;A. Anthimos, *Habitual Residence under the Brussels II bis Regulation*, http://icl-in-greece.blogspot.com/2014_10_19_archive.html; A. Anthimos, *On the Application of Art. 9 & 12 Brussels II bis Regulation in Greece*, http://icl-in-greece.blogspot.com/2014_05_11_archive.html.

293. A. Archontaki & P. Simsive, *Chapter 18. Greece*, in Paul Beaumont et al.(eds), *Cross-Border Litigation in Europe.* (Hart Publishing 2017), pp. 324 ff.

(2) Convention of 19 October 1996 on Jurisdiction, Applicable Law, Recognition, Enforcement and Co-operation in Respect of Parental Responsibility and Measures for the Protection of Children (Ratification: Law 4020/2011). The Convention has been in force in Greece since 1 June 2012.
(3) Convention of 13 January 2000 on the International Protection of Adults (Ratification: Law 4898/2022). The Convention has been in force in Greece since 1 November 2022.
(4) Convention of 30 June 2005 on Choice of Court Agreements (Ratification: Greece is bound by the Convention as a result of the approval by the EU); in force since 1 October 2015.
(5) Convention of 23 November 2007 on the International Recovery of Child Support and Other Forms of Family Maintenance (Ratification: Greece is bound by the Convention as a result of the approval by the EU). In force since 1 August 2014.

C. *Other Multilateral Conventions*

156. Greece is a party to the following multilateral Conventions, which include stipulations governing jurisdiction:

(a) Bern Convention of 7 February 1970 on the International Carriage of Goods (CIM), Passengers and Luggage (CIV) by Rail, ratified in Greece by Royal Decree 334/1972. Jurisdiction is dealt with in Article 44. Greece has also ratified (Law 1593/1986, in force since 1 November 1987) the revision of this Convention effectuated on 9 May 1980, by the '*Convention relative aux transport internationaux ferroviaires*' (COTIF). *See also* Pres. Decree 108/1996 for the Bern 1990 Protocol and Law 3646/2008 for the 1999 Protocol.
(b) Warsaw Convention of 12 October 1929 on the Unification of Certain Rules Relating to International Carriage by Air, ratified in Greece by Necessity Law 596/1937. *See also* Leg. Decrees 4395/1964 and 766/1971, as also Law 1778/1988. Jurisdiction is regulated by Articles 28 and 32. Greece has also ratified (Law 3006/2002) the Montreal Convention of 28 May 1999, which has supplemented the Warsaw Convention. Jurisdiction is treated in Article 33 of the Montreal Convention (*see also* Article 49).
(c) Brussels Convention of 10 May 1952 on the Unification of Certain Rules Concerning Civil Jurisdiction in Matters of Collision of Ships, ratified in Greece by Law 4407/1964.
(d) Brussels Convention of 10 May 1952 on the Unification of Certain Rules Relating to the Arrest of Sea-going Ships, ratified in Greece by Legislative Decree 4570/1966. Particular rules of jurisdiction are included in Articles 4, 5, 7.
(e) Geneva Convention of 19 May 1956 on the contract for the International Carriage of Goods by Road (CMR), ratified in Greece by Law 559/1977. Jurisdiction is governed by Articles 31–33.

(f) Hague Convention of 2 October 1973, in force since 1 August 1976, on the Recognition and Enforcement of judgments related to maintenance Obligations, ratified in Greece by Law 3171/2003. Rules on jurisdiction are included in Articles 7–9.

D. *Conventions Related to Extraterritoriality*

157. Greece is a party to the following multilateral Conventions governing foreign sovereign and diplomatic immunity:

(a) Vienna Convention on Diplomatic Relations of 18 April 1961, ratified in Greece by Legislative Decree 503/1970.
(b) Vienna Convention on Consular Relations of 24 April 1963, ratified in Greece by law 90/1975.

II. Bilateral Conventions

A. *The Irrelevancy of Assimilation Clauses in Bilateral Conventions*

158. A complex of numerous bilateral conventions, comprising clauses assimilating aliens to Greek nationals or providing for free access of aliens in Greek courts, which were of particular significance before 1946, hereinafter cannot have any impact on the determination of jurisdiction of Greek courts, since internal Greek law does not provide for distinctions based on nationality any longer.

B. *Specific Rules in Bilateral Conventions for Jurisdiction in Succession Matters*

159. There are certain particular bilateral conventions which provide rules for the jurisdiction of the courts of the contracting parties with regard to succession:

(a) Convention between Greece and Austria of 1856,[294] ratified in Greece by Law TNΔ'/1856. This convention mostly concerns matters of voluntary jurisdiction when movables are involved.
(b) Convention between Greece and Spain of 21 February/6 March 1919, ratified in Greece by Law 2423/1920.
(c) Convention between Greece and Russia of 17/30 August 1913, ratified in Greece by Law 289/1914.
(d) Convention on Consular Relations, etc., between Greece and Lebanon, ratified in Greece by Legislative Decree 1273/1949.

294. There is an express declaration concerning its application in Austria from 9 Mar. 1951. *See* V. Hoyer-R, Loewe, *Staatsverträge über Rechtshilfe und Vollstreckung* (Wien, Manzsche 1964), p. 135 n. 1. For Austrian bibliography on this convention *see* V. Hoyer-R, Loewe, *Staatsverträge über Rechtshilfe und Vollstreckung* (Wien, Manzsche 1964), p. 135 n. 1.

(e) Convention between Greece and Switzerland of 1 December 1927, ratified in Greece by Law 3610/1926 (Article 10).

C. *Specific Rules for Maintenance Claims and Matters Involving Personal Status*

160. The bilateral Convention between Greece and Cyprus of 5 March 1984, ratified in Greece by Law 1548/1985, provides (Article 27) for an additional special jurisdictional base related to the domicile or residence of the plaintiff when maintenance claims are involved.

The bilateral convention between Greece and (former) Yugoslavia of 18 June 1959, ratified in Greece by Law 4009/1959, includes some particular regulations involving jurisdiction on guardianship (Articles 19, 20), paternity (Article 23), adoption (Article 24, §2) and absentia (Article 25).

Part III. Actions and Claims

Chapter 1. Actions

§1. Definition – Types of Actions – Joinder

I. Definition

A. The Action as a Procedural Act

161. In Greek law, an action is defined as a procedural act entailing a request for judicial protection of a disputed subjective right. An action is thus based on a concrete private right and seeks to restrain interference. The procedural notion of action is, however, distinguished from the substantive claim, which the holder of a subjective right exercises against the obligee.[295] Despite its foundation on a substantive right, an action is addressed against the State rather than the person against whom the private right is exercised. Accordingly, at the side of the private law relationship between the parties, which is based on the subjective right involved, commencement of an action institutes an additional legal relationship between the plaintiff and the State. This relationship is of a public law nature and currently has a constitutional underpinning (Article 20). It marks the right of the plaintiff against the State to obtain a judicial decision on the merits provided that no procedural impediments exist.

B. The Action as a Procedural Document

1. Contents of the Complaint

162. The term action is also used to define the specific complaint which contains the request for judicial protection with regard to civil rights. Thus, the various provisions of the CPC alternately speak of an action, either in the sense of a procedural act or document.

295. On some occasions (*see*, e.g., Arts 946, 1035, 1047, 1346, etc.), in reminiscence of the respective Roman legal concept, the Greek CC still uses the term action in order to refer to the exercise of a substantive claim. A distinction between the substantive and the procedural meaning of the term action is, therefore, drawn.

163. The contents of an action are minutely provided for in Article 216. The typical requirements include name of the court, where the action is raised, designation of the type of the complaint, names and domicile of the parties or their representatives, date and signature, as a rule, by the party's attorney (Articles 117, 118 and 119). The essential elements of the complaint are: (a) specification of the cause of the action by complete reference of the relevant facts supportive to the relief claimed, including determination of the substantive links between the action and the given parties, known as the 'factual basis' of an action (Article 216 §1a); (b) exact description of the object in litigation, when material, e.g., of the disputed movable or immovable (Article 216 §1b); (c) specification of the requested relief (Article 216 §1c), i.e., of its object, amount and type, which basically cannot be subsequently modified (Article 223α). In disputes involving property, the value of the object in litigation should be specified (Article 216 §2a), as well as other elements which can institute the subject matter or the territorial competence of the court (Article 216 §2b). Theoretically, an action need not include statements on applicable rules of law, known as its 'legal basis', since determination of legal issues belongs to the court. However, lawyers most often attempt an extended legal analysis. An action need not specify the means of evidence to be produced.

2. Sanctions

164. An action must necessarily contain factual assertions covering the entire complex of facts which constitute the legal conditions to the relief claimed.[296] Otherwise, it is dismissed as legally unfounded upon the court's own motion at any stage of a proceeding. Moreover, after an action has been brought, amendments regarding its factual basis entailing a change of the cause of the claim are absolutely forbidden (Article 224a CPC).[297] An action which does not include sufficient concretization of the facts referred to is characterized as 'vague' and is dismissed as inadmissible again on the motion of the court.

II. Types of Actions

A. *Criteria of Classification*

165. There are two kinds of criteria to classify the various types of actions: substantive and procedural.

296. G. Mitsopoulos, 'Gedanken zu einigen wichtigen Probleme der Zivilprozessrechtslehre', *ZZP* 1978, pp. 113–127 (121 and n. 21).

297. Only supplements, clarifications and corrections are allowed, to the extent they do not diversify the factual basis of an action (Art. 224 b CPC). Accordingly, this right of the plaintiff mainly concerns the so-called vague actions, but not those considered legally unfounded. In detail, *see* A. Anthimos, *Mutatio & Ementatio Libelli*, in P. Arvanitakis (ed.), *Prozeßrechtsvergleichung und prozessuale Vereinheitlichung, Studia in Memoriam Peter Gilles* (Athens-Thessaloniki, Sakkoulas Publications 2021), pp. 15–42.

According to the traditional criterion originating from Roman law, actions are categorized as being, e.g., personal, hereditary, mixed or as of property or of family law, etc. Such distinctions are currently of limited procedural significance. They are sometimes used by the CPC to determine the scope of certain jurisdictions.

166. The procedural criterion for classifying actions lies with the kind of relief sought. Actions are thus distinguished into three separate types: (a) actions for specific performance, (b) declaratory actions, and (c) constitutive actions, i.e., an action to change a legal relationship.

B. Actions for Specific Performance

167. Actions for specific performance seek the granting of coercive relief. They constitute the most frequently utilized type of action. Coercive relief includes the performance, omission or indulgence of a specified act or the payment of a certain sum of money as determined by substantive rules.

Actions for specific performance must be normally based on a substantive claim which has matured when proceedings are commencing, i.e., on an already instituted substantive right which is no longer subject to a condition or term. However, since 1967, Greek law has introduced a type of legal protection called 'preventive'. Provided that the overall legal relationship already exists and that certain conditions are fulfilled, an action for specific performance can be brought even before a claim has matured (Article 69).

C. Declaratory Actions (Article 70 CPC)

168. A declaratory action aims at the judicial declaration of the existence or non-existence of a legal relationship.[298] Declaratory actions are distinguished into 'positive' and 'negative', depending on whether the plaintiff seeks a judicial affirmation of the existence of the right claimed or the non-existence of the right asserted against him by the defendant. Actions aiming at the judicial determination of facts rather than substantive rights or the meaning of rules of law are, on the contrary, inadmissible.[299]

Pursuant to Article 70, the plaintiff in a declaratory action must manifest a justifiable specific legal interest. This consists of the uncertainty concerning the existence of a right, which results in the plaintiff's need for judicial protection. The

298. K. Beys, 'Das Unterscheidungsmerkmal von Feststellungs-Leistungs- und Gestaltungsklagen und Urteilen', in the *Volume in Honour of G. Mitsopoulos*, I (Athens/Komotini, Sakkoulas 1993), pp. 47–62; S. Delikostopoulos, *Die Klage auf Feststellung vergangener und zukünftiger Rechtsverhältnisse* (München, 1969).

299. There is an exception involving the falsity of documents which can constitute the object of a declaratory action.

prevailing view of Greek case law and doctrine regards declaratory action as a self-standing legal remedy of equal value compared to an action for specific performance. The latter can be granted even if the former is plainly available.[300] Equality between these two types of actions has been mainly based on the similar binding effects in terms of res judicata produced by both types of decisions.

D. Constitutive Actions (Article 71 CPC)

169. A constitutive action aims at the creation, transformation or rescission of a legal relationship. While declaratory actions seek the mere judicial affirmation of the parties' rights in a legally binding manner, constitutive actions create or modify their legal relationships. According to Article 71 CPC, constitutive actions are therefore available only in cases expressly provided for by law. Usual examples of constitutive actions include actions for divorce or for rescission of a juridical act on the ground of a vice of consent.

III. Joinder

A. Joinder of Parties

1. Permissive Joinder

170. An action may join two or more persons as plaintiffs (active joinder) or defendants (passive joinder). Joinder of parties can be either permissive or compulsory (or necessary).[301]

Permissive joinder relies on the volition of the plaintiff, who is allowed to avoid the filing of multiple suits and the rendition of inconsistent decisions with regard to related actions. Pursuant to Article 74 CPC, parties may be joined when the claims by or against them (a) involve a common right or a common obligation[302] or (b) arise out of identical[303] or essentially similar[304] causes of action. By way of exception, when causes of action are only similar rather than identical, the court must enjoy competence for all co-defendants.

---

300. *See* in particular K. Kerameus, 'Das Verhältnis von Feststellungs- und Leistungsklage nach griechischem Zivilprozessrecht', *Festschrift für W. Kralik* (1986), pp. 245–256.
301. G. Mitsopoulos, 'Die notwendige Streitgenossenschaft nach dem Griechischen Zivilprozessrecht', *Festschrift für Fr. Baur* (Tübingen, Mohr 1981), pp. 503–515.
302. Article 74 No. 1 first case. For example: Suits by or against several co-owners (Art. 1113 CC) or coheirs (Art. 1884 CC).
303. Article 74 No. 1 second case. For example, Suit of two passengers in a car, injured in the same road accident, against the driver.
304. Article 74 No. 2. For example: Suit based on several similar contracts by or against several parties.

The plural parties conduct their cases independently. The claims joined remain distinct and can be decided differently (Article 75). When a joinder is not appropriate, the court orders that the claims joined are severed (Article 78 CPC). Permissive joinder in Greece retains an increasing role for reasons of practical convenience.

2. Necessary Joinder

171. Joinder of parties becomes necessary when specific reasons emerging from substantive or even procedural law[305] do not allow the rendering of inconsistent decisions on the merits. All four analytical conditions of necessary joinder provided for by the CPC (in Article 76 §1) are based on the same underlying idea that a joinder should be necessary where a uniform decision on the merits is indispensable to avoid legal or even logical[306] inconsistencies.

Necessary joinder in Greek law has been provided for in two types of cases.[307] First, there are cases where the compulsory plurality of the parties is required by express provisions, e.g., CC[308] or CPC,[309] and where a failure of those parties to comply causes the inadmissibility of the action.[310] Second, there are cases where, despite the absence of any such sanction, necessary joinder may be achieved through impleader on the initiative of one of the interested parties, called impleader of necessary parties (Article 86 CPC), or upon the courts' order (Article 90 CPC). Necessary parties are then deemed to have originally joined the action.

When joinder is necessary, procedural acts by some affect all joined parties, whereas defaulting parties are represented by those who duly participate (Article 76 §1 CPC). Methods of appeal by some affect all necessary parties (Article 76 §4).

B. Joinder of Claims

1. General Features

172. The plaintiff can consolidate in one action any number of claims against the same defendant, whether interrelated or not (Article 218 CPC). Joinder of claims

305. This in particular refers to necessary joinder which is caused by the widened subjective limits of res judicata, i.e., by the fact that the judgment handed down to the relationship of one party to his opponent may have the effect of res judicata with respect to another party. *See* Art. 76, §1, second case.
306. For a dissenting view as to whether the risk of mere logical inconsistencies can base a necessary joinder *see*, however, the majority opinion of *Areios Pagos* 902/1982, in plenary session, *Legal Tribune* 1983, p. 209; *see also Areios Pagos* 710/1978, *Legal Tribune* 1979, p. 535; 797/1980, *Dike* 1981, p. 88.
307. *Areios Pagos* 575/1986, *Legal Tribune* 1987, p. 363; 686/1986, *Legal Tribune* 1987, p. 725; 897/1986, *Legal Tribune* 1987, p. 1213.
308. *See*, e.g., Arts 553, 771, 788, 789, 1116, 1132, 1180a, 1253a.
309. *See*, e.g., Arts 478, 608, 619, 936, §2.
310. The classic example is the action for partition which must be addressed against all other co-owners of the thing in common, under the penalty of inadmissibility (Art. 478 CPC).

can appear in several forms (i.e., joinder of several self-standing claims, joinder of main and accessory claims, joinder of claims in the alternative, subsidiary joinder). This concept in Greek law generally defines the consolidation of either more than one separate object in litigation or of more causes of action. Since the joinder of claims is also designed to avoid the filing of multiple suits, it lies at the plaintiff's discretion. A necessary joinder of claims does not exist in Greek law, with the exception of small claims (Article 467) and the related actions in the sense of Article 31.[311] The court can, however, even on its own motion, order the joinder of more pending claims (Article 246 CPC).

Joinder of claims is allowed if some explicitly provided conditions (Article 218 §1 CPC) are satisfied, namely when the joined claims: (a) are not incompatible (except when one is proposed as a subsidiary claim); (b) all belong to the subject matter or the territorial competence of the seized court; the latter, nevertheless, being in certain cases covered by the special jurisdiction for related actions (Article 31 CPC);[312] (c) all can be adjudicated through the same type of proceedings, ordinary or particular; (d) do not unduly cause a confusion of the proceedings. If the above pre-requisites are not met, severance may be ordered even on the courts' own motion (Article 218 §2 CPC).

2. Subsidiary Joinder

173. Actions which depend on a condition are explicitly prohibited (Article 219 §1 CPC). It is generally accepted that parties must remain unchanged; no subsidiarity as to the person of the defendant can be allowed. However, a joinder of subsidiary claims, claims which are to be examined and decided by the court in case the main claim is rejected, is expressly permitted in Article 219, be it a separate object or a new cause of action, or incompatible to the main claim. The plaintiff may also join a subsidiary claim through an additional complaint (Article 219 §2).

§2. Admissibility

I. The Function of Procedural Prerequisites

174. Courts are allowed to enter into the merits of a case only insofar as a number of procedural conditions are satisfied, which are termed 'procedural prerequisites' and are designed as the necessary requirements for the admissibility of an action. They concern: (a) the seized court (i.e., jurisdiction, international jurisdiction, subject matter and territorial competence); (b) the parties to the action; (c) the object of litigation (i.e., the absence of a lis pendens and a res judicata). Procedural prerequisites must be examined upon the court's own motion at any stage of a proceeding (*cf.* Article 73 CPC). As a rule, the absence of any one of those

311. *See supra*, No. 131.
312. *Supra*, No. 131.

preconditions results in the action's dismissal.[313] Failure of the court to observe a procedural prerequisite may be challenged even by a cassation (*see* Article 559 Nos 4, 5, 14). A decision dismissing an action for lack of a procedural prerequisite produces a res judicata effect only with regard to the procedural issue decided (Article 322 §1b, CPC). This allows the plaintiff to successfully re-raise the same action in case the lacking prerequisite has been satisfied.

175. Procedural prerequisites are distinguished from procedural impediments. In contrast to the former, the latter, while also preventing the court from the examination on the merits, may be taken into account only upon an exception (defence) raised by the interested party. A typical example of a procedural impediment is the submission of a dispute to arbitration (Article 263b CPC).

176. The procedural prerequisites which involve the court have already been discussed. This paragraph will deal with the procedural prerequisites which concern the parties, as extensively provided for by the CPC (Articles 62–68). Those referring to the object of litigation will be treated in the following part.

II. Capacity to Be a Party (Article 62 CPC)

177. In principle, the capacity to be a party is directly dependent on personality, i.e., the capacity to hold rights and be subject to duties according to substantive rules (Articles 34–36, 61–62 CC). All persons, regardless of age (Article 34 CC) and all types of legal entities introduced by substantive law, enjoy the capacity to be a party.[314] The capacity of foreign persons is governed by the law of their nationality or seat (Articles 5, 10 CC).

However, the CPC of 1967, basically following the German prototype, has extended the above capacity to associations of persons devoted to a specific purpose and to civil partnerships, in both cases even e without having been accorded legal personality (Article 62b). According to court rulings, the capacity to be a party has been recognized to the group of the co-owners of a building,[315] to the 'co-ownership' of a ship,[316] to a political party,[317] and to a consortium of business associations.[318]

313. By way of exception lack of competence results in the transfer of a case to the competent court (*see supra*, No. 143). The second court is required to stay the proceedings also in case of pendency of the same dispute before another court. *See infra*, No. 215.

314. K. Beys, *Neue Wege zur Bestimmung der Rechts- bzw.* Parteifähigkeit, *Die hellenische Erfahrung*, in Reinhold Geimer (ed.), Wege zur Globalisierung des Rechts, *Festschrift für Rolf A. Schütze zum 65. Geburtstag*, (Munich, C. H. Beck, 1999), pp. 117–127.

315. *See*, e.g., One-member district court of Thessaloniki 964/1973, *Archives of Judicial Decisions* 1973, p. 655.

316. *See*, e.g., *Areios Pagos* 153/1980, *Journal of Greek Jurists* 1980, p. 462.

317. One-member district court of Athens 12625/1982, *Archives of Judicial Decisions* 1982, p. 591.

318. *See*, e.g., Court of Appeal of Athens 91/1979, *Legal Tribune* 1979, p. 1126; Court of Appeal of Corfu 25/1983, *Hellenic Justice* 1983, p. 694.

III. Capacity to Conduct Proceedings in One's Own Name (Articles 63–67 CPC)

178. Capacity to conduct proceedings, i.e., to perform various procedural acts in one's own name, is again defined by a reference to civil law (Article 63 §1 CPC). This is to be distinguished from the capacity to become a party since it does not correspond to personality any more but rather to the capacity of performing juridical acts (Articles 127–137 CC). Thus, all persons above the age of 18 (Article 127 CC) are basically granted full capacity to perform procedural acts in their own name (Article 63 §1a, CPC) unless they fall into the class of persons with limited (i.e., persons under judicial guardianship), or no capacity (i.e., interdicted because of a permanent mental or physical infirmity, incarcerated for a felony during incarceration). Persons with limited capacity retain the right to perform procedural acts in their own name insofar as they are capable of entering into juridical acts (Article 63 § 1b CPC; e.g., a minor above the age of 15 for actions against his employer for delayed wages). Persons absolutely incapable in the field of civil law can conduct proceedings only through persons indicated by specific substantive provisions (Article 64 §1 CPC).[319] A usual example would include minors who are normally represented by both parents (Article 1510 CC). Accordingly, when becoming parties, legal entities may perform procedural acts through their representatives (Article 63 §2) and parties without legal personality through the persons managing their affairs (Article 63 §3). Foreign persons who lack the capacity to conduct litigation in their own name pursuant to the law of their nationality are deemed capable of doing so before Greek courts when granted such capacity by Greek law (Article 66 CPC).[320]

IV. Representation by Attorney

179. Parties to a civil action who are vested with the capacity to conduct proceedings in their own name or through their legal representative must normally be represented in court by a lawyer, except: (a) in litigation concerning a small claim before the justice of the peace; (b) where there is a need to avoid an imminent danger (Article 94, § 2a CPC; *cf.* Article 36 §1d, Lawyers' Code).[321] To be precise, representation by attorney does not constitute a procedural prerequisite in the sense already discussed but rather a particular condition to the validity of a given procedural act. Since the provided sanction is the rendition of a default decision, the absence of this condition neither prevents the court from examining the merits of the case nor results in the inadmissibility of an action.

---

319. An exception is provided with regard to provisional remedies (Art. 64, §2); *see infra*, No. 252.
320. *See*, i.e., Court of Appeal of Larisa 126/1975, *Dike* 1976, p. 205. An additional exception includes labour disputes (Art. 665 §1 CPC), small claims (Art. 472, §1) and provisional remedies. *See also infra*, Nos 252 and 428.
321. *See also supra*, No. 85.

180. The power of an attorney to represent a litigant is normally conferred through either a notarial act, a duly certified private document, or a personal oral declaration by the given litigant in court (Article 96 §1 CPC).[322] An attorney can perform for his client all procedural acts (Article 97 CPC), except those expressly imposed on the party (e.g., party oath, party examination) or those entailing a disposition of the client's substantive rights or the attack of a document for forgery (Article 98 CPC). An attorney may be granted the express authority to also perform such acts. The power of an attorney may be revoked by the client at any time or renounced (*see* the detailed stipulations of Articles 100–103 CPC).

V. Standing to Sue

181. Standing to sue, i.e., the ability of a person to become a proper party with regard to a given proceeding, an ability which in Greek law is termed 'legitimation', is also regarded as a procedural prerequisite. This is primarily granted to the bearers of the legal relationship in accordance with substantive rules. Although it has been repeatedly stressed that standing to sue must be distinguished from the concept of the legal interest of the parties, it is now generally accepted that the regulation involving legal interest also entails the main guideline of the Code concerning legitimation.[323] Accordingly, the ability to become a plaintiff in a given action accrues to the person claiming to be the holder of the subjective right whose relief is sought by this action (active legitimation). Inversely, the ability of a person to be the defendant again depends on whether this person is claimed to be the bearer of the respective obligation under substantive law (passive legitimation).

182. By way of exception, it is in several instances possible for a person other than the owner of a claim to raise an action in his own name (*Prozessstandschaft*), called 'a non-proper party'. Such actions are admissible only when expressly permitted by law. The most typical example is the 'oblique' (derivative) action by which, under certain conditions, a creditor can enforce the rights of his debtor against third parties in case this latter fails to do so (Article 72 CPC). The original parties can continue the proceeding in case the claim has been assigned during the pendency of an action (Article 225 CPC). However, the power to raise an action in one's own name for the purpose of asserting a right vested in another person cannot be granted by a private agreement.[324]

183. In view of Article 68 CPC, which requires a direct legal interest of the persons involved, individuals cannot sue on behalf of a class. Thus, neither class-actions have been allowed, nor associations aimed at the protection of collective

322. N. Klamaris, Die Prozessvollmacht nach dem griechischen Zivilprozessrecht, in Aderhold et al., *Festschrift für Harm Peter Westermann zum 70. Geburtstag* (Köln, Verlag Dr Otto Schmidt 2008), pp. 389–397.
323. The CPC of 1967 had expressly provided (in its Art. 69) that 'judicial protection can be requested only by persons related to the object of litigation'. This stipulation was removed in 1971.
324. 'Gewillkürte Prozessstandschaft' according to the German term.

social interests have been granted standing to sue.[325] However, Article 10 Law 2251/1994 (Consumer Protection Act) has granted standing to sue consumer associations for the protection of collective rights.[326]

VI. Legal Interest

184. According to Article 68 CPC, judicial protection can be granted only to persons claiming to have a direct legal interest. Although the CPC has not defined the notion of legal interest, this is understood as an additional procedural prerequisite and is generally related to the need for legal protection. Such need must concern already instituted rather than future legal relationships.

§3. Vexatious Litigation

185. The CPC of 1967 has, for the first time, explicitly introduced in Greek civil proceedings a fundamental principle which prohibits abuse of procedural rights.[327] This requires that parties, their legal representatives and their attorneys conduct the proceedings in accordance with the rules of good morals and faith and establishes a general duty of those persons to tell the truth. Article 116 institutes a concrete prohibition for utilizing the rights granted for purposes other than those designed for. The prohibition of the abuse of procedural rights has revealed a higher importance in enforcement proceedings.

Article 116 does not explicitly declare the inadmissibility of the procedural act causing an abuse of rights; this is sanctioned only by pecuniary penalties (Articles 205 No. 2 and 185 No. 1), infrequently ordered by Greek courts. Its practical impact has been therefore quite limited. Thus, the doctrinal discussion which had developed under the old Code of 1835 on whether the prohibition of the abuse of civil rights pursuant to Article 281 CC also extends to the field of civil proceedings and whether this can result in the inadmissibility of the respective acts has retained its practical significance. While a part of the Greek doctrine regards Article 281 CC as of a general scope, courts have denied applying it with regard to procedural rights,

325. For some very specific exceptions to the rule, basically involving unfair competition (Art. 10 Law 146/1914) and collective labour law (Art. 622 CPC) *see* the report of P. Kargados, 'Der gerichtliche Schutz von Gruppeninteressen in Griechenland', *Volume in Honour of N. Vervesos* (Athens/Komotini, Sakkoulas 1991), pp. 201–223; D. Tsikrikas, 'Les actions collectives en droit grec' in *Studia in Honorem Pelayia Yessiou-Faltsi* (Sakkoulas Publications 2007), pp. 733 ff.

326. *See* P. Lakkis, *Der kollektive Rechtsschutz der Verbraucher in der Europäischen Union – dargestellt an der Verbandsklage der Verbraucherverbände nach dem AGBG, dem UWG and dem griechischen Verbraucherschutzgesetz*, Bielefeld 1997; C. Polyzogopoulos, 'The collective Action in Greek Law for the Protection of Consumers', in *Studia in Honorem Pelayia Yessiou-Faltsi* (Sakkoulas Publications, 2007), pp. 438 ff.; P. Arvanitakis, *Der prozessuale Verbraucherschutz im griechischen autonomen und internationalen Recht*, ZZPInt 10 (2005), pp. 111–122; N. Klamaris, 'Der Rechtsmissbrauch im griechischen Zivilprozessrecht', *Festschrift für Fritz Baur* (Tübingen, Mohr 1981), pp. 483–503 (488 ff.).

327. N. Klamaris, 'Der Rechtsmissbrauch im griechischen Zivilprozessrecht', *ibid.*

except in enforcement proceedings, where it is called to application under the formulation that these entail the exercise of a substantive right. According to a wider view, a general prohibition of the abuse of rights in all legal fields, hence, also procedural rights, must be now accepted on the basis of Article 25 §3 of the – Const. of 1975, according to which 'abusive exercise of rights is not permitted'.

186. Legal scholarship almost unanimously accepts that under Article 116 CPC, vexatious litigation is sanctioned also through liability founded on the general tort provisions (Article 914 CC). In the field of enforcement proceedings, such liability is governed by particular stipulations introducing specific conditions regarding culpability (Article 940 CPC). In recent case law, however, there have not been significant illustrations applying this liability, except in some cases of unjustified enforcement proceedings. Besides, *Areios Pagos* had formerly refused to accept reparation of damages provoked by vexatious litigation in favour of a defeated party, as inconsistent with the res judicata effect produced by the decision.

Chapter 2. Claims and Defences

§1. Definition

187. The first appearance of a defendant in civil proceedings is effectuated by his pleadings submitted to the first hearing of the case. These are expected to include the answer to the action (Article 261 CPC). Second, they can furthermore contain various types of exceptions (Articles 262–267) or a cross-action (Article 268).

§2. Defendant's Answer to the Action

188. A defendant's answer on an action consists of his position, affirmative or negative, regarding the truth of the facts which constitute this action's factual basis. Whereas an affirmative reply as to certain factual allegations of the plaintiff is regarded as a judicial confession, a contradiction of the facts alleged in the complaint, called denial of the basis of the action, results in the burden of the plaintiff to prove them. To avoid the risk that an ambiguous answer will be deemed by the court as entailing a tacit confession (Article 261 CPC), a defendant must clearly deny the cause of the action. A denial of the action can be simple or 'justified'. In the latter case, denial is accompanied by assertions referring to specific reasons, which thus broaden the scope of counter-evidence by the defendant.

§3. Exceptions

I. Definition

189. Exceptions are clearly distinguished from an answer on an action. In procedural terms, exceptions involve allegations of new facts, compared to those instituting the cause of the action, which are destined to bring about either the dismissal of the action, entirely or partly, or the suspension of the proceedings. The same term is also used in the area of civil law[328] to define the 'counter-right' of a person exercised against the right of the opponent for the purpose of defence (*exceptio juris*). The procedural meaning of an exception does not necessarily refer to the exercise of a right but rather to the performance of a procedural act.

II. Distinctions

190. There are several criteria to distinguish exceptions. The most important distinctions are in: (a) 'Genuine' exceptions and 'exceptions in improper sense'.[329]

328. Greek law has not developed different legal terminology, e.g., German law (*Einrede*, *Einwendungen*) for those two concepts.

329. This corresponds to the Italian distinction of '*eccezioni in senso proprio*' and of '*eccezioni in senso improprio*' and basically to the German terms '*Einreden*' and '*Einwendungen*'.

Whereas the former constitutes a right and is, hence, raised only by a party who is entitled to rely on this defence pursuant to substantive law (*exceptio juris*), the latter is, as a rule, based on facts and may be taken into account also by the court on its own motion, even in the absence of an allegation by a party (*exceptio facti*). Accordingly, as a rule, 'genuine' exceptions can be raised only by the holder of the respective subjective right (Article 262 §2 CPC); (b) Procedural and substantive exceptions. The former involves the unfolding of the procedure, whereas the latter affects the subjective rights exercised through the action and are based on substantive law. (c) Subversive and dilatory exceptions. Subversive exceptions not only tend to the dismissal of an action but also to the extinction of the substantive claim. Dilatory exceptions are merely aiming at the suspension of proceedings.

III. Rules Governing Exceptions

191. Following the traditional rule that by raising an exception, the defendant becomes the plaintiff (*reus in excipiendo fit actor*), Article 262 §1 CPC requires that an exception consists of similar component parts to those of an action, i.e., of a concrete 'factual basis' and a specific request, being otherwise subject to similar sanctions. This rule, however, applies only with regard to 'genuine' exceptions; no specific request is necessary in other instances. On the basis of substantive rules, an exception can be further challenged through a counter-exception bearing an equivalent structure.

Exceptions of the same defendant may not contradict each other unless pleaded as subsidiary defences, nor can they be inconsistent with the defendant's answer. There is finally a list of exceptions (Article 263: e.g., lack of territorial competence. submission of the dispute to arbitration, impleader), which, under the penalty of inadmissibility, must be raised in the first hearing of the case in all instances.

§4. Cross-Actions

192. A defendant is entitled to advance a cross-action against the plaintiff (Article 268 CPC) as soon as the pendency of the action has been established, provided that (a) the same type of proceedings can be used for both the claim and the counterclaim (Article 268 §3), and (b) this belongs to the subject matter competence of the same or of an inferior court (Article 34 CPC). On the contrary, territorial competence is entirely covered by the special forum for cross-actions.[330] To avoid the filing of multiple suits, in contrast to several European legal systems, the CPC does not require connexity, i.e., that a counterclaim is related to the main claim. Until 2015, a cross-action could be either included in the answer of the defendant, which ought to be filed at least thirty days before the hearing of the case, or raised through a separate document, which ought to be served upon the plaintiff again at least thirty days before the hearing of the case (former Article 268 §4 CPC).

330. *See supra*, No. 132.

Law 4335/2015 has introduced a new distinction between ordinary and particular proceedings. In the context of the former and before all kinds of courts (three-member district courts, one-member district courts and justices of the peace), a cross-action must be raised through a separate document (Article 268 § 4a), which must be filed and served upon the plaintiff or any other party within sixty days after the action has been filed (Article 238 §1a) on penalty of being deemed as non-existent. A separate document is also needed when a cross-action is advanced in the context of particular proceedings. But this must be filed and served on the adversary party at least eight days before the hearing of the case, on penalty of inadmissibility (Article 591 §1g).

In terms of their procedural treatment, cross-actions remain distinct and do not depend on the action.

Chapter 3. Sanctions on Procedural Irregularities

§1. Formal Requirements

I. Definitions

193. A procedural act is deemed as non-existent in the absence of one of its component elements. Typical examples of such acts are, e.g., a service of a procedural document by a private individual, a decision rendered by persons other than those entitled to exercise the judicial function (Article 313 §1a CPC) or which does not satisfy the requirement of publication (Article 313 § 1c). Non-existent procedural acts do not need to be judicially declared as such. However, the non-existence of a judicial decision can be confirmed by a declaratory judgment.[331]

A procedural act is null and void when one or more of the legally provided procedural requirements are lacking. When due to a specific procedural defect it cannot be examined whether a procedural act is legally founded or not, it is called inadmissible. The notion of inadmissibility is most often related to the function of the procedural prerequisites.

II. The Non-existent Judicial Decisions

194. Article 313 CPC grants a declaratory action for the official declaration of the non-existence of a judicial decision in five exclusively specified cases (Article 313 §1), provided that the relevant methods of review have been already exhausted (Article 313 §2). These refer to the lack of some fundamental elements of a judicial decision. They include decisions: (a) by a person not entitled or not any longer entitled to exercise the judicial function; (b) by a civil court on cases which do not belong to the jurisdiction of civil courts; (c) which have not been duly published; (d) against a non-existent natural or legal person; (e) against persons enjoying immunity. Such declaratory actions are not subject to time limitations and do not constitute a necessary condition for the non-existence of the given decision.

The non-existent judicial decision can also be challenged by an objection.

III. Procedural Nullities

A. *Distinction Among Substantive and Procedural Nullities*

195. Pursuant to Article 159 CPC, violations of provisions regulating the procedure or the specific form of procedural acts have, as a consequence, the nullity of the given acts. In Greek law, however, there is a clear distinction between the concept of nullity in the area of substantive and procedural law. Void juridical acts in the sense of substantive law are deemed as non-existent and produce no legal effects

331. *See infra*, No. 196.

(Article 180 CC). Hence, they need not be judicially pronounced as null and void. An action seeking an official declaration of the nullity of a juridical act will result in the rendition of a merely declaratory decision. On the contrary, to safeguard the security of legal proceedings, procedural nullities must be pronounced by the court (Article 159 CPC). Void procedural acts produce all their legal effects unless rescinded by a specific decision, which thus bears a constitutive nature.

B. Types and Conditions of Procedural Nullities

196. There are two types of procedural nullities: (a) those where the judge is obliged to pronounce the nullity of a procedural act, and (b) those which depend on the discretionary power of the judge.

First, the judge is bound to declare a procedural act as null and void, either when the application of the violated procedural provision has been explicitly imposed by statute under penalty of nullity (Article 159 No. 1 CPC) or when the violation of a given procedural condition constitutes a ground of an extraordinary method of review, i.e., of a cassation or of the reopening of a judgment (Article 159 No. 2). The practical impact of this type of procedural nullity is intended to be rather limited. Greek courts have, however, frequently extended the application of this type of nullity by regarding some statutory formulations of an imposing character as equivalent to an express sanction of nullity.

Second, the pronouncement of nullity of all procedural acts, in general, depends on whether an alleged irregularity has caused a specifically defined irreparable 'detriment' to the party pleading it (Article 159 No. 3 CPC). As a rule, the notion of 'detriment' is understood in its procedural sense, i.e., as related to the overall procedural possibilities granted to a party. The court is required to freely evaluate whether reparation of such detriment can be effected only through the pronouncement of nullity.

197. Procedural nullity cannot be pronounced by the court on its own motion; it must rather be invoked by a party (Article 160 §1 CPC). A party who has performed a null procedural act or has provoked its nullity is not entitled to attack it. An express or tacit consent of the interested party removes nullity (Article 160 §2 CPC).

Failure of the court to pronounce a procedural nullity or any violation of the relevant statutory requirements is sanctioned through a ground for cassation (Article 559 No. 14).

§2. Time Limits

198. Procedural nullities must be, as a rule, invoked in the course of the act immediately subsequent to that which is asserted as null and void (Article 160 §3). This rule is again intended to promote the security of proceedings.

Part IV. Proceedings

Chapter 1. Pretrial Proceedings

§1. Provisional Remedies

199. Greek law has not developed a pretrial stage of civil proceedings in the common law sense. The basic field where a court is called to deal with a civil dispute before the main action has been initiated is the domain of provisional remedies. These include various types of court orders, most often also provisionally rendered, that are designed to grant relief even before the main proceeding on a given claim has commenced. In terms of practical relevance, provisional remedies currently occupy a central role within the machinery of Greek civil proceedings. This type of judicial protection is going to be further discussed below.[332]

§2. Pretrial Settlements of the Parties

I. Extrajudicial Settlements

200. Another area of pretrial occupation with a civil dispute lies in the attempts for its extrajudicial settlement.

An extrajudicial settlement by the parties (Articles 871–872 CC), at which attorneys are expected to initially aim (*cf.* Article 35 §3 Lawyers' Code), is a settlement concluded outside judicial litigation. Unlike a judicial conciliation, this does not directly result in avoiding civil proceedings (*cf.* Article 293 §2 CPC) but rather grants a defendant a subversive objection against the causes of the raised claim.

II. Mandatory/Optional Conciliation Attempt

201. Conciliation is generally regarded as a means to avoid the courts' overload and, at the same time, to encourage the peaceful termination of a judicial contest.[333] Although an alternative dispute resolution culture has not yet developed in Greece (in spite of constant complaints of court overload and delays), there has been an

332. *See infra*, Nos 250 ff.
333. P. Yessiou-Faltsi & E. Podimata, *Preliminary or Summary Proceedings: Scope and Importance in Greek Civil Procedure*, *RHDI* 2004, pp. 384 ff.

increased statutory emphasis on a pretrial settlement within the court. The drafters of CPC had not only strongly favoured an attempt at a pretrial conciliation by the judge (former Articles 233 §2, 208, 209–214 CPC) but also envisaged pretrial settlements in court by the parties as the judgment's equivalent in terms of closing a dispute (Articles 212 §4, 293 §1b CPC, still in force). Accordingly, justices of the peace were obliged to attempt conciliation between the parties before any hearing of the case (former Article 208 §1 CPC). The same obligation was imposed on any court (justice of the peace or one-member district court) during the first hearing of a labour case (former Article 667).[334]

Law 4335/2015 has introduced a new set of rules intending to promote extrajudicial settlements.[335] Former Articles 208, 233 §2–4, and 667 have been therefore replaced or removed.

202. For disputes belonging to the subject matter competence of three-member district courts in ordinary proceedings, if they are subject to conciliation in accordance with substantive law rules, Law 2298/1995 (Article 1)[336] had introduced a mandatory pretrial stage (Article 214A CPC), to be applied with regard to actions brought after 16 September 2000. Under the penalty of inadmissibility of any further proceeding, an attempt at conciliation was to be undertaken on the initiative of the plaintiff's attorney.[337] However, this mandatory pretrial stage did not succeed in promoting extrajudicial settlements, mostly due to the reluctance of the parties' attorneys. Consequently, Article 214A CPC has been revised in 2011. An attempt at conciliation on the lawyers' initiative is henceforth optional.[338] The attempt can now take place before all courts of first and second instance, as long as a final decision has not been yet rendered. In case this attempt is successful, the conciliatory agreement is registered in a specific document subject to approval by the President of the three-member district court or the competent judge. This document serves as an executory title. Enforcement proceedings can start immediately.

III. Conciliatory Intervention by the Justice of the Peace

203. A conciliatory intervention by the justices of the peace has been provided for (by Articles 209–214 CPC) to ultimately avoid initiation of a civil proceeding. This enables any party intending to bring a suit to previously request the justice of

334. In addition, a voluntary attempt by any other court was provided for in former Arts 233 §2; 524 §1; 548,; 573 §1 CPC. This was effectuated by summoning the parties, specifically for the aim of achieving a conciliation, at any stage of the proceeding. *See* K. Kerameus, 'The Use of Conciliation for Dispute Settlement', *RHDI* 1979, pp. 41 ff.; the same author, 'The Function of Conciliation as a Means of Avoiding Litigation and Settling a Dispute', *RHDI* 1982–1983, pp. 227–238.
335. *See infra*, Nos 549 ff.
336. As replaced by Art. 6 §2, of Law 2479/1997, and modified by Art. 3 of Law 2915/2001 and Art. 5 of Law 3043/2002.
337. *See* in particular Art. 157A former Lawyers Code in detail providing for the lawyers' fees.
338. *See* A. Anthimos, in Nadja Alexander, Sabine Welsh & Martin Svatos (eds), *EU Mediation Law Handbook* (2017), *Chapter: Greece*, pp. 383–402.

the peace intervention for achieving a conciliation. Before Law 4335/2015, the conciliatory intervention of the justice of the peace was possible, even if this judge had no subject matter competence over the dispute. According to new Article 209 CPC, this institution can now operate only in cases where the justice of the peace has subject matter and territorial competence of the dispute. However, the practical relevance of the conciliatory intervention by the justice of the peace has been minimal. A conciliation concluded in the course of this proceeding constitutes an executory title (Articles 212 §4, 293, 904 §2c CPC).

IV. Practical Relevance

204. Despite the favourable procedural framework, the practical impact of pretrial settlements in Greece has been actually non-existent. The relevance of out-of-court conciliations is also considerably limited. The reasons for this phenomenon lie beyond procedural regulation (costs, unfavourable attitude of litigants and courts, etc.).

§3. Preliminary Administrative Procedure in Real Actions Against the State

205. Commencement of an action in Greek law is not subject to any kind of previous preliminary procedures. By way of exception, a real action against the State regarding immovable property can be admissibly raised only after a specific administrative preliminary procedure has been completed in advance.[339]

339. Article 8, §1, of Emergency Law 1539/1939 'On the Protection of Public Immovable Property'. Article 1 §1 of Legislative Decree 31/1968 has extended this requirement also to real actions against municipalities and village communities.

Chapter 2. Proceedings in First Instance

§1. Adversary Proceedings

I. Ordinary Proceedings[340]

A. *Introduction of the Claim*

1. Registration by the Court – Method of Initiating the Action

206. According to Article 215 §1 CPC, a civil action is commenced at the plaintiff's initiative by two separate procedural acts, i.e., by filing a complaint with the clerk of the court and by serving a copy on the defendant. An action is considered filed with the court only after both acts have been completed.

As soon as the day and time for the hearing of the case have been scheduled, the court clerk, enters the action in the docket (Article 226 §2). Before 2015, the initial service of the action on the defendant included the summoning of the defendant on the fixed day of the hearing). The entering of an action in the docket is not, however, regarded as a necessary element to the initiation of an action.

In the context of the new structure of first-instance proceedings introduced by Law 4335/2015,[341] Article 21, §2 CPC provides that the service of the action from the plaintiff on the defendant must be effectuated within thirty days following filing with the court clerk. This time limit extends to sixty days whenever the defendant or a co-defendant resides or seats abroad or is of unknown residence. In case of failure of the plaintiff to comply with the above time limit, the action is regarded as not filed with the court.

2. Notice – Service of the Complaint

207. Service of the action and the summons on the defendant is effectuated in the same manner as of all other documents, namely with the official delivery of the complaint on the initiative of the plaintiff (Article 123) through a public officer (the bailiff), officially appointed as the functionally competent organ in the territory of the court where the defendant is domiciled or resides (Articles 122 §1; 127 §1). By virtue of Article 122 A CPC, service of documents by digital means is possible. The rule entered into force on 1 January 2022. Service must be certified through a document which has the probative effect of an authentic instrument. The court must

340. K. Makridou, *Civil Justice Reforms in Greece: Case Management, Single-Judge Proceedings and Alternative Dispute Resolution Procedures*, *ZZZ* 2011/2012, pp. 257 ff.; K. Makridou, *Greek Case Management in Light of Other European civil Justice Systems*, *The Journal of Comparative Law*, VII (2012), pp. 227–242; N. Klamaris, *Die wichtigsten aktuellen Reformen in Bezug auf das zivilprozessuale erstinstanzliche Verfahren nach der griechischen ZPO. Zugleich eine kurze kritische Analyse*, in *Fairness Justice Equity: Festschrift für Reinhold Geimer zum 80. Geburtstag* (Munich, C.H.Beck 2017), pp. 335–344; C. Triadafillidis & P. Yiannopoulos, *Das ordentliche Verfahren nach der neuen griechischen ZPO, ZfRV* 58 (2016), pp. 275–279.

341. *See infra*, Nos 217 ff.

deem the facts recorded or witnessed by the bailiff as established erga omnes, provided that he has acted within the scope of his authority (*see* Article 438).[342]

If the recipient of service consents, service may be effected anywhere and at any time (Articles 124 §§1, 2, 125 §1). Otherwise – and this is everyday practice – documents need to be served to the residence or the professional installation (of any kind) of the recipient (Article 124 §2). Residence is defined as the house or the apartment where the recipient usually spends either the day or the night, even if not used as such for a very short time (Article 128 §2). Under these provisions, courts accept that it is the bailiff's duty to check whether the indicated lodging is in fact used by the recipient. Nevertheless, given that tracing the actual residence is not a fact directly discoverable by the bailiff, the recipient has the right to overcome the bailiff's respective confirmation by counterproof (*see* Article 440).[343]

208. The method of service on parties residing (or having a seat) outside of Greece has always followed the French system of the '*remise au parquet*'. According to Article 134 §1 CPC, when the defendant has a residence or a seat abroad, service is effected through the delivery of the action to the public prosecutor of the competent court. The order for service from the part of the plaintiff must then necessarily include the precise address of the defendant abroad (Article 134 §2). The public prosecutor is obliged to send the complaint to the Minister of Foreign Affairs, who must then transmit it to the defendant. Whether this is handed to the defendant on time or not, service is deemed to be complete and capable of producing legal effects as soon as the action is delivered to the public prosecutor (Article 136). The obligatory period of time between the summoning of the defendant and the day of appearance[344] is to be calculated from this fictional service. Furthermore, the first hearing of the case may admissibly follow, regardless of the defendant's complete ignorance. Greek courts, therefore, by using several methods of interpretation, have often accepted the reopening of a default decision, even when a defendant was duly summoned in the sense of the above provisions. Service of process abroad may be avoided if the defendant has appointed a representative ad litem in Greece.[345]

---

342. Article 122 §4 CPC has provided that service of documents through the post, telegraph or even telephone may also be permitted for all or only some documents. This method of service must, nevertheless, be activated by special decrees, based on the proposal of the Minister of Justice, which must also regulate the exact method of effecting and proving it. Until now, this channel has been not used, as such decrees do not yet exist. Only exceptionally Royal Decree 338/1970 has permitted service through the post, but only within territories of justices of the peace in case of absence of a bailiff. For this reason, its practical relevance is obviously minimal.
343. Detailed rules specify which persons are entitled to receive a document (Arts 126, 128, 129), and the method of service in the absence or refusal of those persons (Arts 128, §4, 130, 138); also, the method of service to persons in a hospital or in prison (Art. 131), or in a ship (Art. 132), or to a military (Art. 133).
344. *See infra*, No. 213.
345. A. Anthimos, *Service of Proceedings on the Foreign Party's Attorney as an Alternative to Personal Service*, https://eapil.org/2020/10/05/service-of-proceedings-on-the-foreign-partys-attorney-rather-than-the-party-itself/.

209. A similar method is followed to effect service on persons of unknown residence. In addition, publication of a summary of the document served in two daily newspapers is required (Article 135).

210. Greece ratified the 1965 Hague Convention for the Service of Documents Abroad in 1983.[346] In recent case law, the aforementioned problems have been faced within the scope of Articles 15 and 16 of this Convention. In addition, since 31 May 2001, the method of service on parties living in one of the Member States of the EU was governed by Regulation 1348/2000. This piece of legislation was replaced by Regulation 1393/2007.[347] Starting from 1 July 2022, the new EU Regulation 2020/1784 applies.

In addition, Greece is a party to a number of bilateral conventions governing service abroad.[348] Greek courts initially envisaged such conventions of judicial assistance as only regulating the procedure of transmitting documents abroad, given that service in Greece was considered already complete through the delivery of these documents to the public prosecutor. In recent years, however, a contrary interpretation seems to prevail; when a bilateral convention on service abroad is to be applied, service on the defendant is not regarded as complete unless the complaint has actually been handed over to the defendant abroad. In any case, the legal prevalence and practical predominance of the EU Regulation and the Hague Service Convention have minimized the significance of bilateral treaties concluded by the country.

3. Time Limits

211. According to Article 228 CPC, if not otherwise stipulated, service of the summons on the defendant must normally be completed at least thirty days before

346. *See supra*, No. 29. For the application of the Convention *see* A. Anthimos, *Serving Greek Proceedings to US defendants – A Case Law Survey, Civil Procedure Review*, vol. 6, n. 2: May-August 2015, pp. 99–106; A. Anthimos, *Griechisch-Schweizerischer Zustellungsverkehr in Zivil- und Handelssachen, ZZZ* 2014, pp. 150–152.

347. A. Anthimos, *Fictitious Service in the EU – Requiem for a nightmare?, Czech Yb Int'l Law* 2017, pp. 3–34; A. Anthimos, *Supreme Court 1130/2017 [On the application of Art. 19.2 Service Regulation], International Journal of Procedural Law* 2018, pp. 150–153. With a focus to service of documents in Germany and Austria, A. Anthimos, *Griechisch-Deutscher und Griechisch-Österreichischer Zustellungsverkehr in Zivil- und Handelssachen – Eine Bestandaufnahme der griechischen Rechtsprechung,* in Simon Laimer et al., *Europäische und internationale Dimensionen des Privatrechts, Festschrift für Andreas Schwartze* (Wien, Jan Sramek Verlag 2021), pp. 3–17. *See also* A. Anthimos, *Postal Service from Greece to Germany – Recalling Henderson v. Novo Banco*, https://eapil.org/2022/02/14/postal-service-from-greece-to-germany-recalling-henderson-v-novo-banco/. Of major importance is a recent ruling of the Greek Supreme Court, which defined the time of service at the point of submission of the document to be served to the Greek Transmitting Agency, a solution which gives an end to a huge debate about the interpretation of Art. 215(2) CPC, *see* A. Anthimos, Supreme Court] No. 1182/2022, *International Journal of Procedural Law* 2023 (forthcoming).

348. *See supra*, No. 29.

the hearing. The summoning of the defendant residing abroad must be made at least sixty days before the hearing. In case of joinder of parties, the residence of one of the co-defendants abroad is sufficient for the extension of time for all addressees, regardless of their whereabouts.

4. Procedural Effects: Lis Pendens[349]

212. Initiation of an action produces legal effects at both procedural and substantive levels. Procedural effects have been specifically provided for by Articles 221–224 CPC. Procedural effects commence retrospectively from the time an action has been filed (Article 221 §1 CPC), i.e., provided that it has been subsequently served on the defendant since otherwise the composite act of the initiation of an action has not been brought to completion; hence, it is regarded as non-existent.

213. A primary procedural effect of the initiation of an action is that from the moment it has been filed, it is henceforth considered pending (Article 221 §1a CPC). Lis pendens, which in Greek law is regarded as a (negative) procedural prerequisite to be observed on the court's own motion, will not allow the progress of any other subsequent proceeding regarding the same claim and between the same parties (Article 222 CPC).

214. A foreign lis pendens produces a similar effect, provided that the conditions for the recognition of a foreign decision are not absent. The impact of a pending action in a foreign court on the progress of civil proceedings in Greece is not yet clear in case law.

215. The pendency of an action has further effects: The factual basis of an action may not be amended (Article 224 CPC). Amendments regarding the requested relief are not allowed (Article 223 CPC). Beyond safeguarding the rights of defence, these restrictions are intended to consolidate the subject matter. On the contrary, lis pendens does not prevent the parties from any disposition over the pending claim (Article 225 CPC).

216. The commencement of an action in a civil court constitutes and continues to remain the relevant moment for the determination of the subject matter jurisdiction and the territorial competence of this court (Article 221 §1b CPC). In case of co-existence of more concurrent jurisdictions, commencement of an action before a certain court results in the concentration of competence in this court (Article 221 §1c CPC).

349. E. Moustaira, *Rules for Declining to Exercise Jurisdiction in Civil and Commercial Matters, RHDI* 1994, pp. 173–184.

5. Substantive Effects

217. The substantive effects of the initiation of an action have been exclusively connected to the service of process and are provided for by the CC. Only some of these various effects can be discussed here.

A significant effect is the interruption of the running of prescription (Article 261a CC).[350] Prescription commences to run anew and is again interrupted by the latest procedural act (Article 261 b CC). The same rule applies with regard to an acquisitive prescription (Article 1049 CC). Initiation of an action involving a pecuniary claim also causes the obligation for the payment of interests (Article 346 CC) and, under certain conditions, intensifies the liability of a party (*see*, e.g., Articles 348, 1096, 1097, 1100, 1102, 1103 CC).

B. Progress of Proceedings

1. Preparatory Measures – Written Pleadings – Production of Evidence

218. After a complaint has been filed, the most important procedural documents are the written pleadings of the parties prepared for the hearing of the case. Whether compulsory or solely optional,[351] according to current practice, these constitute the most significant part of the preparatory phase of a civil proceeding. Such pleadings are almost without exception elaborated by attorneys in all instances. Pleadings do not need to be served on the opposing party.

The pleadings of the plaintiff contain: (a) a more detailed presentation of factual allegations, which constitute the factual basis of the action and must have been already included in the complaint rudimentarily;[352] (b) an extended analysis of the legal rules to be applied and of their meaning, most often comprising references to legal scholarly works and to case law; (c) his views as to the evaluation of evidence introduced; (d) specifications or requests as to the means of evidence to be produced. The pleadings of the defendant, as already explained,[353] introduce his answer to the complaint, his exceptions or, eventually, a cross-action.[354]

The time limits for filing pleadings in Greek law have undergone continual changes in the course of various types of proceedings.

Law 4335/2015 (presently in force) brought about a radical change to the preparatory phase of ordinary civil proceedings. Until 1 January 2016, when Law 4335/2015 entered into effect, the interval between the filing of a civil action and the first

350. Prescription, as in all civil law countries, is regarded as belonging to substantive law. In Greek law it is governed by Arts 247–278 CC.
351. *See supra*, Nos 40–41.
352. *See supra*, No. 164.
353. *See supra*, No. 189.
354. *See supra*, No. 194.

hearing of the case was a 'dead'[355] period. The greatest innovation introduced consists in the effective use of the time between the filing of the claim and the first hearing. More specifically, Article 237 §1 CPC provided that the parties are obliged to file their pleadings, as well as their means of evidence in support of their claims or objections, within one hundred days after the filing of the action. Within the same time limit, the plaintiff must also provide evidence that the action has been served on the defendant in due time. Prolongation of this time limit of one hundred days for thirty more days is allowed to all parties whenever the defendant or one of the co-defendants has a residence abroad or is of unknown residence. Very recently, the aforementioned provision was amended again: The deadline for submitting pleadings, evidence, and other pertinent documents is now ninety days following the lapse of the time to serve the proceedings. An extension of time is provided for cross-border service and service to persons of unknown residence: In this case, the deadline is now 120 days following the lapse of the time to serve the proceedings. The rule applies from 1 January 2022 onwards. The intention was to extend the time available for residents abroad; to sum up, according to the old system, the defendant living abroad had 130 days from filing, not from the service of the writ, to file pleadings, evidence, etc. Today, the same person has 180 days from filing, i.e., 60 (from filing to last day for service) + 120 (from termination of the 60-day term from service abroad or to a person of unknown residence). Each party can moreover submit an additional pleading, usually termed 'Addition and Contradiction'. This can in the first place include some further analysis or clarifications, but only regarding allegations already contained in the main pleading. Such restriction is of noteworthy practical significance, in particular as to the exceptions of the defendant. The latter can neither introduce new grounds for objections against the action[356] nor can he raise a counterclaim through an additional pleading (Article 268 CPC). Second, an additional pleading is utilized to contradict the allegations of the adversary party. Additional pleadings in ordinary civil proceedings can be filed only within the next fifteen days from the date of expiry of the 90- or 120-day limit.[357] The case file is closed upon expiry of the above-mentioned 15 days.

219. Failure of the parties to timely submit written pleadings, if compulsory, had since 1985[358] been subject to severe consequences, as this could result in the rendition of a default decision.[359] Article 237 §2c[360] explicitly declares that ' untimely submitted pleadings are not taken into account'. As already noted, according to the latest amendments to CPC,[361] all kinds of documentary evidence,[362] including

355. *See* Ch. Apalagaki, *Presentation of the Draft Reform the Code of the Greek Civil Procedure Code (Ordinary and Special Proceedings of the Courts of First Instance)*, in K. Makridou & G. Dimantopoulos (eds), *Civil Trial of First and Second Instance according to Swiss and Greek Law* (2014), pp. 69 ff. (75).
356. Article 237 §1 CPC.
357. Article 237 §2 CPC.
358. Article 6 of Law 1478/1984 which had modified Art. 239 §1 CPC.
359. A party could require for the postponement of a hearing if a serious obstacle to the timely submission of pleadings had been shown as probable, but only once. *See* Art. 239 §1 CPC.
360. As modified by Law 4335/2015.
361. Article 237 §1 CPC.

sworn attestations,[363] must be attached to the pleadings filed with the clerk. The practical result of this rule is that in trials before the district courts, which are operating within the above-described framework of ordinary proceedings, documentary evidence and sworn attestations must be currently produced within the time mentioned above on penalty of inadmissibility.[364] Additional documentary evidence is allowed only for the contradiction of allegations included in already admissibly filed pleadings. Evidence must be produced at the latest within fifteen days from the aforementioned time limit expiry date, on penalty of inadmissibility.[365]

220. At the initial preparatory stage, and more specifically within fifteen days from the closing of the file, the judge (or judges) entrusted with the case are appointed. The rapporteur is then appointed by the President of the three-member district court.[366] The hearing of the case is set at this same time. The hearing must take place no later than thirty days after the expiry of the aforementioned fifteen-day limit. In practical terms, these rules tend to ensure that the hearing in the context of ordinary proceedings should normally take place no later than forty-five days after closing the file.[367]

221. Although the possibility of using electronic devices was also recognized in previous versions of the CPC, the conduct of an e-trial did not develop due to technical shortcomings in the area of civil proceedings. The ability of the parties to conduct several procedural acts though electronic means is considered an important novelty.[368] New Article 237 §11 provides that the submissions of the parties and other supporting documents can be filed electronically. It is thus expected that the electronic form will gradually replace traditional written submissions.[369]

2. The Trial

222. Two types of civil trials have prevailed in Greek civil proceedings since 1985.[370] Whereas proceedings before the one-member district courts and the justices of the peace were mainly oral, written proceedings dominated trials before the three-member district courts.

Law 2195/2001, as modified by Law 3043/2002, introduced a momentous change to the structure of the Code of 1967/1971/1985. According to this procedural system, all kinds of proceedings in both the one-member and the three-member district

362. *See infra*, Nos 395 ff.
363. *Infra*, No. 411.
364. Article 237 §2c CPC.
365. Article 237 §2 CPC.
366. Article 237 §6 CPC. *See also* Ch. Apalagaki, in K. Makridou G. Diamantopoulos (eds), *Civil Trial of First and Second Instance According to Swiss and Greek Law* (2014), pp. 77 ff.
367. New Art. 237 § 6; Ch. Apalagaki, *supra,* n. 368.
368. Ch. Apalagaki, in K. Makridou & G. Diamantopoulos (eds), *Civil Trial of First and Second Instance according to Swiss and Greek Law* (2014), pp. 78 ff.
369. Ch. Apalagaki, *supra* n. 356.
370. *See also infra*, Nos 412 ff. and *supra*, Nos 40–41.

courts followed the same pattern. This unified model of normal proceedings in all civil courts had been based on the attempt to concentrate all relevant material for the adjudication of civil cases in a single oral hearing. Factual allegations of the parties, as well as means of evidence, were thus introduced during this sole hearing on penalty of inadmissibility. The judge was relieved from the rules dominating rigid evidence in all civil courts, with the exception of those rules which imposed limitations on the use of testimony.[371]

223. Law 4335/2015 started to operate in Greece on 1 January 2016. The main objective of its drafters was to achieve acceleration of ordinary civil proceedings in all courts and by all means. Contrary to the previous system, Law 4335/2015 has followed in the opposite direction. To avoid delays, a new model of a civil trial was adopted, exclusively based on the written pleadings of the parties. The date of the hearing may be announced by the secretary to the parties electronically. The hearing may take place even without the physical presence of the parties and their lawyers (Article 237 §6). Furthermore, on request of the parties or on its own motion, the court may decide that the absent parties or their lawyers are allowed to participate in the hearing and perform remotely valid procedural acts through electronic means of communication.[372]

The examination of witnesses during the hearing is excluded. Testimonies of third persons are allowed only through the instrument of written 'sworn attestations' (affidavits). No additional pleadings or means of proof can be submitted after the closing of the file, even in cases where they are based on facts that occurred subsequently. The court is thus expected to issue a final ruling exclusively based on the written contents of the case file. Only by way of exception is the court allowed to order the examination of witnesses, one for each opposing party, in principle of those third persons who have already given and signed a written 'sworn attestation'. This may occur through a simple judicial order during a supplementary new hearing whenever the court, after studying the written contents of the case file, considers that the examination of witnesses is 'absolutely necessary'. The parties are then allowed within eight days after the examination of the witnesses to proceed by filing additional pleadings, stating their evaluation of evidentiary proceedings. Nevertheless, eventual further allegations of the parties or new means of evidence may not be taken into account.[373] The court can, moreover, on request of the parties or on its own motion, order the examination of witnesses, experts, or the parties themselves, even when they are not present in the courtroom, by using electronic means. The examination of those persons is then deemed to have taken place before the court and has an equal evidentiary value to an examination conducted with the physical presence of the examined persons before the court.[374]

---

371. *Infra*, No. 373.
372. New Art. 237 §13 CPC.
373. *See* the detailed stipulations of new Art 237, §§ 6–9 CPC; C. Apalagaki, in K. Makridou & G. Diamantopoulos (eds), *Civil Trial of First and Second Instance according to Swiss and Greek Law* (2014), pp. 77 ff.
374. Article 237, §13 CPC.

224. The court has discretionary powers to postpone the hearing of a case on the request of a party for a good cause (Article 241: only once). This practice tended to become the rule, as this possibility was very frequently utilized by Greek attorneys. Several later amendments have, therefore, limited the scope of application of the relevant rules and imposed financial penalties on the party claiming postponement of a hearing. Article 237 §6 has now provided that in first instance ordinary proceedings, the postponement of the hearing according to Article 241 is not allowed.

225. The CPC provides for detailed rules – now of limited practical significance after the amendment of 2015 – which are designed to govern oral hearings (Articles 233, 234, 235, 252, 253, 255). Additionally, there are several stipulations enabling the judge to develop an active role during the hearing.[375] Opinions by public prosecutors do not constitute a part of normal proceedings.[376] After the termination of a hearing, the court can order its repetition when further clarifications or supplements are needed (Article 254 §1 CPC).

226. The minutes for each oral hearing include an accurate description of what has occurred during this hearing (questions, replies, allegations, requests and declarations of the parties) and also the testimony of witnesses, experts and parties or their representatives (Article 256 §1 CPC). In addition, expert reports, in case these are oral (oral expertise since 1971 has been an exception permitted only in particular proceedings), or conclusions of direct proof by the court must also be contained. This document, which in some cases may be notified to the parties (Article 257), must be signed by both the presiding judge and the secretary (Article 258 §1).

According to Article 256 §1, the minutes of each oral hearing should be normally kept in handwriting. This task was until 2002 entrusted to the special clerk of the court, the secretary, who worked under the instructions of the judge directing the respective hearing. Furthermore, Article 256 §2 permits these minutes to be kept in shorthand. In such a case, the original text, after being translated, needs to be attached to the official minutes. Finally, Article 256 §3 explicitly provides that the use of voice recording in keeping the minutes of oral hearings is allowed. Since the 2001 amendment, tape recording of the minutes of the single oral hearing in all Greek courts has become the rule.

3. Third Party Proceedings

a. Basic Distinctions

227. In order to safeguard their legal interests, Greek law enables third parties to intervene on their own initiative in pending proceedings in which they were not previously involved. Such intervention is termed 'voluntary'. An intervention by a third party can be involuntary. It may be the result of an impleader, which includes

375. *See supra*, Nos 42–46.
376. *See* more specifically *supra*, Nos 76–77.

an official summoning of a third party to intervene or of a mere third-party notice. Both institutions impose upon the involuntary intervener several burdens if he does not comply.

Interventions are further distinguished in 'principal' and in 'accessory'. Whereas in the former case, the intervener claims for himself the object of the pending proceedings, or part of it, in the latter case, the intervener is merely supporting one of the parties as having a legal interest in his victory.

b. Principal Intervention

228. A principal intervention[377] (Articles 79, 81 CPC) is an action of a third person against both parties in an already pending trial.[378] It is admissible insofar as it involves part or the entire claim in litigation but does not exceed it (Article 79 §1 CPC). For example, when the action involves possession of a thing, the intervener cannot admissibly claim ownership. Before the amendment by Law 4335/2015, a principal intervention could be normally made as late as before the Court of Appeal.[379] Article 79 §1 now provides that a principal intervention can be brought only before the Courts of First Instance.

A principal intervention constitutes a plural procedural relationship between the old and the new parties – a situation to be distinguished from joinder – which results in a binding res judicata effect as to both the original parties and the intervener.

c. Accessory Interventions

229. Once an action is pending, accessory intervention is permissible for any third party claiming a legal interest in the victory of one of the original parties (Article 80 CPC). The condition of legal interest is not only connected to the res judicata effect or other binding effects of the decision against the third party but also extends to any other interest related to the legal rights of the intervener. An accessory intervention is admissible in all stages of the procedure, including proceedings in cassation (Article 80).

Generally, the intervener is not given the position of a full party but rather retains the role of the principal party's assistant. Thus, he must accept the procedural condition which he finds at the time of his intervention (Article 82 a). Due to his relationship with a party, the intervener is moreover precluded from any assertions that the court has wrongly decided the case ('intervention's effect': Article 84a CPC). He can merely argue under certain conditions that the case was badly conducted by the principal party (Article 84b CPC).

377. For the comparative aspects S. Kousoulis, 'Aktuelle Probleme der Hauptintervention', *ZZP* 1988, pp. 211 ff.

378. A principal intervention must be brought in the same manner as an action (Art. 81 §1a CPC). Moreover, according to Art. 81 §2, a principal intervention has similar effects to those of an action.

379. G. Rammos, 'Die Intervention in der Berufungsinstanz nach dem griechischen Zivilprozessrecht' *Volume in Honour of Segni* II (Milano, 1967), pp. 215–221.

230. Following the example of German and Austrian law, the Greek CPC has introduced two types of accessory intervention, the former is termed 'simple', the latter 'self-standing'.

In the case of a simple accessory intervention, the intervener is up to a certain extent subordinate to the principal party he seeks to support. Neither can he make any statements or take any procedural steps which are in contradiction to those of the principal party (Article 82b CPC), nor can he attempt any acts of disposal over the object in litigation. The intervener is, however, not bound to the res judicata effect of the decision as against the opposite party but is merely subject to the 'intervention's effect'. However, he can constitute himself as a principal party and take the position of the one supported if both parties agree (Article 85 CPC).

A self-standing accessory intervention, on the contrary, applies when the judgment between the principal parties is legally effective, also as between the intervener and the opponent party (Article 83 CPC). Hence, while not becoming a full party but still possessing a direct interest in the outcome of the proceeding, the intervener in those cases is relieved from the restrictions as to his procedural position and is permitted to conduct proceedings without regard to the procedural behaviour of the principal party he seeks to support.

d. Impleader

231. Greek law provides for three different types of impleader. These must be distinguished from a third-party notice. First, they include an official summoning of a third party for participating in a pending proceeding; and second, they actually result in extending the proceedings against the third party.

Impleader of third parties must be effectuated through the same mode as of bringing a new action against the impleaded person and has the same effects as an action (Article 89 CPC). The defendant may even file a dilatory exception for the postponement of the hearing in the event the impleaded party fails to enter an appearance until this third person is given the proper time for this purpose (Article 266). Such an exception is inadmissible if filed after the hearing (Article 263 f).

232. According to Article 88 CPC, either parties or principal interveners have the right to issue a summons against a third person if they have a claim for compensation against him in the event of defeat. Being the most important type, this is termed the impleader of the 'procedural guarantor' and presupposes the operation of a previous substantive relationship as among the impleading and the third party impleaded. Such an impleader must always be deemed as entailing an implicit action against the third party and constitutes an additional procedural relationship to the principal action. An impleader of the procedural guarantor, however, may be consolidated even with an incidental action against this third party. Such action will be examined by the court only in case the principal action is successful.

Usually, it is the defendant who claims to be entitled to indemnity by a third party and takes steps to effectuate the participation of this party in the trial. A motor car insurer may be thus impleaded by the defendant in proceedings against his insured, resulting from an accident; a third party may be impleaded by the defendant in case he has been the co-author of the harm to the plaintiff during such an accident, and the defendant claims to be entitled as against him to contribution (Articles 926–927 CC).

There is a detailed regulation in the CPC about the procedural position of such third parties (Articles 277–278). Generally, they are allowed to either solely contest their obligation against the impleading party or intervene in the main proceeding or constitute themselves as principal parties.

233. The second type of impleader is of rather limited practical importance and is called the impleader of 'the real owner or possessor' (Articles 87 and 276 CPC). A defendant in an action *ad rem* can summon a third party when he claims to disturb the plaintiff's possession in exercising the rights of this party (e.g., impleader of the owner by a usufructuary). In this case, the impleaded person becomes a party to the action and the judgment is effective as also against him.

234. As already explained,[380] the third type of impleader involves necessary joinder. According to Article 86, the plaintiff may issue a summons against any other necessary party who refuses to be his co-plaintiff; the defendant has the same right as against both the necessary plaintiffs and the necessary defendants. Impleader of necessary parties results in extending litigation and the effects of the decision to all those impleaded since they automatically become parties and are deemed to have initially joined the action (*see* Article 275, as subsequently revised).

235. Impleader in a pending proceeding normally operates on the initiative of a party who is permitted to compel a third person to participate. The law allows, however, an impleader also by court order (Article 90 CPC) once the requirements for an impleader by a party are met and the court deems that the participation of a third party is necessary. The court does not address an order to the third party directly but rather determines the party on whose initiative the impleader will be effectuated. An impleader based on a court order produces similar effects as any other impleader. Nevertheless, the consequences of the parties' failure to comply with the court order have not been specified by the Code. Hence, there have been dissenting opinions in theory. In practice, the institution is of a rather limited use.

e. Third Party Notice

236. A third-party notice may be served in the course of pending proceedings until a final decision on the merits has been rendered by a Court of First Instance in all situations where a legal interest justifies it (Article 91 §1 CPC). When the requirements for addressing an impleader are missing, courts frequently accept that it must be considered a third-party notice.

Although a third-party notice must be effectuated through a similar mode as the raising of an action, and, hence, as of an impleader (Article 91 §2 CPC), it does not have the same effects of an action or impleader since it does not include any request against the third party and does not result in automatically extending a party role to

380. *See supra*, No. 173.

the third person. Only through an intervention is the latter entitled to participate in the pending proceeding (Article 92a CPC). Once a third-party notice was served before the first hearing of a case, the failure of the recipient to intervene causes the loss of his right to attack the decision through a third party-opposition (Articles 92b and 586–590 of the CPC).[381] On the contrary, the Code does not define any exact consequences of a third party-notice which is served on a third person after the first hearing of an action. It has been, therefore, accepted by means of a teleological interpretation that such a third-party notice must be understood as producing a similar effect to an 'intervention's effect' (Article 84), even when the third party has failed to intervene.

C. Judgment

1. Deliberation

237. A court decision must be delivered only by the judge or the judges before whom the hearing of the case took place (Article 300 CPC). If this is not possible (e.g., because of death, resignation, etc., of the judge), the hearing must be repeated (Article 307). Where the case is not handled by a single judge, the collegiate court deliberates – and votes, if necessary – upon its judgment in secret (Articles 113 §1b, and 300 CPC). Deliberation of the court takes place in chambers, either right after a hearing or, normally, on a subsequent date designated by the president or the presiding judge (Article 301 §1 CPC). This latter appoints a reporting judge, charged with the task of reporting on the whole case during the deliberation, and is likely to play a leading role, being in charge and specifying the order of the discussion and of any voting, which will eventually follow (Article 301 §§1 and 2 CPC). Judgment is reached by majority vote, where opinions on the decision are divided (Article 302 §1a CPC). Junior judges vote before the senior; the president gives his opinion last (Article 301 §3 CPC). When there are more than two opinions, judges must accede to the opinions of the greater number (Article 302 §2 CPC). As already explained,[382] dissenting opinions must be included in the judgment (currently of all courts).

After the deliberation is over, the reporting judge is charged with drafting the judgment electronically, which is then dated and signed in material form by both the presiding and the reporting judge (Articles 304 and 306 CPC). From this duly signed draft, the judgment must be pronounced in open court (Article 304 §2 CPC).

2. Different Kinds of Judgment

238. A judgment s termed as final when it concludes the proceeding in the court which has rendered it. Such judgment is delivered if the case appears ripe (Article 308 §1 CPC) and cannot be revoked by the court after it has been published (Article

381. *Infra*, Nos 311–314.
382. *See supra*, No. 63.

309a CPC). On the contrary, a non-final judgment merely decides over incidental or other preparatory measures during the course of proceedings, e.g., orders the taking of evidence. A non-final judgment may be revoked by the court on its own motion or upon request of a party until a final judgment has been pronounced (Article 309b CPC). Accordingly, as a rule, non-final judgments cannot be attacked through methods of review (Articles 513, 539, 553 CPC).

A final judgment can develop a res judicata effect only when it is no longer subject to ordinary methods of review (this is then termed a formal res judicata(Article 321 CPC). Furthermore, a judgment which can no longer be attacked even by extraordinary methods of review is characterized as 'unappealable'.

3. Formal Aspects of Judgments

239. The authentic text of a judgment is formed after its publication and is signed by the judge who was the president during the hearing (by the single judge or by the president of the panel) and by the clerk of the court (Article 306 §1 CPC).[383] This remains at the court office. Any interested party can obtain copies from the court clerk.

240. The component parts of a judgment are four (Article 305). First, the introductive part includes the names of the judges in collegiate courts, particularly mentioning who was the reporting judge (Article 305 No. 1 CPC) and, among others, the names, professions, and domicile of the parties, their representatives and attorneys, with particular reference as to whether they have entered an appearance and filed any pleadings (Article 305 Nos 2 and 3). Then comes the descriptive part, which includes brief statements on the object of litigation and its procedural course since the action was raised (Article 305 No. 4). The essential other two parts are (Article 305 No. 5): the reasons, the premises of the judicial syllogism which lead to the solution, and the actual decision. The latter is expected to be complete, clear, concrete, and, as a rule, free of conditions. The judgment must finally mention that it was published (Article 305 No. 6).

4. Notice and Service

241. Judgments are served in accordance with the same rules as those provided for all other procedural acts. This is, hence, done on the initiative of the parties (Article 310 §1 CPC), in practice of those who are successful, as time limits for methods of review normally run from service of the judgment on the defeated party. By way of exception, non-final judgments are deemed to have been served when the parties, their representatives or their attorneys were present during publication (Article 310 §2 CPC).

383. Article 306 §§2, 3 CPC includes additional rules covering situations where the president of the hearing is not in the position to sign the judgment.

5. Res Judicata

242. The principal effects of a judgment are res judicata[384] and enforceability.[385] Additionally, judgments have some secondary effects. For example, a judgment no longer subject to ordinary methods of review causes the prolongation of the general statute of limitation to twenty years if the claim was subject to a shorter limitation period (Article 268 §1 CC); when involving a money claim, such judgment can also create a title for a mortgage (Article 1263 CC). However, the probative effects of judgments are explicitly regulated (Article 312 CPC) in view of their character as public documents.

a. Distinctions of Res Judicata

243. Greek law draws a distinction between 'formal' and 'substantive' res judicata. Formal res judicata defines judgments which are no longer subject to regular methods of review. This constitutes a prerequisite to substantive res judicata (Article 321 CPC) in its meaning as a conclusive effect in subsequent proceedings. In this latter sense, res judicata is minutely regulated in Articles 322–334 CPC.

Another distinction currently adopted is between res judicata on substantive and mere procedural issues. A judgment dismissing an action on the ground that a certain procedural prerequisite is lacking can also create a binding effect; this is termed procedural res judicata, as it extends only to the procedural question handled and decided (Article 322 § 1b CPC). A judgment of dismissal on the ground, e.g., that the party lacks the capacity to conduct proceedings does not preclude a subsequent action if it is relieved from the previous procedural defect.

In the following units of this chapter, we will discuss res judicata in its substantive sense, i.e., that which presupposes a judgment on the merits.

b. The Function of Res Judicata

244. According to the prevailing opinion, res judicata is basically understood as a procedural rather than substantive institution securing social peace, certainty and stability in legal relations.[386] In its negative function, res judicata is regarded as a (negative) procedural prerequisite, which does not allow any subsequent court to entertain the merits of a case identical to those already covered by res judicata (*non bis in idem*). Res judicata, thus, bars any subsequent action to obtain the same relief as that already sought. Any such action will be dismissed as inadmissible. In its

384. N. Klamaris, *Die griechische ZPO-Regelung in Bezug auf die Rechtskraft im Umfeld des Eurogrundsatzes der Rechtskraft von Entscheidungen*, in Alexander Bruns et al., *Festschrift für Rolf Stürner zum 70. Geburtstag, 2. Teilband: Internationales, Europäisches und ausländisches Recht* (Tübingen, Mohr Siebeck 2013), pp. 1601–1624.

385. The former is discussed in this chapter, whereas the latter, as also recognition of foreign res judicata, will be dealt with in the chapter of enforcement proceedings.

386. For a trend, which underlines the substantive aspects of res judicata, *see* G. Mitsopoulos, 'Gedanken zu einigen wichtigen Problemen der Zivilprozessrechtslehre', *ZZP* 1978, pp. 113 ff. (124–127).

positive function, res judicata prevents the re-litigation of all issues decided in a previous suit, thus operating as only a partial bar to the subsequent action. The res judicata defence must also be considered by the court on its own motion at any stage of the proceedings (Article 332 CPC). Failure of the court to comply constitutes a ground for cassation (Article 559 No. 16).

c. Object and Objective Limits of Res Judicata

245. Only legal relationships which have been brought to a court through an action, a cross-action, a principal intervention or a set off defence, and have been judicially determined (Articles 322 §1a; 324 CPC), can be covered by the binding effect of res judicata. Neither judicial determinations on factual allegations of the parties nor considerations of a court on the meaning of legal norms can develop this effect. Only the resolution of controversy, not the reasons adduced in the decision, has a conclusive effect on subsequent action.

The operation of res judicata requires identity of the cause of action, i.e., of both the factual and the legal base of the involved claim, and, as a rule, identity of the parties (Article 324 CPC). According to Greek doctrine[387] and case law,[388] it does not lie within the scope of res judicata to preclude re-litigation of a claim when the second action is based on a different legal base. The dismissal of the first action founded on the breach of contract does not bar a second action seeking the same recovery on the ground of tort, or vice versa.

Defences are precluded if already decided or could have been decided in the course of a given proceeding (Article 330b CPC). By way of exception, a defence can be entertained in a subsequent proceeding whenever based on a self-standing claim which can constitute the cause of a principal action (Article 330b CPC).

d. Subjective Limits of Res Judicata

246. Res judicata basically covers the parties and persons who have become the parties' heirs and successors after the proceeding has commenced or terminated (Article 325 Nos 1 and 2 CPC). These persons cannot attack a decision on the ground of malice of a party or of a non-party unless provided for by a particular ground for reopening the decision (Article 333 §1 CPC). A party who does not sue in the same capacity cannot be bound.

On the basis of specific rules, the conclusive effect of a judgment also extends[389] to: (a) possessors or holder in actions involving property regardless of when its possession or detention has commenced (Article 325 No. 3 CPC); (b) the trustee (*fideicommissarius)* under certain conditions in actions between the present heir and a

387. K. Beys, 'Die objektiven Grenzen der Rechtskraft im griechischen Recht', *Festschrift für W. Habscheid* (Bielefeld, Gieseking 1989), pp. 11–21; K. Makridou, *Principles of Preclusion and Res Judicata – Reflections from the Greek and the American Law Perspectives*, in *Issues of Estoppel and Res judicata in Anglo-American and Greek Law* (Νομική Βιβλιοθήκη; Athens 2012), pp. 63–100.

388. Plenary session of *Areios Pagos* 967/1973, *Legal Tribune 1974*, pp. 505–506; *Areios Pagos* 414/1971, *Legal Tribune* 1971, p. 1112; *Areios Pagos* 439/1970, *Legal Tribune* 1970, p. 1289.

389. K. Beys, 'Die subjektiven Grenzen der Rechtskraft und die staatsrechtliche Wirkung des Urteils nach griechischem Recht', *Festschrift für K.H. Schwab* (München, Beck 1990), pp. 61 ff.

third party (Article 326 CPC); (c) heirs in actions involving succession between administrators of vacant succession, liquidators of an estate, or executors of will and a third party (Article 327 §1 CPC); (d) executors of will under certain conditions in actions involving succession between heirs and a third party (Article 327 §2 CPC); (e) the guarantor in actions between the creditor and the principal debtor, once the decision has dismissed the action on the ground of the non-existence of the claim (Article 328 §1 CPC), or vice versa (Article 328 §2); (f) members of legal entities in actions between the legal person and a third party regarding the rights and obligations of the former (Article 329 CPC). This last rule is of particular importance, as it also involves members of various types of commercial companies. In particular, in proceedings for matrimonial disputes and disputes between parents and children, since these involve personal status matters, res judicata is established as a conclusive effect erga. Third parties covered by the res judicata effect of a judgment can attack it only on the grounds of malice of the parties (Article 333 §2e CPC).

Res judicata cannot be understood as further binding non-parties. An effect of res judicata against third parties (*Drittwirkung der Rechtskraft*) has not been accepted in Greece.

e. Collateral Estoppel

247. In contrast to most continental systems, Greek law has introduced (Article 331 CPC) the principle of collateral estoppel, in the sense that it extends res judicata, not only to the principal object of litigation but also to some preliminary issues if these constitute a legal relationship per se. The above rule operates where the decision on such a preliminary legal relationship is a necessary condition to the determination of the main object in litigation,[390] in case this preliminary relationship belongs to the subject matter competence of the court adjudicating over the action.

f. Reformation Action

248. A judgment establishing a res judicata effect can be modified if it involves periodic performances, e.g., payment of maintenance, once the circumstances under which it was pronounced have essentially changed (Article 334 §§1 and 3 CPC). Reformation of res judicata can be then achieved through a specific legal remedy (Article 334 §4) termed 'reformation' action. This can also be based on a subsequent fluctuation of the cost of living (Article 334 §2). Reformation actions have become more frequent in recent years.

6. Interpretation and Rectification of Judgments

249. All kinds of judgments are subject to interpretation or rectification by the court which rendered them upon request of a party or on the court's own motion

390. For example, when the main object in litigation involves an accessory claim for interests, the existence of the main claim constitutes such a preliminary issue.

(only in case of rectification) through a subsequent judgment (Articles 315–320 CPC). Whereas a rectification is permissible to the extent a judgment includes typographical mistakes, a computation error, or has been drawn in an inexact or deficient manner (Article 315), interpretation presupposes that the meaning of the given judgment is ambiguous. This does not authorize the court to make any changes to the essential contents of the judgment (Article 316).

II. Provisional Remedies

A. Introductory Remarks

250. The CPC of 1967 has integrated all measures previously known as either preventive, conservatory or provisional under a unified title for which it seems more appropriate to use the general English term of 'Provisional remedies'.[391]

Legal theory distinguishes within the scope of provisional remedies between two main categories: (a) Conservatory measures, which tend to secure the future satisfaction of a substantive right (Articles 704–727, 737–738); and (b) 'Regulatory' provisional remedies granted in order to provisionally arrange disputed situations through orders for specific acts, omissions or indulgences, e.g., in disputes related to possession, unfair competition, family relations, etc. (Articles 731–735). A particular kind of this second category is the provisional adjudication of claims (i.e., related to maintenance, salaries, damages, etc.) for the prompt relief of weak parties (Articles 728–730).

Provisional remedies are now generally regarded as one of the guaranteed forms of legal protection (Article 20 Const. of 1975). They are treated by the CPC in two parts: a general, stipulating common prerequisites and procedure (Articles 682–703), and a special (Articles 704–738), comprising the detailed regulation with regard to particular remedies. The specific conservatory measures for securing enforcement,[392] which have been included in this special part, are: (a) Judicial security (Articles 704–705); (b) Pre-notice in Mortgage Records of a Real Mortgage (Article 706); (c) Conservatory Attachment (Articles 707–724); (d) Judicial Custody (Articles 725–730); and (e) Sealing, Unsealing, Inventory, Public Deposit of Property (Articles 737–738).

While within the above list, the judge has a discretionary power to select the proper measure for each specific case (i.e., to grant an order for the provisional recordation of a real mortgage instead of the requested attachment) without being bound by the request of the parties (Article 692 §1), it is generally accepted that the enumeration of conservatory measures should be regarded as restrictive in the sense that the judge is not allowed to use measures not specifically provided by the CPC. Furthermore, while the judge is entitled to order more than one measure if

391. P. Kargados, *Summary Adjudication in Hellas*, *RHDI* 1998, pp. 123–156; K. Makridou, *General Principles and Preconditions for the Granting of Provisional Remedies in Greek law,* in F. Carpi, C. Rasia & C. Apalagaki, *Provisional Measures in Italian and Greek Procedural Law*, Greek and foreign civil procedural systems III (Thessaloniki, Sakkoulas Publications 2016), pp. 23 et seq.

392. For more details *see infra*, Nos 433 ff.

needed (Article 692 §2), he is at the same time obliged to select the less oppressive measure for the aggrieved party (Article 692 §3), e.g., to order the deposit of security instead of attachment. On the contrary, regulatory measures for the provisional arrangement of disputed situations have been to a greater extent left to the judge, who may order any proper measure (Articles 732, 735; *see also* 734 §2, involving possession of property) without being dependent on a statutory list.

Conservatory measures must be understood not only as a means for securing future enforcement but also, to a certain extent, as a preliminary phase of enforcement proceedings.

251. From the two main categories of provisional remedies (conservatory and regulatory), one must distinguish matters which, following a particular statutory provision, are adjudicated through the proceeding of provisional remedies, although they do not grant genuine provisional measures per se. Due to the acceleration attained through this procedure, resorting to it has been quite frequently attempted, especially when matters need a quick judgement (e.g., stay of execution proceedings, etc.). *Areios Pagos*[393] has ruled that the provided total restriction of methods of review (Article 699) does not apply to judgements not issuing a genuine provisional remedy.

B. General Prerequisites

1. Substantive Conditions

252. Under the explicit wording of Article 682 §1 CPC, provisional remedies may be granted in order to secure or conserve a substantive right, having already become or eventually expected to become the object of litigation in 'normal' proceedings through a principal action. Hence, the first condition of provisional remedies lies in its reference to a private right, including those dependent on a condition, term, or future claims (Article 682 §1b), which thus becomes the underlying foundation of provisional legal protection. Nevertheless, when the specific remedy of the provisional arrangement of an urgent situation (Article 731–736) comes into question, it should not necessarily need to refer to a specific substantive right. It is sufficient that the whole situation is connected to a legal relationship, even in a wide sense, capable of producing rights and obligations in the future. However, provisional remedies are understood as teleologically connected with the principal action rather than with the underlying substantive right.

The second condition of provisional remedies lies either with the existence of an urgent situation or with the avoidance of an imminent danger (Article 682 §1). Despite some doubts on whether a distinction between the above notions is necessary or even attainable, it is now accepted that while an urgent situation refers to circumstances calling for a prompt provisional arrangement, the avoidance of an

393. 754/1986, plenary session, *Dike* 1986, pp. 664 ff. (665); 317/2016, Civil Procedure Law Review 2016, pp. 272 ff.

imminent danger covers the need to secure future enforcement. Although such clear distinctions may not be found in case law, decisions granting conservatory measures usually tend to find their judgement on the need to avoid imminent danger. The above distinction practically results in granting relief through conservatory measures, even for reasons referring to the future.

2. Procedural Prerequisites: Subject Matter and Territorial Competence

253. Jurisdiction for granting provisional relief in the sense of Article 682 CPC extends only to matters belonging to civil courts, according to the general stipulations of Article 1 CPC, while arbitration is excluded (Article 685). Under this conception, *Areios Pagos* has ruled since 1969 that tax claims of the State may not be protected through conservatory measures of the CPC.

254. One-member district courts enjoy general subject matter competence with regard to provisional remedies (Article 683 §1). Only when subject matter competence for the relevant principal action has been allocated to justices of the peace does competence for provisional remedies also belong to the same courts (Article 683 §2).[394] With regard to actions pending before them, other courts (i.e., three-member district courts and Courts of Appeal) also have authority to order provisional relief (Article 684; *see also* 682 §2). Case law has confirmed this subject matter competence, but only under the strict condition that the requested measure seeks to secure a substantive right which exactly corresponds to the object of litigation in the pending proceedings.

255. In addition to a particular competence of the court located closest to the place of enforcement (Article 683 §4), which goes together even with exclusive jurisdictions, territorial competence for provisional relief depends on general stipulations (i.e., defendant's domicile, seat, court of the situs, performance of a contract, etc.). Requests for provisional remedies may, therefore, be brought to any of the above courts, available at the interested party's option.

256. Procedural prerequisites with regard to the parties are subject to two exceptions: first, persons not generally enjoying the capacity to conduct proceedings (persons below the age of 18, persons being interdicted, or mentally ill) may be granted this capacity when their participation is justified for the avoidance of an imminent danger (Article 63§2 CPC). Second, under the above condition, parties are allowed to conduct litigation in person without being represented by an attorney (Article 94 §2). Both exceptions are, however, of limited practical relevance.

394. The only exception refers to provisional remedies with regard to the possession of property, which have been exclusively entrusted to the justices of the peace (Art. 733 CPC).

3. International Jurisdiction

257. International jurisdiction of Greek courts for ordering provisional remedies is primarily based on territorial competence, according to the general provision of Article 3 CPC. Greek courts enjoy international jurisdiction when located closest to the place of enforcement. This is based on the particular territorial competence recognized in such cases by Article 683 §4 CPC. The needs served by opinions allowing international jurisdiction under a wider scope, despite the lack of any substantial connection between the principal action and Greece, are now regarded as being satisfied only under the condition of the above provision. In any case, according to opinions which now seem to prevail, provisional remedies embodying measures to be materialized outside of the Greek territory do not fall within the international jurisdiction of Greek courts (e.g., pre-notice of mortgage or attachment with regard to real property situated abroad).

C. Procedure for Granting Provisional Remedies

1. Commencement of Proceedings

258. The preliminary stage of proceedings for provisional remedies includes submission of the relevant application, as a rule, in writing (Articles 686 §1; for its necessary elements: 688 §1). The hearing of the case is then scheduled by the competent judge and usually takes place within a few days (Article 686 §2). Although this hearing may take place on any day (even on Sundays or other holidays) and anywhere (even at the judge's home) (Article 686 §3), it is usually carried on during a normal court session. The competent judge also decides whether or through what formalities the opposing party shall be summoned (Articles 686 §2). The use of telephone or electronic communication is not excluded (Article 686 §4). Ex parte proceedings are allowed, but only under extremely urgent circumstances (Article 687 §1). Greek courts make infrequent use of this discretionary power. In disputes involving possession or detention of property, summoning of the adversary is compulsory (Article 734 §1).

2. Main Hearing

259. The main, and also the sole oral hearing,[395] is based on a flexible procedural framework with regard to both the authority of the judge for relying on facts not submitted by the parties (Article 691 §1) and the free admissibility (and

395. This is carried on, as a rule, without the cooperation of a secretary (Art. 690 §2 CPC). Participation of a secretary is compulsory only in disputes involving possession or detention of property (Art. 734 §5). Article 690 §2 provides that the adjudicating judge may allow the tape recording of the proceeding.

evaluation) of any available means of proof (Article 690 §1). Evidence must be brought during the hearing. An affirmative decision is allowed when the allegations of the applicant have been shown as probable (Article 690 §1).

3. Decision on the Application

260. The decision granting or rejecting a provisional remedy is a genuine judicial decision (691 §2). It must, therefore, include brief reasoning, according to Article 92 §3 Const., and also determination of both the provisional remedy ordered and the substantive right or situation secured (Article 691 §§2, 3). The judge may also order for a security to be deposited by the applicant ex officio, thus making provisional relief dependent on its payment (Article 694). The relief granted is not allowed to interfere with the rights of third persons (Article 692 §5).

261. In contrast to an explicit provision of the CPC of 1967, under which the principal action was expected to be brought within thirty days after provisional relief was granted, no specification of a time limit for bringing the main action was provided since 1971.[396] Yet, it belonged to the discretionary power of the judge to fix such a limit, which then could not be less than thirty days (693 §1). Law 4842/2021 has now provided that the principal action must be brought within no less than sixty days following publication of the decision ordering provisional relief unless the court order has allowed a longer time CPC. Upon expiry of the time limit, the provisional remedy is removed as of right, with the exception of cases where the successful applicant has already served an order of payment on his opponent. (Article 693 §2).

262. According to Article 692 §4, provisional remedies must not lead to the full satisfaction of the substantive right which they seek to secure or conserve. This stipulation, however, has created difficulties both in legal theory and case law and has led to the expression of dissenting opinions as to the extent of its application. The question which has emerged is whether this restriction also refers to provisional arrangements of a disputed situation (Article 731). The reason is that most often, such provisional remedies inevitably include full satisfaction[397] (e.g., prohibition of an illegal strike through a provisional measure).

396. This rule does not apply with regard to the 'provisional adjudication of claims', where the successful applicant is obliged to bring the principal action sixty days (Art. 729 §5a, as replaced by Law 4335/2015). Otherwise, the provisional remedy is removed as of right (Art. 729 §5a). For conservatory attachment and custody *see also infra*, Nos 440 and 444.

397. I. Iliakopoulos, *Die Grenzen der Befriedigungsverfügung im deutschen und griechischen Recht* (Lang/Frankfurt 1983); M. Mantzourani – Tschaschnig, *Die Befriedigungsverfügung nach deutschem und griechischem Recht unter besonderer Berücksichtigung des Wettbewerbsrechts* (Lang/Frankfurt 1986).

4. The Provisional Res Judicata

263. According to Article 695, a provisional remedy has a provisional binding effect, but it does not influence the main proceedings. Notwithstanding the above, Greek doctrine, followed by *Areios Pagos*, speaks of a provisional res judicata. Such effect is moreover understood as being subject to the objective and subjective limits, according to the general rules of res judicata.

5. Non-availability of Methods of Review

264. Unless otherwise provided, provisional remedies may not be attacked by any methods of review whatsoever (Article 699).[398] Cassation had been allowed by the Code of 1967, but it was abandoned in 1971. *Areios Pagos*[399] had initially extended such inadmissibility even to the cassation 'in the interest of the law'. This ruling has been however overthrown by a later reverse decision of the same court.[400]

6. Enforcement

265. Provisional remedies may function as executory titles (Article 700) and be enforced in a technical sense only when arranging a disputed situation through orders concerning a specific act, omission or indulgence (Article 731) or when provisionally adjudicating over certain claims (Articles 728 ff.).

D. Revocation of Provisional Remedies

1. Mandatory Revocation

266. With regard to provisional remedies, the function of methods of appeal is substituted to a certain extent by revocation. Provisional remedies are revoked either mandatorily (Article 698) or at the discretion of the judge (Articles 696, 697).

Mandatory revocation of provisional measures is always dependent on the outcome of the main proceedings, thus revealing its conservatory or overall accessory character. A provisional remedy, according to Article 698 §1, is mandatorily revoked wholly or partially either by the judge who issued it or by the judge before whom main proceedings are pending: (a) when a final judgement against the applicant has

398. A single exception is provided in Art. 734 §3, involving appeal against provisional remedies arranging possession or detention of property.
399. 47/1990, plenary session, *Legal Tribune* 1991, pp. 245–246.
400. *Areios Pagos* 13/1999, *Dike* 2000, pp. 517 ff.

been rendered in main proceedings, and it is no longer subject to ordinary methods of appeal, or has been already enforced even provisionally; (b) when a settlement for the main dispute has been agreed; (c) when a period of thirty days following subrogation or termination of main proceedings through an alternative method has lapsed.

2. Revocation on the Discretionary Power of the Judge

267. Revocation of a provisional measure may be ordered on the discretionary power of either the judge who issued it (Article 696) or the court which adjudicates over the main action (Article 697). In the first case, two types of revocation have been formulated, each under a different conception. Revocation may be, in the first place, ordered until the first hearing of the main action if justified through allegations for change of real conditions under which a provisional remedy was issued (Article 696 §3).[401] Inefficiencies with regard to law or evidence and new means of proof may not be taken into account. Revocation, in the second place, functions as a guarantee of the right of defence. It may be requested by any party, or a third person, on the grounds of his non-participation in or non-summoning to the proceedings, even without any allegations of change of real conditions (Article 696 §1).

Revocation of a provisional measure may be ordered by the competent court while proceedings of the main action are pending, without any special conditions required.

E. Provisional Orders

268. The promptest form of provisional judicial protection is administered through the issuing of provisional orders (Article 691A). In terms of practical significance, such orders have been enjoying an increasing influence, though sometimes granted with no sufficient justification. It belongs, indeed, to the discretion of the judge, as soon as the request for provisional remedies has been brought, to issue, even ex officio, this form of prompt relief, usually by a simple note on the application itself, without an obligation to summon the opposing party, except when the judge deems that his appearance is deemed necessary (Article 691A §2). Provisional orders are promptly enforceable (Article 700 §3). Unless otherwise determined by the judge, they expire when the decision on the request for provisional remedies has been rendered (Article 691A §1). According to Article 691A § 2b, when a provisional order has been rendered, the hearing on the application for granting a provisional measure must take place within thirty days.

401. By way of exception this mode of revocation is not permissible with regard to provisional measures involving possession or detection of property (Art. 734 §5).

§2. Default Proceedings

I. General Conditions

A. *A Default Judgment in Case of Failure of Appearance*

269. The rules – governing default proceedings during the last decades underwent successive modifications. Default may result from an inadequate representation of each party to the hearing by a duly appointed lawyer or from any party's failure to duly file pleadings on time (Article 237 §1).[402] The hearing of the case is understood as the commencement of adjudication in the seized court, irrespective of whether the court has also entertained the merits of the case or not (Article 281 CPC).[403]

B. *The Judge Is Obliged on His Own Motion to Examine If Service Was Duly Effected*

270. Absence of either the plaintiff or the defendant (or the intervener) obliges the judge to examine on his own motion whether service of process was actually effected through the proper procedure and time limits (Articles 271, 272). The hearing of the case is otherwise declared inadmissible, and a new service on the absent party is required. In the context of ordinary proceedings, when the defendant fails to enter an appearance, but the action has not been duly served, it is deemed as not having been brought (Article 271 §2). However, a question of due service emerges only when a hearing of the case is fixed upon the motion of the opponent to the absent party (*cf.* Article 272 §1).[404]

Examination of proper summoning is based on the bailiff's certificate of service, presented to the judge by the party serving the notice. This includes the duty of the judge to check whether service of summons was in fact completed to the actual home or place of business of the service recipient.

C. *Remedy of Initial Default by a Party's Later Appearance*

271. According to Article 280 §§1 and 4 CPC, the proper presence of a party at only some stages of the hearing can prevent a default judgment. If the defendant has been absent when the hearing of the case was initiated but has properly participated in a later stage of this hearing, he is not regarded as a defaulting party and must accept what has occurred during his absence (Article 280 §1). As courts have

402. In addition, failure of the party to submit evidence for the payment in advance of certain costs or fees has the same consequences.

403. However, neither a postponement (Art. 241 CPC), nor a transfer of the case on the ground of the incompetence of the seized court (Art. 46 CPC) can constitute a hearing of the case in the sense of Art. 281.

404. *See also* Art. 507 CPC.

accepted, no default judgment may be rendered when an initially defaulting party properly participates in a new, supplementary hearing of the case ordered by the court, which is then deemed to be the continuation of the initial one (Article 254. These rules are now of minor practical importance in the context of the written proceeding introduced by Law 4335/2015. They can be applied only in cases adjudicated in the context of particular proceedings.[405]

II. The Defendant's Default at the Hearing

272. A defendant's default at the hearing of the case results in the rendition of a judgment in favour of the plaintiff (Article 271 §3 CPC). This is effectuated on the basis of an assumed confession from the defendant's absence with regard to the grounds of the action, provided that such a confession is generally permitted (this is not the case in matrimonial disputes). *Areios Pagos* has nevertheless refused to totally assimilate this assumed 'confession' to a genuine means of evidence.

Before proceeding to the rendition of a default decision, the court is obliged to investigate whether: (a) all procedural prerequisites have been met, and (b) the action is legally founded. A prima facie investigation of the claim's factual justification is not required, as the defendant is deemed to confess the grounds for the action.

III. The Plaintiff's Default at the Hearing

273. When the plaintiff fails to make an appearance at the hearing, provided that the defendant has been summoned on the plaintiff's initiative, the action is dismissed (Article 272 §1 CPC). The dismissal of the action, if admissible and legally founded, is then deemed based on substantive grounds. *Areios Pagos* regards such a judgment as capable of producing a substantive res judicata.

IV. Absence of the Parties at Later Hearings

274. Whenever a failure of the parties to appear occurs at a hearing on second instance, Article 524 §§3, 4 CPC distinguishes between the default of the appellee, including the default of the appellant regarding cross-appeals, and the default of the appellant (and of the appellee as to the cross-appeal). Provided that the parties have been duly summoned, the default of the appellant as to the appeal and the default of the appellee as to the cross-appeal result in the dismissal of the appeal or of the cross-appeal, unless the above were held inadmissible (Article 524 §3). On the contrary, the court is required to investigate the merits of the case in situations of default of the appellee or the appellant as regards the cross-appeal; the absent party is then regarded as being present. Investigation of the case may then be based on the

405. *See infra*, Nos 419 ff.

already presented documents and evidence produced at earlier stages of the proceedings.[406] In conclusion, once the appellant fails to make an appearance, the appeal is dismissed (Article 524 §3).

V. Failure of All Parties to Appear

275. If all parties fail to enter an appearance or duly participate in a hearing, the latter is cancelled (Article 260 §1, CPC). For cases coming under rules of ordinary or particular proceedings, the parties are obliged to schedule a new hearing within ninety days after the cancellation of the former one, otherwise, the action is deemed as unfiled (new Article 260 §2). If a hearing is cancelled due to force majeure, a new hearing is scheduled by order of the presiding judge. Registration of the new hearing in the court's docket equals service of process. Information about the parties is also possible through an e-mail sent by a court clerk, however, it is not imperative for the clerk to notify the parties (new Article 260 §4, which was introduced in the wake of the pandemic).

§3. Ex Parte Proceedings

I. Voluntary Jurisdiction

276. The main example of ex parte proceedings in Greek law is voluntary jurisdiction. Its regulation in the CPC includes a series of both general (Articles 739–781) and special stipulations (Articles 782–866). The former provisions are designed to establish an appropriate procedural framework, following the special nature of voluntary jurisdiction, whereas the latter provides for a variety of cases which are specified as matters of voluntary jurisdiction (Article 739)[407] and extend to almost all fields of private law.

Voluntary jurisdiction does not apply to actual parties in the sense of adversary proceedings (in particular Articles 742–759). The application of Articles 1–590 CPC is however not excluded unless it contradicts specific provisions of voluntary proceedings (Article 741).

The ex parte proceeding of voluntary jurisdiction is commenced at the request of an interested person (Articles 747, 748). The application must in some instances be served on the public prosecutor (Article 748 §2). In addition, the judge can order the summoning of any third person who has a legal interest in participation in the proceedings (Article 748 §§3–5). Impleader (Article 753) and principal or accessory interventions (Article 752) of third persons are permissible. Persons who have

406. The same rule applies (Art. 510) and remained after the revision of 2015, in the case of an opposition against default.

407. *Supra*, No. 95.

participated in the proceedings are entitled to attack the decision through the normal methods of review (Articles 760–772), whereas third persons can raise a third-party opposition (Article 773). The latter is the most frequently utilized method of attack in the current judicial practice with regard to voluntary jurisdiction.

II. Orders of Payment

277. Orders of payment are always issued through an ex parte proceeding (Articles 623–630). Such orders primarily constitute an executory title. Therefore, they are briefly discussed in the chapter on enforcement proceedings.

III. Provisional Remedies

278. As already discussed,[408] provisional remedies can be exceptionally granted through an ex parte proceeding.

408. *See supra*, Nos 55 and 258. For the provisional orders *see also* No. 268.

Chapter 3. Review Proceedings

§1. Introductory Remarks

I. Definition

279. Methods of review[409] in Greek law are understood as the procedural acts whereby a party to litigation aggrieved by a judicial decision seeks to have the case reconsidered, entirely or partly, whether before the same court or a court of a superior rank for the purpose of correcting its errors.

II. Distinctions

280. Greek law has developed the basic distinction between methods of review called ordinary and extraordinary. Ordinary methods are usually defined as those which can attack all final judgments on any grounds, irrespective of their relation to fact or to law. However, the unique example of a method of attack which can be applied on such a general scale, and at the same time the most significant type of a review proceeding in Greek law, is the appeal. The second method of review, characterized as an ordinary method, is the opposition against or application to set aside a default judgment, which, naturally, involves only this latter type of decision. Extraordinary methods of review, on the contrary, can be employed against decisions which already have a res judicata effect, solely on the basis of specific grounds exclusively provided for by statute (Articles 544 and 559–560 CPC). These include cassation, covering re-examination of only questions of law, and the reopening of a judgment.

In contrast to the two ordinary methods of opposition and appeal, a common feature of extraordinary methods of review is that they generally do not stay the execution of the judgment attacked. Accordingly, whereas the former two are termed suspending, the extraordinary methods are characterized as non-suspending. Another distinction between methods of attack concerns the court, where these are re-adjudicated. Appeal and cassation are termed as 'devolutive' methods in the sense that they transfer the case to a court of a higher rank, in contrast to the 'non-devolutive' methods, i.e., opposition against default and reopening of judgments, which are addressed to the same court.

III. General Rules

281. Where more methods of review against certain judgments are available, basically, they are to be applied successively, following the order provided by the CPC. Ordinary methods, naturally, must be utilized before the extraordinary. Opposition against default judgments and appeal are, on the contrary, both available at

409. *See supra*, also, No. 52.

the parties' option (*see* Article 513 §1 CPC). Finally, it is accepted by some authors that the reopening of a decision must precede cassation. This order can be overturned when an interested party abandons his right to apply a method which comes first.

282. Judgments can be attacked only through the procedural devices available (*numerus clausus*) and to the extent specifically provided for by statute. Greek courts do not possess an inherent power to determine whether and under which conditions the attack on a judgment can be permissible. However, neither the right of appeal is covered by the guarantee of legal protection nor are restrictions to the methods of review by common legislation regarded as unconstitutional.

IV. Initiation

283. The CPC contains a number of common stipulations specifying the mode of initiating all review proceedings (Articles 495–498). Methods of attack are regarded as having been brought as soon as the relevant written petition has been submitted to the clerk of the court, where the attacked judgment was rendered (Article 495 §1), and its registration to the special Records of Methods of Review kept in each court has been effectuated (Articles 495 §2, and 496).[410] This is the moment when the effects of methods of review are commencing (Article 500). No service on the adversary party is required. In accordance with the principle of the parties' motion, further steps rely on the initiative of the interested party, who is authorized to activate the review proceedings by fixing the date for the hearing before the appropriate court (Article 498 §1). Service of summons on the opposing party must then observe the same time limits as in the case of actions (Articles 498 §2 and 228).

V. Admissibility

284. Legal theory, based on the detailed regulation contained in the CPC, has developed certain prerequisites relevant to the admissibility of all methods of review. The latter is distinguished from their legal foundation and is to be examined on the court's own motion (*see* Articles 532, 577 §2 CPC). These prerequisites are (a) Methods of review must be permissible, i.e., the decision attacked must be appealable,[411] and the persons attacking it must have been parties or interveners to the action, or are their heirs or other successors;[412] (b) the party attacking the decision must have a legal interest, which consists of the prejudice of a losing party,

410. A special Royal Decree (564/1968) provided for the respective details.

411. For the opposition against default *see* Art. 501; for appeal *see* Arts 511–514; for the reopening of judgments *see* Arts 538–541; for cassation *see* Arts 552–555.

412. *See* Arts 502, 516, 542, 556 CPC. However, defaulting accessory interveners are, in principle, not authorized to attack the decision. *See* Art. 502 §2.

whether defeat is total or only partial;[413] (c) application of the appropriate formalities and observance of time limitations provided.[414]

Methods of review are available from the day of publication of a decision (Article 499). However, the time limitations start to run normally the day after a judgment was served on the opponent party (Article 144 §1). Since 1974, these do not run during the month of August (Article 147 §2). Against the same decision, a given method of review can be employed only once by the same party,[415] unless the prior has been withdrawn.

Admissibility of a method of review is to be distinguished from the admissibility of its ground (*see* Articles 533 §1; 549 §1; 577 §3). This distinction is of particular significance with regard to extraordinary methods, as only grounds which are included in the list provided by the CPC (Articles 544 and 559–560) can constitute admissible grounds for attacking a decision.

§2. Opposition Against Default

I. General Aspects: The Abandonment of the Institution of 'Unjustified' Opposition

285. The CPC has explicitly characterized (Article 495, §1) opposition against a default judgment as a method of review.

Until May 1993, opposition against default operated under two types. A principal method of attack on default judgments was the 'unjustified' opposition. All default judgments rendered right after the first hearing of a case, at first or second instance of ordinary proceedings, could be attacked through an opposition, even if the defaulting party had been duly summoned. The availability of this method of attack obviously encouraged the dilatory tactics of the defendant and was, therefore, subject to criticism.

Reopening of a default decision could also be sought through a 'justified' opposition. This type of opposition is based on the fact that the party was not duly summoned and his right to be heard was violated.

Article 501 CPC provides today that opposition on a default judgment is permissible solely on the conditions that the defaulting party was not at all summoned, that this party was not duly or timely summoned, or that the absence of the defaulting party is attributed to circumstances coming under the abstract concept of 'force majeure'. The latter concept has been quite frequently employed in recent years. According to case law, the death of a party, or of a person close to a party or to his attorney, and the sickness of an attorney has been accepted as justifiably preventing

413. *See* Arts 516, 542, 556 CPC.

414. For opposition against default *see*: Arts 503, 505 CPC; for appeal *see*: Arts 518, 520 CPC; for the reopening of a judgment *see*: Arts 545, 547 CPC; for cassation *see*: Arts 564, 566 CPC.

415. *See* the explicit rules of Arts 514, 541 and 555 CPC, regarding appeal, the reopening of a judgment and cassation. In particular *see* N. Klamaris, 'Rechtsvergleichende Betrachtungen zum Grundsatz der Einmaligkeit der Rechtsmittelerhebung', *Festschrift für H. Fasching* (Manzsche, Wien 1988), pp. 269–290.

the appearance of the defaulting party. Force majeure is, however, intended to cover solely limited cases of violation of the right of defence.

Restriction of opposition on default judgments rendered at the first hearing of the case is, however, counterbalanced by another modification which permits a full appeal. In case a default judgment is attacked directly with an appeal, without passing through the stage of opposition, the defaulting party is authorized to present any kind of fresh (legal or factual) material and any kind of fresh evidence (Article 528 CPC).[416]

II. Requirements and Effects

286. Any defaulting party, whether in first or in second instance, including principal interveners, has the right to request the reopening of default under the aforementioned conditions (Articles 501 and 502 CPC). Opposition in ordinary proceedings is subject to a time limit of fifteen days if the defaulting party resides in Greece or sixty days if this party resides abroad or is of unknown residence (Article 503). This period of time begins to run upon service of the default judgment (Article 503 §1). If, however, the defaulting party resides abroad or is of unknown residence, the time period of sixty days does not begin to run unless a summary of the default decision is published in two daily newspapers following service on the public prosecutor (Article 503 §§2–3).

Opposition to default judgments, when successful, results in a new examination of the merits. Both the admissibility of opposition and the substance of the case are treated within a uniform judgment (Article 509, as amended by Article 26 Law 4842/2021).

§3. Appeal

I. General Aspects

287. Appeal in Greek law (Articles 511–537 CPC) is generally envisaged as the means of implementing what is known as the 'principle of two instances' (Article 12 CPC). It is, therefore, intended to be a method of 'complete jurisdiction' in the sense that: (a) it allows a full re-examination of the case by a court of a higher rank on points of both fact and law, whether procedural or substantive; and (b) it does not solely encompass the control of legality and reasoning of the attacked judgment, but also, in case the decision is quashed, it results in a fresh judgment on the merits, a stage which can under certain conditions follow even within the same court. However, appellate proceedings are: (a) in principle restricted to the grounds of complaint against the judgment put forward by the parties (Article 522), a restriction understood as consistent with the dispositive principle and known as the 'devolutive effect'; and (b) as a rule based solely on the material presented at first instance (Article 527).

416. For the rules restricting new facts, *see infra*, No. 292.

II. Conditions to Admissibility

A. Appealability

288. The rule is that all final decisions at first instance of three- and one-member district courts, as well as those issued by justices of the peace, are appealable (Articles 511, 513 §1, CPC). Only decisions of the justices of the peace concerning small claims have been excluded (Article 512). The question of whether the latter must be considered appealable if the grounds of an appeal concern the erroneous application of this type of proceeding (special provisions for small claims), whereas opinions, in theory, are dissenting, has been positively answered by *Areios Pagos*[417] in the context of the principle 'of the most favourable treatment of the parties. Decisions on the allocation of court costs are also not appealable as long as the grounds of appeal do not extend to other parts of the judgment (Article 193 CPC).

Non-final decisions are generally not appealable. These are deemed as having been attacked by the appeal which concerns subsequent final decisions, even if this appeal is not expressly addressed against them (Article 513 §2 CPC). Decisions which are only partly final are also not appealable, except in the case of a cross-action (Article 513 §1b CPC). However, despite this rule, case law has accepted partial appealability in cases of joinder if a final decision has been pronounced only regarding one of the joined parties[418] or one of the joined claims.[419] Default decisions are directly appealable (Article 513 §1).[420]

B. Appeal Period

289. An appeal is available right after the publication of the decision according to the general rule governing all methods of review (Article 499). The appeal period starts to run the day after the judgment of the lower court was served upon the appellant. Time limitations, however, also run against the party on whose initiative service of the judgment was effectuated (Articles 144 and 518 §1). The time to appeal is thirty days when the appellant resides in Greece and sixty days when he resides abroad or is of unknown residence (Article 518 §1). In case no judgment is served, time to appeal runs from the day of publication and is then two years (Article 518 §2). The time periods for attacking default decisions through the ordinary methods of opposition and appeal run simultaneously. To safeguard his right

---

417. 1482/1977, plenary session, *Dike* 1978, p. 289; 109/1981, plenary session, *Legal Tribune* 1981, p. 1276; *cf.* 5/1985, plenary session, *Dike* 1986, p. 72; 754/1986, plenary session, *Dike* 1986, p. 664.
418. There are three successive rulings of the plenary session of *Areios Pagos* involving a permissive joinder and concerning the analogous question with regard to cassation: 401/1981, *Legal Tribune* 1981, p. 1557; 744/1982, *Legal Tribune* 1983, p. 808; 902/1982, *Legal Tribune* 1983, p. 209. *See also Areios Pagos* 22/2009, *Civil Procedure Law Review,* 2009, p. 520.
419. *Areios Pagos* 59/1981, *Legal Tribune* 1981, p. 1255; Court of Appeal of Athens 12182/1988, *Hellenic Justice* 1990, p. 1044.
420. *See also supra*, No. 281.

of appeal against such decisions, since opposition against default must be exclusively based on evidence of improper service of process and can be, hence, unsuccessful, a party is required, besides opposition, to also subsidiarily lodge a timely appeal.

III. Grounds for Appeal

290. Initiation of an appeal follows the general rules discussed above.[421] Among the contents of the respective document, minutely provided for by the CPC (Articles 520, 118–120), a clear specification of the grounds of appeal is expressly demanded. According to standard case law, a general complaint against a decision that it is erroneous does not suffice to admissibly initiate an appellate proceeding. It is, on the contrary, required that a notice of appeal includes specific concretization of at least one error, be it a false interpretation of legal norms or an error related to the facts. Specification of a ground of appeal, generally, as a false evaluation of evidence, without a special concretization of the means of evidence referred to, has, however, been accepted as sufficient.

The appellant is entitled to submit an additional document containing new grounds of appeal on the condition that these concern parts of the judgment already challenged by the initial appeal or those necessarily related to them. In contrast to the initial notice, a document containing additional grounds of appeal, after being filed with the clerk, must be served upon the opposing party at least thirty days before the hearing (Article 520 §2 CPC). Complaints with additional grounds of appeal are widely utilized by Greek attorneys since these are not drafted under the pressure of the time period of thirty days, thus allowing a less stressful study of the questions raised.

IV. Effects

291. The commencement of an appellate proceeding has three effects which are termed: (a) suspensive, (b) devolutive, and (c) 'communicative'. Whereas the first refers to the stay of execution which results from both the time period (Article 519 CPC) and/or the initiation of a proceeding on appeal (Article 521), the second marks the character of an appeal as a 'devolutive' method and in particular the extent of the powers granted to the court of the higher level. This court is thus restricted to the grounds of appeal, including the additional ones put forward by the parties (Article 522 CPC). In Greek law, contrary to other European legal systems, an appellate court is not allowed to interfere with the parts of the judgment in respect of which no appeal was brought. According to current case law, however, the admissibility of the action and its legal foundation as well can be re-examined by an appellate court on its own motion.

421. *See supra*, No. 283.

The 'communicative' effect of an appeal is connected with the right of the respondent to bring a cross-appeal (Article 523 CPC).[422] Legal scholars regard cross-appeals as a genuine method of review, i.e., as a special type of appeal. This institution is intended to allow a respondent who was partly defeated by the attacked judgment to seek its modification in his favour rather than raising merely defences against the appeal, even after the time period for a regular appeal has expired or the respondent has admitted the judgment. To avoid unexpected surprises for the appellant, however, cross-appeals are allowed to challenge only those parts of the judgment which have been already attacked by the appeal or those necessarily related to them (Article 523 §1). Cross-appeals may be only taken by means of a special complaint which is filed with the clerk and then served on the appellant at least thirty days before the hearing of the appeal (Article 523 §2). Whereas the abandonment of the main appeal, or its dismissal as ill-founded, does not affect the cross-appeal, on the contrary, when the main appeal is dismissed as inadmissible, the cross-appeal falls as well, unless filed within the time period provided for a regular appeal (Article 523 §3).

V. Proceeding

292. An appellate proceeding, in principle, follows the rules governing first-instance proceedings (Article 524 §1 CPC). According to Article 524 §2, appellate proceedings are mandatorily oral only once a default judgment is attacked directly by an appeal. With the exception of ancillary requests born later, neither new claims nor cross-actions are admissible (Article 525 §§2, 3 CPC). Amendments of the factual grounds of the action, its cause of action or the requested relief are inadmissible, even if the opposing party consents (Article 526). Re-judgment by the appellate court basically relies on the same rules applied (Article 533 §2) and the same factual allegations submitted at first instance (Article 527). The exceptions to the latter rule before Law 4335/2015 were basically similar to those formulated as exceptions to the principle of concentration operating at first instance (*see* Article 527 Nos 2 and 3).[423] An additional exception refers to factual allegations which are presented as defences against the appeal, as long as these do not result in the alteration of the factual basis of the action (Article 527 No. 1). On the contrary, parties are, as a rule, free to produce new means of evidence, including, under certain conditions, testimony and the examination of the parties (Articles 529 §1, and 530 CPC). Fresh evidence can, however, be excluded at the discretion of the judge when he decides that the delay was designed as part of dilatory tactics or was caused by gross negligence of the party producing it (Article 529 §2).

When a Court of Appeal decides to reverse, it must proceed with the case and decide on the merits. This is an obligation expressly provided for, irrespective of whether the Court of First Instance had also delivered a decision on the merits or not. An exception has been provided in cases where reversal is based on a lack of competence (Article 535 §2).

422. N. Klamaris, *Das Rechtsmittel der Anschlussberufung* (Tübingen 1975).
423. *See supra*, No. 39.

§4. CASSATION

I. General Aspects

293. Cassation in the Greek CPC (Articles 552–582) has been modelled on French law, hence, based on the distinction between fact and law.[424] This method of review brings the attacked decision before the Supreme Court (*Areios Pagos*) and is, accordingly, designed as an extraordinary method restricted to points of law (Article 561 §1). As a rule, it has a non-suspensive character (Article 565). Greek legal doctrine regards cassation principally as a method destined to secure the correct application of legal norms. It has also greatly contributed to the uniformity of their application by decisions of lower courts.[425]

294. Cassation proceedings were initially intended to be strictly limited to points of law. There were gradual developments, however, either based on standard case law or on certain pieces of legislation, which allowed *Areios Pagos* to extend its examination under certain conditions to questions of facts as well. Since 1957, it was explicitly provided that once the attacked decision was reversed, adjudication on the merits followed within the same court, usually in a special panel designed for this purpose. Article 580 §3 CPC, before its amendment in 1993, was also formulated under the same idea.

Law 2172/1993 attempted to restore the character of cassation as a method purely dealing with questions of law. Article 580 §3 CPC was reformulated, except when reversal is based on lack of jurisdiction or of subject matter competence (*see* Article 580 §§1 and 2 CPC), and imposed the general rule that, upon reversal, no further adjudication on the merits within the panels of *Areios Pagos* can follow. Article 580 §3 CPC was amended in 2015 and has restored rules similar to those operating before the 1993 amendment.

To avoid overloading *Areios Pagos* and to achieve acceleration of the proceedings, Law 2915/2001 had initially introduced a pretrial examination of the grounds of cassation by a three-member Judicial Council, consisting of the President of the Supreme Court and two supreme justices, on the basis of an oral proposal by the reporting judge for their dismissal.[426] By order of this Council, the hearing of the case could be cancelled once the grounds of cassation were evaluated to be inadmissible or manifestly ill-founded. The parties, however, reserve the right to apply

424. G. Mitsopoulos, 'La distinction du fait et du droit en procedure de cassation', *RHDI* 1968, pp. 4 ff.; the same author, 'Die Unterscheidung zwischen Tatfrage und Rechtsfrage im Kassationsverfahren', *ZZP* 1968, pp. 251 ff.

425. Bakopoulos A., 'The Role of the Supreme Courts at the National and International Level, Greek Law', in Yessiou-Faltsi (ed.), *The Role of the Supreme Courts at the National and International Level, Reports for the Thessaloniki International Colloquium* (Thessaloniki 1996), pp. 149 ff.; D. Tsikrikas, *Rechtsmittelverfahren im griechischen Recht. Der Einfluss ausländischer Vorbilder auf das griechische Recht – Insbesondere das Rechtsmittel der Kassation unter rechtsvergleichender Betrachtung*, in Althammer/Roth (Hrsg.), *Ausländische Rechtsimplantate im nationalen Zivilprozessrecht* (Mohr Siebeck 2020), pp. 63–82.

426. *Infra*, No. 303.

for the realization of the hearing, bearing the burden of an additional financial penalty, in case the cassation filed was eventually dismissed. Unfortunately, this innovation had a very limited practical impact. After having remained in force for a decade, it was abolished in 2011. Law 4335/2015 has again replaced Article 571 CPC and reintroduced a similar type of pretrial examination of cassations filed, dependent on the discretion of the reporting supreme justice.

II. Conditions

A. Decisions Which Are Subject to Cassation

295. The conditions for filing a cassation are provided for in Articles 552–560, 562, 564, and 566 CPC.

As a general rule, all final judgments of civil courts are subject to a review by cassation (justices of the peace, one-member and three-member district courts, Courts of Appeal, Article 552), whether rendered in contested actions, in default (Article 553 §1), or ex parte proceedings (*see* in particular Articles 769–772), when ordinary methods of review are not, or not any longer available. Reviewability of non- or partly-final decisions is governed by similar rules (Article 553) to those involving appealability.[427] A direct cassation on a judgment of a Court of First Instance is permissible as soon as this judgment is no longer subject to an opposition against default or an appeal. This situation can also result from an abandonment of the aforementioned methods.

B. Time Period

296. When a party resides in Greece, the time period for filing a cassation is thirty days following service to the opposing party (Articles 144 §1 and 564 §1 CPC). This period extends to sixty days if the party resides abroad or is of unknown residence (Article 564 §2 CPC). When the attacked decision is still subject to ordinary methods of review, this time limit starts to run after the time period for raising these methods has been exhausted. In cases where no service of the judgment under review was effected, the time limit for cassation is two years, starting from the date of the judgment's publication (Article 564 §3 CPC.

C. Grounds for Cassation

297. Greek law (Articles 559 and 560 CPC) draws a clear distinction between substantive and procedural grounds of cassation. Whereas a violation of any

427. *See supra*, No. 288.

substantive law rule is, generally, subject to a review in cassation, violations of rules of procedure can be reviewed only within the context of the specifically provided grounds.

Article 559 No. 1 CPC provides for a review in cassation when a substantive rule has been violated, including those involving the interpretation of juridical acts, whether a statute law or a custom, a rule of Greek or of foreign law,[428] a rule of internal or international law. In addition, violations of 'teachings of common experience'[429] are reviewable insofar as these are utilized for the interpretation or application of legal norms. Under the scope of this stipulation, it is generally accepted that a review in cassation is allowed not only for violation of enactments, including any type of statutory rules but also for violation of all rules containing essential provisions of law included in decrees or regulations issued by the executive.

Violation of a substantive rule is understood as encompassing (a) the false interpretation and (b) the erroneous application or non-application of legal norms. Application of the law to the facts found by the lower court is understood as also extending to the legal characterization of facts. For example, whereas the determination of damages suffered by the victim in tort cases constitutes a question of fact and is, therefore, not reviewable, the issue of whether the facts found amount to culpability, as required by Article 914 CC, is reviewable. By reviewing the legal qualification given to facts, particularly in the course of application of the abstract concepts most often contained in several rules of substantive law, i.e., good faith, force majeure, important reason, good morals, abuse of rights, public policy, etc., *Areios Pagos* has exercised a more effective control over the lower courts, despite the difficulties of exact distinctions which emerged quite often. As already explained, review in cassation moreover extends to the violation of rules governing the interpretation of contracts, in particular in the context of Articles 173 and 200 CC, which principally refer to the concept of good faith. In addition, the review of the 'teachings of common experience', applied in the course of determination of points of law, actually results in extending the control of *Areios Pagos* on the application of rules of reasoning by the lower courts.[430]

A violation of the applicable law in the opinion of a judgment does not, however, normally constitute a basis for reversal if the case has been decided correctly. Such error is disregarded and the cassation is dismissed, except if the attacking party claims a legal interest for the avoidance of unfavourable res judicata. Reversal is then restricted solely to the erroneous reasoning (Article 578 CPC).

298. In Greek law, the ground of cassation (Article 559 No. 19) termed 'lack of legal basis'[431] has allowed review of the violation of substantive rules under a certain respect which has been traditionally characterized as 'an oblique violation'.

428. *See supra*, No. 37.
429. For this concept *see supra*, No. 36.
430. G. Rammos, 'Die Verletzung der Erfahrungssätze als Kassationsgrund nach griechischem Zivilprozessrecht', *Festschrift für W. Wengler*, Vol. II (Berlin 1973), pp. 693 ff.
431. G. Mitsopoulos, 'Le manque de base légale du point de vue du Droit Comparé' (Sakkoulas/ Bruylant, 2007); P. Yessiou-Faltsi, 'Ist der "manque de base légale" ein Kassationsgrund, der über die Unterscheidung des materiellen Rechts und des Zivilprozessrechts hinausgeht?', *Festschrift für W. Henckel* (Berlin – New York, W. de Gruyter 1995), pp. 923 ff.

This ground was introduced in Greece under French influence ('*manque de base legale*'). Similarly, a judgment is considered lacking a legal basis – and, according to the current terminology, as having 'obliquely' violated a rule of law – whenever the considerations on the findings of fact therein contained are so defective, inconsistent or insufficient, that *Areios Pagos* cannot examine whether a given rule of substantive law has been correctly applied to the relevant facts or not. Accordingly, lack of legal basis is clearly distinguished from both 'direct' violation of legal norms and absence of reasoning in a judgment. In terms of practical frequency, lack of legal basis is one of the most significant grounds for cassation.

299. Article 559 (Nos 2–18, 20) provides for a list of eighteen exclusively specified '*procedural*' grounds. These concern the non-observance of various procedural rules that are held sufficiently essential to open the way for review in cassation. Such procedural grounds are categorized in five groups which include violations of procedural rules involving: (a) the composition of the court below (Article 559 Nos 2, 3), the jurisdiction of civil courts (Article 559 No. 4), and their subject matter competence (Article 559 No. 5); (b) some fundamental procedural principles, i.e., the right of defence (Article 559 No. 6), publicity of the proceedings (Article 559 No. 7), the rules involving the free disposition of the parties (Article 559 No. 9), and the principle of party presentation (Article 559 Nos 8, 10 and 11); (c) some institutions of the law of evidence, i.e., the conclusive proof produced by certain means of evidence (Article 559 No. 12), the rules governing allocation of the burden of proof (Article 559 No. 13), and the distortion of a document, amounting to the lower courts' holdings apparently and entirely different from the document's clear content (Article 559 No. 20); (d) the existence and the binding effects of judgments, e.g., illegal revocation of a final judgment (Article 559 No. 15), or violations as to the binding effect of res judicata (Article 559 No. 16); (e) procedural nullities, exclusions from procedural rights or the admissibility of procedural acts (Article 559 No. 14). This latter ground, since it can include violations of the requirements of all procedural acts, operates as a procedural ground of a rather generalized scope and is, hence, in practice a frequent basis for attack.

300. Judgments of the justices of the peace, including those rendered by district courts, while functioning as appellate courts, can be reviewed in cassation within a list of more limited grounds. Beyond the violations of any rule of substantive law (Article 560 No. 1),[432] these initially included only three procedural grounds regarding: (a) the proper composition of the court below (Article 560 No. 2, amended by Article 36 Law 4842/2021); (b) violations of jurisdiction and subject matter competence (Article 560 No. 3, amended by Article 36 Law 4842/2021); and (c) the illegal exclusion of publicity (Article 560 No. 4). Law 4335/2015 has allowed a broader control, including those district courts functioning as appellate courts. Article 560 CPC has currently provided for two additional grounds allowing review

432. Following an explicit provision, this ground of cassation cannot operate when small claims are involved.

in cassation, the most important being the lack of legal base (Article 560 No. 6); the second concerning violation of the principle of party presentation (Article 560 No. 5).

III. Proceeding

301. A cassation proceeding is initiated in the same fashion as all other review methods (*see* Articles 495–497 and 566). Additional grounds of cassation can be admissibly indicated through a supplemental complaint which must be filed with the clerk of *Areios Pagos* and, moreover, served on the opposing party at least thirty days before the hearing (Article 569 §2 CPC). To avoid filing inadmissible attacks under the pressure of the initial time period, these are permissible even if the initial complaint does not entail an admissible or a sufficiently concretized ground (Article 569 §1); however, it must be restricted to already attacked chapters of the judgment or those related to them (Article 569 §2).

Despite the character of cassation as a non-suspensive method, in a limited number of cases in which the likelihood of irreparable harm is imminent, the filing of this extraordinary method of review can have the effect of a stay. Suspension of execution may be then ordered, totally or partly, in a special closed proceeding by three supreme justices, including the reporting judge (Article 565 §2 CPC).

302. Cassations are normally entertained by the 'civil' panels of *Areios Pagos*, specifically designed for reviewing questions of law in civil disputes. A cassation can be introduced before the full bench of the court, either after a common decision of the President of *Areios Pagos* and its Public Prosecutor or after a decision by the adjudicating panel (more frequent in practice) when questions of general interest arise, or to secure uniformity of interpretation within the decisions of lower courts (Article 563 §2). The adjudicating panel is moreover obliged to transfer the case to the plenary session of *Areios Pagos* whenever its judgment, whether it reverses the decision of the court below or not, is being delivered with the majority vote of merely one supreme justice or whenever it refuses application of a law due to its unconstitutionality (Article 563 § 2b).[433]

303. The reporting judge is appointed in an early stage of the cassation proceeding, namely, as soon as the date of the hearing is fixed (Article 568 §2 CPC). According to Article 571 CPC ((*see also* Article 568, §2c CPC), the sole task of the reporting supreme justice is to evaluate whether the cassation filed is admissible or not, whether the indicated grounds for cassation are admissible or well-founded, or not, and then, in the latter case, to orally propose the cassation's dismissal.[434]

Upon the request of the party, when the reversed decision has been executed, full restitution must be ordered (Article 579 §2).

433. Transfer in this last case is optional if the issue of constitutionality has been already decided by a previous ruling of the full bench of *Areios Pagos* (Art. 563 §2c CPC.

434. *Supra*, No. 294.

The opinions of *Areios Pagos* are usually brief, contain no references to legal scholarly works or precedents, sporadically cite judgments issued by the same court, exceptionally refer to judgments of the Court of Justice of the EU, and most often appear as mere logical deductions from statutory texts.

IV. Cassation in 'The Interest of the Law'

304. Following the French prototype, Article 557 CPC grants the Public Prosecutor of *Areios Pagos* authority to act as a true party and file a cassation 'in the interest of the law'[435] against any decision of civil courts, even not reviewable through a normal cassation by a party,[436] or despite the expiry of the time limitations provided under the normal circumstances for the cassation by a party. This is introduced before the plenary session of *Areios Pagos* (Article 563 § 2a CPC). A 'cassation in the interest of the law' does not affect the parties. Unless the grounds contained in the petition involve the exceeding of jurisdiction or the lack of subject matter competence, the res judicata effect of the decision by the court below remains binding (Article 557b). Cassation 'in the interest of the law', intended, as in French law, to avoid perpetuation of erroneous precedents, has been utilized by the Public Prosecutors of *Areios Pagos* rather sparingly.

§5. Reopening of Judgments

I. General Aspects

305. Reopening of judgments in Greek law (Articles 538–551 CPC) has been formulated as an extraordinary method of review, basically following the French '*requete civile*' rather than the German '*Wiederaufnahme des Verfahrens*'.[437] Its characteristic feature is that it serves to overthrow the binding effects of res judicata in an extremely limited number of cases (Article 544), either where the continuation of these effects would directly violate fundamental procedural principles or where this appears as a necessary method to remedy mostly unintentional errors by the judge, which on some occasions are rather attributed to the improper conduct by a party. Reopening of judgments is, accordingly, a procedural device quite sparingly utilized. Moreover, its relationship to cassation has not yet been sufficiently clarified.

435. G. Rammos, 'Die Kassation im Interesse des Gesetzes nach dem griechischen Zivilprozessrecht', *Gedächtnisschrift für Rudolf Bruns* (München, Vahlen 1980), pp. 35–44.

436. Also against provisional measures. *See supra*, No. 264.

437. For comparative aspects, *see* G. Rammos, 'Höhere Gewalt, Zufall, Naturereignis und Wiederaufnahme des Verfahrens nach dem griechischen Zivilprozessrecht', *Festschrift für Fr. Baur* (Tübingen, Mohr 1981), pp. 561–572.

II. Conditions

A. Decisions Which Are Subject to a Reopening

306. Final judgments of civil courts (formal res judicata) can be challenged by the extraordinary method of reopening (Article 539), whether rendered in contested or default proceedings, at first or second instance.

B. Time Period

307. For parties residing in Greece, the time period for reopening is sixty days following the day on which the judgment to be reviewed was served (Articles 144 and 545 §1 CPC) or when decisions of the Courts of First Instance are being challenged, from the day the time limits to raise ordinary methods of review have been exhausted. This time limitation becomes one hundred and twenty days once a party resides abroad or is of unknown residence (Article 545 §2). In quite a number of instances, however, these time periods may be considerably extended, in particular when reopening is based on the misconduct of a party, as they then start to run only after some facts which constitute the asserted grounds of reopening have actually occurred (*see* in detail: Article 545 §3). Finally, when no service has been effected, the time period for reopening runs from the publication of the judgment, provided that this is a formal res judicata (Article 545 §5), and is then three years.

C. Grounds for Reopening

308. The grounds for reopening of judgments are generally intended either to remedy grave procedural errors or to protect privileged groups of persons (infants, incompetents, etc.) not properly represented or, finally, to sanction the fraudulent conduct of a party or a judge.

The grounds for reopening which can be characterized of a genuinely procedural nature are: (a) Inconsistency of judgments, i.e., when a subsequent judgment producing the effect of res judicata contradicts an earlier judgment producing this same effect rendered by the same or a different court in a proceeding as between the same parties and on the same cause of action (Article 544 No. 1). As a rule, characterization of judgments as conflicting entirely depends on their dispositive part than rather the reasons adduced. Once the reopening is successful, the second judgment is reversed (Article 549 §2). (b) Inadequate representation of a party, unless a subsequent consent by this party has healed the defects (Article 544 No. 2), or improper representation by one person of parties with contrary interests (Article 544 No. 3), or representation by an attorney without the proper authorization by the party, not covered by a subsequent consent (Article 544 No. 4). (c) Forged judgments, i.e., false statements as to the participation of the number of judges required, lack of a majority opinion and signatures required (Article 544 No. 5). (d) The fraudulent use of an improper service of process on a party as if of unknown residence (Article 544 No. 9).

Four additional grounds, which are more or less directly connected to the substantive contents of the judgment, are: (a) Delivery of a decision based on false testimony, on a false attestation by a party, on a false expert report, on a false oath, or on a false sworn attestation by a witness, on forged documents, provided that such misconduct has been established by an unappealable criminal judgment, or, if this is not possible (e.g., in case of death), through a principal civil action (Article 544 No. 6). (b) Recovery of decisive documents after rendition of the attacked judgment, by which an assertion may be derived, which was submitted or could not be timely presented either because of force majeure or because the party was unaware of their existence during the trial, and was moreover prevented by the other side or by a third party to obtain knowledge of their existence or possession (Article 544 No. 7, as amended by Article 31 Law 4842/2021). (c) Unappealable rescission of the decision of a civil, criminal or administrative court, which supports the attacked decision, having occurred after the last hearing of the case where the attacked decision was rendered (Article 544 No. 8). (d) Bribery of the judge having share in the rendition of the attacked judgement, or any other intentional violation of duty by this judge, which has substantially influenced its contents, provided that such bribery or such violation of duty has been established by an unappealable criminal judgment, or, if this is not possible, through a principal civil action, which, as a rule, must be raised within six months after the rendition of the attacked judgment (Article 544 No. 10).

III. Proceeding

309. A reopening must always be instituted in the same court that rendered the judgment (Article 21 CPC). Neither the time period for seeking reopening nor the institution of the respective proceeding can normally stay execution (Article 546 §1).[438]

A reopening generally proceeds as did the action in the court where it was pending (Article 548).[439] The CPC does not any longer clearly divide the proceeding of reopening into two phases, as was the case under the old Code. According to Article 549, the court first decides whether the grounds of reopening are admissible and legally founded, i.e., the reasons alleged are existent. In the affirmative case, after rescission of the attacked decision, the court at once proceeds to the merits. Upon request by the party who attacks a decision which is reversed and has already been executed, full restitution must be ordered (Article 550). The judgment rendered on

438. There are, however, certain exceptions (Art. 546 §1, e.g., involving matrimonial disputes and disputes regarding the relationship between parents and children or disputes involving a document's falsity, where a stay is automatically granted under the condition that the time limit for instituting the proceeding of reopening runs from service of the judgment challenged. In addition, the adjudicating court can grant a stay on the request of a party (Art. 546 §2). A new para 3 was introduced by Art. 32 Law 4842/2021, extending the stay to the effects of the judgment under the above conditions.

439. As modified by Art. 1, Article 'Third' of Law 4335/2015.

reopening is reviewable only if the reversed judgment was, and, in the affirmative case, is subject to the same methods of review under the same conditions as that judgment (Article 551).

§6. General Opposition and Third-Party Opposition

I. General Opposition

310. A general remedy known as opposition has operated in Greek law (*see* current Articles 583–585 of the CPC) ever since the old Code. Opposition under this wide scope is granted to any third person prejudiced or whose legal interests are endangered by a judicial or extrajudicial act if the opponent was not summoned or did not participate (Article 583). The provisions regarding this general remedy, as well as those involving the specific remedy of third-party opposition, have been included in the 'Third Book' of the CPC under the general title 'Methods of Review and Oppositions' (Articles 495–590). Following this order of the Code, we will briefly examine both devices, although it is generally accepted that these are different in nature from methods of review.

The most renowned types of general opposition are currently oppositions against orders of payment,[440] oppositions to enforcement,[441] and oppositions against tables of classification in enforcement proceedings.[442] All those types, operating within the common framework provided for by the institution of general opposition,[443] are of great practical relevance. General opposition is moreover regarded as a general means to implement the right of legal protection and of defence, even in the absence of a specific remedy.

II. Third-Party Opposition (Tierce-Opposition)

A. General Features

311. Third-party opposition (*tierce-opposition*),[444] introduced in Greek law (Articles 586–590) under French influence, must be understood as the procedural device granted to persons who were not parties to the action for the purpose of attacking a judgment that causes them prejudice and endangers their legal interests (Articles 586 §1 and 583). While also a legal remedy rather than a method of review,

440. *See infra*, No. 464.
441. *See infra*, Nos 487–501.
442. *See infra*, No. 484.
443. In particular as to the mode of their initiation (Art. 585) and territorial competence (Art. 584); *see infra*, Nos 490, 493.
444. To avoid confusion with the institution of a third party-opposition, specifically designed to challenge acts of the enforcement proceedings by third parties claiming a right over the seized property (*see* more particularly *infra*, Nos 496–500), we refer to this special remedy by also juxtaposing its original French name. While the former is exclusively addressed against acts of execution, this latter remedy challenges only final judgments.

third-party opposition is clearly distinguished from the remedy of general opposition since, in contrast to the latter, it can exclusively challenge judicial decisions and not merely judicial or extrajudicial procedural acts. Despite the arguments against its utility, Greek legal authors generally regard third-party opposition as a remedy necessary to protect the legal interests of a third party. It is, moreover, a quite frequent occurrence in legal practice.

B. Requirements

312. The CPC provides for two types of third-party opposition. The first type is open to all third persons who were not parties to the proceeding and are not bound by the res judicata effect of the attacked judgment (Article 586 §1). Third parties must have been, directly or indirectly, prejudiced by the existence of the judgment or threatened with being prejudiced. De facto prejudice is usually sufficient. The second type involves judgments which are final between the original and third parties, on condition that the attacked judgment has been obtained by fraud or collusion (Article 586 §2). The original parties themselves remain excluded.

Final judgments of all types of courts may be attacked (Article 586 §1), even if not already a formal res judicata, with the exception of the decisions of *Areios Pagos* when adjudicating on a cassation. No time limitation for raising a third-party opposition has been provided for by the CPC. *Areios Pagos* has moreover ruled that neither does the general statute of limitations apply in view of the public law character of this remedy.

C. Proceeding

313. Competence of the court to decide on the attack depends on the type of third-party opposition (Article 587). Third-party opposition can be principal when proceedings are brought against the attacked judgment or incidental if raised in the course of other main proceedings, where one party attempts to rely on the judgment while attacked by its opponent. In case of a principal third-party opposition, competence lies in the court that issued the judgment under attack. In the case of an incidental third-party opposition, competence is, on the contrary, vested in the court before which the attack is brought, provided that the latter court is of the same or higher rank than that from which the judgment to be attacked was issued.

A third-party opposition is initiated as a normal action (Articles 588 §2, 585 §1, and 215). Further grounds of opposition are admissible when brought through an additional complaint, provided that this is served on the opposing party within sixty days after the filing of the opposition or, in case of particular proceedings, eight days before the hearing of the case (Article 585). A third-party opposition must be, as a rule, addressed against all initial parties, thus constituting a necessary joinder (Article 588 §1). A third-party opposition does not by itself suspend the effects of the judgment under attack. Upon request of the third party, the court, or the president of the three-member district court, may order a stay of execution for avoiding an essential detriment to the interests of this party (Article 589).

D. Effects

314. When the grounds for a third-party opposition are held to be admissible and well founded, the judgment under attack is not usually quashed but rather modified in order to remove any prejudice to the third party (Article 590a). A third-party opposition has, therefore, only a relative effect, except where an indivisible right is involved (Article 590b).

Part V. Incidents

Chapter 1. Decision on Incidental Matters

§1. Definition and Distinctions: Procedural Treatment

315. The CPC explicitly defines incidents as anything which can hinder, interrupt, abolish or otherwise influence the normal progress of the main proceedings, including enforcement (Article 282 §1). An incidental matter in the above sense can be only understood in connection to a main dispute, provided that one of the parties to the action has a legal interest in the delivery of a decision on both the main dispute and the incident (Article 282 §2).

Legal theory distinguishes between incidents involving mere procedural matters and those related to the substance of a proceeding. Procedural incidents include various preparatory or other matters which influence the normal unfolding of pending proceedings, e.g., the challenge of judges, incidental requests for the forced production of documentary evidence, attacks of procedural acts on the ground of a procedural nullity, attack of a document for falsity, etc. Incidental matters which are related to the substance of a proceeding usually involve a preliminary legal relationship constituting a necessary condition to the adjudication of the main action, for example, the existence of a marriage in maintenance proceedings. The concept of incidents is finally understood as also encompassing cross-actions, interventions, impleader and third-party notice.

Incidental matters are dealt with by the court of the main action, irrespective of the kind of proceedings applied or whether the court would enjoy competence to examine such a matter in an independent action (Article 284 CPC). However, a preliminary legal relationship, which has been incidentally examined, can be covered by the binding effect of res judicata only in cases where the court had subject matter competence (Article 331 CPC).[445]

316. Similar rules apply to the incidental examination of the validity of administrative acts (Article 2 CPC). If the validity of an individual administrative act is challenged before civil courts, the latter is authorized to proceed to its incidental examination (but not to the declaration of its invalidity) when a decision of the competent administrative court has not been yet rendered. This rule is designed to avoid multiple trials and to achieve acceleration. On the contrary, where administrative

445. *See supra*, No. 247.

courts have already examined the validity of the act in main proceedings, the decision pronounced is binding also upon civil courts.[446] Nevertheless, civil courts enjoy the discretionary power to stay their own proceedings upon request by a party or even ex officio when the delivery of decision in a civil dispute depends entirely or partly on a preliminary legal relationship whose adjudication is pending in another civil or administrative court (Article 249 CPC). A similar rule applies with regard to pending criminal proceedings (Article 250 of the CPC).

§2. Incidental Actions

317. The CPC draws a distinction between notions of incidental matters (Articles 282, 284, 285) and incidental actions (Articles 283, 285). The latter are particularly defined as the ancillary applications of either party to a main proceeding against his opponent which are raised during its course before the same court. They can involve requests of a self-standing or non-self-standing character (Article 283 CPC). Incidental applications of a non-self-standing nature can be raised during all stages of the proceedings of first or second instance (Article 283 §2 CPC). On the contrary, when an incidental action includes a self-standing request, this can be brought only at first-instance proceedings. To limit situations where an incidental action can be raised directly before the Courts of Appeal, courts have interpreted the concept of a non-self-standing request narrowly. This is understood as including applications which merely tend to support the main action, e.g., the requests involving the forced production of documents or the declaration of a document's falsity. On the contrary, a subsequent action involving later interests or other fruits of the main claim, or later rents of a lease, or a subsequent request for the declaration of the invalidity of a juridical act instituting a necessary condition to the claim have been considered entailing a self-standing request which cannot be brought directly before a Court of Appeal.

The rules governing incidental applications do not involve cross-actions and principal interventions, as these are subject to a specific regulation.

Incidental actions are, as a rule, tried by the court entertaining the principal case. This court, however, enjoys the discretionary power to deliver a decision solely on the principal dispute if this is ripe and transfer the incidental action to a separate proceeding (Article 285 CPC).

446. For the decisions of the Council of State: Art. 50 §5 Legislative Decree 170/1973 'On the Council of State', codified by Presidential Decree 18/1989. For the decisions of other administrative courts: Arts 196, 197 Code of Administrative Procedure.

Chapter 2. Withdrawal and Discontinuance of Action

§1. The Structure of the Code with Regard to the Subject

I. Possibilities of Terminating the Proceedings on Parties' Volition

318. The CPC devotes a separate chapter to the 'Abolition and Termination of the Trial' (Articles 293–299). This provides for three possibilities of terminating civil proceedings on parties' volition, i.e., (a) on the plaintiff's, (b) on the defendant's, or (c) on both the plaintiff's and defendant's volition. These are: abandonment or withdrawal of the action (Articles 295–297),[447] admission of the action (Article 298), and conciliation (Article 293). Cross-actions, interventions and impleaders, or third-party notices fall within the scope of the same regulation (Article 299). Civil proceedings are terminated without a judgment only in the first (a) and the third (c) cases. In the second (b) case, despite the admission by the defendant, a decision has to be rendered (Article 298).

II. Revocation of Other Procedural Acts

319. The Code also provides for the revocation of other procedural acts, demanding the same requirements (Article 299). This last rule is of particular importance, as it also covers ordinary and extraordinary methods of review.

§2. Abandonment or Withdrawal of Action

I. Substantive and Formal Requirements

A. *Withdrawal of an Action by the Plaintiff Not Including Abandonment of the Substantive Claim*

320. By withdrawing a certain complaint, the plaintiff usually intends to prevent a civil action from dismissal because of failure either to meet the procedural prerequisites or to allege sufficient facts in order to support the claim or to produce the necessary evidence in order to convince the court. It is, thus, more likely that a new action, with the defect remedied, will follow. The CPC regards withdrawal of an action as a one-sided procedural act and, provided that the oral hearing has not yet commenced and the court has not yet examined the merits of the case (Article 294a), as an absolute right of the plaintiff which does not depend on the consent of the defendant. Only at a later stage of the proceedings can the defendant claim a legitimate interest in the termination of the trial through the rendition of a final judgment

447. Abandonment of the action must be understood as also including abandonment of the substantive claim (Arts 296, 297). On the contrary, a mere withdrawal of the complaint has no influence on the substantive claim (Arts 294, 295, 297).

(Article 294b). Once the defendant convinces the court of the probability of such an interest, the unilateral abandonment of the action is regarded as inadmissible.[448]

B. Abandonment of an Action by the Plaintiff, also Including the Substantive Claim

321. A resignation from the substantive claim by the plaintiff, which evidently must also comprise the withdrawal of the action, is again regarded as an exclusive right of the plaintiff. In principle, this does not depend on the consent of the defendant (Article 296a) and, therefore, is also envisaged as a unilateral act. It only depends on the requirements of substantive law, in particular on the capacity of the plaintiff to dispose freely of the substantive right (Article 296a). This last provision has, however, caused a discussion about the exact legal nature of this act.

A resignation from the substantive claim by the plaintiff may be objected by the defendant only exceptionally. It may be inadmissible if the latter demonstrates a legitimate interest in the termination of the proceedings through final judgment (Article 296b). Despite its evident necessity, this last provision has proved to be of very limited practical relevance.

C. Termination of Proceedings Through a Plaintiff's Act Needs to be Formal

322. Termination of civil proceedings by the plaintiff is subject to uniform typical requirements regardless of the exact content of the respective acts. According to Article 297 CPC, the abandonment of an action, regardless of whether it includes a resignation from the substantive right, needs to be explicit and be expressed by the plaintiff either orally, which must be registered in the minutes of the hearing, or in a declaration included in a document which must be served on the defendant, or included in the pleadings.

The above form is also needed when the parties intend to withdraw from other procedural acts (Articles 297, 299).

II. Consequences

A. Withdrawal of an Action Not Including the Substantive Claim

323. The result of withdrawing a certain complaint is that the action is considered not having been brought (Article 295 §1a), and litigation as not pending any

448. Greek courts have accepted the existence of such a legitimate interest most often in cases where the dismissal of the action, due to the lack of evidence from the part of the plaintiff, is highly probable. Such judgments sometimes concern exceptions of lis pendens from the part of the defendant, claiming inadmissibility of a new action on the same claim, due to inadmissible withdrawal of the previous one.

longer. When the consent of the defendant is not required, the proceeding is terminated without a judgment, even when the plaintiff has not yet paid the costs of the procedure, which in any case burdens this party (Article 188 §1). Since the abandonment of the action does not also include the substantive right, a new action with respect to the same claim will be accepted as admissible. The defendant is then to raise a dilatory exception and deny defences unless the costs of the previous proceeding are paid by the plaintiff (Article 295 §2). Greek courts have often interpreted this provision in favour of the plaintiff.

According to Article 263 §1 CC, when an action is abandoned, the interruption of prescription, which has occurred when the process was served (Article 221 CPC), is deemed never to have occurred. The plaintiff, however, can retroactively regain the lost interruption by refiling a new action within six months (Article 262 §2 CC).

324. Restriction to the requested relief occurring during a proceeding is regarded as a partial abandonment of the action (Article 295 § 1b). To the extent such a restriction was attempted, the request is considered not having been brought. This last provision has been a source of interpretative difficulties as to the determination of the subject matter competence of the seized court.

B. Abandonment of an Action also Including the Substantive Claim

325. When the abandonment of an action also includes relinquishment of the substantive claim, pending proceedings are terminated. In addition, every new action with respect to the same claim shall be dismissed since the grounds establishing the cause of action have already disappeared.

§3. ADMISSION

326. The admission of the action by the defendant, also regarded as a one-sided act and as the reverse to the plaintiff's resignation from substantive rights, again depends on the requirements of substantive law, in particular those concerning the capacity of the defendant to dispose over the admitted claim (Article 298a).

The defendant's admission of the action does not need to be formal. It may also be tacit, provided that it can be concluded in a clear way through other acts (Article 298b). Therefore, in case of a defendant's admission, judgment needs to be rendered. Admission by itself does not terminate the proceedings *ipso jure* (Article 298c). Once the defendant admits the action, recognizing totally or even partly the claim of the plaintiff, the court is evidently relieved from any obligation to investigate the case. However, since this act may also be tacit, it is the task of the judge to declare, through the rendition of a judgment, whether and to what extent the conduct of the defendant may be interpreted as conveying an admission. In such a case, the judgment must refer to the exact content of this admission (Article 298c).

The costs of the procedure are allocated by the court to the plaintiff if the defendant did not cause the commencement of civil proceedings (Article 177 CPC); otherwise, it is the defendant's burden to pay all court costs (Article 188 §2).

§4. CONCILIATION

I. Distinctions

327. The main figure of conciliation in the Greek procedural system is the type of judicial conciliation (also termed *court settlement*), the conciliation agreed upon by the parties with respect to a pending civil dispute under the special form required by the CPC (Article 293 §1). Identification of this conciliation as judicial is used in order to distinguish all other settlements of the parties concluded outside of court or outside of litigation, defined as extrajudicial conciliations.[449]

II. Legal Nature

328. Discussions about the legal nature of judicial conciliation in Greece are mainly influenced by the German doctrine about acts producing results in both the substantive and the procedural fields. According to a prevailing opinion, a judicial conciliation must be envisaged as a single act, which nevertheless embodies two unified sides; it is a procedural act and at the same time a contract depending on the rules of civil law. In order to bring forth its effects, a judicial conciliation must at the same time meet the prerequisites of both civil and procedural law. On the contrary, extrajudicial conciliation, bearing features belonging exclusively to civil law, is considered a common contract.

III. Formal and Substantive Requirements

329. A judicial conciliation needs to be expressed in a declaration of the parties either before the court, which adjudicates over the pending action, or before the judge dealing with the administration of evidence. In the former case, the conciliatory agreement of the parties must be registered in the minutes of the proceedings; in the latter case, in the official report of the judge. Judicial conciliation may also follow the form of a notarial instrument (Article 293 § 1b). Limits regarding the competency of notaries are not provided.

When the settlement of the parties does not fulfil the above formal requirements but is concluded in any other form or orally, it may not bring about the same results as a judicial conciliation. It is then regarded as an extrajudicial settlement (Article 293 §2).

Pursuant to Article 293 § 1a, a judicial conciliation must also fulfil substantive law prerequisites: the parties need to have the capacity to dispose freely over the object matter (the substantive claim) of conciliation.

449. For such pretrial settlements *see supra*, Nos 202–206.

IV. Consequences

330. The first effect of judicial conciliation is the termination of pending proceedings (Article 293 § 1b). A decision is not required. For this reason, judicial conciliation is considered not having a res judicata effect. By some authors, it develops either a binding force similar to it, whereas by others, it is only that of a civil contract. In any case, judicial conciliation hinders the parties from bringing the same claim to a new trial.

Its second effect is also similar to that of a judgment: the minutes of proceedings embodying a judicial conciliation before any court are explicitly recognized as an enforceable instrument (Article 904, §2c).[450] Finally, where a judicial conciliation appears in the form of a notarial instrument, it is also enforceable by law (Article 904 §2d).[451]

450. *See infra*, No. 452.
451. *See infra*, Nos 452 and 468.

Chapter 3. Challenge of Judges

§1. Disqualification of a Judge in General

331. A judge can be disqualified either through personal declaration or upon the challenge of a party, or on the courts' own motion, under circumstances which are related to the person of the judge or to the object of litigation (Articles 52–61 CPC).[452] These same rules apply to public prosecutors and court clerks. Experts can be excluded (Articles 376–378) under similar conditions. Disqualification must be ordered through a special decision. Whether the conditions required (Article 52) are fulfilled needs only to be shown as probable (Article 60(1)).

The disqualifying grounds are either of absolute or relative character. The former results in the exclusion of the judge solely upon determination of their existence. They include the relationship of the judge to the parties up to a certain degree (Article 52 §1b, *see also* No. 52(c)), other legal or economic bonds (Article 52 §1a), or certain kinds of previous involvement of the judge to the dispute (Article 52 §1d and e), or a personal interest to the outcome of litigation (Article 52 §1a). The latter refers to 'suspicions of partiality' in general. It is accordingly accepted that it belongs to the discretionary power of the court to determine in each concrete case whether, e.g., the close friendship or the enmity of a judge to a party, in fact, requires disqualification.

§2. Disqualification of a Judge on the Challenge of a Party

332. Once a judge fails to disqualify himself, either party can challenge his participation in the case on the grounds of one of the aforementioned circumstances. A special, incidental proceeding can be initiated, as minutely regulated by Articles 57–61 CPC. Such applications of the parties must be, as a rule, brought five days before the hearing of the case and only exceptionally in the later stages of this hearing (Article 57(1). To avoid abusive applications, Article 57 §§2 and 3 CPC have introduced several numerical restrictions concerning the number of judges who can be admissibly challenged in accordance with the numbers serving in each court. When a judge is challenged, he may not participate in further stages of the proceedings. The issue is decided by the court without his presence (Articles 58, 59).

452. *See also* Arts 14–26 Code of Criminal Procedure; Arts 15–22 Code for the Tax Disputes Procedure; Art. 23 of Law 345/1976 on the Special Highest Court; Arts 17–22 Code of Administrative Procedure.

Part VI. Legal Aid and Legal Costs

Chapter 1. Legal Aid

333. Following the tradition of the previous Code, the CPC devotes a special chapter to legal aid (Articles 194–204) under the title 'benefit of poverty'.

334. In terms of practical application, the 'benefit of poverty' has not operated successfully. Decisions granting this benefit have been very infrequent due to its very narrow scope, the ignorance of the interested parties, and the understandable reluctance of attorneys to support the institution. In light of the right to legal protection, the renovation of the CPC in this respect and the elaboration of a modernized framework of legal aid have been shown as necessary.

335. Law 3226/2004 has introduced a complete system of legal aid for civil or commercial matters. It covers both internal and cross-border disputes (Articles 10 and 11), thus implementing Council Directive 2002/8/EC of 27 January 2003.[453] Pursuant to Article 16 §1 Law 3226/2004, the stipulations on the 'benefit of poverty' of the CPC (Articles 194–204), although not explicitly abolished, should not apply any longer with regard to civil or commercial disputes in case the parties are citizens of a Member State of the EU, or have a domicile or a residence in a Member State (*see* Article 1, §1, of Law 3226/2004). A complete system of legal aid, under Law 3226/2004, means that legal costs (*see* in detail Article 9) of natural persons with a low income, as fixed in Article 1 §2, (not of legal persons), including the costs for the appointment of lawyers, notaries, or bailiffs, if requested (Articles 3, 9 §§1, 2), are undertaken, totally or partly (Article 9 §1), by the State (Articles 12–15), once they have been allocated by the court to these parties (Article 9 §6). Legal aid is granted through a special proceeding (Article 2) designed to verify the economic situation of the applicant through documentary or other means of evidence (Article 2 §§2, 4), separately for each trial, and extends to all instances as well as enforcement proceedings (Article 9 §3). A request for legal aid, additionally, must satisfy the condition, legal remedies, for which it is sought are admissible and not manifestly unfounded, whereas the significance of the case for the applicant should also be estimated by the court (Article 9 §4). The decision granting or refusing legal aid must contain reasons (Article 2 §5) and can be attacked by appeal (Article 8 §2).

453. K. Makridou, *'Lawyers' fees in Greece at a turning point. Recent legislative changes in litigation costs'*, in Mathias Reimann (ed.), '*Cost and Fee Allocation in Civil Procedure*', (Springer 2012), pp. 163 ff.

Law 3226/2004 has finally introduced specific rules regarding requests for legal aid by persons with a domicile or residence in EU Member States (Article 10) and for the transmitting procedures of such requests in other Member States by persons with domicile or residence in Greece (Article 11). Persons domiciled or having a residence in another Member State are entitled to seek legal aid in Greece, even if their income is higher than the limit fixed, in so far as they can prove that they cannot pay the legal costs because of the difference of the standard of living between the State of their domicile or residence and Greece (Article 10 No. 10(a)). Accordingly, pursuant to Article 10 No. 10(b) Law 3226/2004, additional costs for interpreters, official translation of documents and, under certain conditions, travel expenses of persons moving to Greece to support a request for legal aid are also covered. With regard to cross-border disputes, legal aid may consist of the appointment of a legal adviser to assist with the settlement of a dispute before the commencement of court proceedings (Article 10 No. 10(c))

Chapter 2. Legal Costs

§1. General Aspects

336. Legal costs in Greece are relatively low. They comprise the strictly judicial costs, which are several kinds of fees or dues to be deposited in advance, and various extrajudicial expenses, such as the remuneration of attorneys, notaries, bailiffs, experts, etc., and also some other expenses such as witnesses, technical consultants, etc.[454]

The general rule is that each party has to pay the dues and expenses of his own procedural acts in advance (Article 173 §§1–3 CPC). Only in actions seeking maintenance is the defendant, for obvious reasons, obliged to pay the dues and expenses of the plaintiff, as fixed by the court (Article 173 §4 CPC).[455] A second exception was added by Article 6 §4 Law 3625/2007 concerning adults who have become victims of slave traffic or several other illegal acts against their corporal integrity or sexual freedom, punishable by the Criminal Code. The expenses of the adult plaintiff must be paid in advance by the defendants up to EUR 600, as fixed by the judge (new Article 173 §5 CPC). A party who fails to submit evidence of his compliance with these obligations is deemed to be in default of appearance (Article 175 CPC).[456]

§2. Applications of and Deviations from the 'Defeat Principle'

337. Court costs are allocated after the trial, following the 'defeat principle'. According to the main rule, each losing party is charged with his own court costs as well as the costs of his opponent (Article 176 CPC). This rule can basically also apply when each party is only partially successful (*see* Article 178 CPC). The court can then divide the costs in accordance with the degree of the parties' defeat.

Each court is moreover allowed to sometimes deviate from the 'defeat principle' by taking into account whether a party's behaviour has caused the initiation of the suit ('culpability principle'). The court costs are thus charged to the plaintiff whenever a defendant has not provoked the initiation of the trial and has at once confessed or admitted the action (Article 177 CPC). A similar rule can apply in favour of one of the parties in case of partial victory of both parties under specific conditions (Article 178 §2 CPC). Legal costs can be imposed on a victorious party as a penalty, e.g., for violating the duty to tell the truth or for causing the invalidity of a certain judicial act (Article 185).

In terms of practical significance, the most striking example of a departure from the 'defeat principle' concerned cases where 'there are justified doubts as to the outcome of litigation' (Article 179 CPC). The court was then allowed to order that no

454. *Ibid.*, pp. 163 ff.
455. The court, however, cannot exceed the amount of EUR 300. *See* Art. 16 Law 3994/2011, which has modified Art. 173 §4 CPC.
456. *See supra*, No. 269 Fn. 397.

costs would be recovered by the defeated party. Courts indeed resorted very frequently to the 'justified doubts' clause in order to relieve the unsuccessful party from the burden of paying the total amount of costs, most often without sufficient justification. Article 2 §2 Law 2915/2001 has limited the scope of application of this clause by determining that only in cases where the interpretation of the legal norms applied was 'extremely difficult' or in disputes between spouses or certain relatives was the court allowed to depart from the 'defeat principle'. The abolished exception was reinstated by Article 8 Law 4842/2021.

The CPC provides for a complex of minute rules governing the allocation of legal costs in cases of joinder of parties (Article 180), principal interventions (Article 181), accessory interventions (Article 182), conciliation (Article 187), abandonment from a judicial act or the action (Article 188 §1), an admission of the action (Article 188 §2), default (Article 184) and methods of review (Article 183). All these rules basically rely on the principles discussed above.

338. The allocation of the court costs to each party is effectuated through the decision (Article 191 §1) and, normally, must be based on a detailed list of expenses submitted for this purpose by the parties' attorneys (Article 190). Only the necessary costs, whether judicial or extrajudicial, can be recovered (Article 189). In practice, however, such detailed lists of expenses are not often submitted by attorneys, and the whole amount of necessary legal costs is not fully recovered.

Part VII. Evidence

Chapter 1. Burden of Proof

§1. The Allocation of the Burden of Proof

I. General Aspects

A. 'Subjective' and 'Objective' Burden of Proof

339. Burden of proof operates under a subjective and an objective aspect: The first one is related to the determination of the party on whom rests the burden of producing sufficient evidence to the court in order to justify favourable factual allegations. The second is the 'risk of non-persuasion', namely the burden of the party who will otherwise lose the case unless he furnishes enough evidence to satisfy the court up to the appropriate degree of conviction. Insofar as civil proceedings are based on the principle of party presentation, the burden of proof will be allocated to the same party.

B. Significance of the Rules Governing the Burden of Proof

340. A court cannot refuse to decide a case whenever both parties did not produce sufficient proof; it is still obliged to render a judgment, which must be specifically reasoned. Accordingly, the outcome of an action largely depends on the rules governing the burden of proof. When a party bears the burden of proving certain relevant facts and does not succeed in persuading the court of their truth, all claims or defences which rely on those facts will be rejected.

C. The Burden of Alleging the Relevant Facts

341. The burden of proof presupposes a burden of alleging the relevant facts. The latter is related to the obligation of the parties to allege all relevant facts for the foundation of their claims or defences. As a general rule, both the burden of pleading and of proving a certain fact rests on the same party. When a party does not comply with the burden of alleging the relevant facts, an action is dismissed as legally non-founded. The significance of this burden is quite obvious in default proceedings: the court is still obliged to examine whether the action is legally founded and, otherwise, reject it.

II. Rules Regarding the Allocation of the Burden of Proof

342. Unlike in some other legal systems, the Greek CPC provides for a general rule (Article 338) which basically governs the allocation of the burden of proof in all kinds of civil proceedings. According to this stipulation, which is regarded as an official introduction of the 'Norms Theory' ('*Normentheorie*'), developed within the German doctrine, 'Each party is obliged to prove the facts which are required to support his claim or counter-claim' (Article 338 §1). Thus, the operation of this general principle has been connected to the procedure of the application of legal norms. Since the legal effects of a norm can apply only insofar as the overall facts which cause them have been *in concreto* completely fulfilled, the burden of proving these relevant facts rests with the party who seeks the application of a rule in his favour.

Apart from the general rule of Article 338 §1, additional specific rules exist mainly in the CC, which directly provide who bears the burden of proof.

III. Characterization of Rules Related to the Allocation of the Burden of Proof

343. By virtue of the explicit rule (Article 338) which has been included in the CPC, Greek authors usually regard the rules governing the burden of proof as of a procedural nature. This view can also be supported by the fact that among the procedural grounds of cassation, there is one referring to violations of rules allocating the burden of proof (Article 559 No. 13). Following this conception, in conflict cases, the burden of proof should be governed by the *lex fori*.

IV. The Right to Counterproof

344. Evidence produced by a party who bears the burden of proof, called principal evidence, may be opposed by counter-proof. This tends to overthrow the probative effects of the means produced by the party on whom the burden of proof rests. The right to counterproof must be regarded as an integral part of the overall right of defence. It may be effectuated through the same means produced by the party who carries the burden of proof and may be either direct or indirect. It does not have a different subject matter; it rather represents the opposite side of what the other party claims.

§2. Relationship Between Legal Presumptions and Burden of Proof

345. The allocation of the burden of proof is essentially affected by legal presumptions, defined as the consequences that the law draws from a fact that is known about a fact that is unknown. Pursuant to Article 338 §2 CPC, in the absence of a special rule otherwise providing, legal presumptions regarding the existence of a fact may be controverted by any type of evidence. Presumptions shift the burden of proof and at the same time affect the determination of its subject matter. Legal theory, therefore, regards rebuttable legal presumptions as particular rules involving the allocation of the burden of proof. According to the prevailing opinion, a party who seeks to controvert a legal presumption must fully convince the court that reality is contrary to what is deduced by law. The creation of doubts is not sufficient.

While the constitutionality of non-rebuttable presumptions is under question, various rebuttable presumptions exist mostly in the CC (e.g., Articles 38, 424, 941, 944, 980, 1046, 1110, 1111, 1464, 1465, 1765, 1777, 1962, etc.).

Chapter 2. Admissibility of Evidence

§1. Introductory Remarks

I. General Features of the Law of Evidence

346. Greek law has generally maintained that the rules of evidence are an integral part of procedural law.

The Law of Evidence belongs to the second Book of the CPC (Articles 335–465). Whereas its first part (Articles 335–351) provides for general rules dealing with the subject matter of proof (Articles 335, 336, 337), the different types of evidence (Articles 336, §3, 347, 348–351), fundamental principles (Articles 340, 346), and the burden of proof (Article 338), the admissibility of the means of proof is treated extensively in the special part (Articles 352–465).

II. Types of Evidence

A. Rigid, Free, and 'Partly Free' Evidence

347. Evidentiary proceedings in Greek law are carried out through a type of evidence which is known as 'rigid' or 'formal' or 'procedural'. In principle, evidence is expected to be produced through only eponymous means of proof, as specified by Article 339, CPC and solely under the formal procedure provided therein. It must be stressed that although the judge is, as a rule, not free as to the means of proof he can take into account, he is, on the contrary, free as to their evaluation.

348. A total departure from this formal kind of evidence is allowed only where specifically stipulated (*see*, e.g., Articles 8 (determination of the amount in controversy), 337 (foreign law), 469 (small claims), 759 (voluntary jurisdiction)). Evidence is then characterized as 'free', which means that it may be produced through any appropriate means and under a flexible procedure not subject to the requirements of rigid evidence.

349. Since 1984, an intermediate type of evidence, called 'partly free' evidence, has operated successfully in Greece on a rather general scale. It was initially introduced within particular proceedings for disputes involving leases and labour cases and successively extended to disputes related to car accidents, maintenance and custody of children. It was further introduced in ordinary proceedings before the justices of the peace and one-member district courts. Since 1994, the president of the three-member district court had been authorized to order the operation of this type of evidence in ordinary proceedings before the three-member district courts.[457] The 2001 amendment of the CPC has extended application of this type of evidence in three-member district courts during ordinary proceedings, with the exception of

457. *See supra*, No. 222.

cases where the use of testimony is restricted.[458] This same rule also applies after the 2015 amendment of the CPC on the basis of Article 340 §1 CPC.

'Partly free' evidence must be distinguished from both types of rigid and free evidence since, while it allows the evaluation of means of proof which should not be admissible under the normal requirements provided by the Code,[459] at the same time, it does not completely relieve the court from certain rules governing rigid evidence.[460]

B. Direct and Indirect Evidence

350. When the relevant facts necessarily required for the application of a legal norm become a direct object of evidentiary proceedings, evidence is called direct. However, Article 336 §3 of the CPC explicitly allows that the court deduces conclusions as to unknown but relevant facts, from proven facts only indirectly relevant. This type of evidence is called indirect, and the respective logical process of the judge is usually referred to in case law as the deduction of 'judicial presumption'. According to standard case law, indirect evidence is subject to the restrictive rules of testimony by virtue of Article 395 CPC. Contrary to the theoretical objection that a process of reasoning cannot be affected by restrictions, the underlying idea of this conception is to avoid the risks of indirect evidence.

C. 'Preservative' Evidence

351. An extensive regulation (Articles 348–351 CPC) governs evidence produced before the order of the court for the proof taking has been rendered or even before litigation has commenced. This type of evidence is called 'preservative' and may be allowed following the proceeding of provisional remedies (Article 348 §1) with regard to all means, under the circumstances particularly prescribed in Article 348, i.e., asserted danger that a means will be lost or that its utilization will become difficult or asserted need that the current situation of a thing or a work must be confirmed. 'Preservative' evidence may also be based on an agreement of the parties.

III. Free Evaluation of Evidence

352. Unless otherwise explicitly provided, the judge evaluates the means of proof freely and decides in accordance with his inner conviction. The judgment must include the reasons which led the judge to the formation of his conviction (Article 340

458. *See also infra*, No. 373.
459. For example, testimony and presumptions are admissible beyond the restrictions provided for normal cases; or despite some witness incompetencies.
460. The court is, in principle, still bound to estimate only the eponymous means as provided by Art. 339. Also, the rules governing the probative effect of some means (documentary evidence, confessions) are not set aside.

CPC). Means of evidence are in principle regarded as of equal probative effect, even if they consist of presumptions. Within the process of his free evaluation, the judge enjoys a discretionary power to rely on some of them and reject others. Evidence offered by one party may be evaluated to satisfy the burden of proof resting on the adversary (Article 346: principle of the community of the means of evidence).

Weighing of evidence by the judge is subject to review by the Court of Appeal, but such attacks do not constitute any ground for cassation. Although, according to some scholars, failure of the court to sufficiently explain its factual determinations while weighing evidence or contradictory reasoning with regard to this evaluation does provide for a review ground in cassation (lack of legal basis), *Areios Pagos* is steadily rejecting such a ground, by considering that it involves factual determinations which are not subject to a review.

IV. Degree of Persuasion

353. In normal cases, a judge is expected to base his decision on 'fully' convincing evidence according to human standards, which is characterized as 'complete'. Objective theories regarding estimation of probabilities following mathematical or statistical methods have not been accepted as not being in compliance with the principle of free evaluation of evidence under Article 340, which relies on the personal conviction of the judge.[461]

354. Under circumstances specifically prescribed by statute, the court is allowed to be satisfied if the truth of the alleged facts is shown as very probable (Article 347). In such cases, mainly including adjudication over urgent situations or on merely procedural issues, a lower degree of probability is sufficient. Additionally, the court is permitted to utilize any appropriate means of evidence under flexible rules of procedure (free evidence). A significant example is the evidence required for granting provisional remedies (Article 690 §1).[462]

§2. The Means of Proof in Particular

I. General Aspects

A. Enumeration in Article 339

355. Pursuant to Article 339 CPC, there are currently eight means of proof: confessions, direct or tangible evidence, expert reports, documentary evidence,

---

461. G. Mitsopoulos, 'Historisches und richterliches Wissen', *Festschrift für K.H. Schwab* (Beck, München 1990), pp. 337–348 (344). *See*, however, S. Koussoulis, 'Beweismaßprobleme im Zivilprozessrecht', *Festschrift für K.H. Schwab* (München, C.H. Beck 1990), pp. 277–288.
462. *See supra*, No. 259.

examination of parties, testimony, presumptions, and sworn attestations. Party oath, which had been accepted as a separate means by the Code of 1967, was not maintained after the 2001 revision.

Admissibility and the probative effect of these means are, in principle, dependent upon the nature of litigation and the pertinence of a certain means for the proof of the relevant facts. Notwithstanding subsidiary means, i.e., the examination of the parties, all other means may be used simultaneously. Although the enumeration in Article 339 seems restrictive, utilization of presumptions as a means of proof has in fact resulted in relieving the judge to a certain extent from any such limitation.[463]

Each separate means of evidence will be briefly discussed in the next units of this paragraph following the order of the CPC.

B. *Illegally Obtained Evidence*

356. Whether illegally obtained evidence can be evaluated in favour of the party who has produced it has been a point of discussion for many years.[464] Some decisions of *Areios Pagos* had initially refused to declare the inadmissibility of intercepted conversations of spouses in divorce cases, while a part of the case law of the Courts of Appeal had, on the contrary, rejected tapes which had been recorded despite the ignorance of the involved persons, as violating basic constitutional principles (Articles 2 §1; 5 §1). Since 1993, however, *Areios Pagos* has steadily ruled that these means are inadmissible.[465] However, according to Article 370A of the Criminal Code, the use of recording tapes containing telephonic conversations, which have been obtained, despite the ignorance of the interested person, is subject to severe criminal sanctions (*see* §3).

According to the constitutional revision of 2001 (Article 19 §3), the use of means of evidence obtained by violating the confidentiality of communications (Article 19 §§1, 2), the protection of private and family life and the sanctuary of home (Article 9), as well as the protection of the so-called personal data (Article 9A), is prohibited.

II. Confession

A. *Definition and Distinctions*

357. A confession is the statement or the acceptance by a party of the truth of facts unfavourable to him. In Greek law, mainly under French influence, confessions are regarded as self-standing means of proof (Articles 352–354). A confession must be distinguished from an admission. While a confession refers to one or some

463. *See infra*, Nos 408–410.

464. A. Kaissis, *Die Verwertbarkeit materiell-rechtswidrig erlangter Beweismittel im Zivilprozess* (Diss. Heidelberg 1978).

465. *See*, e.g., *Areios Pagos* 1/2001, plenary session, *Dike* 2001, pp. 517 ff.; 17/1993, plenary session, *Hellenic Justice* 1994, pp. 1663 ff.; 18/1995, plenary session, *Legal Tribune* 1996, p. 411; *Areios Pagos* 1/2001, plenary session, *Legal Tribune* 2001, p. 1803.

of the relevant facts which constitute the subject matter of evidence, admissions deal with the claim itself in its entirety (Article 298 CPC). Thus, admissions lead to the termination of litigation,[466] while a confession can only produce evidence of a relevant fact.

358. A confession may be either judicial when effectuated in the course of proceedings, or extrajudicial (Article 352 §2). Depending on its subject matter, a confession is characterized as 'simple' or 'complex'. In complex confessions, which are much more frequent in practice, additional favourable statements tend to avoid the consequences of t unfavourable ones. A confession may be express or tacit when deduced by the judge from the entirety of a party's assertions or his overall behaviour. Article 261 CPC provides that each party must determine his position in connection with the factual statements of the opponent by giving a precise answer about the true or untrue nature of these facts. If not, the court in its own discretion will decide freely, by evaluating the conduct of this party as a whole, whether he has confessed or has denied the grounds for the action.

B. Prerequisites

359. Any party having the capacity to conduct proceedings can make confessions. The intent to confess is also required. In judicial confessions, this may be, however, presumed; in extrajudicial confessions, such intent must be particularly proven.

A party's attorney is entitled to make confessions since such capacity is deemed to be included in an attorney's general powers (Article 97 CPC). A party can remove this power by restricting his general rights (Article 97 §2), or immediately revoke such a confession (Article 99 CPC).

C. Probative Effect of a Confession

360. A judicial confession, whether written or oral, is deemed to produce an absolute degree of certainty with regard to the relevant facts therein included (Article 352 §1 CPC) and is binding on the party who made it. There is no difference between express and tacit confessions as to their probative weight.

Under the present CPC, the significance of the binding probative force of a confession has been considerably limited, as the indivisibility of complex confessions has not been retained. This principle had been developed through case law, based on French influence, although legal theory had always objected to it.[467] The CPC now provides for the separation of complex confessions. A fact confessed by one of the parties in favour of his opponent is deemed as proven, while the part of the

466. For more details *supra*, No. 326.

467. Ch. Fragistas, *Grundzüge des griechischen zivilprozessualen Beweisrechts,* in Rühl – Fragistas, *Rechtspolitische und rechtsvergleichende Beiträge zum zivilprozessualen Beweisrecht* (Berlin 1929), pp. 56 ff.

confession which favours the confessing party, if it consists of a self-standing factual allegation, must still be proven by the latter. If that allegation is not a self-standing one, the probative force of the confession is evaluated freely (Article 353). Initial difficulties regarding the distinction between self-standing and non-self-standing allegations seem to have been overcome. Confessions regarding family law disputes are evaluated freely (Articles 597 §1 CPC).

Extrajudicial confessions need to be proven and are evaluated by the court freely (Article 352 §2 CPC).

D. Revocation of Confessions

361. A confession, judicial or extrajudicial, can be revoked only insofar as the confessing party proves that it has not been based on true facts (Article 354 CPC). Revocation of confessions has been thus related to the reversing of the burden of proof regarding the confessed facts. The judgment on whether a confession is based on true facts relies on the free evaluation of the court.

III. Tangible or Direct Evidence

A. Definition

362. Tangible or direct evidence is effectuated by the court or a reporting judge through an inspection of things or persons, including the parties. It may be ordered at the discretion of the judge, by the court on its own motion, or upon the request of a party when such examination seems indispensable for the determination of facts (Article 355 CPC). The party's request is not binding for the judge; the latter's discretionary power is not subject to a review in cassation.

363. The CPC provides for extensive regulation regarding the place and time of inspection (Article 357), various technical procedures (Article 358), the respective reports (Article 359) and the proceeding after direct evidence has been completed (Article 360). There are also explicit provisions governing the obligation to be subject to direct evidence and the consequences of refusal.

B. Obligation to Cooperate

364. Direct proof is apparently the most secure method of reaching the truth. Nevertheless, difficulties emerge whenever the involved persons fail to cooperate. The relevant questions are governed by a detailed regulation. The general rule is that the parties are in principle obliged to cooperate during direct evidence (Article 361). If not, they are threatened by an evaluation of evidence against them (Article 366) and an obligation to pay damages, expenses and penalties (Article 367).

This rule, which is regarded as a particular application of the parties' duty to tell the truth (Article 116), applies even when the object of direct proof is a person.

Article 362 declares that this person is in principle obliged to tolerate direct proof. However, the court's order may not be enforced specifically. In case direct proof takes place, the judge is obliged to take care and avoid any harm to the health and dignity of the examined person. When an important reason exists, such as a danger concerning the health of the interested person or a possibility of harming his dignity, direct proof does not take place.

Similar rules apply where direct proof concerns the demonstration of a mobile or the visit of an immobile. Direct proof is cancelled if the interested person has an important reason to object to it (Article 365 §1). Specific enforcement is, however, allowed (Article 365 §§2, 3).

C. Probative Effect of Tangible Evidence

365. The results of the inspection may be evaluated freely, following the general rule of Article 340. Since, however, these results are included in a public document (a judicial report or the minutes of a proceeding), it additionally produces the binding probative effects of a public document. The court is thus allowed to weigh freely solely what may be defined as constituting the subject matter of direct proof.

IV. Expert Reports

A. Definition and Distinctions

366. Experts[468] are defined as persons other than the parties who offer to the court evidence of the truth. A precise distinction is drawn between experts and witnesses. Whereas witnesses bring to the court their knowledge about facts they have observed, experts are asked questions of art, science or other technical matters of which they have specialized knowledge. Testimony deals with past facts. Experts express their opinions about present situations. Unlike witnesses, experts can be substituted.

The intermediate category of expert witnesses testify about past facts, which they were, however, capable of conceiving through their special knowledge. The CPC declares that provisions regarding witnesses also apply to expert-witnesses (Article 413). Their competence to testify and privileges to be excluded are treated similarly to those of witnesses.

Expertise is explicitly defined as a means of evidence (Article 339). Still, while all general stipulations regarding those means apply, experts are at the same time characterized as the auxiliary officials of the court (Article 369) who exercise a public function. They are accordingly treated as the court's assistants, e.g., with regard

468. G. Rammos, and Ch. Fragistas, 'L'expertise en Grèce', in *L'expertise dans les principaux systèmes juridiques d'Europe*, Travaux et recherches de l'Institut de Droit Comparé de Paris, Vol. XXXII (1967), pp. 261 ff., and pp. 291 ff.; K. Kerameus, *Die Entwicklung des Sachverständingenbeweises im deutschen und griechischen Zivilprozessrecht*, Prozessrechtliche Abhandlungen, Heft 26 (Diss Berlin, 1963).

to the mode of their appointment or substitution (Articles 370, 372), exclusion (Articles 373, 376), and their various procedural rights (e.g., Articles 369b, 380, 382).

B. Appointment of Experts: Extent of the Discretionary Power of the Judge

367. The CPC devotes a large number of Articles (368–390) to expert reports. Based on the idea that their use may cause excessive expenses or considerable delays to the proceedings, the Code seems to officially recognize that the judge may prefer to use other means. Article 368 draws a delicate distinction between 'special' and 'particular' knowledge. While 'particular' is the knowledge exclusively possessed by specialists, 'special' may also be the knowledge of any other person sufficiently qualified. When matters calling for 'particular' knowledge are to be decided, and expertise has been requested by a party, the court is obliged to use experts (Article 368 §2). However, if the knowledge to be used is considered 'special', the judge has the discretionary power to decide whether to resort to experts or not (Article 368 §1). *Areios Pagos*, however, still following an old tradition, refuses to review decisions of lower courts when they deal with the question of whether a certain issue is calling for 'special' or 'particular' knowledge. Thus, the courts have in fact fully retained their discretion to decide freely when expert reports are really indispensable.

368. Experts are appointed from a particular register kept in court (Articles 371, 372 CPC).[469] The court may, at its own discretion, select any other appropriate persons, public officers or private individuals. The number of experts also depends on the discretionary powers of the judge (Article 368 §1).

C. Probative Weight of Expert Reports

369. Article 387 repeats, in addition to the general principle of the free evaluation of evidence (Article 340), that the opinion of experts is weighed by the court freely. The judge who departs from the result of an expert report must give the precise reasons for this departure. The free evaluation of an expert concerns the results of the investigation. On the contrary, all elements related to its character as a public document, since it is conducted by a person exercising a public function, produce the binding probative effects of public documents.

D. Technical Consultants

370. In contrast to experts, who are appointed by the court, technical consultants are selected by the parties from a circle of persons qualified to be court-appointed

469. Royal Decree 566 of 22/29-8-1968 'On the Mode of Preparing and Keeping the Lists of Experts and Arbitrators'.

experts (Article 391). If the court decides to resort to expert reports, each party is allowed to appoint a technical consultant, who is mainly entrusted to help the parties and express his opinion on the technical matters investigated by the court-appointed experts (Article 392).

E. *Extrajudicial Private Opinions*

371. Private opinions on scientific, artistic or other technical matters regarding various fields of specialized knowledge (e.g., medical questions) are quite frequently presented to Greek courts on the initiative of the parties, even before the proof-taking proceeding has been commenced. According to Article 390, expert opinions related to questions within a pending dispute, when presented to the court upon the initiative of one of the parties, are evaluated by the court freely. The exact characterization of such extrajudicial opinions is, however, disputed. According to successive decisions of the plenary session of *Areios Pagos*,[470] these must rather be regarded as particular kind of documents, which are subject to a specific regulation, than a separate means of evidence.[471]

V. Testimony

A. *Definition*

372. Witnesses are defined as persons, other than the parties, who bring to the court their knowledge about the subject matter of proof. Whether such knowledge has been obtained directly (*testes ex visu*) or through information by other persons (*testes ex naratione*) is not relevant. This is an element to be weighed by the court in the course of the free evaluation of the respective statements.

B. *Statutory Restrictions of Testimony*

373. The CPC considers documentary evidence as more reliable compared to testimony. Under the influence of French law, the CPC of 1835 introduced in Greece what is known as the *limitation to the use of witnesses*.

Article 393 CPC has been now based on the underlying idea that when the object in litigation exceeds a certain amount, admissibility of testimony should be dependent on whether documentary evidence can be attainable. According to this rule),

---

470. 111/1981, *Dike* 1981, p. 311; 205/1981, *Archives of Judicial Decisions* 1981, pp. 268 (269); 848/1981, *Legal Tribune* 1982, p. 441; 12/2005, *Chronicles of Private Law* 2006, p. 40. *See also,* among a series of decisions, *Areios Pagos* 1314/1983, *Dike* 1984, p. 545 and recently *Areios Pagos* 8/2005, Hellenic Justice 2005, 694; 33/2005, *Dike* 2005, p. 765; 609/2007, *Dike* 2007. p. 755.

471. In case an extrajudicial private opinion will be regarded as a separate means, failure of the court to specifically mention that this was evaluated results in a review in cassation on the ground that the court has not taken into account a means produced by the parties (Art. 559 No. 119).

contracts and other collective private acts may not be proven by witnesses if their value is over EUR 30,000.[472] It is assumed that witnesses may freely be used for the production of evidence in all other cases. These include mainly tort cases. Article 393 §1 goes even further by also forbidding the use of witnesses with regard to additional acts when the main act is contained in a document, and their value exceeds EUR 30,000. According to this rule, the existence of, e.g., a condition may not be proven through testimony if the main act is in writing.

Article 393 §2 has also excluded testimony when the facts to be proven are directly contrary to the contents of an existing writing. This last limitation does not depend on the value of the facts to be proven. Its rationale is rather to secure the prestige of documentary evidence.

374. A number of extended exceptions make the basic exclusionary rules of testimony flexible. According to Article 394, testimony is always admissible when: (a) There exists a document which attains a reasonable degree of probability but still not so high as required (Article 394 §1α).[473] This document must be, however, valid and produce a probative effect. (b) The possession of a document is ethically or practically impossible (Article 394 §1b). (c) The document has been lost by chance (Article 394, §1c). If the last condition is met, testimony is also admissible in cases where writing is an essential element for the validity (*ad solemnitatem*) or an exclusive proof (*ad probationem*) of a legal act (Article 394 §2). (d) Testimony is, finally, admissible when the nature of the act or the special conditions under which it was contracted make it necessary (Article 394 § 1d). Commercial transactions may be thus proven by witnesses.

375. In terms of practical significance, the impact of the exclusionary rules of testimony has been considerably decreased. First, in ordinary proceedings before single-judge courts and in the most important particular proceedings, those rules did not apply.[474] Second, the exceptions to these restrictive rules, which are applied by the court on its own motion, can cover a wide range of disputes if interpreted widely. However, pursuant to the 2001 amendment of the CPC (Article 270 § 2b), these exclusionary rules should apply at the side of the newly established system of 'partly free' evidence in all ordinary proceedings,[475] whether before the three-member or the one-member district courts. This same rule also applies (Article 340 §1b) in all courts after the 2015 amendment.

C. *Competence to Give Evidence*

376. The basic rule is that every sane person may give evidence, regardless of nationality or age. Two categories of persons are incompetent witnesses. The first

472. This amount has previously EUR 5,900.
473. An equivalent term to the French 'commencement de preuve par écrit' is used also in Greece.
474. *See supra*, No. 349.
475. *Supra*, No. 349.

category (Article 399) includes persons who are excluded in all cases and are dismissed by the court on their own motion (Article 403 §1). The reason for this general incapacity is the physical or mental condition of certain persons. In addition, clergymen may not testify about facts which came to their knowledge through a confession. The second category (Article 400) includes persons who are dismissed by the court (Article 403 §2) only after an exception of the party against whom the witness is called. Persons who are obliged to keep secret the facts that came to their knowledge during their professional activities (physicians, lawyers, consultants, etc.) are thus not allowed to testify if their client objects. Psychologists were included in the list by Article 19 Law 4842/2021. Before the 2015 amendment, all persons who had a direct interest in the outcome of the case could also be excluded. Public functionaries and the military are finally excluded with regard to confidential facts related to their service.

The competence of children below 14 is entirely dependent on the existence of special reasons which make their testimony indispensable. The court will determine if such reasons exist. In that case, children may give unsworn evidence (Article 405). In matrimonial disputes or in disputes concerning the relations between parents and children, the children of the parties are absolutely incompetent witnesses (new Article 597 §2 No. 2).

D. Obligation to Give Evidence

377. All persons are in principle compellable witnesses. If they are unwilling to give evidence without reason, they are condemned to pay the expenses due to their absence and, at the discretion of the judge, an amount of money as a penalty (Article 398 §2). The judge may not use means of specific enforcement against a witness.

On certain occasions, witnesses may refuse to testify (Articles 401, 403 §3). Professionals enjoy the privilege of refusing to give evidence for all facts that came to their knowledge during their professional activities, even if they are not legally obliged to keep them secret. Relatives of one of the parties up to a certain degree (*see* Article 401 No. 2) may also claim the privilege not to testify. Psychologists have been included in the list by Article 20 Law 4842/2021. Furthermore, there is a privilege against self-incrimination; witnesses may refuse to give evidence about facts which can base a criminal charge against them or their relatives or which harm their dignity (Article 402 No. 1). Witnesses are also not obliged to testify about facts which convey a professional or artistic secret (Article 402 No. 2).

Since 2015, the examination of witnesses can also be conducted through video conference (Article 393 §3 CPC).

E. Probative Weight of Testimony

378. In accordance with the principle of free evaluation of evidence (Article 340), testimony is weighed by the court freely, irrespective of the number of witnesses or any other conditions.

VI. Examination of the Parties

A. General Aspects

379. The means called examination of the parties consists of the statements of one or more parties given through the procedure provided for testimony with regard to the facts related to the subject matter of proof (Articles 415–420 CPC). This was introduced in 1967, mainly following the German and Austrian examples (*Parteivernehmung*) for the purpose of replacing party oaths put by the court.

The examination of the parties is ordered by the court on its own motion or upon the request of a party (Article 416). Utilization of this means relies on the discretionary power of the court, whether of first instance or of appeal. In cases of parties lacking the capacity to conduct proceedings or of legal entities or of bankruptcy, the discretionary power of the court also covers determination of the person to be examined (Article 415 §§2–4, CPC).

Parties, as a rule, give unsworn evidence. However, notwithstanding certain exceptions (Article 417 §1b and §2), the court has the power to require either that one or all of the parties testify on oath with regard to some or all of the contested facts or that they subsequently reconfirm on oath the unsworn evidence they have already given (Article 417 §1α).

B. The Subsidiary Character of the Examination of the Parties: The Amendment of 1984

380. Examination of the parties was initially designed as a subsidiary means of proof. According to the previous version of Article 415 §1, the parties, as a rule, could be examined only when the contested facts had not been sufficiently proven, despite the use of other means. Legal theory had, nevertheless, accepted that the examination of the parties may be used as a main means of proof when other means do not exist.

Subsidiarity of the examination of the parties was probably the basic reason that Greek courts did not initially take full advantage of this means. It caused a remarkable delay in the unfolding of the overall proceedings since the parties could be examined only in a second stage of the evidentiary procedure after the other means had been exhausted without furnishing sufficient evidence. The courts, therefore, sometimes attempted to produce evidence by using their authority to order the personal appearance of the parties, which normally serves for the clarification of pleadings.

381. Under the aforementioned circumstances, the examination of the parties failed to achieve the success expected by the drafters of the Code.

The subsidiary character of the examination of the parties as a means of evidence has been abandoned by the 2011 amendment. Presently, according to Article 237 §13 CPC, the court on its own motion or upon a request by the parties, can decide to examine the parties even without their presence in the courtroom. The examination is transmitted simultaneously with sound and vision in the courtroom and the place where the parties are present. The examination of the parties is then deemed to have taken place before the court and has the same probative force as if it has taken place in the presence of the parties before the court.

C. *Distinction from Other Interrogatories of the Parties and from Testimony*

382. An obligation of the parties to appear when considered by the court necessary is provided by Article 245 §1 CPC. Legal theory draws a precise distinction between personal appearance of the parties and their examination.[476] A personal appearance of the parties under these stipulations merely aims toward interrogatories for the clarification of their factual statements. The examination of the parties is moreover destined to produce evidence.

383. The distinction between testimony and the examination of the parties is drawn from four respects. First, the rules which limit the use of witnesses may not possibly apply when parties are examined. Second, parties, as a rule, give unsworn evidence (Article 417 §1), whereas witnesses must testify on oath (Article 408). Third, the examination is not compulsory for the parties. According to Article 419 §2, no coercive measures can be used. Nevertheless, the parties who object to appear or to be examined will face the probability of an unfavourable outcome since their conduct during the examination is freely evaluated by the court (Article 420). Finally, whereas testimony is the main means, the examination of the parties had been initially designed as a subsidiary means of evidence. Solely, the procedure of receiving the evidence is in both means similar (Article 416).

D. *Probative Weight of the Examination of the Parties*

384. The examination of the parties is freely weighed by the court, even if they testify on oath. Failure of the summoned party either to appear without good cause in order to give sworn or unsworn evidence, or to testify or to answer the interrogatories or, finally, any differences between the unsworn and subsequent sworn evidence are also subject to a free evaluation by the court (Article 420 CPC).

VII. Party Oath

385. The CPC of 1967 maintained a kind of party oath, which was imposed by the court only on the initiative of the parties. The other type of party oath, known as judicial under the CPC of 1835 because it was put to a party on the court's own motion, had been partly abandoned.

476. K. Polyzogopoulos, *Parteianhörung und Parteivernehmung in ihrem gegenseitigen Verhältnis* (Diss. Tübingen, 1976).

In the context of the 2001 amendment, Articles 421–431, which provided for the operation of party oath as a separate means of evidence, were abolished because of their anachronism. Party oath has also been removed from the list of Article 339.[477] Currently, Articles 421–424 CPC have been utilized to treat the means of 'sworn attestation' in detail.[478]

VIII. Documentary Evidence

A. *Definitions and Distinctions*

386. In Greek law, documents are basically defined as human works which are destined to preserve the memory of past facts through the use of letters. They are generally regarded as more reliable means of evidence than testimony and have developed a continuously increasing practical significance, in particular during the recent decades, as documentary evidence under the CPC has also encompassed various means of technology.

Documents as means of evidence are understood in contradistinction to commercial papers and to writings which constitute an essential element for the validity of an act.[479] One must also distinguish documents which are destined to certify the operation of procedural acts. Even if containing evidentiary means, e.g., minutes or written reports on testimony, inspections by the court, expertise, etc., these are not governed by the rules of documentary evidence but rather by the means which they certify, e.g., testimony, expertise, etc.

387. A basic distinction of documentary evidence is in *public* and *private* instruments.

Public documents are those drawn by a competent public official or functionary or any other competent person exercising a public function within the scope of his authority in compliance with the prescribed legal formalities (Article 438 CPC). Practically significant type of public instruments are the notarial acts. All other writings are characterized as private.

Public documents are generally distinguished from private in three respects:

(a) as to the presumption of authenticity;
(b) as to the circle of persons against whom they produce their probative effects;
(c) as to the certainty of date. These important differences will be briefly discussed below.

477. *Supra*, No. 355.
478. *See* No. 411. Since 1 Jan. 2002, former Arts 425–431 CPC are not any longer effective.
479. Examples from the CC: Arts 498 (donation needs a notary deed); 1211 (agreement for pledge must be dressed either in the notarial form or in the form of a private document that has a certain date), etc.

B. Authenticity of Documents

1. Presumption of Authenticity of Public Acts

388. Public acts are regarded as authentic when they are in fact made by the public official who appears to have signed them and when the events therein recorded by the public official as having occurred in his presence have actually taken place before him. Public acts are presumed to be genuine insofar as they have not been attacked for falsity (Article 455 CPC). Although not irrebuttable, the presumption of the authenticity of public documents cannot be overturned by counterproof. A public document needs to be attacked through the institution of a special proceeding to determine its falsity (*see* Articles 460–465 CPC). The burden of proving the falsity lies then on the party attacking it.

2. Authenticity of Private Writings

389. Private writings are regarded as genuine when they have been actually made by the party who appears to have signed them and when they have not been subsequently altered. Unlike public documents, private writings are not presumed authentic. Once their authenticity has been contested by the party against whom private instruments are introduced, the party who relies on these documents bears the burden of proof (Article 457 §1 CPC).

C. Persons as to Whom a Document can Produce Evidence

390. Public documents can produce evidence against the world (Article 438), not only against the person who has signed them but also in his favour. On the contrary, private writings produce evidence only against their author (Article 447 *e contrario*). This rule is subject to two exceptions: (a) Private writings which are introduced by the adversary party can produce evidence also in favour of the party who has signed them (Article 447, *see also* Article 346); (b) Bookkeeping records of enterprises or of other professionals under certain conditions can be used also in their favour (Articles 447, 444).

D. Certainty of Date: Authentication of Private Writings

391. The date of a public document is binding both on the parties and on any third person unless attacked for falsity (Article 438). Private writings, on the contrary, have a certain date only as to the parties of the document, that is only against their authors (Article 446 *e contrario*). Once contested, the truth of the date of a private instrument as to third persons must be proven.

392. Private instruments can acquire a certain date as against third persons from the time the following conditions have been met (Article 446):

(a) When authenticated by a notary or another competent public official in the course of the exercise of his duties.
(b) When one of the signatories has died.
(c) When the essential contents of the private writing have been included in a public document.
(d) When another similar event has occurred which clearly proves the certainty of the date (e.g., incapacity to use handwriting).

E. *Probative Effect of Documentary Evidence*

1. Public Documents

393. Public documents are conclusive evidence regarding the performance of all acts that the public official states he has performed or of any event that this official records as having occurred in his presence (Article 438a CPC). Such conclusive proof can be overthrown only through an attack for falsity. No means of counterproof are admissible (Article 438b). In principle, a public act is also conclusive proof as to facts whose truth had to be examined by the official who signed it. However, conclusions recited by the public official can be contested and disproved through any means of evidence, including testimony (Article 440). No proceeding for the determination of falsity is required.

With regard to their main contents (Article 441), public acts which are executed in order to record the formation of or to confirm a juridical act prove conclusively as against the world the contents of the stated declarations (Article 441 §1), even if consisting of conditions which are not necessary to the act recited, provided that they are directly related to it (Article 441 §2). Counterproof is admissible through any type of evidence, except testimony, since this belongs to the scope of the exclusionary rule of Article 393 §2.

394. The probative effect of the main contents of other public documents which do not embody juridical acts but include mere attestations is not directly stipulated in the Code. It is, however, generally accepted that the statements therein recited which entail extrajudicial confessions of the involved parties are to be evaluated freely in accordance with the relevant provision (Article 352 §2 CPC). All other statements which favour a party or declarations of third persons are under certain conditions evaluated freely.

2. Private Writings

395. Insofar as their genuineness has been accepted through an actual or a presumed recognition or has been proven, private writings which are duly signed and, generally, drawn up in compliance with the provided formalities, are conclusive evidence that the statements which they contain have been made by the person who appears to have signed them (Article 445 CPC,). This binding probative effect can be overcome by any means of counterproof (Article 445 *in fine*), again except testimony (Article 393 §2). Accordingly, the prevailing opinion attributes to both public and private writings a similar binding probative effect.

Likewise, the respective public documents and private writings which do not contain juridical acts can be evaluated under certain conditions freely.

3. Foreign Public Acts

396. Pursuant to Article 439 CPC, all documents which have been drawn up by competent foreign public officials or functionaries or by other persons exercising a public function, provided that they are regarded as public following the law of the place where they were made, have a binding probative effect as the equivalent domestic public acts (Article 438). No authentication is required.

F. Mechanical Reproductions

397. Article 444 §1 No. 3 CPC has explicitly provided that photographs, films, recording tapes and all other kinds of mechanical portrayals are to be considered private documents. Hence, the proceeding of contesting the authenticity of private documents or of attacking them because of falsity applies to these mechanical reproductions; they also produce conclusive evidence about the facts they record unless another form of counterproof overcomes this effect (Article 448 §2). Photographed documents or photocopies have the same probative effect as the original if their accuracy is properly verified, e.g., by a lawyer (Article 449 §2).

Whether a telex or a fax can also be characterized as a private document under the scope of Article 444 §1. No. 3 CPC has been a point of discussion in recent years. Whereas there have been dissenting opinions as for the procedural treatment of a telex, the fax has not as yet created similar difficulties. However, the rapid progress of digitalization has made the above means redundant.

Electronic documents are governed by Law 4727/2020. Under certain conditions, an electronic signature should be compared to a real one.[480] Greek courts have often considered electronic documents as mechanical portrayals, in the sense of Article 444 §1(c) CPC, and have thus accepted that these have the probative effect of a private writing (Article 445). An explicit rule covering all kinds of electronic documents has now been inserted into the CPC (Article 444 §2).

480. I. Igglezakis, *Electronic documents as legal means of evidence in Greece* (*RHDI* 2002), pp. 531–539.

G. Bookkeeping Records of Enterprises or of Other Professionals

398. There are some special rules governing the probative force of bookkeeping records of enterprises, lawyers, notaries, bailiffs, physicians, pharmacists and midwives (Article 444 §1(b & c)). First, such entries are characterized as private writings (Article 444 §1) and, hence, produce conclusive evidence. Second, by way of exception, this probative effect can also be produced in favour of their author (Article 447). However, the exact scope of the binding probative effect of bookkeeping records depends on the person against whom they have been introduced (Article 448 §1 CPC). Against persons obliged to keep similar records, all facts therein recorded are deemed established. Counterproof is admissible. As for other persons against whom they have been produced, they can bring about conclusive proof only with regard to the amount of the contested claim, whenever this has been already proven through other means, and only within a time limit of one year since this was recorded.

IX. Presumptions as Self-Standing Means of Evidence

A. The Dual Meaning of the Term Presumption

399. The term presumption is currently understood under two meanings. Beyond indicating indirect proof (or 'evidence through presumptions'), as the deductive reasoning process of the judge (Article 336 §3 CPC),[481] this term has been used in Article 339 to also define all various means which can produce direct or indirect evidence, although they do not constitute part of the means which have been included within this specific statutory list.[482] This notion has been considered also covering those means which are not in full compliance with the specific requirements of each one of the other means, as provided by the Code, in order to be admissibly utilized as such.

B. Admissibility of Presumptions

400. Admissibility of presumptions is subject to rules which have been partly formed through a permanent practice. First, presumptions are not admissible where testimony has also been excluded (Article 395). According to the prevailing opinion in case law, seeking to secure the right to counter-roof of the party against whom presumptions were used, it was moreover required that testimony has been explicitly ordered through the decision which had ordered the proof taking.[483] The practical relevance of these conditions, however, had been considerably reduced since 1984, as the exclusionary rules of testimony did not actually apply to proceedings

481. *See supra*, No. 350.
482. *See supra*, No. 355.
483. *See supra*, Nos 372 ff. and *infra*, No. 412.

in t single-judge courts.[484] After the 2001 amendment, on the contrary, they have regained their significance. With the exception of particular proceedings, the utilization of presumptions has not remained free from the restrictions provided for the use of testimony in ordinary proceedings.[485] This also applies after the 2015 amendment on a general scale (Articles 395, 424 CPC). Second, presumptions cannot be utilized when contrary to fundamental principles of the law of evidence. Third, presumptions cannot be admissibly evaluated when their production overturns the conditions provided for by the rules governing the eponymous means.[486]

Greek courts have extensively utilized presumptions in recent years. Examples from a quite rich series of cases include: decisions of criminal courts; testimony taken in another proceeding, mainly criminal; various attestations of third persons provided that their genuineness is not contested and that they are not made in view of a proceeding; incomplete testimony; expertise of another proceeding, etc.

C. Probative Effect

401. Presumptions are weighed by the judge freely, in accordance with the general rule of Article 340. A court is allowed to rely on presumptions instead of other means, even on its own motion, when they produce more reliable evidence.

X. 'Sworn Attestations'

402. By way of exception, in proceedings before one-member district courts and justices of the peace, sworn depositions of witnesses (affidavits) given before a justice of the peace or a notary have been accepted as admissible means, on the condition that they have been effectuated before the hearing of the case and the adversary party was summoned at least two working days in advance. In terms of practical relevance, these attestations have in recent years been playing a significant role, as they operated in both ordinary and some particular proceedings.

Law 2915/2001 extended application of 'sworn attestations' to all first-instance ordinary proceedings, whether before three-member or the one-member district courts, on the additional condition that the use of testimony was permissible.

During the 2011 amendment, 'sworn attestations' were added to the list of eponymous means of evidence provided by Article 339. Law 4335/2015 has inserted four new provisions (Articles 421–424), which contain detailed rules governing the taking of evidence through 'sworn attestations' before a justice of the peace, a notary or even a consul. Lawyers were added to the list by Article 21 Law 4842/2021.

---

484. *See supra*, Nos 349 and 373 ff.
485. *See supra*, No. 375.
486. For example, Letters encompassing unsworn testimony of their authors written in view of a trial (*see*, *Areios Pagos* 1211/1975, *Legal Tribune* 1976, pp. 518 (519); 884/1976, *Legal Tribune* 1977, p. 340); attestations before a notary or the justice of the peace without summoning the other party (*see*, e.g., *Areios Pagos* 239/1975, *Legal Tribune* 1975, p. 654). In both cases those means have been regarded as violating the procedural guarantees of the means of testimony.

These are now considered admissible means again on the condition that the adversary party has been summoned at least two working days in advance (new Article 422 §1 CPC), while the parties if they so wish, may be present (Article 422 §2). Each party can now admissibly submit three 'sworn attestations' and two more as means of counter-proof in each instance (new Article 422 §3, as amended by Article 22 Law 4842/2021). In addition, many rules governing testimony can also apply (new Article 423 §1), including the rules excluding testimony. Article 424, which regulates the non-consideration of sworn attestations due to non-abidance of procedural requirements, was amended by Article 23 Law 4842/2021. The new provision lists four alternative conditions for non-admissibility of sworn attestations, thus providing more clarity to the letter of the rule.

Chapter 3. Administration of Evidence Before and After the 2015 Amendment

§1. The Evidentiary Proceedings Before 2001

403. Before the 2001 amendment, whenever the president of the three-member district court decided that this was the appropriate proceeding with regard to a specific case,[487] the first hearing of the case was followed by a non-final decision which contained a brief reasoning and was principally expected to rule on the admissibility and the legal foundation of the parties' requests Article 341 §2 CPC.

§2. Evidentiary Proceedings Before the 2015 Amendment[488]

I. Abolishment of the Decision Ordering Evidence in 2001

404. Law 2915/2001 introduced a uniform proceeding for all first-instance district courts. To achieve acceleration, an explicit rule provided for one single oral hearing, during which, as a rule, the entire stage of the administration of evidence was expected to be carried through. A final decision was then rendered on the basis of the evidence produced during this hearing. This also included reasoning on the admissibility and the legal foundation of the action. The judge was expected to have been informed about the action and the allegations of the parties before the oral hearing, as well as about their means of evidence, in particular about the subject matter and the burden of proof.

II. The Taking of Evidence

405. The taking of evidence was administered before the whole panel of the court. Means of evidence had to be introduced during the oral hearing, whereas the parties were requested to appear in person. They were examined, if needed, on the discretionary power of the judge.[489] The judge was principally obliged to rely on the means included within the list of Article 339 and also the rules dominating rigid evidence.[490] He was moreover allowed to evaluate supplementarily the same means, even though they did not satisfy the requirements provided by the Code,[491] as well as extrajudicial sworn attestations.[492] Supplementary utilization of the two latter categories of means of evidence has been, however, allowed only as long as exclusionary rules of testimony did not apply. The judge was obliged to examine at least one

487. *See supra*, No. 222.
488. N. Klamaris, *Die wichtigsten Grundlagen des Beweisverfahrens nach griechischem Zivilprozessrecht*, in *Zwischenbilanz – Festschrift für Dagmar Coester-Waltjen zum 70. Geburtstag* (Bielefeld, Gieseking 2015), pp. 1025–1036.
489. *See supra*, No. 381.
490. *See supra*, No. 347.
491. *See supra*, No. 349.
492. *See supra*, No. 411.

witness for each side from those who had appeared before him during the hearing. Direct evidence and expertise could be ordered through an oral announcement of the court. As a rule, all evidence was expected to be produced during this single oral hearing. However, on the discretionary power of the judge, an order for the taking of supplementary evidence could be issued.[493]

III. Introduction of Documentary Evidence

A. *Time of Introduction*

406. All documentary evidence had to be introduced at least twenty days before the hearing, on penalty of inadmissibility. Documents ought to be attached to the pleadings which were filed with the clerk. Delayed documents were however not entirely excluded. They could be produced even in proceedings of appeal under certain conditions.[494]

B. *Forced Production of Documents*[495]

407. Parties are obliged to produce documents which they have utilized or to which they have referred during a proceeding (Article 450 §1 – CPC). Furthermore, according to Article 450 §2, every party or any other person who possesses relevant documents for the production of evidence is obliged to demonstrate them before the court, except if an important cause can justify a refusal. The law indicates that such a just cause may be admitted in all cases in which there is a privilege for witnesses to refuse to testify.

The forced production of documentary evidence is ordered by the court on the application of a party (*see* Article 451). The order can be addressed either to a party or to a third person. Forced production of documents may be effectuated through specific enforcement (Articles 452, 941, 946 CPC).

IV. Evidentiary Proceedings Before One-Member Courts

408. In proceedings before one-member district courts and justices of the peace, all evidence was produced in one single oral hearing.[496] After the 2001 amendment

493. For details *see* Art. 270, §5.
494. *Supra*, No. 292.
495. A. Koutsouradis, *Die Informationsbeschaffung im materiellen Recht und im Prozeßrecht. Gezeigt am Beispiel des griechischen Rechts*, in *Recht und Rechtsdurchsetzung – Festschrift für Hans Ulrich Walder* (Zürich, Schulthess Juristische Medien 1994), pp. 25–47; D. Tsikrikas, *Örtliche und internationale Zuständigkeit der griechischen Gerichte bei einer Klage auf Akteneinsicht und Urkundenvorlage*, *ZZPInt* 2007, S. 109–117.
496. *See supra*, No. 413.

of the CPC, evidentiary proceedings before one-member courts were governed by the same rules as those applying to three-member district courts.[497]

§3. Evidentiary Proceedings after the 2015 Amendment

409. The rules governing the administration of evidence have been modified by Law 4335/2015. In the context of the written procedure before the first-instance courts introduced by Article 237 CPC with regard to the ordinary proceedings,[498] all kinds of documentary evidence, as well as 'sworn attestations', had to be submitted within one hundred days[499] from the filing of the action (Article 237 §1 CPC). New evidence could be produced only in reply to the initial submissions within fifteen days from the date of expiry of the one hundred-day time limit (new Article 237 §2 CPC). A main characteristic of this new type of evidentiary proceedings in Greek law concerns the fact that the use of testimony in the context of ordinary proceedings before the first-instance courts has been now allowed only exceptionally. Pursuant to Article 237, §6 CPC, this can occur only when, on the basis of the contents of the file and at the discretion of the judge, the examination of witnesses before the court is absolutely necessary. As a rule, this concerns one witness for each side from those persons who have already submitted 'sworn attestations'. Another main feature of the 2015 amendment is the differentiation which has been introduced between particular and ordinary proceedings, as Law 4335/2015 with regard to particular proceedings has basically maintained the type of evidentiary proceeding operating under former Law 2915/2001[500] (Article 591 CPC). Article 237(1) CPC has been recently amended by Law 4842/2021. The novel version extends the time for producing evidence to 90 (for residents in Greece) or 120 days (for residents abroad or persons of unknown whereabouts) following the lapse of the term to serve the claim to the defendant. Hence, the connecting point is the service, not the filing of the claim anymore. Fresh evidence may be produced only in reply to the initial submissions within 15 days, starting from the date of expiry of the 90- or 120-day time limit, respectively (Article 237 §2).

497. *Supra*, Nos 413–414.
498. *See supra*, Nos 218 ff.
499. In case the defendant or another joined party resides abroad, or is of unknown residence, this time limit extends to 130 days (new Art. 237, §1d CPC).
500. *See supra*, Nos 413 ff.

Part VIII. Particular Proceedings

Chapter 1. General Aspects

410. Particular proceedings have been operating in Greece at the side of ordinary proceedings ever since the old CPC. These were gradually introduced through special legislation to attain immediacy, orality and acceleration. The CPC of 1967 integrated several of those particular proceedings in its fourth Book, designed to institute the appropriate type of procedures with regard to the nature of certain disputes. Particular proceedings are henceforth understood as a special type of proceedings which operate parallel to ordinary in order to satisfy specific procedural goals.

The major significance of particular proceedings must be attributed to two reasons: First, to the continual creation of new particular proceedings which were added to the CPC by special statutes, basically following the guidelines of the particular proceedings for labour disputes, as this has operated quite successfully. Thus, to counterbalance the inadequacies of traditional mechanisms, a wide range of civil disputes was removed from the scope of ordinary and placed in particular proceedings. Second, to the actual extension of particular proceedings for labour disputes to the totality of disputes (belonging first to the subject matter competence of single-judge courts and then to the three-member district courts), formerly adjudicated through the traditional model of ordinary proceedings. On the basis of these developments, one-member district courts and justices of the peace were normally entertaining disputes under a speedy and simplified proceeding. Even three-member district courts applied this same proceeding.

Before the 2015 amendment, the rules for particular proceedings were defined in former Articles 591–681D. These ninety-three Articles contained several repetitions, as well as many internal references between different types of particular proceedings, which were gradually introduced through the years. To avoid unnecessary repetitions, Law 4335/2015 has restructured the fourth Book of the CPC by creating only three groups of particular proceedings. However, this reorganization has not caused essential modifications.

The first group (Articles 592–613 CPC) treats the overall family disputes; the second (Articles 614–622B) covers the particular proceeding introduced for some disputes of financial character, like those emerging from negotiable instruments, lease and condominiums, the use of cars, labour contracts, and contracts involving the remuneration of certain professionals; the third group (Articles 623–645) treats the orders of payment and the orders for the return of a leased immovable.

411. The relationship between ordinary and the various types of particular proceedings is governed by the general rule of Article 591 §1, recently amended by Article 39 Law 4842/2021. Rules regulating ordinary proceedings (Articles 1–590 CPC) still apply unless they are not in compliance with specific provisions of particular proceedings. The operation of appropriate provisions of a particular proceeding is regarded as a procedural prerequisite. The court examines whether a case has been introduced pursuant to the proper proceeding; if not, it proceeds accordingly on its own motion (Article 591 §6 CPC). With the exception of orders of payment, all other particular proceedings have been designed as the only type of legal protection available. Parties are, hence, not entitled to select between several procedural possibilities.

The general goal of most particular proceedings is the institution of a flexible framework dominated by the principles of orality and immediacy in the context of the concentration of the procedure in a unique oral hearing. A second general characteristic is the emphasis on the model of a more active judge, who is partly relieved from the strict rules of ordinary proceedings. A third common trait of most particular proceedings is the introduction of special rules involving methods of review. In the proceedings for matrimonial disputes and disputes between parents and children, however, one must especially observe certain restrictions to the principles of the party's free disposition and presentation.

Chapter 2. The Main Characteristics of Each Particular Proceeding

§1. The Proceeding for Family Law Disputes

412. All disputes relating to divorce, annulment of marriage, declarations on the existence or non-existence of marriage, the personal relationship of the spouses during marriage, as well as agreements on cohabitation according to Law 3719/2008 (Article 592 §1 CPC), are adjudicated through the particular proceeding for family disputes.[501] This provides for some flexible rules regarding the capacity to conduct proceedings in one's own name (Article 594). In addition, some means of proof are to a considerable extent either restricted or treated differently (new Article 597 §2). The defaulting defendant is deemed to be present (Article 595). This stipulation allows the court, despite this party's absence, to enter the merits of the case. Public prosecutors can, in some instances, act as parties (Articles 603 §2, 604). Finally, international jurisdiction[502] and res judicata[503] are governed by specific rules (Articles 601, 605).

413. In contrast to the aforementioned disputes, a divorce 'by consensus' could be initially granted through the proceeding of voluntary jurisdiction (*see* former Article 1441 CC). Article 1441 CC has been replaced by Article 22 of Law 4509/2017. According to the detailed rules of this Article, a divorce 'by consensus' can now be granted by a notarial deed.

414. Disputes relating to the (a) challenge of paternity, (b) challenge of maternity,[504] (c) recognition of the existence or non-existence of the relationship of parent and child or parental care, (d) recognition of paternity of children born out of wedlock, (e) recognition of the existence or non-existence or the nullity of a voluntary recognition of children born out of wedlock, or the challenge of such a voluntary recognition, (f) recognition of the existence or non-existence or of the nullity of adoption or its termination, and (g) recognition of the existence or non-existence of guardianship, are also entertained through the proceeding for family disputes (Article 592 §2 CPC). In addition, pursuant to Article 607, a non-rebuttable presumption has been established in order to support the determination of paternity or maternity.[505] Disputes involving alimony of children can be joined (Article 610 CPC).

415. Furthermore, pursuant to Article 592 §3 CPC, disputes involving (a) maintenance and some other money claims according to family obligations, (b) the exercise of parental care, and (c) the use of the family home and the partition of movable property between the spouses when the marital life is disturbed, are also handled

501. A. Koutsouradis, 'Die Ehestreitigkeiten nach griechischem Zivilprozessrecht', *Volume in Honour of G. Mitsopoulos* (Athens/Komotini, Sakkoulas, 1993), pp. 737–756.

502. *See supra*, No. 148. For the forum of matrimonial disputes in particular *see supra*, No. 125.

503. *See supra*, No. 243.

504. Initially added by Art. 5 §3, Law 3089/2002, effective since 23 Dec. 2002. *See also* the newly introduced Arts 1458 and 1464 CC.

505. *See supra*, No. 364.

through the particular proceeding for family disputes. The court is authorized to establish personal contact with the child involved if needed (Article 612 CPC).

§2. The Proceeding for Orders of Payment

416. Orders of payment are granted through a particular ex parte proceeding (Articles 623–636A CPC), which is further discussed in the chapter on enforcement.[506]

§3. The Proceeding for Certain Categories of Money Claims

417. All disputes directly emerging from negotiable instruments, such as bills of exchange, promissory notes, cheques, etc., can be adjudicated through this particular proceeding (Articles 614 §8, 622B). Consistently with the substantive function of negotiable instruments, this proceeding is designed to achieve acceleration. It requires an immediate submission of the negotiable instruments (Article 622B) on penalty of inadmissibility of the action, whereas all allegations must be immediately proven, the action being otherwise dismissed.

418. Disputes concerning (a) all kinds of lease of things (Article 614 §1 CPC) and (b) the relationship between proprietors of apartments in condominiums or these persons and the condominium's managers (Article 614 §2 CPC) must also observe the particular proceeding for money claims.

419. Labour disputes (Article 614 §3) are now treated in this particular proceeding (Articles 614–622B), whose main institutions, especially those concerning the wider admissibility of evidence (former Article 671) in a unique oral hearing, were gradually used on an extended scale.[507] Some of the other peculiarities of this proceeding are: standing to sue, or the right to intervene is also granted to trade unions, chambers or other associations (Article 622),[508] which can thus protect their members; when default occurs, parties are deemed to be present and the court proceeds to the examination of the merits (Article 621 §2b).

420. Disputes involving the remuneration of certain professionals (Article 614 §§4, 5) are also handled through the particular proceeding for money claims (Article 622A).

421. The same proceeding applies to disputes arising out of the use of cars and car insurance contracts (Article 614 §6).

506. *See infra*, No. 464.
507. *Supra*, Nos 23, 349.
508. Law 3189/2003 (Art. 9, §1) had inserted Art. 675A to the CPC, which granted their right to bring an intervention even in the context of cassation proceedings.

422. Law 2145/1993 instituted a new particular proceeding in order to accelerate adjudication of actions seeking monetary compensation or reparation of moral damage for injury provoked by press, radio, television, or, generally, all actions tending to the protection of personality against such infringements. The above actions are now handled through the newly created proceeding for money claims (Article 614 §7).

§4. SPECIAL RULES FOR CERTAIN TYPES OF DISPUTES: SMALL CLAIMS

423. The CPC has distinguished between particular proceedings and 'special rules'. The latter involve small claims (Articles 466–471),[509] actions seeking for an account (Articles 473–477), and actions for partition (Articles 478–494).

For an action to be handled through the simplified and flexible procedure of small claims (Articles 468–471), operating in Greece on the basis of special legislation of Austrian origin since 1925, it must belong to the subject matter competence of the justices of the peace, and not concern actions in rem related to immovables (Article 466 §1 CPC). In order to reach the substantial truth in a cheaper and speedy manner, justices of the peace are relieved (Article 469 §2 CPC) from any procedural formalities. Currently, small claims' value must not exceed the amount of EUR 5,000. Starting from 1 January 2022, a new system of case management has been introduced by Articles 24–25 Law 4842/2021, which amended Articles 468–469 CPC. The action must be served within ten days following filing to the defendant. If the defendant resides abroad or is of unknown residence, service shall have to be completed within thirty days following filing. The novel reform provides for e-filing corridors by using standardized documents (Article 468 §4 CPC). However, the e-filing system depends on the publication of pertinent ministerial ordinances, which have not been issued yet.

The special rules which involve the actions on accounting and partition are mostly of a highly technical nature.

509. K.D. Kerameus, *Die Erledigung geringfügiger Streitigkeiten nach griechischem Recht*, *RHDI* 1977, pp. 91–108 = Studia Iuridica III (Athens, Sakkoulas/Kluwer 1995), pp. 200–218.

Part IX. Conservatory Measures and Enforcement of Judgments

Chapter 1. Conservatory Attachment

§1. General Remarks

424. The CPC has provided for a complex of conservatory measures which may be ordered following the procedure for provisional remedies and tend to secure future enforcement.[510] These include judicial security; provisional recordation of a real mortgage; conservatory attachment; judicial custody; and sealing, unsealing, inventory and public deposit of property.

In this chapter, we are going to discuss the main points of the aforementioned measures, following the order of the CPC.

§2. The Conservatory Measures

I. Judicial Security

A. *Definition*

425. The mildest among conservatory measures is 'judicial security' (Articles 704–705; 162–168 CPC). This tends to the public deposit, either of a fixed amount of money or of commercial papers or even of a bank guarantee (Articles 163–164), which is destined to be used for the future satisfaction of the contested claim as soon as the creditor has attained an enforceable title. When a public deposit has been effected, a real right of pledge is established in order to secure the claim for which this measure was ordered (Article 166). Nevertheless, a judgment ordering a security deposit in the above sense is technically not regarded as an executory title per se. It rather functions as a burden on the debtor for compliance under the penalty of

510. P. Yessiou-Faltsi & E. Podimata, *Preliminary or Summary Proceedings: Scope and Importance in Greek Civil Procedure*, *RHDI* 2004, pp. 407 ff.; N. Klamaris, *Die einzelnen Sicherungsmaßnahmen im Rahmen des provisorischen Rechtsschutzes nach dem griechischen Zivilprozessrecht,* in: *Rechtslage – Rechtserkenntnis – Rechtsdurchsetzung. Festschrift für Eberhard Schilken zum 70. Geburtstag* (Munich, Verlag C.H. Beck 2015), pp. 339–352.

a more burdensome conservatory measure (e.g., pre-notice of mortgage, attachment), which will be otherwise imposed by the judge instead of the non-deposited security.

B. Proceeding

426. A judge may order the public deposit of a security under the general prerequisites and through the procedure followed for all provisional remedies. Within the scope of the procedure's general principles, under which the judge is not bound to the applicant's request (Article 692 §1) and may order the less oppressive kind of provisional relief (Article 692 §3), judicial security operates in two forms, optional and compulsory.

In the first case, it belongs to the discretionary power of the judge to order the deposit of a security in favour of the applicant, although he has not requested this form of protection when both the debtor's compliance and its efficaciousness seem probable.

In the second case, if another, more oppressive, conservatory measure has been ordered, its substitution through judicial security becomes compulsory for the judge who has issued it or who adjudicates over the main action when the debtor brings a special request to this end. It must be, however, stressed that this substitution retains its compulsory character only to the extent the securing of a money claim, or of a claim capable of being converted in money terms, is being requested (Article 705 §1). In such a case, while the debtor does not comply, the former, more oppressive measure remains. Conflicting interests of the litigants seem in this manner to be equally served. Therefore, when the former conservative measure has been ordered for securing non-money claims, which may not be converted into money, its substitution is again relied on the discretion of the judge, who must then particularly determine whether judicial security may sufficiently secure that claim (Article 705 §2).

C. Effects

427. When the creditor obtains an executory title, the conservatory measure of judicial security, upon the rendering of a special judicial order (Article 168), is transformed into a means of enforcement. Satisfaction of the secured claim then follows the general rules for the privileged position of the real right of pledge.

II. Pre-notice of Mortgage

A. Definition and Requirements

428. Pursuant to Greek law perceptions, mortgage (Articles 1257–1345 CC) is a real right established on the debtor's or even a third person's immovable property in order to secure the satisfaction of a creditor's claim by way of priority on the thing (*see* definition by Article 1257). The pre-notice of a mortgage secures only a priority right for obtaining a mortgage (Article 1277a CC). It is, however, subject to exactly the same requirement of inscription to the 'Mortgage Registry' as a genuine mortgage, the sole difference being an explicit reference to a pre-notice (Article 1276 CC). The latter is expected to convert to a mortgage as soon as a final judgment for the secured claim has been obtained. In such a case, mortgage is deemed inscribed as from the date of the pre-notice (Article 1277b CC).

Pursuant to Article 706 CPC, pre-notice currently operates as one of the conservatory measures. While this is most often sufficiently effective, it is indeed at the same time, less oppressive for the debtor than attachment. The reason is that pre-notice of a mortgage on immovable property does not hinder the transfer of ownership or other real rights.

B. Proceeding

429. The principal title for a pre-notice is the judgment issuing this conservatory measure (Article 706). Pre-notice is, accordingly, ordered by the competent judge (Article 706 §1) upon affirmation of the general prerequisites and again through the proceeding of provisional remedies, also depending on successful assertions by the applicant on the existence of an imminent danger (Article 682). A judgment allowing the inscription of a pre-notice must also specify the exact amount of the claim secured (Article 706 §2). Pre-notice is then established upon the inscription of the judgment to the Mortgage Registry (Articles 1274, 1276 CC).

A pre-notice may also be established through the sole inscription of an order of payment to the Mortgage Registry without any previous judgment issuing this conservatory measure (Article 724). Hence, beyond their enforceability, orders of payment can *ipso jure* confer a title for inscribing a pre-notice. This also applies to judgments, which are still subject to ordinary methods of appeal.

While private will may not typically confer a title for a pre-notice, in contrast to mortgage (Article 1261 CC), procedural tactics in Greece tend to practically establish such an additional method, most often in order to avoid the increased expenses of a conventional mortgage, despite some reservations expressed in theory. This is very frequently attempted through the participation and prompt consent of the opposing party before the competent judge (Article 687 §2). Thus, an essentially unopposed order for issuing this conservatory measure is at once attained.

The most effective method, enjoying considerable practical relevance, consists of the prompt rendering of an order in favour of the applicant, which provisionally prohibits further transfer of ownership or establishment of a mortgage with regard to an immovable, under the penalty of invalidity (Article 176 CC), until the judgment on the requested pre-notice has been rendered. This provisional order is also noted in the Mortgage Registry (*see* now new Article 691A(3) CPC.

C. *Effects*

430. The inscription of a pre-notice has both substantive and procedural effects. On the one hand, pre-notice interrupts prescription of the money claim (Article 1280 CC) and grants a priority for establishing a mortgage. On the other hand, pursuant to Article 41 of the Introductory Law to the CPC, it enjoys equal procedural treatment to a mortgage. Hence, creditors secured through a mere pre-notice are also entitled to announce their claims (Article 972 CPC). Thus, when distribution of the proceeds, derived from the public auction, is effected, they enjoy equally preferential treatment to those secured through a mortgage, as from the date of the pre-notice (Articles 976, 977 and 1007 §1).[511] The subsequent conversion of the pre-notice into a full mortgage, or at least the acquisition of an enforceable instrument, is a condition of this preferential treatment (Articles 1007, §1b, and 978). Pre-notice is converted into a mortgage upon the claim being adjudicated by a final judgment (Article 1277 CC) and upon the relevant inscription in the Mortgage Registry within the next ninety days (Article 1323 No. 3 CC). When pre-notice has been inscribed on the basis of an order of payment, it may be converted into a mortgage upon expiration of the two successive time limits for raising an opposition (Articles 632, 633 §2) or upon rejection of such an opposition (Article 29 Introductory law of the CPC).[512] It is furthermore accepted that under the above two conditions, even pre-notices which have been inscribed on the basis of a specific judgment (Articles 706, 682) may now be converted into a mortgage based on the order of payment.

III. Conservatory Attachment

A. *Definition and Requirements*

431. The most restrictive and, therefore, most effective conservatory measure within Greek law is conservatory attachment (Articles 707–724 CPC). This refers to the seizure of all kinds of the debtor's property (Article 707), allowed by the competent court, in order to secure a money claim exclusively, upon affirmation of the general prerequisites and through procedure of provisional remedies, before an executory title has been obtained. The lack of an enforceable instrument is hence substituted through a judgment, which must specify the exact amount of the claim secured (Article 708).

Compared to the pre-notice of a mortgage, attachment must be distinguished in three respects: first, its object may extend to all property (movables, immovables, other real rights, ships, aeroplanes, claims, and other special assets), hence, it is not limited to immovables (Article 707); second, in contrast to a pre-notice, by suspending the debtor's power of disposal (Article 715 §1), attachment results in prohibiting transfer of the seized property; third, attachment may not secure precedence of satisfaction, when the proceeds of the future auction will be distributed. Unlike

511. *See infra*, Nos 483–484.
512. *See infra*, No. 464.

both pre-notice and judicial security, attachment may not lead to the establishment of a real security right, neither of a real mortgage nor a pledge. It belongs, nevertheless, to the discretionary power of the judge whether attachment will be ordered for all property of the debtor *in abstracto* or with respect to some particular objects, this specification being for evident reasons compulsory, solely when attachment involves ships or aeroplanes (Article 709). It must be finally stressed that pursuant to Article 715 §5, and due to the restrictive character of attachment, the creditor is subject to a limit of thirty days for bringing the main action under the penalty of its prompt removal.

Like pre-notice of a mortgage, attachment may also be effected on the basis of an order of payment (new Article 724 §1) for the purpose of securing the claim, without the issuing of conservatory measures being necessary. Since the 2015 amendment, this possibility has also been recognized by creditors who have obtained a decision subject to ordinary methods of appeal. Attachment may, nevertheless, be suspended if payment or non-existence of the claim has been shown as probable (new Article 724 §2). When attachment is based on an order of payment, the creditor is moreover not subject to a time limit for bringing the main action (Article 715 §5(c)).

B. Proceeding

432. The CPC covers attachment through a detailed regulation. Proceedings differ with regard to movables or real rights on movables possessed by the debtor (Article 711), claims or movables possessed by a third person (Article 712), ships or aeroplanes or real rights on those movables (Article 713) and immovables (Article 714). The above extensive regulation is based on the different modes of seizure within enforcement proceedings, including exceptions to the principle of attachability (*see* Article 710). The attached property is subject to guardianship under judicial control (Articles 716–718). The debtor's capacity for its disposal is suspended (Article 715 §1).

C. Effects

433. The ultimate goal of attachment is fulfilled when the creditor has obtained an enforceable title for the claim provisionally secured. Under this condition, he may be satisfied by promptly commencing enforcement on the attached property (Article 722). On the contrary, when enforcement proceedings have been commenced by another creditor, satisfaction of creditors secured by attachment may be effected only through their provisional participation in the distribution of the proceeds of the auction (Article 723). Upon eventual acquisition of an executory title, their actual payment may be realized.

IV. Custody

A. *Definition and Proceeding*

434. In contrast to attachment, custody is a conservatory measure which secures future enforcement of non-money claims. As a self-contained remedy, dependent on the general prerequisites (Articles 682 ff.) of all other measures of provisional relief, custody must be distinguished from other forms of guardianship treated in various provisions of the CC (i.e., Articles 831–833, 359–360, 1226). Its scope comprises all kinds of movable or immovable property, including enterprises (Articles 725 §1). It even extends to commercial or other professional books, documents, or other objects when the applicant has a right to request their use for the production of evidence (Article 725 §2) through the particular action provided by the CPC (Articles 450–453).

A general clause (Article 725) allows custody in all kinds of disputes regarding the aforementioned property, whether based on real or personal rights. This conservatory measure, therefore, has also been enjoying considerable practical relevance.

B. *Effects*

435. Beyond appointment of a custodian by the court and subordination of the involved property under his administration (Article 726), custody leads to a provisional prohibition of property transfer (Articles 727, 715 §1). Likewise, in attachment, such suspension of the debtor's capacity to dispose of his property is exceptionally subject to the condition that the main action is brought before the competent court within the next thirty days. Otherwise, the conservatory measure automatically expires (Articles 727, 715 §5).

Similarly, as in attachment, when the creditor has obtained an enforceable instrument with regard to the secured claim, he may be satisfied through normal enforcement proceedings (Articles 727, 722 §1).

V. Sealing, Unsealing, Inventory and Public Deposit of Property

436. Sealing, unsealing, inventory and public deposit of property, when ordered as conservatory measures (Articles 737–738), also seek to secure future enforcement. Although they do not effect the capacity of disposal over the involved property, they are successively used as preparatory measures in case there is a danger that otherwise enforcement cannot be successful.

§3. Judicial Review

437. An order for a preliminary seizure or another conservatory measure is not subject to a judicial review by methods of appeal. It may be, however, revoked as for all other provisional remedies.[513]

513. *See supra*, Nos 264 and 267.

Chapter 2. Enforcement of Judgments

§1. Enforcement of Domestic Judgments

I. Introductory Remarks

A. Methods of Enforcement in the Greek Law of Execution

438. Greek law[514] provides for several methods of execution primarily based on the nature of the creditor's claim. Each of these methods is activated by special means, applied to the particularities of the enforced obligation. The various methods and means of enforcement, as well as the rules applicable to each, are included exclusively in the Special Part of the eighth Book of the CPC, dedicated to the Law of Enforcement (Articles 904–1054).[515] The Introductory Law to the Code (Articles 1, 4, 52) has abolished most of the previous special pieces of legislation dealing with execution. However, as a matter of government policy, some special laws, introducing specific rules when the State or special legal entities are involved, are still operating. Of great practical significance are: (a) the 'Code of Collecting Public Revenues' (Law 4978/2022) and (b) the 'Special Legislation on Corporations', which extends to banks (Legislative Decree of 17 July 1923).

Following the German and Austrian patterns, and unlike the Romanic law system, Greek law has adopted the principle of 'execution *in natura*', which applies not only to money but also to non-money claims.

514. The initial numbers 441–445, 464–465 and 469–477 of Ch. 2, §1, were based on a previous elaboration by Dr Leda Pipsou, (now) ordinary Professor of Law, University of Thessaloniki. The author wishes to thank her and acknowledge her kind and effective contribution.

515. N. Klamaris & G. Orfanidis, 'Die Zwangsvollstreckung der gerichtlichen Entscheidungen und die Vollstreckungsmittel der Gerichte nach dem griechischen Zivilprozessrecht', *RHDI*, 1985–1986, pp. 335–358 (343 ff.); P. Yessiou-Faltsi and L. Pipsou, 'The Law of Execution Faced with the Social Phenomenon of "Overrunning into Debt", Taking into Account the EEC Member States' Law', A National Report for Greece, *Actualités du droit*, Revue de la Faculté de Droit de Liège, 1995, pp. 689 ff.; same authors, in de Leval (ed.), *Seizure and Overindebtedness in the European Union, Civil Procedure in Europe* I (Kluwer Law International 1997), pp. 323 ff.; D. Tsikrikas, *Bemerkungen zur Struktur und Funktion des griechischen Vollstreckungsrechts*, *ZZP Int* 1996, p. 119 et seq.; P. Yessiou-Faltsi, *Prinzipien der Einzelzwangsvollstreckung in der griechischen im Vergleich zur deutschen Zivilprozeßordnung*, in *Festschrift für Hans Friedhelm Gaul zum 70. Geburtstag* (Bielefeld, Gieseking 1997), pp. 815–830. On constitutional challenges in the field of compulsory execution, *see* P. Arvanitakis, *Verfassungsrechtliche Probleme der Zwangsvollstreckung zur Befriedigung privatrechtlicher Ansprüche nach griechischem Recht*, *ZZP* 111 (1998), pp. 463–485. *See also* N. Klamaris, *Zum Stand des griechischen Zwangsvollstreckungsrechts. Eine zusammenfassende Skizze*, *ZZP* 2008, pp. 475–502. Focusing on the amendments introduced by Law 4335/2015, C. Apalagaki, *Griechisches Zwangsvollstreckung und die Reform der ZPO durch das Gesetz 4335/2015*, in *Fairness Justice Equity: Festschrift für Reinhold Geimer zum 80. Geburtstag* (C.H.Beck 2017), pp. 2–30.

B. Specific Performance

439. The CPC draws a clear distinction between specific performance, which concerns all kinds of non-money claims, and enforcement to satisfy a money claim. The methods of execution, as well as the means applicable to each, constitute a '*numerus clausus*', and they may not be modified or replaced by agreements between the parties.

Specific performance applies to obligations to deliver or hand over movable (Articles 941 and 942) or immovable (Article 943) property, as well as to obligations to perform (Articles 945, 946, 949), or not to perform or not to oppose a certain act (Article 947). Provisions made for specific performance do not deprive the debtor of the right to seek compensation if enforcement was impossible or did not lead to successful results (Article 948).

C. Means of Enforcement of Money Claims: Attachment, Compulsive Administration of Property, Imprisonment

440. To effectuate methods of enforcement of money claims, the CPC provides three ordinary means. The most common in practice is attachment. Among the two additional means, the first is a form of receivership, called compulsive administration of the debtor's immovables or business (Articles 1034–1046). The second consists of the debtor's imprisonment (Articles 1047–1054). Although abolished by the CPC of 1967 for humanistic reasons, the institution actually survived in commercial life through special legislation. Upon the major amendment of the CPC in 1971, imprisonment was integrated again into the Code as an effective means to compel, indirectly, satisfaction of money claims. Imprisonment was imposed by the final decision, which ought to be a *formal* res judicata for a period of up to one year and for claims which exceed the amount of EUR 30,000,[516] only on merchants for commercial debts. Since the 2011 amendment, imprisonment is now allowed only in tort claims. In addition to its rather infrequent practical use, the constitutionality of imprisonment is under question.[517] While the theory is unanimously against this means, *Areios Pagos* has on some occasions accepted it. Since 1997, after ratification of the Covenant on Civil and Political Rights (Law 2462/1997),[518] Greek courts steadily accepted, on the basis of Article 11[519] that imprisonment can be utilized only in case the debtor is in the position to satisfy his creditor but refuses to do so.

The question of the constitutionality of imprisonment for debts against the State was brought before the Special Highest Court of Greece after the rendition of

516. *See* Min. Dec. 12082/2004, effective since 20 Feb. 2009.
517. K. Beys, 'Die verfassungsrechtlichen Grenzen der Zwangsvollstreckung im griechischen Recht', *ZZP* 1988, pp. 165 ff.
518. *Supra*, No. 29.
519. 'No one shall be imprisoned merely on the ground of inability to fulfil a contractual obligation.'

conflicting judgments on the issue by the two Supreme Courts,[520] i.e., the Council of State[521] and *Areios Pagos*[522] With its leading ruling 1/2010,[523] the Special Highest Court decided that imprisonments for claims of the State violate Article 2, §1, of the Constitution.[524]

D. *'Oath of Manifestation'*

441. The CPC provides a subsidiary means, called 'oath of manifestation', suitable for the discovery of the debtor's property (Article 952). According to Article 941 §2, this institution may also be used in specific enforcement for the purpose of discovering the particular movable. The debtor is compelled to take the oath through a procedure before the justice of the peace, which operates under the special rules provided for voluntary jurisdiction (Articles 861–866 of the CPC). If the debtor fails to appear without good cause, or if he refuses to take the oath, the court, at the creditor's request, may order his imprisonment (Article 864).

II. Main Organs of Execution

442. The main organ to levy execution and perform various other related functions is the bailiff, particularly defined as a 'judicial functionary'. Additionally, in execution to satisfy a money claim, a principal role is given to the notary, usually called 'clerk of the public auction'. The bailiff is the principal organ of both direct specific performance and execution to satisfy a money claim, with limited exceptions, related to specified types of enforcement (i.e., in judgments ordering the declaration of will, Article 949). However, the only authorized organ to conduct public auctions is the notary (Articles 959 §1; 998 §1; 1012 §1 CPC).

Organs of execution are appointed by the creditor (Article 927). The enforcing activity of the bailiff is currently considered purely public in nature. This is confirmed not only by the public law nature of the rules that govern the execution system but also by the public nature of the creditor's right to resort to public authorities to enforce his claim. The enforcement activities of the bailiff are effectuated by the creditor's request to the State rather than by any private law contractual arrangements between the creditor and the bailiff.

520. For the jurisdiction of the Special Highest Court under these circumstances *see supra*, No. 73.
521. Majority opinion of the decisions 250 and 252/2008, in plenary session, *Harmenopoulos* 2008, pp. 471 ff. Dissent of three Supreme Justices. According to these decisions, the means of imprisonment is not compatible with the Constitution.
522. 1/2009, in plenary session, *Theory and Practice of Civil Law* 2009, pp. 469 ff. *Areios Pagos* confirmed once again the constitutionality of Law 1867/1989, as subsequently modified.
523. *See Theory and Practice of Civil Law* 2010, pp. 463 ff. Dissent by 5 Supreme Justices.
524. 'Respect and protection of the value of the human being is the primary obligation of the State'.

III. The Executory Title as a General Prerequisite of Execution

A. *General Remarks*

443. Greek legal theory has defined executory titles as the documents which incorporate claims capable of being materialized through enforcement proceedings. According to Article 904 §1 CPC, executory titles are: (a) Final judgments and judgments of every Greek court which have been declared as provisionally enforceable; (b) Arbitral awards; (c) Minutes of proceedings before any Greek court embodying a conciliation or allocation of court costs; (d) Notarial documents; (e) Orders of payment and orders for the return to the lessor of a leased immovable (Articles 637–645), rendered by Greek judges; (f) Foreign titles declared enforceable; (g) Orders or acts recognized by statute as executory titles. The above list is evidently not restrictive due to its last provision which allows additional categories of executory titles. Nevertheless, it still has a binding character in the sense of prohibiting the creation of executory titles through private agreements.

Executory titles are regarded as a fundamental prerequisite of execution proceedings. Their role is understood in two directions: On the one hand, they specify the limits of the right of execution with regard to the corresponding obligation of the State. On the other hand, they serve as the base of the procedure by determining the persons and the substantive claim involved.

B. *Judicial Decisions*

1. Kind of Decision

444. Article 904 §2a refers to judicial decisions in general; it is understood as covering only judgments for specific performance (*see* in particular the more concrete wording of Article 916). Nevertheless, despite the lack of enforceability, declaratory actions were quite popular in Greece for the understandable reason that they were exempted from the court deposit slip imposed on the actions for performance. Procedural tactics tended to surpass this disadvantage by using declaratory decisions as a public document, which permitted the rendition of an order for payment (Article 623), being an executory title per se (Article 630). Currently, declaratory actions are no longer exempted from fees.

445. Only judgments terminating proceedings before a certain court, even partially, may operate as executory titles, no matter if against a defaulting party or on the basis of the defendant's admission (Article 298 CPC). When a civil claim is involved, any judgment, whether rendered by a civil, an administrative or a criminal court, may be used as an executory title and thus support enforcement proceedings according to the CPC, e.g., judgments of criminal courts ordering the reparation of damages caused by a criminal act.

2. Final Judgments Which Are a Formal Res Judicata

446. A final judgment is certainly the principal judiciary title. This term must be understood as encompassing any judgment which is not or is not any longer subject to the ordinary methods of review (opposition against default judgment and appeal). This is a significant point in a judgment's procedural maturity, as it also results in the effect of res judicata.[525]

A judgment may be or become a formal res judicata in several ways. If both parties are present during the proceeding, a court's decision may be at once a formal res judicata, either when an appeal is not allowed (e.g., small claims proceedings) or when this decision has been rendered by a Court of Appeal. Moreover, in some very particular cases (e.g., determination of compensation after expropriation of private property), the direct subordination of a certain dispute to the Courts of Second Instance results in the immediate rendition of such a decision. Normally, judgments become a formal res judicata either when the ordinary methods of review have not been used timely or, although used, they have been rejected. Formal res judicata of a judgment may lastly result through discontinuance either of the methods of review already used (Articles 294, 297, 299 CPC) or of the right to attack per se (Articles 296, 298, 299).

C. Provisionally Enforceable Judgments

1. General Remarks

447. Articles 907–914 CPC, through a rather extensive regulation, provide for provisional execution, thus establishing the statutory basis for the development of what may be described as a frequent practice in Greece. Provisional execution occurs even before a judgment has become a formal res judicata, regardless of any ordinary methods of review (opposition or appeal), which may still be used or which have already been used and are still pending. It suffices that this judgment has been explicitly declared as provisionally enforceable.

2. General Requirements

448. Provisional execution in its technical sense may be based only on a judgment for specific performance. The question of whether declaratory judgments or those ordering the formation of a certain legal relationship may also profit from such a possibility, in the sense of an earlier execution, has been quite often raised. While the prevailing opinion seems to remain negative, there are also voices in theory and in practice which tend to support the necessity of provisional execution, even in a wide sense, with regard to all kinds of judgments.

525. *See supra*, Nos 239 and 240.

449. The underlying idea of a provisional execution, more particularly expressed in Article 908 §1 CPC, is to avoid damage to the successful party due to unjustified delay of enforcement. It is also taken into account whether the methods of review allowed are expected to have a successful outcome or not. However, according to Article 908 §2 CPC, the court must examine whether irreparable damage to the defeated party seems to be probable due to an early execution. It is the judge's task to carefully estimate the conflicting interests of the litigants.

450. Provisional enforcement presupposes an explicit court order, which must be included in the judgment's text. Declaration of a judgment as provisionally enforceable may be ordered only upon the party's request (Article 907 CPC), which is admissible even during proceedings on opposition or appeal (Article 913 §1 CPC).

3. Kinds of Provisional Execution

451. The CPC distinguishes between optional and compulsory provisional execution. The former, covering a wide scope of cases indicatively listed in Article 908 (judgments based on an admission by the defendant, on confession, on public or accepted private documents; judgments for maintenance, intellectual property, torts, labour or commercial matters, possession, etc.) relies on the discretion of the judge, who is called to decide, by estimating the conflicting interests already discussed (nr. 458), whether enforcement proceedings must be allowed promptly. The latter, comprising certain judgments restrictively mentioned in Article 910 (judgments ordering the return of a leased thing or the payment of rent by the lessee when in delay; judgments with regard to bills of exchange, promissory notes and checks; judgments involving maintenance or retarded salaries, in both cases only for the time after filing of the action and three months before), obliges the judge to order provisional execution on the successful party's request, without any further examination of eventual damages to the adversary. When the order of provisional execution belongs to the discretion of the judge, he may additionally order, on request of the defeated party, payment of security by the successful party before the commencement of provisional execution (Article 911), a practice followed infrequently.

The above distinction of provisional execution, being a historical relic, does not seem sufficiently justified any longer, particularly if one takes into account that since 1971, suspension of provisional execution in both kinds, optional and compulsory, is equally attainable.

4. Exclusion of Provisional Execution

452. Article 909 CPC excludes provisional execution in only a limited number of cases. The most important of these restrictions are the prohibition of provisional enforcement against the State, town municipalities and village communities (Article 909 No. 1) or for claims involving court expenses (Article 909 No. 2). According to a former opinion of *Areios Pagos*, this restrictive provision involving provisional execution against the State must be understood as referring to only non-money claims, since execution for money claims against the State is entirely forbidden (by Article 8 Law 2097/1952 regarded as being still in force); and, despite its special character, it must be extended to all legal persons, enjoying by virtue of a special provision the privileges of the State. The scope of this restrictive regulation had been excessively broadened. Currently, the question has been raised on whether prohibition of provisional enforcement against the State can still be operative. This is in light of Article 94 §4 Const., introduced in 2001, which explicitly declares that judicial decisions should also be enforced against the State and all other legal persons of public law; in addition, on the basis of the consideration that Article 8 of Law 2097/1952 is henceforth unconstitutional.[526]

5. Suspension of Provisional Execution

453. Suspension of provisional enforcement, regardless of its character as optional or compulsory, is allowed only when the provisionally enforceable judgment has already been admissibly attacked through an opposition against default or through an appeal (Articles 912–913 CPC). In such a case, the court which rendered a provisionally enforceable judgment is called, upon request of the defeated party, to re-estimate the conflicting interests and to anticipate whether the success of the method of review already used seems probable (Article 912 §1). The court may order the suspension of provisional execution on condition of a security to be deposited by the defeated party. Suspension of provisional enforcement may also be ordered even by the adjudicating court of the opposition or appeal (Article 913 §1).

According to standard practice, suspension of provisional enforcement is promptly decided through an ex parte provisional order of the court in the first stage. Nevertheless, a regular hearing on the request for suspension requires the summoning of the opponent (Article 912 §2 CPC).

D. Arbitral Awards

454. Arbitral awards are considered executory titles only upon their filing (in paper or electronic) with the clerk of the one-member district court (Article 893 §2 CPC), without being subject to any additional proceedings whatsoever. Arbitral awards may not be attacked by normal methods of appeal (Article 895 §1 CPC). The only review allowed is through other arbitrators, if agreed by the parties (Article 895 §2), a method of rather limited practical importance. Hence, unless otherwise provided, arbitral awards result promptly in a res judicata effect (Article 896) and are accordingly directly enforceable. Despite dissenting opinions on whether enforcement proceedings should be suspended when an action to set aside an arbitral award (action for annulment in the Greek version, *see* Articles 897–900) has been brought,[527] and the rulings of *Areios Pagos* against such a possibility, the law

526. *Areios Pagos* 21/2001, in plenary session, *Dike* 2002, pp. 20 ff.
527. *Infra*, Nos 549–550.

has explicitly provided for such a suspension (through the proceeding for provisional remedies), when the award has been attacked through both an action for annulment and an action for the recognition of its non-existence (Article 901).[528] Suspension is ordered when the aforementioned actions are likely to be successful.

E. Orders of Payment

455. The particular proceeding for orders of payment is a quite effective method to obtain a prompt enforceable instrument with regard to money claims (Articles 623–636A).[529] Orders of payment, exclusively for money claims deriving from commercial papers, modelled mainly on German law, have been known in Greece since 1953. The CPC has extended the possibility for obtaining a payment order to all money claims when based on a public or even private document, the claim does not depend on a condition, term or counter-performance, and the amount of money to be paid has been definitely fixed. A payment order can also be obtained on the basis of a provisional measure, granted after an admission by the defendant or a confession (Article 623). Article 636A has been added to the CPC in 2017, which, under certain conditions, extends the possibility of obtaining an order of payment for salary claims.

An order of payment may be rendered either by the justice of the peace or the one-member district court, depending on the value of the claim (Article 625), after ex parte proceedings (Articles 626–630), and is at once enforceable (Article 631). Enforceability is not suspended, even by opposition of the debtor (Article 632 §3),[530] unless the latter brings a separate request to the judge who has rendered the order of payment. The judge may, at his own discretion, grant an order for suspension until a final decision on the opposition has been rendered and also make suspension dependent on the deposit of a security (Article 632 §3b). Furthermore, a payment order may result in res judicata only if it is served on the debtor for a second time, i.e., and the debtor does not bring an opposition within a second term provided by law (Article 633 §2).

During the last twenty years, payment orders have steadily expanded in frequency. Under Article 1 §2 of Council Regulation (EC) 1896/2006 on the European Order of Payment, this national proceeding can continue to operate. However, since the 2015 amendment, the enforceability of a payment order against a person who

528. *Infra*, No. 549.
529. P. Yessiou-Faltsi & E., Podimata, *Preliminary or Summary Proceedings: Scope and Importance in Greek Civil Procedure*, *RHDI* 2004, pp. 397 ff.; K. Makridou, *The Enforcement of Payment Orders Under Greek Law*, *ZZZ* 2016, pp. 39 et seq.
530. The creditor's nationality may not be exploited as an opposition ground: In the case between a Kosovar limited liability company and a Greek SA, the Greek Supreme Court was confronted with the question, whether the non-recognition of Kosovo by the Hellenic Republic may be considered a valid ground for opposition against a payment order issued by a Greek court. The Supreme Court dismissed the final appeal, confirming the rulings issued by the instance courts, *see* A. Anthimos, *Greek Supreme Court No. 1938/2017, International Journal of Procedural Law* 2019, pp. 132–134.

resides or has a seat abroad or is of unknown residence is, by way of exception, suspended as far as the time limit for raising an opposition has not expired. During this time limit, only provisional remedies against these persons are permissible (Article 631). This new rule aims at the adjustment of Greek law with the spirit of the case law of the CJEU.[531]

F. Foreign Judgments

456. In order for judgments of foreign courts to operate as domestic enforceable titles, they need a local *exequatur* (Article 905).[532] This applies to all judgments rendered in the world, with the exception of EU Member States. The EU has produced vast legislation by virtue of which exequatur has been made redundant in specific matters (*see* Regulation 805/2004, on the European Enforcement Order;[533] Regulation 1896/2006, on the 'European Order of Payment'; European Small Claims Regulation 861/2007; Maintenance Regulation 4/2009; Regulation 1215/2012, so-called Brussels I bis Regulation).

G. Foreign Arbitral Awards

457. To be enforceable in Greece, a foreign arbitral award must receive an *exequatur* through proceedings similar to foreign judgments' (Article 906). Conditions for enforcement are provided in Article 903 CPC.[534]

H. Provisional Remedies

458. Provisional remedies, when including claims capable of enforcement in a technical sense, are enforced through normal enforcement proceedings (Article 700 §1 CPC).[535] The relevant procedural requirements are, however, subject to some simplifications (Article 700 §2) aiming at the acceleration of execution.

Provisional orders with regard to requests for provisional remedies, which are rendered by a court ex officio promptly after the above requests have been brought (new Article 691A), including those rendered during proceedings of voluntary jurisdiction (Article 781), may be enforced in the same manner (Article 700 §3).[536]

531. In detail A. Anthimos, *Greek Payment Orders against Foreign Residents*, *International Journal of Procedural Law* 2016, pp. 327–340.
532. *See infra*, No. 505 ff.
533. Yessiou-Faltsi, 'Effects of the European Enforcement Order on the Enforcement Law in Europe', in *Festschrift in Honour of Professor Kozyris* (Sakkoulas Publications, 2007), pp. 579 ff.; same author, 'The European Enforcement Order after Five Years of Experience in Greece', *RHDI* 2008, pp. 735 ff.
534. *See infra*, Nos 551 ff.
535. *See also supra*, No. 265.
536. *See supra*, No. 268.

Enforceability of provisional remedies has a significant practical impact. Resort to such proceedings has become quite popular in Greece, particularly in recent years.

I. Notarial Documents

459. Notarial documents are considered enforceable instruments when embodying declarations of will by the interested parties.[537] Elaborated primarily by the notaries, as the functionally competent organs,[538] they must comply with specific typical requirements.[539] While as a kind of public document, they also produce an increased probative effect, their role as enforceable instruments derives exclusively from the explicit provision in Article 904 §2 CPC.

Notarial documents may operate as enforceable instruments only with regard to money claims or to obligations regarding the delivery of property (Articles 941–943). On the contrary, they may not support enforcement proceedings for the performance of a specific act or omission.

J. Awards Issued by Administrative Authorities for the Collection of Public Revenues

460. Law 4978/2022 ('Code for the Collection of Public Revenues') establishes a particular enforcement procedure to be applied when the claim under performance belongs to the State or some other legal persons enjoying an equally privileged treatment. Awards of the competent administrative authorities, confirming such debts, operate as enforceable instruments without being previously subject to judicial examination.

K. Orders for the Return to the Lessor of a Leased Immovable

461. Articles 637–645 have introduced an ex parte proceeding designed to operate for the protection of the lessor.[540] This applies only to the rental of immovable property. It allows the lessor to obtain an enforceable instrument rather promptly for the return of the leased thing in case of unjustified delay of rent payment. The structure of this proceeding is basically similar to the proceeding for the orders of payment.

---

537. Article 1 §1a of Law 2830/2000 'On the Code of Notaries'.
538. Articles 2, 4 of Law 2830/2000 'On the Code of the Notaries'.
539. Articles 8–11 of Law 2830/2000 'On the Code of the Notaries'.
540. P. Yessiou-Faltsi & E., Podimata, *Preliminary or Summary Proceedings: Scope and Importance in Greek Civil Procedure, RHDI* 2004, pp. 405 ff.

IV. The Executory Formula

462. In order for enforcement proceedings to be commenced, an enforceable instrument must carry the executory formula. This contains an official command addressed to the organs of enforcement in the name of the Greek people for executing the instrument (Article 918 CPC). There is a detailed regulation about the competent organs to inscribe the executory formula on the instrument (Article 918 §2 CPC). In case of judicial instruments, this is effected by the judge, who has rendered the title, or the president of the court (Article 918 § 2a). An executory formula on notarial documents is inscribed by the notary who has drawn them up (Article 918 2c).

463. A complete copy of the enforceable instrument, bearing the executory formula, is issued to the creditor who claims a legal interest (Article 918 §3) by the court clerk or, in case of notarial documents, by the notary. The issuance of more than one copy is permissible for a good cause (Article 918 § 3b). In case of a refusal involving the right to obtain one or more authorized copies, the matter is brought before the one-member district court (Article 918 §5 CPC).

V. Other Prerequisites to Execution

A. Prerequisites Involving the Enforced Claim

464. Enforcement proceedings are not allowed when the claim sought to be enforced depends on a suspensive condition or a term (Article 915 CPC). Hence, enforcement acts may be nullified unless fulfilment of the condition or expiration of the term has in advance been proven by a public or private document, having a probative effect against the debtor (Articles 915b and 924a CPC).

465. The amount of the claim must be exactly defined in the enforceable instrument (Article 916 CPC). For the protection of the debtor, subsequent determination of the amount of the claim through other documents or by a third person is not allowed.

B. Prerequisites Involving Persons Entitled to or Subject to Enforcement

466. Subjective limits of the enforceability of an executory title are determined following the respective provisions involving subjective limits of res judicata (Article 919 CPC). In addition, pursuant to Article 920 CPC, executory titles involving general or limited partnerships may be directly executed against general partners in accordance with the relevant substantive law stipulations, even if they were not parties to the pertinent proceedings.

C. Service of the Copy of the Instrument to Be Enforced

467. Initiation of enforcement proceedings is marked by the service of a precept on the debtor, comprising a formal notice inviting him to voluntary execution (Article 924 CPC). This is included at the end of the certified copy of the enforceable instrument issued to the creditor, which is served on the debtor. If the debtor does not comply within the next three working days (Article 926 §1),[541] the creditor may proceed to execution.

468. The service of the precept has both procedural and substantive effects. The sole procedural effect is the formal commencement of enforcement proceedings. The substantive effects include interruption of prescription (Article 264 CC) and cause the consequences of delayed performance (Articles 340 ff. of the CC).

469. A precept lapses if enforcement proceedings are not commenced within one year after its service (Article 926 §2 CPC).

VI. Initiation of the Main Enforcement Proceedings

470. The main phase of enforcement proceeding, including the operation of execution acts, is commenced and also advanced further on the initiative of the creditor (Article 927 CPC). This is effectuated through the delivery of the enforceable instrument to a bailiff, serving within the territory of the district court where the property of the debtor is located. The bailiff is then vested with the authority to proceed to enforcement.

VII. Proceedings in Enforcement for Money Claims

A. General Remarks

471. Enforcement on property to satisfy a money claim primarily operates through forced liquidation of assets. This is carried out in several steps: First, the debtor's goods are attached. Second, other creditors may intervene. Third, the debtor's assets are liquidated after their sale in a public auction. And fourth, the proceeds of liquidation are distributed amongst the petitioning and other announced creditors. The main points of these steps are extensively treated by the CPC (Articles 953–1033).

541. Enforcement against the State or against a legal person of public law is permissible sixty days after service of the enforced decision on the Minister responsible for payment or on the competent authority of the legal person (Art. 4 § 2 3068/2002). For the conditions of enforcement against a foreign state, *see* K. Beys, *Die Zwangsvollstreckung gegen einen ausländischen Staat im hellenischen Recht*, in *Grenzüberschreitungen – Beiträge zum Internationalen Verfahrensrecht und zur Schiedsgerichtsbarkeit; Festschrift für Peter Schlosser zum 70. Geburtstag* (Tübingen 2005), pp. 37–48.

To achieve acceleration of the execution process of money claims, which suffered from long delays, a series of legislative initiatives have brought about radical changes to enforcement proceedings (Laws 4335/2015, 4472/2017, 4475/2017, the latter two replaced by Law 4512/2018, Law 4842/2021, and Law 4912/2022). A large number of t former rules which treated the preliminary steps to the public auction were simplified, and electronic means have been introduced as the sole vehicle for conducting public auctions without the physical presence of the parties involved or their lawyers

B. The Various Types of Attachments

472. The – CPC provides four types of attachments: (a) Attachment of movables in the possession of the debtor (Articles 953–958);[542] (b) Garnishment, which also extends to chattels of a debtor that are not in his possession (Articles 982–991B); (c) Attachment of land, which also covers attachment on ships and aircraft (Articles 992–997); (d) Attachment of the debtor's special assets, like copyrights, patents and film exploitation rights (Articles 1022–1033).

C. Distribution of Sale Proceeds

1. The Principle of Proportional Distribution

473. In contrast to the German system of distribution, which is governed by the criterion of temporal priority of multiple attachments (*Präventionsprinzip*),[543] Greek law follows the Romanic system of proportional distribution.[544] Distribution is, in principle, based on equality, allotting to each creditor a proportional percentage of his claim.[545]

2. General and Special Priorities

474. The system of proportional distribution has been amended recently (Law 4842/2021). It is seriously affected by two kinds of priorities: (a) the general priorities, which permit the preferential satisfaction of claims from all kinds of assets liquidated in the public auction (Articles 975, 1007); and (b) the special priorities,

542. G. Stoikos, *Die Zwangsvollstreckung wegen Geldforderungen in das bewegliche Vermögen im deutschen und im griechischen Recht* (Diss. Tübingen, Sofort-Druck 1987), pp. 76 ff.

543. Ch. Fragistas, Das *Präventionsprinzip in der Zwangsvollstreckung*, Beiträge zum Zivilprozess, 11. Heft (Manheim/Berlin/Leipzig, Bensheimer 1931).

544. G. Orfanidis, Die Konkurrenz von Gläubigern im griechischen Zwangsvollstreckungsrecht, in *Grenzüberschreitungen – Beiträge zum Internationalen Verfahrensrecht und zur Schiedsgerichtsbarkeit; Festschrift für Peter Schlosser zum 70. Geburtstag* (Tübingen, Mohr Siebeck 2005), pp. 669–682.

545. P. Yessiou-Faltsi, 'Das Ausgleichsprinzip im griechischen Zwangsvollstreckungsrechts im Unterschied zum deutschen Prioritätsprinzip', *ZZP* 1993, pp. 215 ff.

which lead to the preferential satisfaction of claims only from the liquidation of special assets, which are related to the claim (new Articles 976, 977, 1007). Since the collision among privileged creditors is almost unavoidable, several general or special priorities are classified within each group in a hierarchical order. The costs and expenses of the enforcement proceedings are paid in advance (Article 975 §1).

As a general rule, creditors enjoying general priorities rank before creditors enjoying special priorities (Article 977 §1). However, in the event of collision among creditors with general priorities and creditors secured with real rights or creditors seeking the satisfaction of claims concerning the necessary expenses to preserve the object of sale (Articles 977 §1b; 1007, §1b), the sale proceeds are divided into two parts. The percentage of general priorities is limited only to one-third of the sale proceeds so that the remaining two-thirds are reserved for the satisfaction of special priorities (Articles 977, §1b; 1007, §1b). This system, defined as the 'system of sale proceeds' separation, is designed to sustain the efficaciousness of real security rights. Before the 2015 amendment, solely after satisfaction of these two 'privileged' groups of creditors was the satisfaction of 'ordinary' creditors allowed. Article 977 §3 CPC has now provided that ordinary creditors may be satisfied on any occasion from the 10% of the sale proceeds. Another new stipulation (Article 977A has however excluded such possibility for future claims. New Article 977A favours all future creditors who will be secured by a new real right.

475. Where the sale proceeds are insufficient to satisfy all creditors, the distribution is accomplished by the 'table of classification' (Article 974). This is a public instrument drawn by the notary who has conducted the public auction, indicating the order in which the claims must be satisfied. Parties are entitled to bring in an opposition against the table of classification (Article 979, §2a). The grounds apply to both violations of the rules of classification and substantive objections to the classified claim itself. This opposition may lead not only to the judicial declaration of a classification's nullity but also to the classification of the opposer.

VIII. Judicial Review

A. The Court Is Not an Organ of Execution

476. Greek law does not provide for the involvement of the court in the actual enforcement proceedings, i.e., as an organ directly managing the execution process and its acts. The judge rather retains a controlling function when questions of irregularities have been brought by the persons involved through an opposition (Articles 933–937).

477. Despite its limited authority, the court is not entirely absent during enforcement proceedings. In the first place, enforcement may commence only on the basis of an 'executory formula' issued by the judge.[546] Second, in a rather long series of cases, intervention of the judge is provided for issuing 'regulatory measures of

546. *See supra*, No. 471.

enforcement'. These include, e.g., suspension (stay) of enforcement (Articles 912 §2; 1000), permission for effecting acts of enforcement during holidays or at night (Article 929 §3), permission for an auction of movables found in the seized immovable (Article 943 §3), disputes over the price of the first bid of the seized object (Article 954 §4), disputes with regard to guardianship of the seized object (Articles 956 §§§4, 5, 6), etc. Such regulatory measures are granted either through proceedings of provisional remedies (so in Articles 912 §2; 929 §2; 943 §3; 944; 954 §4; 956 §§§4, 5, 6; 966 §3; 1000; 1019; 1034 §2; 1039 §4; 1040; 1041; 1046; 1050; 1053, etc.) or through the procedure of voluntary jurisdiction (so in Articles 941 §2 and 861–866; 950 §1 and 861–866; 952; 1023–1026; 1028 §2; 1029 §§1, 2; 1030 §1; 1033).

B. *Opposition to Enforcement*

1. General Remarks on the Opposition of the Debtor

478. Opposition to enforcement must be primarily understood as an exclusive remedy of the debtor against the acts of execution (Articles 933–935, 937 CPC). This is regarded as a particular form of the widely formulated remedy, also known under the general term of opposition, given to any person offended by a judicial or extrajudicial act if not summoned or not having participated (Articles 583–585).[547] Opposition to enforcement constitutes an independent proceeding of cognitive character, being the sole remedy given to the debtor. Any other action for declaring the nullity of execution acts is therefore regarded as inadmissible. This defensive character affects some significant procedural stipulations, in particular territorial competence. It does not, however, influence default: the procedural treatment of a default debtor during the opposition proceeding remains similar to that of a default plaintiff.

479. Opposition to enforcement functions within the general scope of 'procedural nullities' (Articles 159–161 CPC).[548] While the grounds of opposition may admissibly concern both substantive and procedural irregularities, its request refers exclusively to a particular act of enforcement, which, following its character as a procedural act, is claimed to be void under the general stipulations for procedural nullities. Exactly as in all other cases of procedural irregularities, declaration of a concrete act of enforcement as null and void most often depends on whether the opposing debtor successfully claims that an alleged irregularity has caused a specifically defined irreparable detriment (Article 159 No. 3). Otherwise, nullity may be determined by the court solely either when the violated stipulation has been explicitly imposed under the penalty of nullity (Article 159 No. 1), or when its violation may constitute a ground for cassation (Article 159 No. 2). This flexible system of relying, to some extent, on the evaluation of the judge, evidently aims at avoiding unjustifiable nullities. It may, nevertheless, also lead to legal insecurity.

547. *See supra*, No. 310.
548. *See supra*, Nos 195–199.

2. Subject Matter Competence

480. Article 933 §1 CPC assigns subject matter competence to one-member district courts and the justices of the peace. Three-member district courts never judge on oppositions to enforcement, even when having adjudicated over the enforced claim. One-member district courts have a regular subject matter competence (Article 933, §1 *in fin*), covering all oppositions to enforcement, whether proceedings are based on judicial decisions or other executory titles. Nevertheless, when enforcement proceedings are based on judgements rendered by a justice of the peace, oppositions to enforcement must be brought before the same court (Article 933 §1). Before the 2015 amendment, the exact scope of the subject matter competence of the justices of the peace had led to dissenting opinions within case law as to whether the relevant criterion for allocating oppositions to the justices of the peace should extend to other executory titles as well, either rendered by those courts (i.e., orders of payment) or produced during proceedings before them (i.e., judicial conciliations). The present provision has settled this question by allowing an affirmative answer.

3. Territorial Competence

481. Territorial competence depends on the stage of enforcement, and particularly on the specific act which is being attacked through the opposition (new Article 933 §3). When an opposition seeks declaration of nullity of solely the precept, which has been served on the debtor, while no further enforcement proceedings have been initiated, territorial competence is being determined as if the opposing debtor is the defendant in normal proceedings. The opposition is then brought before the courts, either of the debtor's domicile or of other exclusive or concurrent jurisdictions (Articles 933 §3; 584). As soon as subsequent enforcement acts have been effected, e.g., attachment, an exclusive jurisdiction of the place of execution is established to satisfy the prevailing need to concentrate all litigation related to enforcement. Territorial competence of the court of execution is absolutely exclusive in the sense that it prevails over other exclusive jurisdictions.

4. Grounds of Opposition

482. Proceedings to oppose execution may be based on three types of grounds (Article 933 §1): (a) inefficiencies of the executory title, (b) irregularities of the acts of execution, and (c) objections referring to the creditor's right to enforcement:

(a) The debtor may first contest the formal or even the substantive validity of the executory title by, e.g., claiming nullity of the notarial document, procedural irregularities of the order of payment (Article 630), or of the executory formula (Article 918), procedural inefficiencies of the document incorporating a judgment (Articles 305–306), etc.

(b) The debtor may challenge the formal regularity of each one of the acts of execution. This wide category of grounds refers to all violations of procedural requirements (*modus executionis*), beginning from the formalities of the precept and its service (as accompanied by the copy of the enforceable instrument) and covering conditions of all successive steps until the auction is completed. It therefore enjoys the most extended practical relevance.

(c) The debtor may raise all substantive objections, e.g., referring either to the non-existence of the obligation sought to be enforced (e.g., nullity, simulation) or to its discharge or unenforceability.

Distinction between the aforementioned three types of grounds is to a certain extent necessary. A legal definition of a certain ground as belonging to each category is related to the length of the time limit within which the opposition proceedings must be commenced (Article 934). Grounds referring to the enforced obligation may, furthermore, be under certain conditions inadmissible.[549]

5. Time Limitations

483. In order to restrict invalidities of enforcement proceedings and safeguard the efficaciousness of execution, Article 934 CPC has introduced a system of 'gradual' time limitations for bringing oppositions against acts of enforcement, depending on the asserted grounds. Despite some initial difficulties caused by the need to exactly classify the grounds of opposition, this rather complex system has been operating quite effectively.

Article 934 §1 provides that all grounds of opposition may be admissibly brought within forty-five days after attachment. Finally, proceedings to oppose the regularity of the auction itself in enforcement of money claims must commence (a) within thirty days in the case of movables and (b) within sixty days after transcription at the Registry of the transfer in case of immovables (Article 934 §1b). In enforcement proceedings for non-money claims, the time limitation for contesting the regularity of the last act of execution is thirty days after its performance.

6. Rules of Procedure

484. Proceedings to oppose acts of enforcement are commenced and further unfolded exactly as a normal civil action (Article 585 §1). The opposing debtor is moreover allowed to bring further grounds of opposition against the same act of enforcement through an additional complaint, on the condition that this is served on the opposing party, when a particular proceeding is applicable, eight days before the hearing of the case (Article 585 §2). Beyond some particular rules of procedure exclusively related to oppositions against enforcement (Articles 933, 937), which we will discuss below, proceedings follow the normal pattern. The adjudication of

549. *See infra*, Nos 494–495.

oppositions currently operates under the particular proceeding for money claims unless otherwise provided (Article 937 §3 CPC).

485. Enforcement proceedings of instruments enjoying a res judicata effect may not be admissibly attacked through grounds of opposition, including objections to the obligation under enforcement, which have been already covered by the preclusion principles of this effect (Articles 933 §4; 330). This rule in the first place refers to all final judgements, which are no longer subject to ordinary methods of review (Article 321), and to arbitral awards (Article 896). It may additionally cause preclusion of grounds in enforcement proceedings, which are based on orders of payment. Beyond preclusion, which may normally result from a final decision rejecting an opposition to orders of payment (Article 632), this may be attained through a quasi res judicata effect, which in Greek law has been recognized (Article 633, §2) to such orders, if they have been successively served on the debtor twice, without been attacked by an opposition (Article 632) within the limits of time provided. This quite original institution of Greek law evidently aims at restricting unjustified oppositions and thus accelerating execution of orders of payment.

486. The two next restrictive rules of opposition proceedings must also be approached as means for acceleration.

First, grounds of opposition related to the extinction of the claim are inadmissible unless promptly proven. After some dissenting opinions of lower courts, *Areios Pagos* supported a narrow interpretation of the notion of 'prompt proof' by ruling that, under the above restriction, only confessions and documentary evidence are admissible means of evidence. The above is now embedded in the law (Article 933 §5).

Second, grounds of opposition which could have possibly been brought in previous opposition proceedings, may not be henceforth admissibly included in a subsequent opposition (Article 935). This rule is understood as establishing an absolute form of the concentration principle.

487. Three more peculiarities of opposition proceedings remain to be discussed (Article 937). (a) An accessory intervention of creditors is admissible, even without invoking a particular legal interest (Article 937 §1a). (b) Methods of review, with the exception of opposition against default judgments in first and second instance, are permissible (Article 937 §1b, as amended by Law 4842/2021). (c) Finally, the possibility of lodging an appeal within the term provided by law, or the appeal already lodged, does not suspend the enforcement process (Article 937 §1c).

C. Third Party Opposition

1. Particular Features

488. Through a specific remedy known as 'a third-party opposition', validity of enforcement acts may be challenged by any third party if he claims to have a right over the seized property, which may be exercised against the debtor (Article 936, §1). Legal protection obtained by raising a third-party opposition, therefore, goes far beyond both the protection of ownership or of other rights, granted through actions normally available under the CC (e.g., a revendicatory action), and the protection attained through a normal opposition of the debtor (Article 933). The particular feature of a third-party opposition lies in its mixed effects. While it tends to the recognition of the substantive rights of the third party, an affirmative judgment may simultaneously lead to the nullity of enforcement.

2. Grounds of a Third-Party Opposition

489. The grounds of a third-party opposition, first defined through a general stipulation (Article 936 §1), refer to all substantive rights of a third person infringed by the enforcement proceedings which may be exercised against the debtor. The above provision is listing an indicative list which includes: (a) Real rights (Article 936 § 1a), such as ownership and personal servitudes (in particular usufruct and habitation, Articles 1142–1191 CC); (b) Prohibition of disposing the attached property designed for the protection of the third party, causing the nullity of disposal (Article 936 § 1b); (c) Possession of the third party unless proven by the petitioning creditor that the debtor has a predominant real right (ownership) (Article 936 §1b). This last provision evidently tends to relieve the third party from the burden of proof of his ownership by reversing and allocating it to the petitioning creditor.

Legal scholarship has been interpreting third party's rights rather widely, which may be protected by this remedy. Thus, even the personal rights of a third party, which under certain conditions may be exercised against the bidder (e.g., right of a lessee), have been regarded as admissible grounds of third-party opposition, though only leading to the appropriate limitations of rights on the attached property. Supported by legal doctrine, *Areios Pagos* has ruled[550] that third-party opposition is designed to also protect rights of third persons in a wide sense, comprising all possibilities or powers granted by substantive law. This formulation was used in order to protect rights of a third party deriving from a pre-contract. More specifically, it was accepted that the exercise of the debtor's right of ownership, which is realized through an attachment, must not violate the prohibition of abuse of rights against a third party (Article 281 CC), otherwise instituting a ground for attacking enforcement proceedings in favour of a third person. However, a third party who has purchased property from a debtor, alienating his or her assets in fraud of creditors, is not entitled to bring a third-party opposition if an action for revocation (*Actio Pauliana*, Articles 939–946 CC) raised by the petitioning creditor, has been successful (Article 936 §3).

550. *Areios Pagos* 448/1984, plenary session, *Legal Tribune* 1985, p. 61; *Areios Pagos* 1151/1981, *Journal of Greek Jurists* 1982, p. 773.

3. Subject Matter and Territorial Competence

490. In contrast to the opposition of the debtor, subject matter competence for adjudicating over a third-party opposition is determined by the value of the property claimed by the third-party (Articles 936, §1b, in fine; Articles 7–11 CPC). Territorial competence is again determined by the place of enforcement.

4. The Compulsory Parties

491. Third-party opposition must be addressed against both the petitioning creditor and the debtor under penalty of inadmissibility (Article 936 §2). A necessary joinder of parties is thus instituted, subject to the particular regulation within the CPC (Articles 76–77).

5. Time Limitations

492. Third-party opposition is no longer available after termination of enforcement proceedings. The third party may henceforth seek protection only through the relevant actions granted by substantive law. But even then, he is subject to a limitation of time which differs depending on the kind of property sold. It is one year for movables, running from the time they were delivered to the bidder, and five years for immovables, running from the transcription of their transfer to the Transcription Registry (Article 1020 CPC).

D. Suspension of Enforcement

1. Conditions

493. Before the 2015 amendment, when enforcement proceeding was opposed, be it by the debtor (Article 933) or a third party (Article 936), it could be further suspended (former Articles 938–939). Although granted through a separate proceeding, after a special request of the opposing party, suspension was, as a rule, entrusted to the discretion of the judge, who was expected to be adjudicating over the opposition.

Former Article 938 CPC was abolished in 2015. Suspension of enforcement for money claims was not any more permissible. The only possibility given to the debtor, or a third party, was to bring a relevant request to the Court of Appeal, adjudicating over this party's appeal, when the opposition brought before the first-instance court was unsuccessful. The landscape changed once again by Law 4842/2021: Article 938 has been reinstated. Suspension is now allowed in first-instance opposition proceedings, save one very important exception: Suspension proceedings are not allowed with respect to attachment of immovables, which predominates court practice.

2. Procedure: Provisional Order

494. Proceedings before the Court of Appeal for deciding on requests for suspension follow the rules used for issuing provisional remedies (new Article 938 §2; Articles 686 ff. CPC), thus operating quite rapidly. A provisional order of the court, in the form of an act preventing continuation of enforcement until the decision on the requested suspension can be rendered, is also permissible (new Article 691A CPC). Such orders are rather frequent and, sometimes, not sufficiently justifiable.

3. Effects

495. Suspension of enforcement has two effects. On the one hand, it prohibits performance of acts of execution under penalty of nullity declared by the competent court. On the other hand, it suspends or interrupts all time limits which have been provided with regard to the above acts (Article 939 §2).

§2. Recognition and Enforcement of Foreign Judgments

I. Rules Applicable in the Absence of a Treaty

A. General Remarks

1. The Doctrinal Foundation of the Recognition and Enforcement of Foreign Judgments

496. In Greek law,[551] recognition of the binding effects and enforcement of foreign judgments is an obligation having its source in an international custom which

551. G. Maridakis, *Die Vollstreckbarkeit ausländischer Urteile in Griechenland*, *RabelsZ* 1930, pp. 506–512; G. Economou, 'Greece', in D. Campbell (gen. ed.), *International Execution Against Judgment Debtors*, Vol. I (London, Sweet and Maxwell/Callaghan 1993), pp. 1–24 (3); D. Evrigenis & K. Kerameus, 'Report on the Accession of the Hellenic Republic to the Community Convention on Jurisdiction and the Enforcement of Judgments', *Official Journal of the European Communities*, C 298, Vol. 29/1986; S. Vrellis, '*Reconnaissance et exécution de decisions étrangères tant judiciaire qu'arbitral – Le système en vigueur et ses améliorations*', Greek National Report to the 8th World Conference of Civil Procedure in Utrecht 1987, in *Justice and Efficiency*, Special Volume (ed. by IΔME/Athens 1988), II, pp. 399 ff.; P. Yessiou-Falsi, in Rossides, Hadji & Marketos, *Doing Business in Greece* (American Hellenic Institute Foundation, Waschington D.C.), §24.2; N. Klamaris, *Enforcement of Court Orders and Judgments: Greece,* in Walter, Gerhard (Hrsg.), *Recognition and Enforcement of Foreign Judgments Outside the Scope of the Brussels and Lugano Conventions* (The Hague, etc., 2000), pp. 275 et seq.; Ph. Kozyris, 'Conflict of Laws, International Jurisdiction, and Recognition and Enforcement of Judgments and Awards', in Kerameus & Kozyris (eds), *Introduction to Greek Law*, third edition (Kluwer Law International/Sakkoulas, 2008), pp. 379 ff., Bendermacher-Geroussis A., *Anerkennung und Vollstreckung ausländischer Entscheidungen über die Sorge der Person der Kinder und die Unterhaltspflicht*, *RHDI* 1955, pp. 45–50, Christopoulos, Th., *Requirements for the Enforcement of Foreign Judgments in Greece,*

has been developed through parallel, national statutory regulations. As long as Greek public policy is not violated, foreign courts worldwide are regarded as equal to domestic ones. Accordingly, foreign judgments are basically expected to produce similar effects to the judgments of Greek courts.[552]

2. Distinction Between Recognition and Enforcement

497. Greek law clearly distinguishes between recognition and enforcement.

Since recognition refers to the binding effects of a foreign judgment attributed basically by foreign law, these are understood as automatically extending to Greece by the time they have been produced abroad. Recognition of a res judicata effect, thus, does not need to be declared through a special proceeding. In principle, this may be effected by any court or other authority (judicial, administrative, ecclesiastical, etc.) even incidentally, ex officio and automatically, when the interested party is basing his request on the binding force of the foreign judgment (Article 323 CPC).[553] On the contrary, since enforceability of a foreign instrument may not be regarded as *ipso jure* extending in Greece, but it rather requires a constitutive domestic act to move the coercive mechanisms of the State, enforcement of a foreign judgment must be declared through a special proceeding (Article 905) which results in vesting the foreign title with a local *exequatur*. A foreign judgment declared enforceable in Greece may be amended by virtue of a petition to modify the foreign judgment, which most of the time is a decision ordering child support.[554]

3. Characterization of the Foreign Judgment

498. Any act of the judicial organs of a foreign State which terminates a proceeding related to a private law dispute falls within the scope of the provisions regulating recognition and enforcement of foreign judgments.[555] Primarily, decisions of all foreign civil courts are included, i.e., special, commercial or labour courts, regardless of whether composed by professional or lay judges, but not those of international courts. Decisions of criminal or administrative courts are excluded unless

RHDI 1948, pp. 348–357; A. Millionis, *Praxis der Vollstreckung deutscher Urteile in Griechenland nach dem EuGVÜ,* RIW/AWD 1991, pp. 100–103; D. Tsikrikas, *Anerkennung und Vollstreckung ausländischer gerichtlicher Entscheidungen und Schiedssprüche nach dem griechischen Zivilverfahrensrecht, ZZPInt* 2018, pp. 79–100; A. Anthimos, *Reconocimiento y ejecución de sentencias extranjeras en Grecia, Revista de Derecho Comunitario Europeo* 1999, pp. 209–218.

552. The above does not apply to administrative acts, *see* Douga A., *On the Recognition of Foreign Administrative Acts in Greece, RHDI* 2014, pp. 741–764.

553. One of the most controversial issues is the recognition of foreign last names, *see* A. Anthimos, *Recognition of Surnames in Greece – Where do we go from here?*, https://conflictoflaws.net/2019/recognition-of-surnames-in-greece-where-do-we-go-from-here/.

554. A. Georgiades, *Die Abänderung ausländischer Urteile im Inland, Xenion Zepos II* (1979), pp. 189 et seq.

555. P. Massouridis, 'The Enforcement of Foreign Judgments in Greece', *RHDI* 1970, pp. 186–224 (187–188).

they involve compensation under civil law. What is relevant is not the character of the organ which has rendered a foreign act but rather its nature as a judicial decision over a private dispute.

According to the prevailing opinion, characterization of a court as a State civil court and of a dispute as of private law follows the law of the place where the decision is sought to be enforced.

B. *The Basic Provisions of the CPC on Recognition and Enforcement of Foreign Judgments – EU Regulations*

499. The CPC includes four separate provisions regulating the effects of foreign judgments: (a) Article 323 governs recognition of judgments rendered in foreign contentious proceedings; (b) Article 905 §4 involves the recognition of foreign judgments related to personal status; (c) Article 905 §§1–3, covers the *exequatur* proceeding; and (d) Article 780 specifically treats the effects of foreign decisions regarding matters of voluntary jurisdiction. In addition, recognition of foreign arbitral awards is regulated by Article 903, and the obtaining of a local *exequatur* in such a case by Article 906. This will be discussed in the chapter on arbitration.

Decisions of EU Member States courts are recognized and enforced on the basis of a series of EU Regulations. These are the following:

- Council Regulation (EC) No. 44/2001 of 22 December 2000 on jurisdiction and the recognition and enforcement of judgments in civil and commercial matters ('Brussels I').
- Council Regulation (EC) No. 2201/2003 of 27 November 2003 concerning jurisdiction and the recognition and enforcement of judgments in matrimonial matters and the matters of parental responsibility, repealing Regulation (EC) No. 1347/2000 ('Brussels IIa').
- Council Regulation (EC) No. 4/2009 of 18 December 2008 on jurisdiction, applicable law, recognition and enforcement of decisions and cooperation in matters relating to maintenance obligations.[556]
- Council Regulation (EU) 2016/1103 of 24 June 2016 implementing enhanced cooperation in the area of jurisdiction, applicable law and the recognition and enforcement of decisions in matters of matrimonial property regimes.
- Council Regulation (EU) 2016/1104 of 24 June 2016 implementing enhanced cooperation in the area of jurisdiction, applicable law and the recognition and enforcement of decisions in matters of the property consequences of registered partnerships

556. A. Douga & V. Koumpli, *On the Regulation of Maintenance Obligations in Greece*, *RHDI* 2014, pp. 931–960; A. Anthimos, *The Court of Appeal of Piraeus on the Non-Recognition of a Dutch Judgment on Maintenance*, https://eapil.org/2020/11/11/the-court-of-appeal-of-piraeus-on-the-non-recognition-of-a-dutch-judgment-on-maintenance/.

- Council Regulation (EU) No. 650/2012 of the European Parliament and of the Council of 4 July 2012 on jurisdiction, applicable law, recognition and enforcement of decisions and acceptance and enforcement of authentic instruments in matters of succession and on the creation of a European Certificate of Succession.
- A second set of EU Regulations has abolished wholly or partially exequatur proceedings, allowing direct enforcement of foreign judgments. These are the following:
  - Council Regulation (EU) No. 1215/2012 of the European Parliament and of the Council of 12 December 2012 on jurisdiction and the recognition and enforcement of judgments in civil and commercial matters (recast) ('Brussels I (recast)').
  - Council Regulation (EU) 2019/1111 of 25 June 2019 on jurisdiction, the recognition and enforcement of decisions in matrimonial matters and the matters of parental responsibility, and on international child abduction (recast).
  - Council Regulation (EC) No. 4/2009 of 18 December 2008 on jurisdiction, applicable law, recognition and enforcement of decisions and cooperation in matters relating to maintenance obligations.[557]
  - Council Regulation (EC) No. 805/2004 of the European Parliament and of the Council of 21 April 2004 creating a European Enforcement Order for uncontested claims.
  - Council Regulation (EC) No. 1896/2006 of the European Parliament and of the Council of 12 December 2006 creating a European order for payment procedure.
  - Council Regulation (EC) No. 861/2007 of the European Parliament and of the Council of 11 July 2007 establishing a European Small Claims Procedure Council Regulation (EU) No. 655/2014 of the European Parliament and of the Council of 15 May 2014 establishing a European Account Preservation Order procedure to facilitate cross-border debt recovery in civil and commercial matters.[558]

C. The Prerequisites to Recognition

1. The Res Judicata Effect of the Foreign Judgment

500. A prerequisite to the operation of a foreign res judicata in Greece is that the respective judgment does have the claimed res judicata effect in accordance with the law of the State where this judgment has been rendered (Article 323 No. 1). However, the notion of res judicata is being understood pursuant to the conception

557. A. Douga & V. Koumpli, *On the Regulation of Maintenance Obligations in Greece*, *RHDI* 2014, pp. 931–960; A. Anthimos, *The Court of Appeal of Piraeus on the Non-Recognition of a Dutch Judgment on Maintenance*, https://eapil.org/2020/11/11/the-court-of-appeal-of-piraeus-on-the-non-recognition-of-a-dutch-judgment-on-maintenance/.
558. A. Anthimos, *Implementation of the EAPO in Greece*, https://conflictoflaws.net/2017/implementation-of-the-eapo-in-greece/.

of Greek law. Any decision of a foreign civil court can be recognized, be it declaratory, constitutive, or a decision for a specific performance, irrespective of whether it accepts or dismisses the action or has been rendered in default proceedings.

2. The International Jurisdiction of the Foreign Court

501. The foreign court must have had the authority to adjudicate the case under the internal rules governing the jurisdiction of Greek courts (Article 323 No. 2). Neither the rules actually applied by the foreign court nor the foreign court's subject matter or territorial competence are relevant. It is instead sufficient that the foreign court has territorial competence pursuant to a Greek rule, regardless if this constitutes only a concurrent or even an exorbitant jurisdiction.

Facts which established the jurisdiction of the foreign court can be re-examined insofar as this does not include a re-examination on the merits. Under this determination of the indirect jurisdiction of Greek courts, a foreign judgment is recognized if, e.g., the defendant's domicile (Article 22), the domicile of one of the joined defendants (Article 37), or the place of a contract's formation, or performance (Article 33), or the place of the defendant's property (Article 40), are located within the State where this judgment was rendered. Despite the lack of an explicit provision, a foreign decision will not be, however, recognized when Greek courts claim to have an exclusive jurisdiction over the case.[559]

3. Protection of the Right of Defence

502. A default decision rendered by a foreign court against an alien can be recognized in Greece insofar as the losing party has enjoyed equal opportunities to those available to nationals involving his right of defence (Article 323 No. 3). Service must have been effected in accordance with the law of the country where the decision was rendered. However, despite this rather restrictive provision, both legal theory and courts regard violations of the right of defence as also involving Greek public policy.[560]

4. Inconsistent Decisions

503. A domestic res judicata always has prevalence over a foreign res judicata (Article 323 No. 4). A decision cannot be recognized and a foreign res judicata cannot be imported in Greece when contrary to a domestic res judicata binding the same parties, which has developed even subsequently. On the contrary, a domestic lis pendens involving the same dispute cannot prevent the recognition of a foreign judgment.

559. Ch. Fragistas, 'La compétence internationale exclusive en droit privé', *Studi in onore di Antonio Segni II* (Milano 1967), pp. 199 ff. (204, 211–212).

560. *See infra*, No. 514.

5. Violation of Public Policy

504. A foreign decision cannot be recognized in Greece when contrary to good morals or public policy (Article 323 No. 5).[561] The scope of public policy is distinguished on the one hand from the domestic notion of public policy (Article 3 CC: rules of *jus cogens*), and on the other hand from the international public policy in its function as an impediment to the application of foreign law. The reservation of Greek public policy, as a condition to the recognition of foreign decisions, has been regarded as extending to both procedural and substantive issues (procedural and substantive public policy). In order to describe the notion of public policy while examining the prerequisites of recognition, Greek courts usually follow the definition given by a classical author:[562] A foreign decision is regarded as contrary to public policy when the development of its effects within the Greek territory imports conditions which are directly inconsistent with the current moral, State and economic order as the foundation of everyday life.

505. Violations of procedural public policy have been most often connected with due service of process and the protection of the right of defence. A default judgment will not be recognized, either when the defendant has not been served or when he has not been granted a reasonable time before his appearance in court. Greek courts, however, have frequently applied these prerequisites within a rather narrow scope. It has been thus accepted that the lack of financial means to support an appearance of the defaulting party abroad, the development of a res judicata effect through a default judgment which has not been previously served, the initial service of process in a foreign language or following the stipulations involving defendants of unknown residence when this was not the case, are not sufficient facts as such to base refusal of recognition of default judgments. Differences in the applied foreign procedural law involving evidentiary proceedings have also not been considered entailing violations of public policy. Foreign decisions lacking reasoning can also be recognized when this defect does not entail a violation of the right of defence or substantial public policy. A request for a preliminary ruling is pending before the CJEU concerning 'quasi' anti-suit injunctions.[563]

561. In detail, A. Anthimos, *Der verfahrensrechtliche ordre public im griechischen internationalen Zivilprozeßrecht Griechenlands*, *IPRax* 2000, pp. 327–331; A. Anthimos, *Der prozessuale ordre public bei der Anerkennung und Vollstreckung ausländischer Gerichtsentscheidungen nach deutschem und griechischem Zivilprozeßrecht und nach dem Europäischen Gerichtsstands- und Vollstreckungsübereinkommen,* in: Apostolos M. Anthimos Marc-André Delp & Harald Harazim, *Harmonisierungsprobleme im europäischen Wirtschaftsrecht,* (Baden, Nomos Verlag, 2000), pp. 11–153, and more recently, A. Anthimos, *The Public Policy Defence in the Recognition and Enforcement of Foreign Judgments in Greece*, *International Journal of Procedural Law*, Vol. 12 (2022), No. 2, pp. 296 et seq.

562. G. Maridakis, *Enforcement of Foreign Judgments According to the Law in Force in Greece*, 3rd ed. (Athens 1970), §41 (in Greek).

563. *See* A. Anthimos, *Greek Supreme Court No. 820/2021*, *International Journal of Procedural Law* 2022, pp. 136–142; A. Anthimos, *Awaken the Guardian: UK damages for breach of a choice of court agreement violate Greek public policy*, https://conflictoflaws.net/2019/awaken-the-guardian-uk-damages-for-breach-of-a-choice-of-court-agreement-violate-greek-public-policy/; A. Anthimos, *From Anti-Suit Injunctions to 'Quasi' Anti-Suit Injunctions and Declaratory Relief for Breach of a*

506. Despite the lack of any explicit provision involving the application of the law called for by the Greek conflict rules, in cases related to the personal status of Greek nationals (especially to divorce), Greek courts, exceptionally, have quite often considered the application of a substantive regulation other than Greek law, e.g., if providing grounds for divorce unknown to Greek law, as violating public policy.[564] Nevertheless, the recent family law reform has been to a great extent preventing the appearance of such situations.[565] In a similar fashion, foreign adoption decrees are recognized as a rule.[566] Same-sex marriage or custody orders concerning same-sex couples are however not tolerated by Greek public policy.[567] The latter has been however reversed in the second instance.[568]

6. No Re-Examination of the Merits

507. The CPC does not provide for any kind of re-examination of the merits. Also, neither corrections nor an official interpretation of the foreign decision is allowed.

7. No Reciprocity

508. Reciprocity has never been a condition for recognition under Greek law.

8. No Examination of the Applicable Law

509. No requirement is provided as to whether the law applied by the foreign court would have been also applicable pursuant to the Greek conflict rules. Unless

---

Choice of Court Agreement: A Whiter Shade of Pale?, https://conflictoflaws.net/2020/from-anti-suit-injunctions-to-quasi-anti-suit-injunctions-and-declaratory-relief-for-breach-of-a-choice-of-court-agreement-a-whiter-shade-of-pale/.

564. Legal theory and some judicial decisions are, however, satisfied when the applicable substantive law under a foreign conflict rule can lead to similar solutions (*théorie de l'équivalence des solutions*).

565. A. Anthimos, *Rabbinical Divorce Recognized in Greece*, http://icl-in-greece.blogspot.com/2014_11_02_archive.html; A. Anthimos, *Recognition of an Egyptian Khul'a Divorce in Greece*, http://icl-in-greece.blogspot.com/2016_10_16_archive.html. *See* however A. Anthimos, *Talaq v Greek Public Policy: Operation Successful, Patient Dead …* , https://conflictoflaws.net/2018/talaq-v-greek-public-policy-operation-successful-patient-dead/. A fresh judgment changed again the course, *see* A. Anthimos, *Talaq Reloaded: Repudiation Recognized if Application Filed by the Wife,* https://conflictoflaws.net/2019/talaq-reloaded-repudiation-recognized-if-application-filed-by-the-wife/.

566. A. Anthimos, *Winds of Change in the Recognition of Foreign Adult Adoption Decrees*, *International Journal of Procedural Law* 2017, pp. 163–165.

567. A. Anthimos, English Custody Orders Violate Greek Public Policy if the Parents Form a Same-Sex Couple, https://eapil.org/2021/02/03/english-custody-orders-violate-greek-public-policy-if-the-parents-form-a-same-sex-couple/.

568. A. Anthimos, *Greek Court Recognizes UK Custody Order to the Non-biological Parent in the Context of a Married Same-Sex Couple*, https://conflictoflaws.net/2022/greek-court-recognizes-uk-custody-order-to-the-non-biological-parent-in-the-context-of-a-married-same-sex-couple/.

no violation of Greek public policy is involved, neither the substantive rules actually applied by the foreign court nor their dissimilarity to the respective Greek legislation are relevant, even if, under domestic conflict rules, Greek substantive provisions of *jus cogens* would have been applicable.

D. Enforcement of a Foreign Judgment

1. Prerequisites

510. Prerequisites to enforcement of a foreign decision in Greece are, in principle, similar to the requirements of recognition (*see* Article 905 §3 CPC). The sole difference consists in the condition of enforceability instead of a foreign res judicata (Articles 905 §§2 and 3).

2. The Enforceability of the Foreign Judgment in Particular

511. A foreign decision can be declared enforceable in Greece if it is enforceable in accordance with the law of its origin (Article 905 §2 CPC). Unless contrary to public policy, the foreign instrument does not need to also satisfy the conditions of enforceability under domestic law. What is relevant is the time when the domestic *exequatur* is granted; instruments, which in this time have ceased to be enforceable after successful methods of review, cannot be vested with enforceability.[569]

Enforceability is related to decisions which can be enforced in a technical sense (decisions for specific performance) and on that specific phase of a decision's procedural maturity which permits its enforcement. While a foreign judgment needs to be enforceable only under the law of its origin, it has been, on the contrary, accepted that whether provisionally enforceable foreign instruments can also be executed in Greece, is a question to be judged under Greek law. This is connected to the definition of the notion of enforceability and, in particular, to the question of whether this notion also includes provisional enforcement.

Despite the lack of an explicit provision, the prevailing opinion supports granting *exequatur* to foreign decisions which are only provisionally enforceable in accordance with the law of their origin, even in cases where domestic law would not allow provisional enforcement. Thus, in order to declare the enforceability of an instrument, Greek courts neither examine whether a foreign decision has been matured to res judicata in accordance with the law of its origin nor demand that the methods of review provided by the foreign law against a decision have been exhausted.

---

569. *See* A. Anthimos, *Enforcing a First Preferred Ship's Mortgage from St. Vincent & the Grenadines in Greece*, http://icl-in-greece.blogspot.com/2014_09_28_archive.html. The same applies, if the foreign judgment is not anymore enforceable after granting *exequatur*. In this case, the foreign judgment execution is not anymore possible in Greece, ad hoc A. Anthimos, *Greek Supreme Court No. 767/2019, International Journal of Procedural Law* 2021, pp. 351–353: No execution of a Baltimore expired money judgment, even if previously given full faith and credit in Greece.

3. The *Exequatur* Proceeding

512. The *exequatur* proceeding provided by Article 905 §1 CPC tends to adopt the foreign judgment as such. It has been considered exclusive, in the sense that any new action before a domestic forum seeking a decision of the same nature, based on the foreign proceeding, for the purpose of substituting the foreign decision with a domestic one, would be rejected as inadmissible. The results obtained through this proceeding can thereafter not be invalidated in another proceeding.

513. Exclusive subject matter competence has been allocated to the one-member district Courts of First Instance for the request to obtain *exequatur*. Territorial competence belongs either to the courts of the debtor's domicile or, if this is absent, of the debtor's residence; in cases where the debtor is neither a domiciliary nor a resident of Greece, the request is brought in the one-member district court of Athens (905 §1). Relevant for legal entities is their seat.

514. A request for enforcement is not subject to time limitations. According to some decisions, a delayed application seeking *exequatur* does not entail, as such, a prohibited abuse of rights on the part of the creditor.

515. The *exequatur* proceeding operates under the specific rules designed for matters of voluntary jurisdiction (Articles 905 §1b, 740 to 781). The defendant does not need to be served. The judge may, however, order his summoning (Article 748 §3), a practice followed rather infrequently. If the defendant does not appear, his absence is not deemed as a confession of the assertions included in the application (Article 754).

The application to obtain an *exequatur* must be supported by: (a) the foreign instrument accompanied by a Greek translation; (b) assertions and evidence involving its enforceability in the country of origin, i.e., an official certificate of the foreign courts' officer that no methods of review have been used, or that they have been dismissed; (c) in case of a default decision, evidence of the notification on the defendant. If the defendant appears, he may only contest the *exequatur's* prerequisites. On the contrary, he may not admissibly bring objections against the claim under enforcement, i.e., assert subsequent payment. Such objections may be only raised through an opposition to enforcement.

516. The decision which grants *exequatur* is of a constitutive nature. Beyond revocation (Articles 758, 779), it is subject to all methods of review provided for cases of voluntary jurisdiction, i.e., to an appeal (Articles 761–766), to a reopening (Articles 767–768), to a cassation (Articles 769–772) and, additionally, in case the defendant has not participated in the proceeding, to a third-party opposition (Articles 773–775).

E. Enforcement of Other Executory Instruments

517. Foreign executory instruments of a similar or an equivalent nature to those provided by Greek law (Article 904 CPC), when rendered by the competent organs in accordance with the law of their origin, are vested with *exequatur* on the condition that they are enforceable under the law of origin and are not contrary to good morals or Greek public policy (Article 905 §2).[570]

F. *The Specific Proceeding for the Recognition of Decisions Involving Personal Status*

518. In order to satisfy practical needs and in view of the doctrinal support to the application of the *exequatur* proceeding by analogy also for the recognition of foreign judgments involving personal status, a paragraph (§4) was added to Article 905 in 1971.[571] This has expressly provided that decisions of foreign courts involving personal status are recognized by virtue of the particular proceeding used to declare the enforceability of foreign judgments. While the prevailing theoretical opinion regarded the application of this proceeding as a mere availability at the party's option, *Areios Pagos* ruled in favour of its compulsory nature.

G. *Recognition of the Effects of Foreign Decisions on Voluntary Jurisdiction*

519. The effects of a foreign decision on matters which under Greek law would have been characterized as belonging to voluntary jurisdiction are recognized under conditions provided in Article 780 CPC, which differ from those required for contentious matters. Unless otherwise provided by international conventions, these conditions are the following: (a) The decision must have applied the same substantive rules which would have been applicable under Greek conflict rules and must have been rendered by a court having jurisdiction under the law of the State whose substantive rules were applied; (b) it is not contrary to good morals or public policy.

II. International Treaties

A. *Multilateral Conventions*

520. Greece ratified the EU Convention on Jurisdiction and Enforcement of Judgments in Civil and Commercial Matters of 1968/1978/1982 by Law 1814/1988, the San Sebastian Convention of 1989 by Law 2004/1992[572] and the 1996 Accession Convention for Austria, Sweden and Finland by Law 2727/1999.[573] The

570. *See* A. Anthimos, *Is a Maltese Ship Mortgage an Authentic Instrument for the Purposes of Article 57 of the Brussels I Regulation?*, https://eapil.org/2021/04/13/is-a-maltese-ship-mortgage-an-authentic-instrument-for-the-purposes-of-article-57-of-the-brussels-i-regulation/.
571. Focusing on German divorce decrees, P.C. Filios & D. Henrich, *Zur Anerkennung deutscher Scheidungsurteile in Griechenland, IPRax* 1985, pp. 150–151.
572. *Supra*, No. 157.
573. These conventions are replaced by Regulations 44/2001 and 1215/2012.

1988 Lugano Convention was ratified by Law 2460/1997, in force since 26 February 1997.[574] The new Lugano Convention started to operate in its revised version of 15 October 2007 on 1 January 2010.[575]

Enforcement of judgments or other enforceable instruments involving civil or commercial matters originating from EU Member States was initially treated under Regulation 44/2001,[576,577] and currently under Regulation 1215/2012 (recast Regulation).[578] Regulation 1215/2012 applies to legal proceedings instituted and documents formally drawn up or registered as authentic instruments after 10 January 2015 (Article 66 §1). Judgments given in proceedings instituted before this date are governed by Regulation 44 (Article 66, §2). Under the Brussels I Regulation, the exequatur proceeding operated on the basis of specific rules designed for matters of voluntary jurisdiction.[579]

Recognition and enforcement of Judgments in Matrimonial Matters and in Matters of Joint Parental Responsibility for Children was initially the object of Council Regulation 1347/2000, replaced by Regulation 2201/2003.[580] Since 01 August 2022, the latter has been replaced by Regulation 2019/1111.[581]

574. Greece has been condemned by the ECHR for violation of the right to judicial protection in the course of recognition and enforcement of child support, *see* A. Anthimos, *Case of Matrakas And Others v Poland and Greece*, ECHR, 7 Nov. 2013 [case Nr. 47268/06], http://icl-in-greece.blogspot.com/2014_02_09_archive.html. *See also* A. Anthimos, *On the Significance of Translation Inaccuracies in the Field of the Lugano Convention (and Beyond ...)*, http://icl-in-greece.blogspot.com/2016_10_09_archive.html.

575. *See Official Journal of the European Union*, No. L 339/1 of 21 Dec. 2007.

576. E. Vassilakakis, *Die Anwendung des EuGVÜ und der EuGVO in der griechischen Rechtsprechung*, *IPRax* 2005, pp. 279-284; A. Anthimos, *Reconocimiento y ejecución de sentencias extranjeras según el Reglamento Bruselas I en Grecia, Anuario Español de Derecho Internacional Privado* 2014, pp. 587–607; A. Anthimos, *Europäisches Zivilprozessrecht in Griechenland – Überblick über die Rechtsprechung griechischer Gerichte in den Jahren 2012-2014, GPR* 2015, pp. 291–295.

577. *See* in detail Frangou & Georgios, *Vollstreckung ausländischer Entscheidungen in Griechenland – Die Anwendung des europäischen Zivilprozessrechts durch die griechische Rechtsprechung, Internationales und europäisches Privat-und Verfahrensrecht*, Band 18, (NOMOS Verlag 2017), (Zugl.: Dissertation Heidelberg 2016),A .. In a case concerning the declaration of enforceability of a UK costs order, the Supreme Court of the Hellenic Republic decided that the 'excessive' nature of the sum (compared to the subject matter of the dispute) does not run contrary to public policy. This judgment signals a clear-cut shift from the previous course followed both by the Supreme and instance courts. The decisive factor was the principle of mutual trust within the EU, *see* A. Anthimos, *Greek Supreme Court No. 579/2019, International Journal of Procedural Law* 2020, pp. 83–85. *See also* A. Anthimos, *Greek Supreme Court on Enforcement of UK Divorce Financial Payment, The European Legal Forum* 2021, pp. 29–31.

578. A. Anthimos, *Recognition and Enforcement of Foreign Judgments According to the Brussels* I-*bis Regulation in Greece*, *YbPIL* 2015, pp. 345–364; A. Anthimos, *Denegación del reconocimiento y la ejecución en el Reglamento Bruselas I bis, Anuario Español de Derecho Internacional Privado* 2015, pp. 375–393; A. Anthimos, *First Contacts with the Application for Refusal of Enforcement in Greece,* https://eapil.org/2022/08/29/first-contacts-with-the-application-for-refusal-of-enforcement-in-greece/.

579. *See supra*, No. 524. *See also* A. Anthimos, Exequatur *proceedings according to the Brussels I Regulation in Greece*, *RHDI* 2014, pp. 1007–1021.

580. *See* OJ, No. L 338/1 of 21 Dec. 2003. In detail, E. Vasilakakis & V. Kourtis, *The Impact and Application of the Brussels II bis regulation in Greece*, in K. Boele-Woelki (ed), *Brussels II bis: Its Impact and Application in the Member States* (Oxford, Antwerp 2007) pp.133–143.

581. OJ L 178/2.7.2019, pp. 1–115.

B. Other Multilateral Conventions

521. Other multilateral conventions governing the enforcement of foreign judgments to which Greece is a party include: (a) The Conventions on the International Carriage of Goods, Passengers and Luggage by Rail[582] (Article 56); (b) the New York Convention of 20 June 1956, on the Recovery Abroad of Maintenance (Articles 5 and 6);[583] (c) the European Convention of 20 May 1980 (Luxembourg) on the Recognition and Enforcement of Decisions Concerning Custody of Children and on Restoration of Custody of Children (Law 2104/1992); (d) the Hague Convention of 2 October 1973, on the Recognition and Enforcement of Decisions Relating to Maintenance Obligations, in force since 1 August 1976, which has been ratified by Law 3171/2003 and has started to operate on 1 February 2004. On the contrary, the Hague Convention of 1 February 1971 on the Recognition and Enforcement of Foreign Judgments in Civil and Commercial Matters was not signed by Greece.[584] Greece signed, but never ratified, the Hague Convention of 15 April 1958 on the Recognition and Enforcement of Decisions Relating to Maintenance Obligations towards Children.

C. Bilateral Conventions

522. Both Articles 323 and 905 CPC feature a reservation clause in favour of the application of international conventions.[585] Accordingly, international conventions prevail over internal law when they are more favourable to the request for recognition or enforcement (*see also* Article 28 Const.).[586] Greek authors, based on the rationale of these treaties, which is understood as tending to secure recognition and enforcement, accept that domestic rules continue to apply when the requirements of the CPC are more favourable with regard to a specific request for recognition or enforcement.

523. A number of bilateral conventions govern the mutual recognition and enforcement of foreign judgments[587] with EU Member States and other countries around the globe. Concerning the first group, the Hellenic Republic has signed treaties with the Federal Republic of Germany (Law 4305/1963),[588] Cyprus (Law 1548/

582. *See supra*, No. 158.
583. *Supra*, No. 29.
584. Ch. Fragistas, 'Deux conventions multilaterales recentes sur la reconnaissance des jugements étrangers', *Rivista di diritto internazionale privato e processuale* 1968, pp. 745 ff.
585. *See also* the explicit rule of Art. 2 of the Introductory Law of the CPC. *See also* A. Anthimos, *ibid*, pp. 201 ff. (pp. 202–205).
586. *See supra*, No. 29.
587. For the detailed list, *see supra*, No. 29.
588. K. Kerameus, 'Rechtsmittelfestigkeit und Vollstreckung von ausländischen Entscheidungen', *Festschrift für W. Wengler*, Vol. II (1973), pp. 383–395; A. Pouliadis, *Die Bedeutung des deutsch-griechischen Vertrags v. 4.11.1961 für die Anerkennung und Vollstreckung deutscher Entscheidungen in der griechischen praxis*, *IPRax* 1985, pp. 357–369; P. Yessiou-Faltsi, 'Die Anerkennung und Vollstreckung deutscher Gerichtsurteile in Griechenland aus der Sicht eines griechischen Juristen', *ZZP* 1983, pp. 67–89; A. Anthimos, *Zum verbleibenden Wert des Deutsch-Griechischen*

1985), Bulgaria (Law 841/1978),[589] Czechoslovakia (Law 1323/1983), Hungary (Law 1145/1981), Poland (Law 1184/1981), Romania (Legislative Decree 429/1974),[590] Croatia and Slovenia (Legislative Decree 4007/1959).[591] These continue to operate only for matters outside the scope of application of European Regulations.

In addition, Greece has bilateral ties with the following countries: Albania: Treaty on Judicial Assistance of 17 May 1993, ratified by Law 2311/1995;[592] Armenia: Treaty on Judicial Assistance of 21 November 2000, ratified by Law 3007/2002; China: Treaty on Judicial Assistance of 1 October 1994, ratified by Law 2358/1995; Georgia: Treaty on Judicial Assistance of 10 May 1999, ratified by Law 2813/2000; Lebanon: Treaty on Judicial Assistance of 5 April 1975, ratified by Law 1099/1980; Ex-Soviet Union;[593] Treaty on Judicial Assistance of 21 May 1981, ratified by Law 12421982; Syria: Treaty on Judicial Assistance of 2 June 1981, ratified by Law 1450/1984; Tunisia: Treaty on Judicial Assistance of 12 April 1993, ratified by Law 2228/1994; Ukraine: Treaty on Judicial Assistance of 2 July 2002, ratified by Law 3281/2004; (former) Yugoslavia:[594] Treaty on Mutual Recognition and Enforcement of Judgments of 18 June 1959, ratified by Legislative Decree 4007/1959.

Anerkennungs- und Vollstreckungsvertrags von 1961, *IPRax* 2015, pp. 361–363; G. Sinanides, *Die Anerkennung deutscher Scheidungsurteile in Griechenland*, Bielefeld, Univ., Fak. für Rechtswiss., Diss., 1980; A. Anthimos, *Greek Supreme Court No. 1395/2018*, *International Journal of Procedural Law* 2019, pp. 339–342.

589. A. Anthimos, *Recognition and Enforcement of Foreign Judgments in the Field of Bilateral Conventions of Greece with Balkan States*, *Balkan Yearbook of European and International Law* (2021) 2020, pp. 201 ff. (pp. 211 ff.).

590. A. Anthimos, *ibid*, pp. 201 ff. (pp. 209–211).

591. Croatia and Slovenia apply the 1959 convention between the Hellenic Republic and (ex) Yogoslavia in matters not covered by EU Regulations.

592. A. Anthimos, *ibid*, pp. 201 ff. (pp. 206–209).

593. E. Vassilakakis, Recognition and Enforcement of Foreign Judgments in Cases of State Succession: The Paradigm of the 1981 Convention between Greece and the Former USSR on Judicial Assistance in Civil and Criminal Matters (with Dr P. Yiannopulos), *Currents – Journal of International Economic Law* 2003, pp. 31–36; A. Anthimos, *Recognition of Russian Personal Status Judgments in Greece: A Case Law Survey*, *Russian Law Journal* Vo. II (2014), Issue 3, pp. 49–61.

594. A. Anthimos, *Balkan Yearbook of European and International Law* (2021) 2020: pp. 201 ff. (pp. 212–215).

Part X. Out-of-Court Dispute Resolution

Chapter 1. Arbitration

§1. Current Relevance

524. The CPC devotes Book VII to arbitration (Articles 867–903).[595] Under this detailed regulation, arbitration is generally regarded as a mechanism for resolving private disputes parallel to State jurisdiction.

To counterbalance deficiencies and delays of State courts, the resort to arbitration has been a steadily increasing occurrence, particularly in commercial or international litigation.[596] Not only private contracts but also most contracts of the Greek State or of legal entities of public law with private individuals, evidently involving disputes of a high value, encompass arbitral clauses. According to the practice followed, contracts between the Greek State and domestic or foreign companies of particular significance are vested with the structure of a 'formal' law, providing for arbitration as an exclusive method A number of such contracts are formed based on special pieces of legislation for the protection of foreign investments. A special statute had been initially provided for this purpose by Article 112 of the 1952 Const., to be enacted only once. The respective Legislative Decree 2687/1953, which followed, has been now recognized by Article 107 §1a of the 1975 Const.

595. G. Oikonomopoulos, 'Greece', in P. Sanders (gen. ed.), *International Commercial Arbitration*, Vol. I (Union Internationale des Avocats, 1956), pp. 270–323 (in English and French); K. Kerameus, 'Probleme des griechischen Schiedsverfahrensrechts aus rechtsvergleichender Sicht', *ZZP* 1979, pp. 413 ff.; A. Foustoukos, *L'arbitrage-interne et international – en droit privé hellénique* (Paris 1976); the same author, 'Greece' in P. Sanders (gen. ed.), *Yearbook of Commercial Arbitration*, Vol. V (International Council for Commercial Arbitration, The Hague, 1980), pp. 57–83, XI (1986), pp. 69–72, VII (1987), pp. 367–368, XIII (1988), pp. 417–419; S. Koussoulis, Die internationale Schiedsgerichtsbarkeit in Griechenland, in: Peter Gottwald (Hrsg.), *Internationale Schiedsgerichtsbarkeit: Generalbericht und Nationalbericht = Arbitrage international = International Arbitration*, Veröffentlichung der Wissenschaftlichen Vereinigung für Internationales Verfahrensrecht e.V., Bd. 9 (Bielefeld, Gieseking 1997), pp. 405–420; A. Foustoukos and S. Koussoulis, 'Greece' in P. Sanders (ed.), *International Handbook on Commercial Arbitration* (The Hague, 2001); G. Verveniotis, *Construction and Arbitration. Cases from the Greek Experience* (Athens-Komotini 2000); N. Deloukas, 'The Arbitration in Greece', In G. Levi (ed.), *Arbitration* (Milano 1991), pp. 103 ff; A. Dimolitsa, 'Arbitration Agreements and Foreign Investments, The Greek State Between Contractual Commitment and Sovereign Intervention' *RHDI* 1989–1990, pp. 259 ff.

596. K. Kerameus, 'Aktuelle Probleme der internationalen Handelsschiedsgerichtsbarkeit unter Berücksichtigung der Rechtslage in Griechenland', in the coll. Vol. *Les particularités nationales de d'arbitrage commercial international* (1987); same author, 'Arbitrage International et Ordre Juridique Hellénique', *Revue de l'Arbitrage* 1987, pp. 35–48.

Articles 867–902 CPC govern domestic arbitration. International arbitration is now treated by Law 5016/2023, replacing Law 2735/1999,[597] which introduced in Greece the rules of the UNCITRAL Model Law on International Commercial Arbitration.[598]

§2. Types of Arbitration: Constitutionality

525. Neither Article 8 §1 Const. 1975, which guarantees the legal judge, nor Article 20 §1, which guarantees the right of individuals to obtain legal protection before the courts, preclude the establishment of alternatives to proceedings before ordinary courts, and the derogation of State jurisdiction, when based on the litigants' will, by reference of disputes to arbitration. Voluntary arbitration is, therefore, not regarded as incompatible with the Const. In addition, the guaranteed freedom of individuals to develop their personality (Article 5 Const.) confirms the spirit of the Const. as not being against any such agreement of the parties.

526. Compulsory arbitrations are, on the contrary, regarded as unconstitutional. Compulsory arbitration is primarily understood as that imposed on a party through the volition of merely one or some of the parties of the other side. Article 7 §1 Introductory Law of the CPC has explicitly repealed all pieces of special legislation providing for compulsory arbitration in private disputes.

527. Compulsory arbitration in the above sense must be, however, distinguished from the type of obligatory arbitration provided for by contracts, usually between the Greek State and other foreign or domestic companies, when these are vested in a 'formal law', as explained above. Pursuant to Article 46 Introductory Law of the CPC, contracts which have been included in 'formal' laws and have provided for the resolution of private disputes exclusively through arbitration remained in force. The most striking examples of this kind of obligatory arbitration are indeed those referring to the protection of foreign investments, pursuant to Legislative Decree

597. For a French and English translation of this Law by A. Dimolitsa and S. Kousoulis *see* Loi 2735/1999 'Arbitrage Commercial International'/Law 2735/1999 'International Commercial Arbitration', *RHDI* 1999, pp. 586 ff.

598. K. Kerameus, 'The New Greek Law on International Commercial Arbitration', *RHDI* 1999, pp. 583 ff.; S. Koussoulis, 'Actual Problems of International Arbitration. The Greek Law in Comparison with the UNCITRAL Model Law', *RHDI* 1999, pp. 479 ff. *See also* Calavros, *Das UNCITRAL-Modellgesetz über die internationale Handelsschiedsgerichtsbarkeit,* Bielefeld 1988, S. Koussoulis, 'Actual Problems of International Arbitration. The Greek Law in Comparison with the UNCITRAL Model Law', *RHDI* 1996, pp. 479–500; N. Klamaris, *Hauptunterschiede zwischen der Regelung der Schiedsgerichtsbarkeit in der griechischen ZPO (Art. 867-903) und der Regelung der Internationalen Handelsschiedsgerichtsbarkeit im (griechischen) Gesetz 2735/1999. Ein innerstaatlicher Überblick und Vergleich,* in *Grenzüberschreitungen – Beiträge zum Internationalen Verfahrensrecht und zur Schiedsgerichtsbarkeit; Festschrift für Peter Schlosser zum 70. Geburtstag* (Tübingen, Mohr Verlag 2005), pp. 383–398; K. Makridou, The public policy defence in International Arbitration under Greek Law, *ZZP* International 18 (2013), pp. 175 ff.

2687/1953, as remained in force according to the Const. of 1975. According to legal theory, having a contractual basis, the exclusive submission to arbitration of disputes emerging from such formal laws may not be considered violating the Const.

528. The aforementioned types of compulsory and obligatory arbitration are clearly distinguished from institutional arbitration. This latter, as long as it is based on the volition of all parties, has not created any doubts.

§3. Institutional Arbitration

529. Institutional arbitration has been explicitly provided for by Article 902 CPC.[599] Chambers of Commerce[600] and Engineers, the Stock Exchange, and Professional Associations, which are legal persons of public law, are allowed to organize permanent arbitral tribunals established by a presidential decree for concrete disputes upon the proposition of the Minister of Justice and the Minister who has the supervision of the institutions mentioned above. This decree can, among other things, also regulate the procedure before the permanent arbitral tribunals and the selection of arbitrators (Article 902 §2). Institutions which can organize such permanent arbitral tribunals may even be entrusted to propose a compulsory list from which the parties will be obliged to select their arbitrators.

530. From the permanent arbitral tribunals organized by many of the above institutions, we may note the following examples:

(a) The permanent arbitral tribunal at the Maritime Chamber (Royal Decree 447/1969) for the settlement of disputes concerning maritime matters within the scope of private law.
(b) The permanent arbitral tribunal at the Chamber of Engineers (Presidential Decree 723/1979. Its jurisdiction extends to disputes deriving from technical matters, e.g., the execution or the preservation of constructions which are supervised by engineers – members of the Chamber (Article 2 §2).
(c) The permanent arbitral tribunal provided by Presidential Decree 91/2020 at the Bar Association of Athens. This permanent arbitral tribunal has the jurisdiction to adjudicate private law disputes, except those falling under the scope of Article 614 §3, i.e., labour disputes (Article 1).

599. A. Foustoukos, 'Une nouvelle institution permanente d'arbitrage en Grèce', *Revue de l'arbitrage* 1974, pp. 418–423. According to the data of the Greek 'Institute of Arbitration' at the Law Faculty of Democritos University in Komotini, based on the 1,855 arbitral awards in the area of the District Court of Athens during the years 1969–1987, the awards of the Permanent Arbitral Tribunals consist of the 2.3% of the total number.

600. A. Kaissis, *Die Schiedsgerichtsordnung der Deutsch-Griechischen Industrie- und Handelskammer*, in *Ars aequi et boni in mundo – Festschrift zum 80. Geburtstag von Rolf A. Schütze* (München, 2015), pp. 213–220.

(d) The permanent arbitral tribunal provided by Presidential Decree 68/2020 at the Bar Association of Thessaloniki.[601]

§4. Arbitrable Disputes

531. The general rule is that all private law disputes are arbitrable when the parties enjoy the power to freely dispose the object in litigation (Article 867a).[602] Only labour disputes are explicitly excluded (Article 867b) for reasons of public interest to avoid situations where the acceptance of the arbitration agreement can be the result of pressure.[603] Also, disputes involving personal status cannot be settled through arbitration.[604]

601. For the permanent arbitral tribunals at the Bar Associations of Piraeus, *see* Presidential Decree 199/1984; Larissa, *see* Presidential Decree 305/1984; Patra, *see* Presidential Decree 415/1985; Ioannina, *see* Presidential Decree 122/1987; Chania, *see* Presidential Decree 476/1987; Chalkida. *see* Presidential Decree 398/1988.
602. This stipulation is understood widely and, hence, as also covering cases which belong to voluntary jurisdiction, if they bear the nature of a genuine dispute. According to most authors, administrative disputes are in principle not arbitrable.
603. Following its rationale, the exception is interpreted narrowly.
604. A divorce cannot be pronounced through an arbitral award, even if granted ‘by consensus’.

Chapter 2. Arbitration Agreement and Party Autonomy

532. The CPC does not draw any distinctions between an arbitration agreement, i.e., an agreement involving already existing disputes, and an arbitral clause, i.e., an agreement referring to future disputes. On the sole condition that the legal relationship, out of which the future arbitrable disputes are expected to arise (Article 868), has been already born, both types of agreements have been now integrated, whether involving present or future disputes, under a uniform institution known as the 'arbitration agreement'. This must be necessarily in writing, be it in public or private instrument,[605] unless the interested parties voluntarily participate in the arbitration procedure, even in the absence of a document (Article 869).

533. There have been dissenting opinions as to the exact legal nature of the arbitration agreement. Whereas, according to one opinion, this must be characterized as a procedural contract, in view of its effects which are mainly procedural, some authors regard the arbitration agreement as a contract of a sui generis or of a mixed character. Article 869 §2 CPC explicitly declares that the arbitration agreement is treated by the provisions governing civil law contracts. The capacity of the parties to enter into arbitration agreements is, thus, basically dependent on substantive law requirements.

According to the prevailing opinion, the arbitration agreement must be handled as a self-standing contract, which is not affected by the deficiencies of the main contract, where it is included. And vice versa: the deficiencies of the arbitration clause do not affect the main contract; they result in state adjudication of the dispute.[606]

605. Article 869 CPC explicitly provides that telegrams, telex and fax can be also accepted.
606. A. Anthimos, *Pathological Clauses in International Sports Arbitration and Return to Civil Proceedings*, https://eapil.org/2020/09/03/pathological-clauses-in-international-sports-arbitration-and-return-to-civil-proceedings/.

Chapter 3. Composition of Arbitral Tribunal

534. Parties are as a rule free to choose their arbitrators.[607] According to Articles 871–878 CPC, the appointment of the arbitrators is based upon the volition of the parties, as expressed in the arbitration agreement. If a party has not appointed the arbitrators and the arbitration agreement does not provide otherwise, the one-member district Court of First Instance appoints the arbitrator upon request (Article 878 §1). For this reason, an arbitrator's list is prepared every year by the three-member district courts and kept at every one-member district court of the country (Article 879 §1). According to Royal Decree 566/1968, which regulates the composition of the arbitrators' list, all individuals who are considered appropriate to carry out arbitration may be registered. The arbitrators are to be registered in groups in accordance with their specialty.

According to Article 871A CPC,[608] the parties are allowed to entrust, by a clause in the arbitration agreement, professional judges with the adjudication of their possible controversies, who can thus act also as arbitrators. What is not allowed is the appointment of a professional judge as an arbitrator personally (*see* Article 871A §4). Judges of a specific court are currently appointed to act as arbitrators by turn, following the order of seniority (Article 871A).

The parties may designate one or more arbitrators, in even or uneven numbers, who need not be Greek nationals. In practice, the appointment of one, or sometimes three arbitrators, is more usual. An entire court can be also appointed (Article 871 §1). Unless otherwise provided, when more persons are named arbitrators, they must also appoint the 'presiding' arbitrator (Article 874).[609] Arbitrators need not accept their assignment (Article 880 §1). Also, they may resign after acceptance for a good cause upon permission from the one-member district court (Article 880 §2). Once an arbitrator has been appointed, revocation of his assignment must be based on unanimous consent by all parties (Article 883 §1). Arbitrators can be challenged on the basis of similar grounds to those of judges (Article 883 §2).

607. The 'Greek Institute of Arbitration' at the Law Faculty of Democritos University in Komotini had collected data concerning the professions of the arbitrators in the area of the District Court of Athens during the years 1969–1987. According to this data, 47.8% of the arbitrators were engineers, 18% were judges, 21.3% were advocates, and 3.8% were university professors. To the panel of the arbitral courts sometimes participated the president (0.7%), or the Vice President (0.3%) of the Chamber of Engineers. 8% of the arbitrators exercised other professions.

608. The 'presiding' arbitrator in Greek law does not exercise the functions of the umpire of English law. *See* A. Foustoukos, 'Greece', in P. Sanders (gen. ed.), *Yearbook of Commercial Arbitration,* Vol. V (International Council for Commercial Arbitration, The Hague 1980), p. 71 and n. 1 (the author uses the expression 'chairman').

609. The 'presiding' arbitrator in Greek law does not exercise the functions of the umpire of English law. *See* A. Foustoukos, 'Greece', in P. Sanders (gen. ed.), *Year Book of Commercial Arbitration,* Vol. V (International Council for Commercial Arbitration, The Hague 1980), p. 71 and n. 1 (the author uses the expression 'chairman'); A. Koutsouradis, 'Grundsätze und Besonderheiten der Beweisaufnahme nach griechischem Schiedsverfahrensrecht', in the Vol. *Les particularités nationales de l'arbitrage commercial international* (1987).

Arbitrators are entitled to remuneration, part of which must be paid in advance (Article 882 §1). The arbitrators' fees are subject to essential limits in accordance with the value of the object in litigation (Article 882 §2). Arbitrators are liable for fraud or gross negligence while carrying out their duties (Article 881).

Chapter 4. Interim Measures and Preliminary Awards

535. Arbitrators can neither grant nor revoke or modify provisional remedies (Article 889 §1, CPC). The arbitration agreement, however, does not prevent the parties from seeking provisional relief from the courts (*see* Article 889 §2).[610]

610. I. Germanos, *Einstweiliger Rechtsschutz durch staatliche Gerichte bei Vorliegen einer Schiedsvereinbarung in Deutschland und Griechenland, RHDI* 2010, pp. 989–1001.

Chapter 5. Conduct of Arbitral Proceedings

536. Unless otherwise provided by the arbitration agreement, arbitrators are required to determine the kind of procedure to be followed and also the place and time of the arbitration (Article 886 § 1b). It is, accordingly, accepted that the proceeding for provisional remedies can be applied as well. Arbitrators, however, are not entitled to disregard fundamental procedural guarantees. Both sides must enjoy equal rights and have the same obligations; both must receive equal treatment and be given an adequate opportunity to submit evidence and to be heard before the arbitrators (Article 886 §2).[611] Also, representation by an attorney cannot be excluded (Article 886 §3b). *Areios Pagos*[612] has ruled that the arbitrators are not allowed to rely on private cognizance over the controversial facts, this being inconsistent with their task as adjudicators.[613]

If there is more than one arbitrator, all arbitrators must act jointly (Article 886 §1a). The proceeding is presided by the 'presiding' arbitrator (Article 886 §3a) and is supported by a court clerk appointed by the arbitrators, who prepares the minutes of the hearings. Unless otherwise provided by the arbitration agreement, as long as the parties have been duly summoned, the arbitration procedure can advance further, despite the non-appearance of one or of all parties or their failure to present factual allegations or means of evidence (Article 887 §1).

Witnesses and experts can be examined under oath or not (Article 888 §1a). Arbitrators are, however, not entitled to use coercive measures while administering the evidence procedure (Article 888 §1b). Upon request by the arbitrators, the evidentiary procedure can be carried out by the justice of the peace (Article 888 §3).

537. The parties are basically free to agree on the applicable law on the substance of the dispute (Article 890 §1) or even submit the dispute to an adjudication *ex aequo et bono*, i.e., grant the arbitrators the power to decide as '*amiables compositeurs*'. Only the rules involving public policy cannot be disregarded (Article 890 §2). When such an agreement is absent, the decision by the arbitrators must be based on the provisions of substantive law (Article 890 §1).

The Arbitrator authorities are primarily governed by the submission. Unless the parties have otherwise agreed, arbitrators are granted the competence to rule on their own jurisdiction,[614] i.e., including examination of the validity of both the main contract and the arbitration agreement and of preliminary questions (Article 887 §2). On the basis of the generally accepted autonomous character of the arbitration agreement, arbitrators are entitled to decide on its validity, irrespective of their decision as to whether the main contract is valid or not, provided that the parties have

611. A. Koutsouradis, 'Grundsätze und Besonderheiten der Beweisaufnahme nach griechischem Schiedsverfahrensrecht', in *Les particularités nationales de l'arbitrage commercial international* (1987) = Νομικά Μελετήματα I (1987), pp. 181 ff.
612. 1509/1982, *Dike* 1984, pp. 322 ff.
613. A. Koutsouradis, 'Zur Frage der Verwendung privaten Wissens durch den Schiedsrichter', *Konkurs-Treuhand – und Schiedsgerichtswesen* 1984, pp. 573–578.
614. K. Kalavros, 'Grundsätzliches zum Rechtsverhältnis zwischen Schiedsrichtern und Parteien nach griechischem Recht', *Festschrift für W. Habscheid* (Gieseking, Bielefeld 1989), pp. 65–78..

not agreed otherwise. This ruling can be, however, reviewed by the courts in the context of the action for setting aside the award.

538. When an action is brought in court despite the arbitration agreement, the other side must invoke the latter's existence in his pleadings or at the hearing and before raising any other defence (Article 263b; *cf.* also Article 870). Failure of the party to comply, grants the court competence over the dispute. When a party invokes the submission, the court is obliged to refer the case to arbitration (Article 264), provided that the arbitration agreement has been incidentally examined and held as valid.

Chapter 6. Arbitral Award

539. Unless the submission does not provide otherwise, the arbitrators and the 'presiding' arbitrator deliberate in common and deliver their decision by majority (Article 891a). Whenever a majority opinion cannot be attained, the opinion of the 'presiding' arbitrator prevails (Article 891b). The award must be in writing (Article 892 §1); starting from 1 January 2022, arbitrators may deliver and sign their award digitally by using a certified electronic signature (Article 892 §1, as amended by Article 55 Law 4842/2021. The award must contain reasons (Article 892 §2e). However, the parties may conclude an agreement stating that the reasoning of the award is not needed (Article 892 § 2b).

Arbitral awards are not reviewable through normal methods; they can become at once res judicata and, upon their filing with the clerk of the one-member district court, are promptly enforceable. Enforcement proceedings of arbitral awards follow the normal pattern.[615]

615. *See supra*, No. 463.

Chapter 7. Recourse Against Arbitral Award

540. The principal method for setting aside the award under Greek law is the 'action for annulment' (Article 897).[616] An additional remedy for declaring the non-existence of the award (Article 901) covers some fundamental defects, i.e., the absence of an arbitration agreement (Article 901 §1a), the non-arbitrability of the dispute (Article 901 §1b), and the inexistence of the party (individual or legal entity) against whom the arbitration proceeding was instituted (Article 901 §1c). It is, therefore, a rare occurrence.

The grounds for annulling the award (Article 897) can be categorized as involving: (a) the arbitration agreement, i.e., cases where the arbitration agreement is null and void (Article 897 No. 1), or where the award has been pronounced after the arbitration agreement has ceased to produce legal effects (Articles 885 and 897 No. 2); (b) the arbitrators, i.e., cases where the arbitrators have been appointed in violation of the conditions provided for by the arbitration agreement or the law, or where the parties have revoked the arbitrators' assignment, or where the arbitrators have delivered their decision despite their disqualification (Article 897 No. 3), or where the arbitrators, while rendering the award, have exceeded their authority granted by the arbitration agreement or by the law (Article 897 No. 4); (c) the procedure before the arbitrators, i.e., violations of the principle of equality of the parties or of defence, or the rules governing the delivery of the award (Articles 897 No. 5; 886 §2; 891; 892), and the existence of grounds for the reopening of the decision (Article 897 No. 8); (d) the award itself, i.e., cases where the award is contrary to public policy or good morals (Article 897 No. 6),[617] or it is not intelligible or contains inconsistent provisions (Article 897 No. 7). Neither the false interpretation, nor the erroneous application of substantive law per se can constitute grounds for annulling arbitral awards.

541. Actions for annulling arbitral awards are entertained by the Courts of Appeal where the award was rendered (Article 898 §1 CPC). On the basis of the 2015 amendment, the procedure to be followed is the one stipulated under Article 614 CPC, i.e., particular proceedings for money claims. A review in cassation is permissible. The hearing before *Areios Pagos* must take place within three months after a party has taken further steps before this court. The time period to bring the action is three months following service of the award; otherwise, it is considered inadmissible (Article 899 §2). A party cannot waive his right to bring an action for annulling an arbitral award before the latter has been rendered (Article 900).

Despite the narrow scope of the institution, the actions for setting aside arbitral awards are very frequent in practice.[618]

---

616. K. Kerameus, 'Einschränkungen der Klage auf Aufhebung von Schiedssprüchen', *Festschrift für H. Fasching* (Wien, Manzsche, 1988), pp. 257–268.

617. Kaissis, A., *Zum Begriff des ordre public bei der Aufhebung von Schiedssprüchen in Griechenland*, in *Grenzüberschreitungen – Beiträge zum Internationalen Verfahrensrecht und zur Schiedsgerichtsbarkeit; Festschrift für Peter Schlosser zum 70. Geburtstag* (Tübingen, 2005), pp. 321–328.

618. *See also* Kerameus, 'Judicial Organization and Civil Procedure', in Kerameus & Kozyris (ed.), *Introduction to Greek Law,* third edition (Kluwer Law International/Sakkoulas, 2008), pp. 370–372.

Chapter 8. Recognition and Enforcement of Awards

§1. Characterization of an Award as Foreign

542. The CPC contains two Articles governing recognition (Article 903) and enforcement (Article 906) of foreign arbitral awards.[619] Application of these provisions requires that an arbitral award is characterized as foreign. In the absence of a direct specification by the Code, there have been dissenting opinions as to the criteria of this characterization.[620] According to the currently prevailing opinion in both theory and case law, it is the applicable law which is considered decisive, rather than the place of arbitration or the nationality of the parties or of the arbitrators. When arbitral awards have been or are to be rendered pursuant to the conditions provided for by foreign law rather than by the Greek CPC, these are considered foreign.

§2. Recognition of Foreign Arbitral Awards under the CPC

543. In contrast to enforcement, recognition of a foreign award does not need to be declared through a particular proceeding; it can rather be effected incidentally in the course of any other proceeding (Article 903), provided that the requirements of recognition are not absent.

The res judicata effect of foreign arbitral awards can be recognized in Greece if the following conditions are fulfilled: (a) the arbitration agreement on which the arbitral award was based is valid under the law by which it is governed (Article 903 No. 1). Accordingly, the validity of this agreement must be determined following the applicable law pursuant to the Greek choice of law rules (*see* Article 25 CC). (b) The subject matter of the award is arbitrable under Greek law (Article 903 No. 2). (c) The award may not be challenged by any methods of review or other legal remedies, and there is no pending proceeding questioning its validity (Article 903 No. 3). In contrast to methods of review, which do not need to have been exercised, an action for setting aside the award can prevent its recognition only as long as it is already pending. A foreign award does not need to be enforceable under the law of the place where it was rendered. (d) The losing party has not been deprived of his

619. A. Foustoukos, 'La reconnaisance et l'exécution en Grèce des sentences arbitrales étrangères après la recente réforme du droit de l'arbitrage', *Revue de l'arbitrage* 1974, pp. 265–289; same author, 'Greece' in P. Sanders (gen. ed.), *Yearbook of Commercial Arbitration*, Vol. V (International Council for Commercial Arbitration, 1980); I. Horomides, 'The Enforcement of Foreign Arbitral Awards in Greece', *Arbitration International* 1987 (Vol. 3, No. 3, July 1987); S. Vrellis, 'Reconnaissance et exécution de decisions etrangères tant judiciaire qu'arbitral – Le système en vigueur et ses améliorations', Greek National Report to the 8th World Conference of Civil Procedure in Utrecht 1987, in *Justice and Efficiency*, Special Volume (ed. by IΔME/Athens 1988), II, pp. 399 ff. (433–441); P. Massouridis, 'The Enforcement of Foreign Judgments in Greece', *Révue hellénique de droit international* 1970, pp. 187 ff. (201–207); D. Tsikrikas, *Anerkennung und Vollstreckung ausländischer gerichtlicher Entscheidungen und Schiedssprüche nach dem griechischen Zivilverfahrensrecht*, *ZZPInt* 2018, pp. 79 –100.

620. Ch. Fragistas, 'Arbitrage étranger et arbitrage international en droit privé', *Revue critique de droit international privé* 1960, pp. 1 ff.

right of defence during the arbitral proceeding (Article 903 No. 4). (e) The foreign award is not contrary to a domestic judgment binding the same parties on the same cause of action (Article 901 No. 5). (f) The award is not contrary to public policy or good morals (Article 903 No. 6). Greek courts hold that the lack of reasons does not violate this condition. There is, on the contrary, no control as to the correct application of the rules of law to the substance of the dispute by the arbitrators. *Areios Pagos*[621] has, however, ruled that arbitral awards adjudicating payment of punitive damages, without measuring whether the awarded penalties are disproportionate or not, violate Greek public policy.

544. According to Article 45 §1f Law 5016/2023 on International Commercial Arbitration, recognition and enforcement of all foreign arbitral awards is effected following the requirements of the New York Convention of 1958 (ratified in Greece by Legislative Decree 4220/1961). Accordingly, while the proceeding for obtaining *exequatur* is still regulated by Article 906 CPC[622] in light of Article 7 §1 New York Convention (applicability of the more favourable rules), the conditions for recognition or enforcement provided by the CPC can be henceforth operative only, and insofar they are more favourable in comparison to the New York Convention.

§3. Enforcement of Foreign Arbitral Awards

545. A foreign arbitral award can be executed in Greece upon its declaration as enforceable through a proceeding similar to that applied to foreign judgment and legal instruments (Article 906, referring to the *exequatur* proceedings under Article 905 CPC). The prerequisites to enforcement are the same as those required for recognition.[623]

§4. International Treaties

I. Multilateral Conventions

546. As already noted,[624] Greece is a party to the Geneva Conventions of 1923 and 1927, to the New York Convention of 1958,[625] and to the Washington Convention of 1965 on the Settlement of Investment Disputes. On the contrary, Greece is

621. 1260/2002, *Legal Tribune* 2003, pp. 1020 ff. *See* E, Vassilakakis, 'Enforceability of Foreign Arbitral Awards Adjudicating Punitive Damages in Greece' in *Festschrift Kozyris* (Sakkoulas Publishers, 2007), pp. 493 ff.; C. Triadafyllidis, *Anerkennung und Vollstreckung von punitive damages Urteilen nach kontinentalem und insbesondere nach griechischem Recht, IPRax* 2002, pp. 237 ff.
622. *See infra,* No. 542.
623. *See supra,* Nos 552 and 553.
624. *See supra,* No. 29.
625. B Patkos, 'The United Nations Convention of 1958 on the Recognition and Enforcement of Foreign Arbitral Awards in the Light of the Greek Civil Procedure Code of 1971', *RHDI* 1974, pp. 295–306; K. Makridou, Interpretation *and Application of the New York Convention in the Republic of Greece,* in George A. Bermann (ed.), *Recognition and Enforcement of Foreign Arbitral Awards*

not a party to the European Convention on Commercial Arbitration of 21 April 1961. The New York Convention of 1958 is applied by Greek courts almost exclusively. A significant number of awards emanating from diverse foreign courts of arbitration have been recognized and declared enforceable in Greece.[626]

II. Bilateral Conventions

547. There is a number of bilateral conventions on the recognition and enforcement of foreign arbitral awards between Greece and: (a) the United States of America (USA): Treaty of Friendship, Commerce and Navigation, dated 3 August 1951 and ratified by Law 2893/1954 (Article 6, §2); (b) Albania: Treaty on Judicial Assistance of 17 May 1993, ratified by Law 2311/1995 (Articles 23 §1c, and 25); (c) Armenia: Treaty on Judicial Assistance of 21 November 2000, ratified by Law 3007/2002 (Articles 17 §1d, and 18 §2); (d) China: Treaty on Judicial Assistance of 1 October 1994, ratified by Law 2358/1995 (Articles 20c, and 26); (e) Cyprus: Treaty on Judicial Assistance of 5 March 1984, ratified by Law 1548/1985 (Articles 21, 23 and 24); (f) Georgia: Treaty on Judicial Assistance of 10 May 1999, ratified by Law 2813/2000 (Article 28); (g) Germany: Treaty on Mutual Recognition and Enforcement of Judgments, etc., dated 4 November 1961, and ratified by Law 4305/1963 (Article 14 §1); (h) Hungary: Treaty on Judicial Assistance of October 1979,

– *The Interpretation and Application of the New York Convention by National Courts* (Springer 2017), pp. 379–416. With respect to public policy, *see* G. Mitsopoulos, *Die Unvereinbarkeit des ausländischen Schiedsspruchs, der auf Schadensersatz wegen Unterlassung einer Überversicherung eines Schiffes erkennt, mit dem griechischen ordre public*, in *Festschrift für Gottfried Baumgärtel zum 70. Geburtstag* (Heymann; Cologne 1990), pp. 381–388; E. Vassilakakis, *Recognition or Enforcement of Foreign Arbitral Awards and State Succession: The Ghostly Paradigm of the Agreement between Greece and Yugoslavia in Comparison to the New York Convention of 1958*, *Croatian Arbitration Yearbook* 2009, pp. 281–297.

626. A. Anthimos, *Enforcement of an ICC award and a Swiss Supreme Court judgment*, http://icl-in-greece.blogspot.com/2014_06_08_archive.html; A. Anthimos, Declaration of enforceability of a CAS award in Greece, *LEX Sportiva* 2014, pp. 118 et seq.; A. Anthimos, *Reconocimiento y ejecución de un laudo de Tribunal de Arbitraje Deportivo (CAS) en Grecia, Arbitraje – Revista de arbitraje comercial y de inversiones* 2015, pp. 270–275, and recently A. Anthimos, *Enforceability of CAS Awards in Greece – A Short Survey*, *The European Legal Forum* 2022, pp. 101–103; A. Anthimos, *New York Convention applies to the recognition and enforcement of Basketball Arbitral Tribunal awards,* https://conflictoflaws.net/2020/new-york-convention-applies-to-the-recognition-and-enforcement-of-basketball-arbitral-tribunal-awards/; A. Anthimos, *Recognition and enforcement of an arbitral award by the International Commercial Arbitration Court at the Ukrainian Chamber of Commerce and Industry (ICAC at the UCCI)*, http://icl-in-greece.blogspot.com/2014_04_13_archive.html; A. Anthimos, *Greece safe harbor for CIETAC awards*, http://icl-in-greece.blogspot.com/2014_04_20_archive.html; A. Anthimos, *Enforcement of a JAG award in Greece*, http://icl-in-greece.blogspot.com/2014_04_27_archive.html. *See* however A. Anthimos, *Failure to Demonstrate the Existence of an Arbitration Agreement Impedes Enforcement of an ICC Award,* http://icl-in-greece.blogspot.com/2014_10_12_archive.html; A. Anthimos, *No Exequatur for an ICA Award in Greece*, http://icl-in-greece.blogspot.com/2014_06_01_archive.html; A. Anthimos, *Excess of Authority as a Ground of Refusal for an AAA Award in Greece*, https://conflictoflaws.net/2022/excess-of-authority-as-a-ground-of-refusal-for-an-aaa-award-in-greece; A. Anthimos, *Bitcoin and Public Policy in the Field of International Commercial Arbitration,* https://conflictoflaws.net/2022/bitcoin-and-public-policy-in-the-field-of-international-commercial-arbitration/.

ratified by Law 1149/1981 (Articles 24, 26, 27); (i) Lebanon: Treaty on Judicial Assistance, dated 5 April 1975, ratified by Law 1099/1980 (Article 10); (j) Romania: Treaty on Judicial Assistance, dated 19 October 1972, ratified by Legislative Decree 429/1974 (Articles 22, 23, 27 and 28); (k) Syria: Treaty on Judicial Assistance, ratified by Law 1450/1984 (Article 28); (l) Tunisia: Treaty on Judicial Assistance, dates 12 April 1993, ratified by Law 2228/1994 (Article 28 §1c); (m) Ukraine: Treaty on Judicial Assistance, dated 2 July 2002, ratified by Law 3281/2004 (Article 20, §2); (n) (former) Yugoslavia: Treaty on Mutual Recognition and Enforcement of Judgments, dated 18 June 1959, ratified by Legislative Decree 4007 /1959 (Articles 1 to 7).

Bilateral treaties often refer to the New York Convention of 1958 (*see* the treaties with Albania (Article 25); China (Article 26); Germany (Article 14 §1); Georgia (Article 28); Hungary (Article 26); Romania (Article 27); Syria (Article 28); Ukraine (Article 20 §2)). Certain treaties, however, require the application of the conditions involving foreign judgments by analogy (*see*, e.g., the treaties with Cyprus (Article 23), Lebanon (Article 10), and former Yugoslavia (Article 4)).

III. Relationship to Domestic Law

548. According to Article 903 CPC, international conventions prevail over domestic law. It is, however, accepted that domestic law can be applied instead of a convention, where its requirements are more favourable compared to those of a convention with regard to a concrete request for recognition or enforcement.[627]

627. *See also* Art. 7, §1, of the New York Convention *supra*, No. 544.

Chapter 9. Mediation

§1. Legislation/Definitions

549. The institution of mediation has passed three stages in Greece. In December 2010, the Greek Parliament enacted the law on 'Mediation in Civil and Commercial Matters' (Law 3898/2010) to be applied to both domestic and cross-border disputes. This law was in part designed to meet the European Directive's requirements for cross-border dispute mediation (Directive 2008/52 EC of the European Parliament and the Council of 21 May 2008 on 'Certain Aspects of Mediation in Civil and Commercial Matters').[628] Several by-laws were, however, needed to address a number of pending issues. In light of the Mediation Act 2010, the definition of mediation was differentiated from conciliation.[629]

Starting from 17 January 2018, mediation in civil and commercial matters was exclusively regulated by a new Mediation Act, embedded within a colossal law, covering a series of legislative matters (Articles 178–206 of Law 4512/2018), with the exception of voluntary court-annexed mediation.[630]

The aforementioned law was seriously challenged by judges and lawyers alike, leading to a new law (Law 4640/2019),[631] which is still in force.

§2. Rights That Can Be Subject to Mediation-Mediation Agreement-Mediation Procedure-Settlement Agreement

550. In addition to being consistent with the European Directive's requirements, the 2019 Act aims at offering a fully regulated system of a structured process whereby the parties try to settle a dispute out of court. The new rules include, among others, regulations on the permissibility of mediation (Article 3), the referral to mediation (Article 4), several procedural issues, the enforceability of mediation agreements (Article 8), the impact of mediation on statutes of limitations (Article 9), accreditation requirements for mediators (Article 12), and the mediator's duties (Article 13: impartiality, independence and neutrality). However, the most spectacular novelty of the 2019 Mediation Act consists of the introduction of a mandatory mechanism of mediation with regard to a certain number of private disputes. Under penalty of

628. Directive 2008/52/EC aims at promoting and facilitating mediation in the EU as an alternative method of resolving disputes at both the internal and cross-border levels.

629. *See* in detail A. Anthimos, *Greece*, in Giuseppe De Palo & Mary B. Trevor, *EU Handbook on Mediation* (OUP 2012), pp. 148–161; A. Anthimos, in Nadja Alexander, Sabine Welsh & Martin Svatos (eds), *EU Mediation Law Handbook* (2017), Chapter: Greece, pp. 383–402; G. Diamantopoulos & V. Koumpli, *On Mediation Law in Greece*, *RHDI* 2014, pp. 361–394; Ch. Apalagaki, *Alternative Streitbeilegung im griechischen Zivilverfahren,* in *Rechtslage – Rechtserkenntnis – Rechtsdurchsetzung: Festschrift für Eberhard Schilken zum 70. Geburtstag*, (Munich, C.H.Beck, 2015), pp. 199–206; K. Makridou, *Speeding up Civil Litigation in Greece Through ADR Methods,* in *Tatsachen – Verfahren – Vollstreckung: Festschrift für Isaak Meier zum 65. Geburtstag* (Schulthess Juristische Medien, 2015), pp. 449 ff.

630. *See* No. 551.

631. Mediation in civil and commercial cases – Further harmonization of Greek legislation to the provision of EU Directive 2008/52.

inadmissibility of judicial proceedings Article 6 provides that for certain disputes, specifically enumerated in this rule, a preliminary recourse to mediation is compulsory.[632]

Although the stage of mandatory recourse to mediation does not preclude the right of judicial protection at the end, it provoked negative reactions during the second stage (2018) emanating from Bar Associations and scholars, raising issues of unconstitutionality and contravention to Article 6 §1 of the Convention for the Protection of Human Rights. As a result, following an opinion issued by *Areios Pagos* (full bench),[633] Article 19 Law 4566/2018. provided that Article 182 Law 4512/2018, providing for mandatory mediation, would not start to operate until 16 September 2019.

Meanwhile, the above issues have been solved, and the 2019 Act is fully operative. The main findings during a nearly five-year application are not entirely enticing: Voluntary recourse to mediation is not prospering, and the obligatory stage of preliminary mediation session, according to Article 6, results in fewer mediation agreements and pretty much a stay of proceedings due to the omission of a considerable part of lawyers to follow the procedure provided in the Mediation Act.

§3. Judicial Mediation

551. Article 214B, inserted in the CPC in 2012, has adopted the institution of judicial mediation. This continues to apply even after the introduction of the Mediation Act. It is understood as a distinct mechanism of mediation which can function in parallel with the structured process provided by the Mediation Act. Judicial mediation can apply to private law disputes either before the initiation of a judicial proceeding or while this is still pending (Article 214B §1). As a rule, one or more of the presidents of first or second instance courts (Article 214B §2) are appointed as mediators to each court for a period of two years. These judges are there to act as mediators whenever the interested parties voluntarily submit a written application to this end (Article 214B §3). In addition to this voluntary mechanism of judicial mediation, any court before which a case is pending is allowed to encourage the parties to resort to mediation (Articles 214B §4, 214C, as added to the CPC in 2015). In case a mediation agreement is attained, is registered in a specific document, which, after being signed by the mediator, the disputants and their attorneys, and has been deposited to the secretariat of the competent court, can serve as an enforceable instrument (Article 214B §3).

§4. Practical Relevance of Mediation

552. Until today, despite the existence of a strong legal foundation for the future of mediation and the multiple arrays of options offered to litigants, a mediation

632. A. Anthimos, *New Law on Mediation in Civil and Commercial Maters – Some Cross Border Issues*, http://icl-in-greece.blogspot.com/2018_01_21_archive.html.

633. *Areios Pagos* 34/2018, *Civil Procedure Law Review* 2018, pp. 287 ff.

culture is only gradually developing in Greece. Presently, the statistical data as to the practical relevance of mediation are not delivering to the extent expected by devout mediation proponents: The statistics issued by the Central Mediation Committee for the year 2021 refer to a 7.63% success rate in the realm of obligatory mediation sessions under Article 6. No statistics exist with regard to voluntary mediation attempts. Thus, to predict the success or failure of mediation does not currently seem possible.

Bibliography in Languages Other Than Greek

§1 Books or General Works

Bolos, A. *Die Pfändung von Bankkonten im griechischen Recht*. zugl. Diss. Berlin, Berlin, 2004

David, R. & Brierly J., *Major Legal Systems in the World Today*. 3rd ed. London: Stevens, 1985.

Delikostopoulos, S., *Die Klage auf Feststellung vergangener und zukünftiger Rechtsverhältnisse*. München, 1969.

Dickopf, K., *George Ludwig von Maurer 1790–1872 – Eine Biographie*. Kallmünz, 1960.

Foustoukos, A., *L'arbitrage-interne et international – en droit privé hellénique*. Paris, 1976.

Fragistas, Ch., 'Greece', *International Encyclopedia of Comparative Law*. Vol. I. National Report, Tübingen: Mohr, 1978 = *Legal Studies*, Vol. IV. Athens/Komotini: Sakkoulas, pp. 2387–2413.

Fragistas, Ch., *Das Präventionsprinzip in der Zwangsvollstreckung,* Beiträge zum Zivilprozess, 11 Heft. Bensheimer, Manheim/Berlin/Leipzig, 1931.

Georgopoulos, D. & Reinecker H., 'Zivilgerichtsbarkeit und Zwangsvollstreckung in Griechenland'. in the Vol. of B. Kuru et al. *Zivilgerichtsbarkeit und Zwangsvollstreckung in den Ländern Türkei, Griechenland, Spanien, Portugal und Schweiz.* Stuttgart: Deutscher Sparkassenverlag, 1978, pp. 87–157.

Hoyer, V. & Loewe R., *Staatsverträge über Rechtshilfe und Vollstreckung*. Wien: Manzsche, 1964.

Iatrou, A., *Civil and Criminal Proceedings in Greece*. Athens: Sakkoulas, 1981.

Iliakopoulos, I., *Die Grenzen der Befriedigungsverfügung im deutschen und griechischen Recht*. Lang/Frankfurt, 1983.

Mantzourani – Tschaschnig, M., *Die Befriedigungsverfügung nach deutschem und griechischem Recht unter besonderer Berücksichtigung des Wettbewerbsrechts*. Lang/Frankfurt, 1986.

Kaissis, A., *Die Verwertbarkeit materiell-rechtswidrig erlangter Beweismittel im Zivilprozess*. Diss. Heidelberg, 1978

Kerameus, K.D., *Die Entwicklung des Sachverständingenbeweises im deutschen und griechischen Ziviprozessrecht*. Köln: Karl Heymanns Verlag, 1963.

Bibliography in Languages Other Than Greek

Kerameus, K.D., *Enforcement in the International Context*. Recueil des Cours. Vol. 264. Academy of International Law, 1997.

Kerameus, K.D. & Koussoulis S., 'Civil Justice Reform: Access, Costs, and Delay. A Greek Perspective'. in A. A. Zuckerman (ed.), *Civil Justice in Crisis*. Oxford University Press 1999, pp. 363–384.

Kerameus, K.D., *Enforcement Proceedings*. Chapter 10, Vol. XVI. Comparative Civil Procedure, International Encyclopaedia of Comparative Law, 2003.

Kerameus, K.D. & Kozyris P.J. (eds), *Introduction to Greek Law*. 3rd ed. New York/ Athens: Kluwer Law International/Sakkoulas, 2008.

Klamaris, N., *Das Rechtsmittel der Anschlussberufung*. Tübingen, 1975.

Koussoulis, S., *Beiträge zur modernen Rechtskraftlehre*. 1986.

Lakkis, P., *Der kollektive Rechtsschutz der Verbraucher in der Europäischen Union – dargestellt an der Verbandsklage der Verbraucherverbände nach dem AGBG, dem UWG and dem griechischen Verbraucherschutzgesetz*. Bielefeld, 1997.

Mainas, P., *Die Eventualmaxime nach griechischem Recht*. Diss. Köln, 1970

Makridou, K. & Diamantopoulos G. (eds), *Civil Trial of First and Second Instance according to Swiss and Greek Law*. Athens-Thessaloniki: Sakkoulas Publications, 2014.

Maniotis, D. & Tsantinis S., *Civil Justice in Greece,* Nagoya University Comparative Study of Civil Justice, Vol. 6. Tokyo, Japan: Jigakusha Publishing Corporation, 2010.

Mitsopoulos, G., *Le manque de base légale du point de vue du droit comparé*. Athens/Bruxelles: Sakkoulas/Bruylant, 2007.

Mitsopoulos G., *Topique, nouvelle rhétorique et science du droit, Académie d' Athènes*. Centre de Recherche sur la Philosophie Greque. Athènes, 2008.

Polyzogopoulos, K., *Parteianhörung und Parteivernehmungen in ihrem gegenseitigen Verhältnis*. Diss. Tübingen, 1976.

Rizopoulos, V., *Investitionen in Griechenland und Schiedsgerichtsbarkeit. Investitionsverträge zwischen Staat und Privatunternehmen*. zugl. Diss. Köln 2002, Berlin, 2004

Sinanides, G., *Die Anerkennung deutscher Scheidungsurteile in Griechenland*. Bielefeld, Univ., Fak. für Rechtswiss., Diss., 1980.

Stoikos, G., *Die Zwangsvollstreckung wegen Geldforderungen in das bewegliche Vermögen im deutschen und im griechischen Recht*. Diss. Tübingen, Sofort-Druck, 1987.

Tekidou, D., *Der Vollstreckungszugriff auf Bankkonten. Eine rechtsvergleichende Betrachtung des griechischen und deutschen Rechts*. Europäische Hochschulschriften, Reihe 2, Bd. 4142; zugl. Diss. Hannover 2004, Frankfurt/ M. u.a., 2005.

Verveniotis, G., *Construction and Arbitration. Cases from the Greek Experience*. Athens-Komotini, 2000.

Zweigert, K. & Kötz H., *Einführung in die Rechtsvergleichung*. Vol. 1. Tübingen: Mohr, 1971 = Introduction to Comparative Law, Vol. 1. Oxford: Clarendon Press, 1987.

§2 Special Essays, Articles, Reports

Essays or articles of Greek proceduralists, treating special fields or problems of Greek Civil Procedure or Judicial Organization, are often published in foreign collective volumes (mostly '*Festschrifte*') or periodicals. The *Zeitschrift für Zivilprozess* is one of the best examples. Most of these are referred to within the respective chapters of this book.

Prof. K., Beys. in his report for the Passau Congress, 1989 (*see* the volume edited by W, Habscheid. *Das deutsche Zivilprozessrecht und seine Ausstrahlung auf andere Rechtsordnungen.* Gieseking, Bielefeld 1991), has presented a complete chronological list of monographs or essays written by Greeks in German (until 1989). *See* K, Beys. 'Die Ausstrahlung des deutchen zivilprozessualen Denkens auf das griechische Recht der Privatrechtsstreitigkeiten', pp. 300–332 (328 n. 125). *Dike* 1989, pp. 401–441 (434 note 125).

National reports of Greek scholars for procedural Congresses in English, German or French have been regularly published in the '*Revue hellénique de droit international*'. Greek national reports for the 8th World Conference of Civil Procedure in Utrecht, 1987, have been published by the Institute of Procedural Studies (*Justice and Efficiency, The Contribution of the Greek Science of Procedural Law to the 8th World Conference of Civil Procedure*, Vols I–II, Athens 1987).

In particular, an updated list of special essays, articles and reports is the following:

Anthimos, A., *Greece*, in Giuseppe De Palo & Mary B. Trevor, EU Handbook on Mediation. OUP, 2012, pp. 148–161.

Anthimos, A., *Reconocimiento y ejecución de sentencias extranjeras en Grecia. Revista de Derecho Comunitario Europeo* 1999, pp. 209–218.

Anthimos, A., *Der verfahrensrechtliche ordre public im griechischen internationalen Zivilprozeßrecht Griechenlands. IPRax* 2000, pp. 327–331.

Anthimos, A., *Der prozessuale ordre public bei der Anerkennung und Vollstreckung ausländischer Gerichtsentscheidungen nach deutschem und griechischem Zivilprozeßrecht und nach dem Europäischen Gerichtsstands- und Vollstreckungsübereinkommen.* Hanover 1994, in *Anthimos/Delp/Harazim*, Harmonisierungsprobleme im europäischen Wirtschaftsrecht. Nomos Verlag, Baden, 2000, pp. 11–153.

Anthimos, A., *Declaration of Enforceability of a CAS Award in Greece.* LEX Sportiva 2014, pp. 118 et seq.

Anthimos, A., *Reconocimiento y ejecución de sentencias extranjeras según el Reglamento Bruselas I en Grecia. Anuario Español de Derecho Internacional Privado* 2014, pp. 587–607.

Anthimos, A., *Griechisch-Schweizerischer Zustellungsverkehr in Zivil- und Handelssachen. ZZZ* 2014, pp. 150–152.

Anthimos, A., *Recognition of Russian Personal Status Judgments in Greece: A Case Law Survey.* Russian Law Journal Vol. II. 2014, Issue 3, pp. 49–61.

Anthimos, A., *Exequatur Proceedings According to the Brussels I Regulation in Greece. Revue Hellénique de Droit International* 2014, pp. 1007–1021.

Anthimos, A., *Zum verbleibenden Wert des Deutsch-Griechischen Anerkennungs- und Vollstreckungsvertrags von 1961. IPRax* 2015, pp. 361–363.

Anthimos, A., *Serving Greek Proceedings to US defendants: A case law survey.* Civil Procedure Review, vol. 6, no. 2. May–August 2015, pp. 99–106.

Bibliography in Languages Other Than Greek

Anthimos, A., *Denegación del reconocimiento y la ejecución en el Reglamento Bruselas I bis. Anuario Español de Derecho Internacional Privado* 2015, pp. 375–393.

Anthimos, A., *Recognition and Enforcement of Foreign Judgments According to the Brussels I Regulation in Greece. YPIL* 2015, pp. 345–364.

Anthimos, A., *Europäisches Zivilprozessrecht in Griechenland – Überblick über die Rechtsprechung griechischer Gerichte in den Jahren 2012–2014.* GPR 2015, pp. 291–295.

Anthimos, A., *Reconocimiento y ejecución de un laudo de Tribunal de Arbitraje Deportivo (CAS) en Grecia, Arbitraje – Revista de arbitraje comercial y de inversiones* 2015, pp. 270–275.

Anthimos, A., *Fictitious Service in the EU – Requiem for a nightmare?. Czech Yb Int'l Law* 2017, pp. 3–34.

Anthimos, A., *Greek Payment Orders Against Foreign Residents. International Journal of Procedural Law* 2016, pp. 327–340.

Anthimos, A., in Nadja, Alexander, Sabine Welsh & Martin Svatos (ed.), *EU Mediation Law Handbook.* Kluwer law 2017, pp. 383–402.

Anthimos, A., *Winds of Change in the Recognition of Foreign Adult Adoption cecrees. International Journal of Procedural Law* 2017, pp. 163–165.

Anthimos, A., *Frischer Wind in der Anerkennung ausländischer Volljährigenadoptionen in Griechenland – (zu Plenum des Areopags 9/2016). IPRax* 2017, pp. 419–420.

Anthimos, A., *The Supreme Court Recognizes a French ordonnance de référé. International Journal of Procedural Law* 2017, pp. 318–319.

Anthimos, A., *Supreme Court 1130/2017 [On the application of Art. 19.2 Service Regulation]. International Journal of Procedural Law* 2018, pp. 150–153.

Anthimos, A., *Nichtanwendung der EUGVVO 2001 für einen KV-Bescheid in Griechenland (zu LG Thessaloniki, 19.12.201 – 19865/2017). IPRax* 2019, pp. 343 ff.

Anthimos, A., *Greek Supreme Court No. 1938/2017. International Journal of Procedural Law* 2019, pp. 132–134.

Anthimos, A., *Greek Supreme Court No. 1395/2018. International Journal of Procedural* Law 2019, pp. 339–342.

Anthimos, A., *Regulation BIa: A standard for Free Circulation of Judgments and Mutual Trust in the European Union (JUDGTRUST) – National Report GREECE,* 2019, https://www.asser.nl/media/795624/greece_report.pdf.

Anthimos, A., *Greek Supreme Court No. 579/2019.* International Journal of Procedural Law 2020, pp. 83–85.

Anthimos, A., *Recognition and Enforcement of Foreign Judgments in the Field of Bilateral Conventions of Greece with Balkan States. Balkan Yearbook of European and International Law* (2021) 2020: pp. 201–224.

Anthimos, A., *Greek Supreme Court on Enforcement of UK Divorce Financial Payment.* The European Legal Forum 2021, pp. 29–31.

Anthimos, A., *Griechisch-Deutscher und Griechisch-Österreichischer Zustellungsverkehr in Zivil- und Handelssachen – Eine Bestandaufnahme der griechischen Rechtsprechung, in: Simon Laimer • Christoph Kronthaler • Bernhard A. Koch*

(Hrsg). Europäische und internationale Dimensionen des Privatrechts, Festschrift für Andreas Schwartze. Jan Sramek Verlag, Wien 2021, pp. 3–17.

Anthimos, A., *Greek Supreme Court No. 423/20198.* International Journal of Procedural Law 2021, pp. 157–159.

Anthimos, A., *Greek Supreme Court No. 767/2019. International Journal of Procedural Law* 2021, pp. 351–353.

Anthimos, A., Mutatio & Ementatio Libelli, in Paris Arvanitakis (ed.), *Prozeßrechtsvergleichung und prozessuale Vereinheitlichung, Studia in Memoriam Peter Gilles.* Athens-Thessaloniki: Sakkoulas Publications, 2021, pp. 15–42.

Anthimos, A., *Enforceability of CAS Awards in Greece – A Short Survey. The European Legal Forum* 2022, pp. 101–103.

Anthimos, A., *The Public Policy Defence in the Recognition and Enforcement of Foreign Judgments in Greece. International Journal of Procedural Law* 2022, pp. 296–313.

Anthimos, A., *Greek Supreme Court No. 820/2021. International Journal of Procedural Law* 2022, pp. 136–142.

Anthimos, A., *Supreme Court No. 1182/2022. International Journal of Procedural Law* 2023 (forthcoming)

Apalagaki, Ch., *Presentation of the Draft Reform the Code of the Greek Civil Procedure Code (Ordinary and Special Proceedings of the Courts of First Instance).* in Makridou & Dimantopoulos (eds), *Civil Trial of First and Second Instance according to Swiss and Greek Law* 2014, pp. 69 ff.

Apalagaki, Ch., *Griechisches Zwangsvollstreckung und die Reform der ZPO durch das Gesetz 4335/2015*, in *Fairness Justice Equity: Festschrift für Reinhold Geimer zum 80. Geburtstag*, C.H.Beck 2017, pp. 25–30.

Apalagaki, Ch., *Alternative Streitbeilegung im griechischen Zivilverfahren*, in *Rechtslage – Rechtserkenntnis – Rechtsdurchsetzung: Festschrift für Eberhard Schilken zum 70. Geburtstag*, Munich : C.H.Beck, 2015, pp. 199–206.

Arvanitakis, P., *Verfassungsrechtliche Probleme der Zwangsvollstreckung zur Befriedigung privatrechtlicher Ansprüche nach griechischem Recht. ZZP* 111 (1998), pp. 463–485.

Archontaki, A. & Simsive P., *Chapter 18. Greece*, in Paul Beaumont et al. (eds), *Cross-Border Litigation in Europe.* Hart Publishing 2017, pp. 315–327.

Arvanitakis, P., *Der prozessuale Verbraucherschutz im griechischen autonomen und internationalen Recht. ZZPInt* 10 (2005), pp. 111–122.

Bakopoulos, A., 'The Role of the Supreme Courts at the National and International Level, Greek Law', in Yessiou-Faltsi (ed.), *The Role of the Supreme Courts at the National and International Level.* Reports for the Thessaloniki International Colloquium 1996, pp. 149 ff.

Baumgärtel, G., 'Welche Anregungen vermag das neue griechische ZPGB für die in Deutschland geplante Prozessbeschleunigung zu geben?'. *Zeitschrift für Zivilprozess* 1968, pp. 6 ff.

Bendermacher-Geroussis, A., *Anerkennung und Vollstreckung ausländischer Entscheidungen über die Sorge der Person der Kinder und die Unterhaltspflicht. Revue hellénique de droit international* 1955, pp. 45–50.

Beys, K., 'Die verfassungsrechtlichen Grenzen der Zwangsvollstreckung im griechischen Recht'. *Zeitschrift für Zivilprozess* 1988, pp. 165 ff.

Bibliography in Languages Other Than Greek

Beys, K., 'Die objektiven Grenzen der Rechtskraft im griechischen Recht'. *Festschrift für W. Habscheid,* Bielefeld: Gieseking 1989, pp. 11–21.

Beys, K., 'Die subjektiven Grenzen der Rechtskraft und die staatsrechtliche Wirkung des Urteils nach griechischem Recht'. *Festschrift für K.H. Schwab*, München: C.H. Beck 1990, pp. 61 ff.

Beys, K., 'Die Ausstrahlung des deutschen zivilprozessualen Denkens auf das griechische Recht der Privatrechtsstreitigkeiten, Ein Beitrag zur Geschichte der griechischen Prozessrechtswissenschaft'. in *Grundlagen-berichte für die Tagung der Wissenschaftlichen Vereinigung für Internationales Verfahrensrecht, Verfahrensrechtsvergleichung und Schiedsgerichtswesen e.V. (Passau 1989), Veröffentlichungen der Wissenschaftlichen Vereinigung für Internationales Verfahrensrecht e.V.* Bd. 5, Bielefeld: Gieseking 1991, pp. 300–332.

Beys, K., 'Das Unterscheidungsmerkmal von Feststellungs-Leistungs- und Gestaltungsklagen und Urteilen'. in *Volume in Honour of G. Mitsopoulos*. Athens/Komotini: Sakkoulas 1993, pp. 47–62.

Beys, K., *Der Bereich der Privat- und Verwaltungsrechtsstreitigkeiten im hellenischen Recht.* in *Festschrift Für Hideo Nakamura Zum 70. Geburtstag am 2. März 1996* (Tokyo, 1996; de Gruyter; Reprint 2013), pp. 51–72.

Beys, K., *Grundgedanken des griechischen Zivilprozeßrechts in ihrer Fortentwicklung durch die EMRK. ZZP* 109 (1996), pp. 29–60.

Beys, K., *Neue Wege zur Bestimmung der Rechts- bzw. Parteifähigkeit. Die hellenische Erfahrung*, in Reinhold Geimer (ed.), *Wege zur Globalisierung des Rechts, Festschrift für Rolf A. Schütze zum 65. Geburtstag*. Munich: C. H. Beck 1999, pp. 117–127.

Beys, K., *Die Zwangsvollstreckung gegen einen ausländischen Staat im hellenischen Recht.* in *Grenzüberschreitungen – Beiträge zum Internationalen Verfahrensrecht und zur Schiedsgerichtsbarkeit. Festschrift für Peter Schlosser zum 70. Geburtstag.* Tübingen: Mohr Siebeck 2005, pp. 37–48.

Christopoulos, Th., *Requirements for the Enforcement of Foreign Judgments in Greece. Revue international de droit comparé* 1948, pp. 348–357.

Coutsoumaris, Th., 'Le nouveau Code de procedure civil hellénique', *Revue international de droit comparé* 1970, pp. 530–536.

Deloukas, N., 'The Arbitration in Greece', In G. Levi (ed.), *Arbitration.* Milano 1991, pp. 103 ff.

Diamantopoulos, G. & Koumpli V., *On Mediation Law in Greece, Revue hellénique de droit international* 2014, pp. 361–394.

Dimolitsa, A., 'Arbitration Agreements and Foreign Investments, The Greek State Between Contractual Commitment and Sovereign Intervention'. *Revue hellénique de droit international* 1989–1990, pp. 259 ff.

Dimolitsa, A. & Kousoulis S., *Loi 2735/1999 'Arbitrage Commercial International'/Law 2735/1999 'International Commercial Arbitration'. Revue hellénique de droit international* 1999, pp. 586 ff.

Douga, A., *On the Recognition of Foreign Administrative Acts in Greece. Revue hellénique de droit international* 2014, pp. 741–764.

Douga, A. & Koumpli V., *On the Regulation of Maintenance Obligations in Greece. Revue hellénique de droit international* 2014, pp. 931–960.

Economou, G., 'Greece'. in D. Campbell (gen. ed.), *International Execution Against Judgment Debtors*. Vol. I. London: Sweet and Maxwell 1993.

Evrigenis D. & Kerameus K., Report by on the Accession of the Hellenic Republic to the Community Convention of Jurisdiction and the Enforcement of Judgements in Civil and Commercial Matters', Official Journal of the European Communities, C 298/6.

Filios, P.C. & Henrich D., *Zur Anerkennung deutscher Scheidungsurteile in Griechenland. IPRax* 1985, pp. 150–151.

Foustoukos, A., 'La reconnaisance et l'exécution en Grèce des sentences arbitrales étrangères après la recente réforme du droit de l'arbitrage', *Revue de l'arbitrage* 1974, pp. 265–289.

Foustoukos, A., 'Une nouvelle institution permanente d'arbitrage en Grèce', *Revue de l'arbitrage* 1974, pp. 418–423.

Foustoukos, A., 'Greece'. in P. Sanders (gen. ed.), *Yearbook of Commercial Arbitration*. Vol. V. International Council for Commercial Arbitration, The Hague, 1980, pp. 57–83, XI (1986), pp. 69–72, VII (1987), pp. 367–368, XIII (1988), pp. 417–419.

Foustoukos, A. & Koussoulis S., 'Greece' in P. Sanders (ed.), International Handbook on Commercial Arbitration. The Hague, 2001.

Fragistas, Ch., *Grundzüge des griechischen zivilprozessualen Beweisrechts*. in Rühl – Fragistas, Ch., *Rechtspolitische und rechtsvergleichende Beiträge zum zivilprozessualen Beweisrecht*. Berlin 1929, pp. 56 ff.

Fragistas, Ch., 'L'usage qui est fait par la jurisprudence du droit comparé'. *Revue hellénique de droit international* 1950, pp. 30 ff.

Fragistas, Ch., 'Le Droit Musulman en Grèce'. *Annales de la Faculté de Droit d'Istanbul* 1955, pp. 129 ff.

Fragistas, Ch., 'Arbitrage étranger et arbitrage international en droit privé'. *Revue critique de droit international privé* 1960, pp. 1 ff.

Fragistas, Ch., 'La compétence internationale exclusive en droit privé'. *Studi in onore di Antonio Segni II*, Milano 1967, pp. 199 ff. (204, 211–212).

Fragistas, Ch., 'Deux conventions multilaterales recentes sur la reconnaissance des jugements étrangers'. *Rivista di diritto internazionale privato e processuale* 1968, pp. 745 ff.

Fragistas, Ch., 'Nationaux et étrangers en droit de Procedure Civil de la Grèce'. *Thesaurus Acroasium, Vol. IV, Miscellanea in Honour of D.S. Constantopoulos*. Institute of International and Public Law and International Relations, Thessaloniki, pp. 543 ff.

Frangou, G., *Vollstreckung ausländischer Entscheidungen in Griechenland – Die Anwendung des europäischen Zivilprozessrechts durch die griechische Rechtsprechung*. Internationales und europäisches Privat-und Verfahrensrecht, Band 18, NOMOS Verlag 2017, Zugl.: Dissertation Heidelberg 2016.

Georgiades, A., *Die Abänderung ausländischer Urteile im Inland. Xenion Zepos II* 1979, pp. 189 et seq.

Germanos, I., *Einstweiliger Rechtsschutz durch staatliche Gerichte bei Vorliegen einer Schiedsvereinbarung in Deutschland und Griechenland. Revue hellénique de droit international* 2010, pp. 989–1001.

Bibliography in Languages Other Than Greek

Grammaticaki-Alexiou, A., *Mixed Jurisdictions. Revue hellénique de droit international* 1985–1986, pp. 315–321.

Horomides, I., 'The Enforcement of Foreign Arbitral Awards in Greece'. Vol.3, No. 3, Arbitration International July 1987.

Igglezakis, I., *Electronic documents as legal means of evidence in Greece. Revue hellénique de droit international* 2002, pp. 531–539.

Kaissis, A., *Wandlungen des Bankgeheimnisses in Griechenland am Beispiel der Pfändbarkeit von Bankeinlagen.* in *Festschrift für Erik Jayme,* Munich: Sellier European Law Publ.,2004, pp. 1475–1486.

Kaissis, A., *Zum Begriff des ordre public bei der Aufhebung von Schiedssprüchen in Griechenland.* in *Grenzüberschreitungen – Beiträge zum Internationalen Verfahrensrecht und zur Schiedsgerichtsbarkeit; Festschrift für Peter Schlosser zum 70. Geburtstag*, Tübingen: Mohr Siebeck, 2005, pp. 321–328.

Kaissis, A., *Die Schiedsgerichtsordnung der Deutsch-Griechischen Industrie- und Handelskammer.* in *Ars aequi et boni in mundo – Festschrift zum 80. Geburtstag von Rolf A. Schütze,* München: C.H. Beck, 2015, pp. 213–220.

Kalavros, K. 'Grundsätzliches zum Rechtsverhältnis zwischen Schiedsrichtern und Parteien nach griechischem Recht'. *Festschrift für W. Habscheid* Bielefeld: Gieseking, 1989, pp. 65–78.

Kargados, P., 'Der gerichtliche Schutz von Gruppeninteressen in Griechenland', *Volume in Honour of N. Vervesos,* Athens/Komotini: Sakkoulas, 1991, pp. 201–223 = *Revue hellénique de droit international* 1982–1983, pp. 257–270.

Kargados, P., *Rules Declining to Exercise Jurisdiction in Civil and Commercial Matters in Greece: Forum Non Conveniens and Foreign Choice of Jurisdictional Clauses. Revue hellénique de droit international* 1994, pp. 161–162.

Kargados, P., *Summary adjudication in Hellas. Revue hellénique de droit international* 1998, pp. 123–156.

Katephores, N., *Darf die richterliche Prozessleitung den Kläger zur Stellung der erforderlichen Anträge veranlassen (grZPO Art. 224–236). ZZPInt* 12 (2007), pp. 119–125.

Kerameus, K., 'Rechtsmittelfestigkeit und Vollstreckung von ausländischen Entscheidungen'.Vol. II. *Festschrift für W. Wengler* 1973, pp. 383–395.

Kerameus, K., 'Civil Procedure in Greece'. 2. *Southern University Law Review* 1976, pp. 175–195 = *Legal Studies.* Thessaloniki: Sakkoulas, 1980, pp. 216–236.

Kerameus, K., *Die Erledigung geringfügiger Streitigkeiten nach griechischem Recht. Revue hellénique de droit international* 1977, pp. 91–108 = *Studia Iuridica III.* Athens: Sakkoulas/Kluwer, 1995, pp. 200–218.

Kerameus, K., 'The Use of Conciliation for Dispute Settlement'. *Revue hellénique de droit internationale* 1979, pp. 41–53.

Kerameus, K., 'Probleme des griechischen Schiedsverfahrensrechts aus rechtsvergleichender Sicht'. *Zeitschrift für Zivilprozess* 1979, pp. 413 ff.

Kerameus, K., 'The Function of Conciliation as a Means of Avoiding Litigation and Settling a Dispute'. *Revue hellénique de droit international* 1982–1983, pp. 227–238.

Kerameus, K., 'National Report for Greece'. in Sh. Shetreet & J. Deschênes (eds), *Judicial Independence the Contemporary Debate.* Dordrecht/Boston/Lancaster: Martinus Nijhoff Publishers, 1985, pp. 123–140 (123) = *Judicial Independence in Greece*. Studia Iuridica III, Athens: Sakkoulas/Kluwer, 1995, pp. 137–154 = *Judicial Independence in modern legal developments – A Report on Greek law. Revue hellénique de droit international* 1982–83, pp. 535–346.

Kerameus, K., *Revisibilität ausländischen Rechts. Zeitschrift für Zivilprozess* 1986, pp. 166 ff. = Studia Iuridica III, Athens: Sakkoulas/Kluwer, 1995, pp. 427–447.

Kerameus, K., 'Das Verhältnis von Feststellungs- und Leistungsklage nach griechischem Zivilprozessrecht'. *Festschrift für W. Kralik* 1986, pp. 245–256 = Studia Iuridica III, Athens: Sakkoulas/Kluwer, 1995, pp. 219–234.

Kerameus, K., 'Aktuelle Probleme der internationalen Handelsschiedsgerichtsbarkeit unter Berücksichtigung der Rechtslage in Griechenland'. in the coll. Vol. *Les particularités nationales de d'arbitrage commercial international* 1987 = Studia Iuridica III, Athens: Sakkoulas/Kluwer, 1995, pp. 532–546.

Kerameus, K., 'Neuere Entwicklungen des Zivilprozessrechts in Griechenland'. in Fenge, H. & Papantoniou N. (Hrsg.), *Griechisches Recht im Wandel, Neuere Entwicklungen des Familienrechts und des Zivilprozessrechts.* Darmstadt: Luchterhand, 1987,. pp. 17–31 = Studia Iuridica III, Athens: Sakkoulas/Kluwer, 1995, pp. 107–124.

Kerameus, K., 'Arbitrage International et Ordre Juridique Hellénique'. *Revue de l'Arbitrage* 1987, pp. 35–48 = Studia Iuridica III, Athens: Sakkoulas/Kluwer, 1995, pp. 563–575.

Kerameus, K., 'Aktuelle Probleme der internationalen Zuständigkeit im Bereich des Brüsseler Übereinkommens von 1968 und die Deutsch-Griechischen Rectsbeziehungen'. in *Vorträge, Reden, Berichte, Europa-Institut der Universität des Saarlandes* 198, 1987 = Studia Iuridica III, Athens: Sakkoulas/Kluwer, 1995, pp. 515–531.

Kerameus, K., 'Einschränkungen der Klage auf Aufhebung von Schiedssprüchen'. *Festschrift für H. Fasching.* Wien: Manzsche, 1988, pp. 257–268 = Studia Iuridica III, Athens: Sakkoulas/Kluwer, 1995, pp. 295–310.

Kerameus, K., 'Das Brüsseler Gerichtsstandsübereinkommen und das griechische Recht der internationalen Zuständigkeit'. *Festschrift für G. Baumgärtel.* Köln/Berlin/Bonn/München: K. Heymanns, 1990, pp. 215–227 = Studia Iuridica III, Athens: Sakkoulas/Kluwer, 1995, pp. 532–546.

Kerameus, K., *The Examination of an Arbitration Agreement by T State Courts While Arbitration is Pending. Revue hellénique de droit international* 1989–1990, pp. 217–232.

Kerameus, K., *Judicial Activism in Greece*, in *Studi in onore di Vittorio Denti II*, Padova 1994, pp. 255–269 = Studia Iuridica III, Athens: Sakkoulas/Kluwer, 1995, pp. 155–166.

Kerameus, K., 'The New Greek Law on International Commercial Arbitration'. *Revue hellénique de droit international* 1999, pp. 583–585 = Studia Iuridica V, Athens: Sakkoulas/Kluwer, 2008, pp. 165–167.

Kerameus, K., *Civil Justice in Greece.* in Fazzalari, Elio & Fortin Pierre (eds), *Civil Justice in the Countries of the European Union.* London/Trenton: CEDAM, 1998, pp. 189–217 = Studia Iuridica V, Athens: Sakkoulas/Kluwer, 2008, pp. 3–30.

Bibliography in Languages Other Than Greek

Kerameus, K., *Pouvoirs du juge et réforme procédurale. Considérations sur l'expérience hellénique*, in *Nouveaux juges, nouveaux pouvoirs?, Mélanges en l'honneur de Roger Perrot*. Paris: Dalloz, 1997, pp. = Studia Iuridica V, Athens: Sakkoulas/Kluwer, 2008, pp. 54–65.

Kerameus, K., *Statut et responsabilité des huissiers de justice en droit hellénique*. in K. Boele-Woelki (ed.), *Comparability and Evaluation: Essays on Comparative Law, Private International Law, and International Commercial Arbitration in Honour of Dimitra Kokkini-Iatridou*, Springer 1994, pp. 205–210 = Studia Iuridica V, Athens: Sakkoulas/Kluwer, 2008, pp.110–117.

Kerameus, K., *Problèmes actuels des voies d'exécution civile en droit hellénique*. in *L'exécution XXIIIème Colloque des Instituts Judiciaires De Colloque des instituts d'études judiciaires Édité par Institut d'études judiciaires*. Paris: L'Harmattan', 2003, pp. 61–70 = Studia Iuridica V, Athens: Sakkoulas/Kluwer, 2008, pp. 213–218.

Kiousis, P., 'Greece'. in Ph. R. Weems, *Enforcement of Money Judgments Abroad*. New York: Bender, 1992, pp. Greece 1–20.

Klamaris N., 'Der Rechtsmissbrauch im griechischen Zivilprozessrecht'. in *Festschrift für Fritz Baur*. Tübingen: Mohr Siebeck, 1981, pp. 483–503.

Klamaris N., 'Rechtsvergleichende Betrachtungen zum Grundsatz der Einmaligkeit der Rechtsmittelerhebung'. *Festschrift für H. Fasching*, Wien: Manzsche, 1988, pp. 269–290.

Klamaris, N., 'Das neue griechische Gerichtsverfassungsrecht oder "Die Rache der Wittelsbacher"'. *Festschrift für W. Habscheid*. Bielefeld: Gieseking, 1989, pp. 161–166.

Klamaris, N., *Die prozessuale Aktualität in Griechenland*. in *Festschrift für Wolfram Henckel zum 70. Geburtstag*. Berlin, New York: Walter de Gruyter, 1995, pp. 437–454.

Klamaris, N., *Die Grundstruktur des griechischen Zwangsvollstreckungsrechts als des effektiven Teils des prozessualen Grundrechts auf Justizgewährung*. in *Festschrift Für Hideo Nakamura Zum 70. Geburtstag am 2. März 1996*. Tokyo: de Gruyter, 1996, Reprint 2013, pp. 253–280.

Klamaris, N., *Enforcement of Court Orders and Judgments: Greece*, in Walter & Gerhard (Hrsg.), *Recognition and enforcement of foreign judgments outside the scope of the Brussels and Lugano Conventions*. The Hague, etc., 2000, pp. 275 et seq.

Klamaris, N., *Die aktuellen bzw. bevorstehenden Reformen im Bereich des griechischen Zivilprozeßrechts. Reformtendenzen und verabschiedete ZPO-Modifizierungen*. in Rolf A. Schütze., *Einheit und Vielfalt des Rechts, Festschrift für Reinhold Geimer zum 65. Geburtstag*. München: Verlag C.H. Beck, 2002, pp. 437–447.

Klamaris, N., *Hauptunterschiede zwischen der Regelung der Schiedsgerichtsbarkeit in der griechischen ZPO (Art. 867-903) und der Regelung der Internationalen Handelsschiedsgerichtsbarkeit im (griechischen) Gesetz 2735/1999. Ein innerstaatlicher Überblick und Vergleich*. in *Grenzüberschreitungen – Beiträge zum Internationalen Verfahrensrecht und zur Schiedsgerichtsbarkeit; Festschrift für Peter Schlosser zum 70. Geburtstag*. Tübingen: Mohr Verlag, 2005, pp. 383–398.

Klamaris, N., *Zum Stand des griechischen Zwangsvollstreckungsrechts.* Eine zusammenfassende Skizze, *ZZP* 2008, S. 475–502.

Klamaris, N., *Die Prozessvollmacht nach dem griechischen Zivilprozessrecht.* in Aderhold et al. (Hrsg.), *Festschrift für Harm Peter Westermann zum 70. Geburtstag.* Köln: Verlag Dr Otto Schmidt, 2008, pp. 389–397.

Klamaris, N. *Die griechische ZPO-Regelung in Bezug auf die Rechtskraft im Umfeld des Eurogrundsatzes der Rechtskraft von Entscheidungen.* in: Alexander Bruns et al. (Hrsg.), *Festschrift für Rolf Stürner zum 70. Geburtstag, 2. Teilband: Internationales, Europäisches und ausländisches Recht.* Tübingen: Mohr Siebeck, 2013, pp. 1601–1624.

Klamaris, N., *Die wichtigsten Grundlagen des Beweisverfahrens nach griechischem Zivilprozessrecht.* in *Zwischenbilanz – Festschrift für Dagmar Coester-Waltjen zum 70. Geburtstag.* Bielefeld: Gieseking, Bielefeld 2015, pp. 1025–1036.

Klamaris, N., *Die einzelnen Sicherungsmaßnahmen im Rahmen des provisorischen Rechtsschutzes nach dem griechischen Zivilprozessrecht.* in *Rechtslage – Rechtserkenntnis – Rechtsdurchsetzung. Festschrift für Eberhard Schilken zum 70. Geburtstag.* Munich: Verlag C.H. Beck, 2015, pp. 339–352.

Klamaris, N., *Die Verfahrensgrundsätze nach dem griechischen Zivilprozessrecht.* MDR 2016, S. 947–951.

Klamaris, N., *Die wichtigsten aktuellen Reformen in Bezug auf das zivilprozessuale erstinstanzliche Verfahren nach der griechischen ZPO. Zugleich eine kurze kritische Analyse.* in *Fairness Justice Equity: Festschrift für Reinhold Geimer zum 80. Geburtstag.* Munich: C.H.Beck, 2017, pp. 335–344.

Klamaris, N. & Estratiou P.M., Access to Justice as a Fundamental Right. *Revue hellénique de droit international* 1998, pp. 291–310.

Klamaris, N. & Orfanidis G., 'Die Zwangsvollstreckung der gerichtlichen Entscheidungen und die Vollstreckungsmittel der Gerichte nach dem griechischen Zivilprozessrecht'. *Revue hellénique de droit international* 1985–86, pp. 335–358.

Kousoulis, S., 'Aktuelle Probleme der Hauptintervention'. *ZZP* 1988, pp. 211 ff.

Koussoulis, S., *Die internationale Schiedsgerichtsbarkeit in Griechenland.* in Peter Gottwald (Hrsg.), *Internationale Schiedsgerichtsbarkeit: Generalbericht und Nationalbericht = Arbitrage international =* International Arbitration, Veröffentlichung der Wissenschaftlichen Vereinigung für Internationales Verfahrensrecht e.V., Bd. 9. Bielefeld: Gieseking, 1997, pp. 405–420.

Koussoulis, S., 'Beweismaßprobleme im Zivilprozessrecht'. *Festschrift für K.H. Schwab.* München: C.H. Beck, 1990, pp. 277–288.

Koussoulis, S., 'Actual Problems of International Arbitration. The Greek Law in Comparison with the UNCITRAL Model Law'. *Revue hellénique de droit international* 1996, pp. 479–500.

Koutsouradis, A., 'Zur Frage der Verwendung privaten Wissens durch den Schiedsrichter'. *Konkurs-Treuhand – und Schiedsgerichtswesen* 1984, pp. 573–578

Koutsouradis, A., 'Grundsätze und Besonderheiten der Beweisaufnahme nach griechischem Schiedsverfahrensrecht'. in *Les particularités nationales de l'arbitrage commercial international* (1987) = *Νομικά Μελετήματα I* (1987), pp. 181 ff.

Bibliography in Languages Other Than Greek

Koutsouradis, A., 'Die Ehestreitigkeiten nach griechischem Zivilprozessrecht'. *Volume in Honour of G. Mitsopoulos.* Athens/Komotini: Sakkoulas, 1993, pp. 737–756.

Koutsouradis, A., *Die Informationsbeschaffung im materiellen Recht und im Prozeßrecht. Gezeigt am Beispiel des griechischen Rechts.* in *Recht und Rechtsdurchsetzung – Festschrift für Hans Ulrich Walder.* Zürich: Schulthess Juristische Medien, 1994, pp. 25–47.

Lambrinakis, E., 'Innovations interessantes du nouveau Code de procédure civile hellénique entré en vigneur le 16 Septembre 1968'. *Revue trimestrielle de droit civil* 1971, pp. 320–325.

Magliveras, K., 'Fact Finding: A Greek Perspective'. in D.L. Carey Miller & Paul R. Beaumont (eds), *The Option of Litigating in Europe*, United Kingdom Comparative Law Series. The British Institute of International and Comparative Law, London, 1993, pp. 87–107.

Makridou, K., 'Lawyers' fees in Greece at a turning point. Recent legislative changes in litigation costs', *World Congress of the International Academy of Comparative Law.* Washington, DC, July 2010, the Greek Report, Volume in: Mathias Reimann (ed.), 'Cost and Fee Allocation in Civil Procedure'. Mathias Reimann, Springer 2012, pp. 163 ff. = *Revue hellénique de droit international* 2010, pp. 113–128.

Makridou, K., *Greek Case Management in Light of Other European Civil Justice Systems. The Journal of Comparative Law*, Vol. VII. 2012, pp. 227–242.

Makridou, K., 'Civil justice reforms in Greece: case management, single-judge proceedings and alternative dispute resolution procedures', *ZZZ* 2011/2012, pp. 257 ff.

Makridou, K., *Principles of Preclusion and Res Judicata – Reflections from the Greek and the American Law perspectives.*in *Issues of Estoppel and Res judicata in Anglo-American and Greek Law.* Athens: Νομική Βιβλιοθήκη, 2012, pp. 63–100.

Makridou, K., *The Public Policy Defence in International Arbitration under Greek Law. ZZP International* 18 (2013), pp. 175 ff.

Makridou, K., *Speeding Up Civil Litigation in Greece Through ADR Methods.* in Tatsachen – Verfahren – Vollstreckung: *Festschrift für Isaak Meier zum 65. Geburtstag.* Schulthess Juristische Medien, 2015, pp. 449 ff.

Makridou, K., *General Principles and Preconditions for the Granting of Provisional Remedies in Greek Law.* in F., Carpi, C. Rasia & C. Apalagaki, *Provisional measures in Italian and Greek Procedural Law; Greek and foreign civil procedural systems III.* Thessaloniki: Sakkoulas Publications, 2016, pp. 23 et seq.

Makridou, K., *The Procedural Treatment of Foreign Law in Greek Civil Trials: Questions of Fact or Questions of Law?. ZZP International* 2016, pp. 143 ff.

Makridou, K., *The Enforcement of Payment Orders under Greek Law. ZZZ* 2016, pp. 39 et seq.

Makridou, K., Interpretation and Application of the New York Convention in the Republic of Greece. in George A. Bermann (ed.), *Recognition and Enforcement of Foreign Arbitral Awards – The Interpretation and Application of the New York Convention by National Courts.* Springer 2017, pp. 379–416.

Maridakis, G., *Die Vollstreckbarkeit ausländischer Urteile in Griechenland. RabelsZ* 1930, pp. 506–512.

P. Massouridis, 'The Enforcement of Foreign Judgments in Greece'. *Revue hellénique de droit international* 1970, pp. 186–224.

Michaelides-Nouaros, G., 'Les systèmes juridiques des peuples Européens'. *Revue hellénique de droit international* 1957, pp. 40 ff.

Millionis, A., *Praxis der Vollstreckung deutscher Urteile in Griechenland nach dem EuGVÜ. RIW/AWD* 1991, pp. 100–103.

Mitsopoulos, G., 'La distinction du fait et du droit en procedure de cassation'. *Revue hellenique de droit international* 1968, pp. 4 ff.

Mitsopoulos, G., 'Die Unterscheidung zwischen Tatfrage und Rechtsfrage im Kassationsverfahren'. *Zeitschrift für Zivilprozess* 1968, pp. 251 ff.

Mitsopoulos, G., 'Considérations sur la théorie de la Procédure Civile'. in the Vol. *Estudios de derecho procesal en honor de Niceto Alcalá – Zamora y Castillo.* Universidad Nacional Autónoma de Mexico, 1975, pp. 801–815.

Mitsopoulos, G., 'Zum Einfluss der neuen griechischen Verfassung auf die griechische Zivilprozessordnung'. *Festschrift für Bosch.* Bielefeld: Gieseking, 1976, pp. 699–707.

Mitsopoulos G., 'Gedanken zu einigen wichtigen Probleme der Zivilprozessrechtslehre'. *Zeitschrift für Zivilprozess* 1978, pp. 113–127.

Mitsopoulos G., 'Die notwendige Streitgenossenschaft nach dem griechischen'Zivilprozessrecht'. *Festschrift für Fr. Baur.* Tübingen: Mohr Siebeck, 1981, pp. 503–515.

Mitsopoulos, G., *Der Einfluss der Verfassung auf das Zivilprozessrecht. Revue hellénique de droit international* 1982–1983, pp. 219–226.

Mitsopoulos, G., 'Historisches und richterliches Wissen'. *Festschrift für Karl Heinz Schwab zum 70. Geburtstag.* München: C.H. Beck, 1990, pp. 337–348.

Mitsopoulos, G., *Die Unvereinbarkeit des ausländischen Schiedsspruchs, der auf Schadensersatz wegen Unterlassung einer Überversicherung eines Schiffes erkennt, mit dem griechischen ordre public.* in *Festschrift für Gottfried Baumgärtel zum 70. Geburtstag.* Cologne: Heymann, 1990, pp. 381–388.

Moustaira, E., *Rules for Declining to Exercise Jurisdiction in Civil and Commercial Matters. Revue hellénique de droit international* 1994, pp. 173–184.

Nerlich, J. & Papaioannou B., *Rechtsanwälte in Griechenland.* in Martin Henssler & J. Nerlich (Hrsg.), *Anwaltliche Tätigkeit in Europa*; Schriftenreihe des Instituts für Anwaltsrechts. Bonn: NOMOS, 1994, pp. 195–210.

Oikonomopoulos G., 'Greece'. in P. Sanders (gen. ed.), International Commercial Arbitration, Vol. I (Union Internationale des Avocats, 1956), pp. 270–323 (in English and French).

Orfanidis, G., *Die Konkurrenz von Gläubigern im griechischen Zwangsvollstreckungsrecht.* in *Grenzüberschreitungen – Beiträge zum Internationalen Verfahrensrecht und zur Schiedsgerichtsbarkeit; Festschrift für Peter Schlosser zum 70. Geburtstag.* Tübingen: Mohr Siebeck, 2005, pp. 669–682.

Papaphilippou, D., *Guarantees for Judicial Independence. Revue hellénique de droit international* 1980, pp. 203–240.

Bibliography in Languages Other Than Greek

Patkos, B., 'The United Nations Convention of 1958 on the Recognition and Enforcement of Foreign Arbitral Awards in the Light of the Greek Civil Procedure Code of 1971'. *Revue hellénique de droit international* 1974, pp. 295–306.

Polyzogopoulos, C., 'The collective Action in Greek Law for the Protection of Consumers'. in *Studia in Honorem Pelayia Yessiou-Faltsi.* Thessaloniki: Sakkoulas Publications, 2007, pp. 438 ff.

Polyzogopoulos, C., *Außergerichtliche Streitschlichtung. Die griechische Lösung.* in Alexander Bruns, et al., *Festschrift für Rolf Stürner zum 70. Geburtstag*, 2. Teilband: Internationales, Europäisches und ausländisches Recht. Tübingen: Mohr Siebeck, 2013, pp. 1745–1759.

Pouliadis, A., *Die Bedeutung des deutsch-griechischen Vertrags v. 4.11.1961 für die Anerkennung und Vollstreckung deutscher Entscheidungen in der griechischen praxis. IPRax* 1985, pp. 357–369.

Rammos, G., 'Das Rechtsmittelverfahren nach dem Entwurf einer neuen griechischen Zivilprozessordnung'. *Zeitschrift für Zivilprozess* 1961, pp. 241 ff.

Rammos, G., 'Der Gang des Erkenntnisverfahrens nach dem Entwurf der neuen griechischen Zivilprozessordnung'. *Zeitschrift für Zivilprozess* 1965, pp. 241 ff.

Rammos, G., 'Die Intervention in der Berufungsinstanz nach dem griechischen Zivilprozessrecht'. in *Volume in Honour of Segni II.* Milano, 1967, pp. 215–221.

Rammos, G., 'Die Verletzung der Erfahrungssätze als Kassationsgrund nach griechischem Zivilprozessrecht'. in *Multitudo Legum Ius Unum II Festschrift für Wilhelm Wengler zu seinem 65. Geburtstag Vol. II.* Berlin: Inter Recht, 1973, pp. 693 ff.

Rammos, G., 'Die Entscheidungsbegründung im griechischen Verfahrensrecht', in the volume: *Die Entscheidungsbegründung in europäischen Verfahrensrechten und im Verfahren vor internationalen Gerichten.* (Wien/New York: Springer, 1974, pp. 399–422.

Rammos, G., 'Die Kassation im Interesse des Gesetzes nach dem griechischen Zivilprozessrecht'. in *Gedächtnisschrift für Rudolf Bruns.* München: Vahlen, 1980, pp. 35–44.

Rammos, G., 'Höhere Gewalt, Zufall, Naturereignis und Wiederaufnahme des Verfahrens nach dem griechischen Zivilprozessrecht'. *Festschrift für Fr. Baur.* Tübingen: Mohr, 1981, pp. 561–572.

Rammos, G. & Fragistas, Ch., 'L'expertise en Grèce', in the collected work: *L'expertise dans les principaux systèmes juridiques d'Europe, Travaux et recherches de l'Institut de Droit Comparé de Paris, Vol. XXXII (1967)*, pp. 261 ff. and pp. 291 ff.

Spiliotopoulos, E., 'Judicial Review of Legislation Acts in Greece', *Temple Law Quarterly*, Vol. 56 (1983), pp. 463–502.

Stürner, R., 'Das deutsche (österreichische) Zivilprozess und seine Ausstrahlung auf andere Rechts-ordnungen', in W. Habscheid (ed.), Das deutsche Zivilprozessrecht und seine Ausstrahlung auf andere Rechtsordnungen. Bielefeld: Gieseking, 1991, pp. 27–28.

Tompaidis J. & Voulgarakis K., in Professional Secrecy of Lawyers in Europe, Compiled by the Bar of Brussels (Cambridge University Press 2013), pp. 200–221.

Triadafyllidis, C., *Anerkennung und Vollstreckung von punitive damages Urteilen nach kontinentalem und insbesondere nach griechischem Recht. IPRax* 2002, pp. 237 ff.

Triadafillidis, C. & Yiannopoulos P., *Das ordentliche Verfahren nach der neuen griechischen ZPO. ZfRV* 58 (2016), pp. 275–279.

Tsikrikas, D., 'Les actions collectives en droit grec'. *Studia in Honorem Pelayia Yessiou-Faltsi.* Sakkoulas Publications, 2007, pp. 733 ff.

Tsikrikas, D. *Bemerkungen zur Struktur und Funktion des griechischen Vollstreckungsrechts. ZZPInt* 1996, pp. 119 et seq.

Tsikrikas, D., *Örtliche und internationale Zuständigkeit der griechischen Gerichte bei einer Klage auf Akteneinsicht und Urkundenvorlage. ZZPInt* 2007, S. 109–117.

Tsikrikas, D., *Die Entstehung und Entwicklung des griechischen Zivilprozessrechts im rechtshistorischen und rechtsvergleichenden Zusammenhang. ZZPInt* 2011, pp. 111–133.

Tsikrikas, D., *Anerkennung und Vollstreckung ausländischer gerichtlicher Entscheidungen und Schiedssprüche nach dem griechischen Zivilverfahrensrecht. ZZPInt* 2018, pp. 79–100.

Tsikrikas, D., *Rechtsmittelverfahren im griechischen Recht. Der Einfluss ausländischer Vorbilder auf das griechische Recht – Insbesondere das Rechtsmittel der Kassation unter rechtsvergleichender Betrachtung.* in Althammer & Roth (Hrsg.), *Ausländische Rechtsimplantate im nationalen Zivilprozessrecht.* Mohr Siebeck 2020, pp. 63–82.

Vassilakakis, E., 'Enforceability of Foreign Arbitral Awards Adjudicating Punitive Damages in Greece'. in *Festschrift Kozyris*. Sakkoulas Publishers, 2007, pp. 493 ff.

Vassilakakis, E., *Recognition and Enforcement of Foreign Judgments in Cases of State Succession: The Paradigm of the 1981 Convention between Greece and the former USSR on Judicial Assistance in Civil and Criminal Matters (with Dr P. Yiannopulos).* Currents – Journal of International Economic Law 2003, pp. 31–36.

Vassilakakis, E., *Die Anwendung des EuGVÜ und der EuGVO in der griechischen Rechtsprechung. IPRax* 2005, pp. 279–284.

Vassilakakis, E., *Recognition or Enforcement of Foreign Arbitral Awards and State Succession: The Ghostly Paradigm of the Agreement between Greece and Yugoslavia in Comparison to the New York Convention of 1958. Croatian Arbitration Yearbook* 2009, pp. 281–297.

Vasilakakis E. & Kourtis V., *The Impact and Application of the Brussels II bis regulation in Greece.* in K. Boele-Woelki (ed.), *Brussels II bis: Its Impact and Application in the Member States.* Oxford: Antwerp, 2007, pp.133–143.

Vrellis, S. 'Reconnaissance et exécution de decisions étrangères tant judiciaire qu'arbitral – Le système en vigueur et ses améliorations'. Greek National Report to the 8th World Conference of Civil Procedure in Utrecht 1987, in Institute of Procedural Studies (ed.), *Justice and Efficiency.* Athens 1988, pp. 399 ff.

Vegleris, Ph., 'La Constitution, le loi et les tribunaux en Grèce'. *Annales de la Faculté de Droit de Liege* 1967, pp. 439 ff.

Bibliography in Languages Other Than Greek

Vekris, I., 'The Legal System of Greece'. in K.R. Redden, *Modern Legal Systems Cyclopedia*, Vol. 3, Part 1, *Country Studies*. Buffalo/New York: Hein, 1990, No. 3.140.3–3.140.45. Parts §§1.4–6 treat the 'Greek Judicial System', 'Legal Education' and the 'Greek Bar'.

Yessiou-Faltsi, P. & Pipsou, L.-M., 'The Law of Execution: National Report for Greece'. in de Leval (ed.), *Seizure and Overindebtedness in the European Union*. Kluwer Law International, 1997.

Yessiou-Faltsi, P., 'Les bases constitutionelles de l'organisation judiciaire en Grèce'. *Revue hellénique de droit international* 1979, pp. 62–87.

Yessiou-Faltsi, P., 'The Production of Evidence in the Case According to the Greek CPC'. *Revue hellénique de droit international* 1979, pp. 88–111.

Yessiou-Faltsi, P., 'Le droit á la preuve'. *Revue hellénique de droit international* 1984, pp. 275–307.

Yessiou-Faltsi, P., *Judicial Responsibility in Greece*, *Revue hellénique de droit international* 1982–83, pp. 281–312.

Yessiou-Faltsi, P., 'Das Ausgleichsprinzip im griechischen Zwangsvollstreckungsrecht im Unterschied zum deutschen Prioritätsprinzip'. *Zeitschrift für Zivilprozess* 1993, pp. 215 ff.

Yessiou-Faltsi, P., 'Ist der "manque de base légale" ein Kassationsgrund, der über die Unterscheidung des materiellen Rechts und des Zivilprozessrechts hinausgeht?'. *Festschrift für W. Henckel*. Berlin – New York: W. de Gruyter, 1995, pp. 923 ff. = Η δικονομική έννομη τάξη III [Procedural Legal Order Vol. III], Thessaloniki: Sakkoulas Publications, 2009, pp. 631–651.

Yessiou-Faltsi, P., 'Judicial Review of Unconstitutional Legislation in Greece'. *Festschrift Für Hideo Nakamura Zum 70. Geburtstag am 2. März 1996 (Tokyo, 1996; de Gruyter; Reprint 2013)*, pp. 697 ff.

Yessiou-Faltsi, P., *Prinzipien der Einzelzwangsvollstreckung in der griechischen im Vergleich zur deutschen Zivilprozeßordnung*. in *Festschrift für Hans Friedhelm Gaul zum 70. Geburtstag*. (Bielefeld: Gieseking, 1997, pp. 815–830.

Yessiou-Faltsi, P., 'The Public Trial in Ancient Athens: Basic Principles of Contemporary Significance'. *Volume in Honour of A. Manessis*, III. Athens: Sakkoulas publications, 1999, pp. 315–342 = in English in: Kojima et al. (eds), Europe's Judicial Systems, Past and Future. Tokyo: Chuo University Press, 1998.

Yessiou-Faltsi, P., 'Civil Procedure in Greece (Nineteenth, and Twentieth Centuries)'. in C.H. van Rhee (ed.), *The Law's Delay*. Antwerp/Oxford/New York: Intersentia, 2004, pp. 377–391 = Η δικονομική έννομη τάξη III Procedural Legal Order Vol. III, (Thessaloniki: Sakkoulas Publications, 2009, pp. 81–103.

Yessiou-Faltsi, P., 'International Jurisdiction: According to the Greek Code of Civil Procedure'. in *Toward comparative law in the 21st century: the 50th anniversary of the Institute of Comparative Law in Japan*, ed. by the Institute of Comparative Law in Japan. Tokyo: Chuo Univ. Press, 1998, pp. 659–684 = Η δικονομική έννομη τάξη III [Procedural Legal Order Vol. III], Thessaloniki: Sakkoulas Publications, 2009, pp. 205–235.

Yessiou-Faltsi, P., *Wirkungen einer internationalen Zuständigkeitsvereinbarung bei einer Streitgenossenschaft*. in Rolf A. Schütze (ed.), *Einheit und Vielfalt des Rechts, Festschrift für Reinhold Geimer zum 65. Geburtstag*. Munich: C.H. Beck,

2002, pp. 1547–1568 = H δικονομική έννομη τάξη III [Procedural Legal Order Vol. III], Thessaloniki: Sakkoulas Publications, 2009, pp. 237–260.

Yessiou-Faltsi, P., *Die Auslandszustellung durch «rémise au parquet» – Auslegungsfragen aus griechischer Sicht.* in Pelayia Faltsi et al., *Recht in Europa: Festschrift für Prof. Dr Dr h.c. Hilmar Fenge zum 65. Geburtstag.* Hamburg: Verlag Dr Kovac, 1996, pp. 159–171 = H δικονομική έννομη τάξη III [Procedural Legal Order Vol. III], Thessaloniki: Sakkoulas Publications, 2009, pp. 293–310.

Yessiou-Faltsi, P., *Greek Law on Service Abroad of Judicial and Extrajudicial Documents.* H δικονομική έννομη τάξη III [Procedural Legal Order Vol. III, Thessaloniki: Sakkoulas Publications, 2009, pp. 311–326.

Yessiou-Faltsi, P., *Date and Means by which a Greek Court Becomes Seised of a Proceeding.* H δικονομική έννομη τάξη III [Procedural Legal Order Vol. III], Thessaloniki: Sakkoulas Publications, 2009, pp. 327–337.

Yessiou-Faltsi, P., *Die Anerkennung und Vollstreckung deutscher Gerichtsurteile in Griechenland aus der Sicht eines griechischen Juristen. Zeitschrift für Zivilprozess* 1983, pp. 67 et seq. = H δικονομική έννομη τάξη III [Procedural Legal Order Vol. III], Thessaloniki: Sakkoulas Publications, 2009, pp. 339–366.

Yessiou-Faltsi, P., Anerkennung ausländischer Personenstandsentscheidungen nach autonomem griechischen Recht. in *Festschrift für Walter H. Rechberger zum 60. Geburtstag.* Wien/New York: Springer Verlag, 2005, pp. 733 et seq. = H δικονομική έννομη τάξη III [Procedural Legal Order Vol. III], Thessaloniki: Sakkoulas Publications, 2009, pp. 367–388.

Yessiou-Faltsi, P., *Versäumnisverfahren und Versäumnisurteil nach griechischem Recht bei Zustellung des Verfahrenseinleitenden Schriftstückes im Ausland.* in Reinhold Geime (ed.), *Wege zur Globalisierung des Rechts – Festschrift für Rolf A. Schütze zum 65. Geburtstag.* Munich: C. H. Beck, 1999, pp. 997 et seq. = H δικονομική έννομη τάξη III [Procedural Legal Order Vol. III], Thessaloniki: Sakkoulas Publications, 2009., pp. 597–611.

Yessiou-Faltsi, P., *Grenzüberschreitender einstweiliger Rechtsschutz nach autonomem griechischen Recht.* in *Grenzüberschreitungen: Beiträge zum internationalen Verfahrensrecht und zur Schiedsgerichtsbarkeit: Festschrift für Peter Schlosser zum 70. Geburtstag.* Tübingen: Mohr Siebeck, 2005, pp. 1141 et seq. = H δικονομική έννομη τάξη III [Procedural Legal Order Vol. III], Thessaloniki: Sakkoulas Publications, 2009, pp. 751–770.

Yessiou-Faltsi, P., *Date and Means by which a Greek Court Becomes Seized of a Proceeding for the Purposes of the European Judgments Conventions and Regulation Nr. 44/2001.* in *Magister Artis Boni et Aequi. Studia in honorem JÁNOS, Németh.* Budapest: ELTE, 2003, pp. 1003 et seq. = H δικονομική έννομη τάξη III [Procedural Legal Order Vol. III], Thessaloniki: Sakkoulas Publications, 2009, pp. 935–950.

Yessiou-Faltsi, P., *Die Folgen des Europäischen Vollstreckungstitels für das Vollstreckungsrecht in Europa*, in Gottwald, Peter (ed.), *Perspektiven der justiziellen Zusammenarbeit in Zivilsachen in der Europäischen Union*, Veröffentlichungen der Wissenschaftlichen Vereinigung für Internationales Verfahrensrecht, Band 15, Bielefeld, 2004, pp. 213 et seq. = H δικονομική έννομη τάξη III [Procedural Legal Order Vol. III], Thessaloniki: Sakkoulas Publications, 2009, pp. 1056–1102.

Bibliography in Languages Other Than Greek

Yessiou-Faltsi, P., *Effects of the European Enforcement Order on the Enforcement Law in Europe.* in *Χαρμόσυνο Φαίδωνα I. Κοζύρη / Justice in Particular: in honour of Professor P.J. Kozyris.* Athens: Sakkoulas Books, 2007, pp. 579 et seq. = Η δικονομική έννομη τάξη III [Procedural Legal Order Vol. III], Thessaloniki: Sakkoulas Publications, 2009, pp. 1151–1193.

Yessiou-Faltsi, P., 'The European Enforcement Order after Five Years of Experience in Greece'. *Revue hellénique de droit international* 2008, pp. 735 ff.

Yessiou-Falsi, P., in Rossides, Hadgi & Marketos (eds), *Doing Business in Greece.* (American Hellenic Institute Foundation, Volume I, Waschington D.C.), §24 = Η δικονομική έννομη τάξη IV [Procedural Legal Order Vol. IV], Thessaloniki:Sakkoulas Publications, 2009, pp. 223–242.

Yessiou-Falsi, P., *Feststellungsklagen und Anerkennung ausländischer Entscheidungen.* in Prof. Dr Dr h.c. Reinhold, Prof. Dr Dr h.c. Rolf A. Schütze & Ass. Prof. Mag. Dr Garber (Hrsg.), *Europäische und internationale Dimension des Rechts: Festschrift für Daphne-Ariane Simotta.* Vienna: Lexis Nexis, 2012, pp. 731 et seq. = Η δικονομική έννομη τάξη V [Procedural Legal Order Vol. V] Thessaloniki: Sakkoulas Publications, 2019, pp. 49–64.

Yessiou-Falsi, P., *Der Zahlungsbefehl der griechischen ZPO als Vollstreckungstitel innerhalb der EU. in Rechtslage – Rechtserkenntnis – Rechtsdurchsetzung: Festschrift für Eberhard Schilken zum 70. Geburtstag.* München: C.H. Beck, 2015, pp. 827 et seq. = Η δικονομική έννομη τάξη V [Procedural Legal Order Vol. V] Thessaloniki: Sakkoulas Publications, 2019, pp. 461–477.

Yessiou-Falsi, P., *Die Abendstunde des persönlichen Arrestes als Exekutionsmittel zur Befriedigung von Geldforderungen im griechischen Recht.* in Alexander Bruns et al., *Festschrift für Rolf Stürner zum 70. Geburtstag, 2. Teilband: Internationales, Europäisches und ausländisches Recht.* Tübingen: Mohr Siebeck, 2013, pp. 1869–1882 = Η δικονομική έννομη τάξη V [Procedural Legal Order Vol. V] Thessaloniki: Sakkoulas Publications, 2019, pp. 1069–1086.

Yessiou-Falsi, P., *Deutsche Urteile über die Vaterschaftsfestellung von nichtehelichen Kindern aus der Sicht der griechischen öffentliche Ordnung.* in Hilbig-Lugani et al., *Zwischenbilanz – Festschrift für Dagmar Coester-Waltjen zum 70. Geburtstag.* (Mohr Siebeck; 2015), pp. 913 et seq. = Η δικονομική έννομη τάξη V [Procedural Legal Order Vol. V, (Sakkoulas Publications; Thessaloniki 2019), pp.1153–1165.

Yessiou-Faltsi, P. & Pipsou L.M., 'The Law of Execution Faced with the Social Phenomenon of "Overrunning into Debt", Taking into Account the EEC Member States' Law'. A National Report for Greece, *Actualités du droit, Revue de la Faculté de Droit de Liège* 1995.3, pp. 689 ff.

Yessiou-Faltsi, P. & Pipsou L. M., in *de Leval (ed.), Seizure and Overindebtedness in the European Union, Civil Procedure in Europe I* (Kluwer Law International 1997), pp. 323 ff.

Yessiou-Faltsi, P. & Podimata E., Preliminary or Summary Proceedings: Scope and Importance in Greek Civil Procedure. *Revue hellénique de droit international* 2004, pp. 383–422.

Yessiou-Faltsi, P. & Tamamidis A., *Recent Tendencies in the Position of the Judge. Revue hellénique de droit international* 1999, pp. 459–484.

Zepos, P., 'The Greek Legal System'. *Revue hellénique de droit international* 1961, pp. 1 ff.

Zepos, P., 'The Historical and Comparative Background of the Greek Civil Code' Civil Code. *Inter-American Law Review* 1961, pp. 285–299.

Zepos, P., 'Mixed Jurisdiction in Greece'. *The American Journal of Comparative Law* 1974, pp. 221–229.

§3 Translations of Legislative Texts

Gesetzbuch ueber das Zivil-Verfahren, Beilage zu Nr. 22 des Regierungsblattes, Nauplia 1834; Gerichts – und Notariats – Ordnung, Beilage zu Nr. 13 des Regierungsblattes, Nauplia 1834.

Baumgartel, G. & Rammos G. (eds), *Das griechische Zivilprozess-Gesetzbuch mit Einführungsgesetz.* unter Mitarbeit von K., Beys, L. Sinaniotis & S. Delikostopoulos, Köln/Berlin/Bonn/München: C. Heymanns V. KG., 1969. The translation is based on the original text and the initial enumeration of the Code (1967). *See supra*, No. 23A new edition, following the subsequent modifications of the Code, is expected to appear.

§4 Periodicals

Two Greek periodicals have been publishing articles or reports also related to Civil Procedure in languages other than Greek (French, English, German). The first is '*Revue hellénique de droit international*', edited since 1948 by the 'Greek Institute of International and Foreign Law' in Athens. The second was *Dike* (monthly) from 1970 to 2009. A special annual edition of the monthly review *Dike*, under the title 'Dike International', appeared since 1994 in German and English. An international edition of the Hellenic Review of European Law appears every December published by the Centre of International and European Economic Law. Both '*Revue hellénique de droit international*' and 'Dike International' are not anymore operative.

§5 Internet Publications

Anthimos, A., *Case of Matrakas and Others v. Poland and Greece ECHR.* 7.11.2013 [case Nr. 47268/06], http://icl-in-greece.blogspot.com/2014_02_09_archive.html.

Anthimos, A., *Greece No Forum for Summary Proceedings Against Facebook*, http://icl-in-greece.blogspot.com/2014_02_23_archive.html.

Anthimos, A., *Recognition and Enforcement of an Arbitral Award by the International Commercial Arbitration Court at the Ukrainian Chamber of Commerce and Industry (ICAC at the UCCI)*, http://icl-in-greece.blogspot.com/2014_04_13_archive.html.

Anthimos, A., *Greece Safe Harbor for CIETAC Awards*, http://icl-in-greece.blogspot.com/2014_04_20_archive.html.

Anthimos, A., *Enforcement of a JAG Award in Greece*, http://icl-in-greece.blogspot.com/2014_04_27_archive.html.

Anthimos, A., *On the Application of Art. 9 & 12 Brussels II Bis Regulation in Greece*, http://icl-in-greece.blogspot.com/2014_05_11_archive.html.

Bibliography in Languages Other Than Greek

Anthimos, A., *International Jurisdiction Issues in the Aftermath of the Sea Diamond Accident*, http://icl-in-greece.blogspot.com/2014_05_25_archive.html.

Anthimos, A., *No Exequatur for an ICA Award in Greece*, http://icl-in-greece.blogspot.com/2014_06_01_archive.html.

Anthimos, A., *Enforcement of an ICC Award and a Swiss Supreme Court judgment*, http://icl-in-greece.blogspot.com/2014_06_08_archive.html.

Anthimos, A., *Greek Supreme Court on the Interpretation of Art. 23 & 24 Brussels I Regulation,* http://icl-in-greece.blogspot.com/2014_08_03_archive.html.

Anthimos, A., *Defamation Through Wikipedia Postings*, http://icl-in-greece.blogspot.com/2014_09_07_archive.html.

Anthimos, A., *Enforcing a First Preferred Ship's Mortgage from St. Vincent & the Grenadines in Greece*, http://icl-in-greece.blogspot.com/2014_09_28_archive.html.

Anthimos, A., *Failure to Demonstrate the Existence of an Arbitration Agreement Impedes Enforcement of an ICC Award,* http://icl-in-greece.blogspot.com/2014_10_12_archive.html.

Anthimos, A., *Habitual Residence under the Brussels II bis Regulation,* http://icl-in-greece.blogspot.com/2014_10_19_archive.html.

Anthimos, A., *Rabbinical Divorce Recognized in Greece*, http://icl-in-greece.blogspot.com/2014_11_02_archive.html.

Anthimos, A., *Refusal to Accept Greek Proceedings by a Greek Living in Germany (Art. 8 Service Regulation*, http://icl-in-greece.blogspot.com/2016_08_07_archive.html.

Anthimos, A., *No Application of Brussels I Regulation for the Enforcement of a Belgian Judgment in Greece,* http://icl-in-greece.blogspot.com/2016_10_02_archive.html.

Anthimos, A., *On the Significance of Translation Inaccuracies in the Field of the Lugano Convention (and Beyond …),* http://icl-in-greece.blogspot.com/2016_10_09_archive.html.

Anthimos, A., *Recognition of an Egyptian Khul'a Divorce in Greece*, http://icl-in-greece.blogspot.com/2016_10_16_archive.html.

Anthimos, A., *Online Defamation, Centre of Interests, and Place of Harmful Event,* http://icl-in-greece.blogspot.com/2016_10_23_archive.html.

Anthimos, A., *New Law on Mediation in Civil and Commercial Maters – Some Cross Border Issues*, http://icl-in-greece.blogspot.com/2018_01_21_archive.html.

Anthimos, A., *Implementation of the EAPO in Greece*, https://conflictoflaws.net/2017/implementation-of-the-eapo-in-greece/.

Anthimos, A., *Sharia Law in Greece: Blending European Values with Islamic Tradition*, https://conflictoflaws.net/2018/sharia-law-in-greece-blending-european-values-with-islamic-tradition/.

Anthimos, A., *Talaq v Greek Public Policy: Operation Successful, Patient Dead …* , https://conflictoflaws.net/2018/talaq-v-greek-public-policy-operation-successful-patient-dead/.

Anthimos, A., *Recognition of Surnames in Greece – Where Do We Go from Here?*, https://conflictoflaws.net/2019/recognition-of-surnames-in-greece-where-do-we-go-from-here/.

Anthimos, A., *Talaq Reloaded: Repudiation Recognized if Application Filed by the Wife*, https://conflictoflaws.net/2019/talaq-reloaded-repudiation-recognized-if-application-filed-by-the-wife/.

Anthimos, A., *Awaken the Guardian: UK Damages for Breach of a Choice of Court Agreement Violate Greek Public Policy*, https://conflictoflaws.net/2019/awaken-the-guardian-uk-damages-for-breach-of-a-choice-of-court-agreement-violate-greek-public-policy/.

Anthimos, A., *First Contact of Greek Courts with the 2005 Hague Choice of Court Convention,* https://conflictoflaws.net/2020/first-contact-of-greek-courts-with-the-2005-hague-choice-of-court-convention/.

Anthimos, A., *From Anti-Suit Injunctions to 'Quasi' Anti-Suit Injunctions and Declaratory Relief for Breach of a Choice of Court Agreement: A Whiter Shade of Pale?*, https://conflictoflaws.net/2020/from-anti-suit-injunctions-to-quasi-anti-suit-injunctions-and-declaratory-relief-for-breach-of-a-choice-of-court-agreement-a-whiter-shade-of-pale/.

Anthimos, A., *New York Convention Applies to the Recognition and Enforcement of Basketball Arbitral Tribunal Awards*, https://conflictoflaws.net/2020/new-york-convention-applies-to-the-recognition-and-enforcement-of-basketball-arbitral-tribunal-awards/.

Anthimos, A., *Pathological Clauses in International Sports Arbitration and Return to Civil Proceedings*, https://eapil org/2020/09/03/pathological-clauses-in-interna tional-sports-arbitration-and-return-to-civil-proceedings/.

Anthimos, A., *Service of Proceedings on the Foreign Party's Attorney as an Alternative to Personal Service*, https://eapil.org/2020/10/05/service-of-proceedings-on-the-foreign-partys-attorney-rather-than-the-party-itself/.

Anthimos, A., *The Court of Appeal of Piraeus on the Non-Recognition of a Dutch Judgment on Maintenance*, https://eapil.org/2020/11/11/the-court-of-appeal-of-piraeus-on-the-non-recognition-of-a-dutch-judgment-on-maintenance/.

Anthimos, A., *English Custody Orders Violate Greek Public Policy if the Parents Form a Same-Sex Couple*, https://eapil.org/2021/02/03/english-custody-orders-violate-greek-public-policy-if-the-parents-form-a-same-sex-couple/.

Anthimos, A., *Is a Maltese Ship Mortgage an Authentic Instrument for the Purposes of Article 57 of the Brussels I Regulation?*, https://eapil.org/2021/04/13/is-a-maltese-ship-mortgage-an-authentic-instrument-for-the-purposes-of-article-57-of-the-brussels-i-regulation/.

Anthimos, A., *Postal Service from Greece to Germany – Recalling Henderson v. Novo Banco*, https://eapil.org/2022/02/14/postal-service-from-greece-to-germany-recalling-henderson-v-novo-banco/.

Anthimos, A., *Excess of Authority as a Ground of Refusal for an AAA Award in Greece,* https://conflictoflaws.net/2022/excess-of-authority-as-a-ground-of-refusal-for-an-aaa-award-in-greece/.

Anthimos, A., *Bitcoin and Public Policy in the Field of International Commercial Arbitration*, https://conflictoflaws.net/2022/bitcoin-and-public-policy-in-the-field -of-international-commercial-arbitration/.

Bibliography in Languages Other Than Greek

Anthimos, A., *Greek Court Recognizes UK Custody Order to the Non-biological Parent in the Context of a Married Same-Sex Couple*, https://conflictoflaws.net/2022/greek-court-recognizes-uk-custody-order-to-the-non-biological-parent-in-the-context-of-a-married-same-sex-couple/.

Anthimos, A., *First Contacts with the Application for Refusal of Enforcement in Greece*, https://eapil.org/2022/08/29/first-contacts-with-the-application-for-refusal-of-enforcement-in-greece/.

Anthimos, A., *The Greek Supreme Court has Decided: Relatives of Persons Killed in Accidents are Immediate Victims*, https://conflictoflaws.net/2023/the-greek-supreme-court-has-decided-relatives-of-persons-killed-in-accidents-are-immediate-victims/.

Index

The numbers here refer to paragraph numbers.

Index

Index

Index

www.ingramcontent.com/pod-product-compliance
Lightning Source LLC
LaVergne TN
LVHW011113300926
849160LV00008B/366
9789403544175